John Hildreth

New Voices in the American Theatre

NEW VOICES

IN THE

AMERICAN THEATRE

Foreword by Brooks Atkinson

THE MODERN LIBRARY · NEW YORK

CONTENTS

FOREWORD

by Brooks Atkinson

THIS VOLUME includes six notable American dramas that were produced in New York from 1947 to 1954. Most of us have been accustomed to regarding this period as undistinguished in the arts of the stage. That is relatively true. For the ten or twelve years that followed the first World War were a time of unequaled plenty. Those were the years when the American drama came of age. Led by Eugene O'Neill, the drama compensated all at once for many years of superficial theatre writing. The "adult dramatists," as we called them then, were in a hurry. They raised the quality of theatre writing to a level that has served as the standard ever since.

The abundance and excitement of those years may never be repeated. Indeed, it may never be necessary again to accomplish so much so rapidly. For the arts of the theatre are now intimately related to the culture of the country; at its best, the drama has artistic stature. The plays in this volume represent the steady development of the theatre's attitudes towards American civilization.

They also represent increasing virtuosity in craftsmanship. Most of them would have been regarded as "experimental" a quarter of a century ago. For most of them have broken with the old formula of the "well-made play" in the interest of freer, more poetic, more subjective forms. Even George Axelrod's "The Seven Year Itch," an immensely successful popular comedy, is written in terms of fantasy. But audiences have found nothing remarkable about imaginative forms. The forms are not self-conscious or eccentric: they are the logical ways to express the specific material.

Most of these plays show a serious attitude towards life and lack intellectual self-confidence. They were written in a time of emotional and political insecurity; and in a time that has been more and more interested in the secrets of the mind. In 1947, when the first of the plays appeared on Broadway, it was already apparent that the awful catastrophe of the war was leading into a period of uncertainty and peril. If the nation had been in a triumphant mood, the plays would probably have been exuberant and outgoing. That was the mood of the twenties—a rather foolish mood, now that we look back on it. But it gave most playwrights a feeling of participating in an expanding civilization in which great things were going to be accomplished.

O'Neill, wedded to tragedy, introspective, pessimistic, was the chief exception to the prevailing spirit of optimism. It is significant that he is the one dramatist from the twenties who speaks most convincingly to contemporary audiences. For this is a period in which we have been turned back on ourselves and have to consider the inadequacies of the mind to deal with the problems of the world. There is more depth than breadth to the intellectual attitudes of today.

When "A Streetcar Named Desire" was produced on December 3, 1947, Tennessee Williams was already known as author of "The Glass Menagerie," which had been put on two years before. "Streetcar," as it is known in the trade, confirmed the impression that a new talent of first importance had come into the theatre. Mr. Williams is a man of his times. He has a terrifying knowledge of the human mind and of the fears that haunt it. He knows the difference between pleasant social appearances and the tragic loneliness of individuals. He is also a master of theatre forms. He uses actors as orchestra conductors use instrumentalists to express moods and tones and to develop themes with spontaneity. There is nothing mechanical about his craftsmanship.

Although "Streetcar" is a drama that burns with passion, it is, in essence, a cold requiem spoken over the spirit of a Southern gentlewoman who has lost her way in the heartless modern world. The original production, which was directed by Elia Kazan, included Marlon Brando as Stanley, Jessica Tandy as Blanche, Karl Malden as Mitch and Kim Hunter as Stella. It was a memorable production of a memorable drama. "Streetcar" won the Critics Circle Award and the Pulitzer Prize in 1948.

Arthur Miller's "Death of a Salesman" was generally recognized as a masterpiece when it appeared on February 10, 1949. There has never been any reason to revise the first impression. Of the six writers represented in this volume, Mr. Miller is the one who participates most actively in the intellectual life of today. He is preoccupied with the relationship between the individual and the great forces of politics and industry. In "All My Sons," in 1947, he had dramatized the tragedy of a wartime munitions manufacturer who had cheated on the quality of his product; and in "The Crucible," in 1953, he dramatized the Salem witch trials of 1692 that in many ways parallel the assault on civil liberties today.

"Death of a Salesman" has a universal theme. It dramatizes the tragedy of an obscure shoe salesman who makes false choices in life and prepares his own destruction. "Attention, attention must be paid to such a person," says his wife to her boorish sons when she recognizes the depth of his anguish. The power, the knowledge and the sincerity of "Death of a Salesman" have persuaded millions of people to pay attention to the tragedy of this victim of the American cant about success. This is another of the dramas staged by Elia Kazan. Lee Cobb as Willy Loman and Mildred Dunnock as his loyal wife gave profoundly moving performances. Mr. Miller's drama won the Critics Circle award in 1949.

When "Come Back, Little Sheba" was produced in New York in 1950, it accomplished two things: it introduced William Inge to New York as an original theatre writer, and it made Shirley Booth a dramatic actress. Mr. Inge is a regional writer. In his later plays, "Picnic" and "Bus Stop," even more specifically than in "Come Back, Little Sheba," he confines himself to Middle Western characters absorbed in their own affairs.

"Come Back, Little Sheba" is a bare, almost clinical character study of a middle-aged couple who are intellectually ill-assorted but who survive a shattering crisis that will presumably stabilize their future. Each one learns something fundamental about their life together. In the first act the play is reticent almost to the point of dullness. But in the second act the wild human impulses that have been lying dormant violently explode. The first act hardly prepares the theatregoer for the furies Mr. Inge lets loose in a commonplace Middle Western home.

This is the act that released Miss Booth from long servitude to worldly comedy roles; and it is also the act that brought sudden distinction to Sidney Blackmer's amiable acting career. He played the part of a lonely chiropractic who had been a dipsomaniac. She played his slatternly though good-natured

wife. In the second act something struck both of them with
the force of a bomb. It was Mr. Inge beginning his career
in the Broadway theatre.

All Mr. Axelrod has in mind in "The Seven Year Itch" is
an evening of giddy entertainment. A summer bachelor,
whose wife and children are in the country, timidly succumbs
to the sociable charms of a blonde who is living in the apartment overhead. There is nothing especially novel about the
story. But the form in which it is written gives it another
dimension. By the use of daydreams, fantasticated in style,
Mr. Axelrod dramatizes the skittish mind of his summer
bachelor. "The Seven Year Itch" is like a comic psychoanalysis. In the original production, which opened on November
20, 1952, Tom Ewell played the central part with great light-
ness, ingenuity and humor. The fact that other actors have
successfully played the part indicates that "The Seven Year
Itch" is no vehicle, but a highly original antic written by a
versatile young man who knows how to improvise in the
theatre.

Although "Tea and Sympathy," produced on September
30, 1953, was the first play by Robert Anderson to reach
Broadway, many people had already seen an earlier play, "All
Summer Long," when it was produced in Washington by the
Arena Stage that spring. "All Summer Long" reached New
York a season later. "Tea and Sympathy" is a tender, percep-
tive drama about a likable prep school student who is falsely
suspected of being homosexual. It can be appreciated as a
literal portrait of the barbarism of life in a preparatory school
for boys. But to many people it has deeper significance. It
dramatizes the brutality of public opinion—the cynical ac-
ceptance of unproven charges, the helplessness of the individual, the sanctimoniousness of the mob, the loneliness of
a person exiled from society, the need for understanding and
pity.

This is the third of the plays in this volume that were directed by Mr. Kazan, who crystallizes the meaning of every
script he stages. When "Tea and Sympathy" was first produced it was beautifully acted by a cast that included Debo-
rah Kerr, John Kerr and Lief Erickson. But audiences have
continued to find beauty in Mr. Anderson's drama when
other actors have played the leading parts. For "Tea and

Sympathy" is a fully-wrought drama that can stand on its own feet as literature and theatre.

Herman Wouk dramatized "The Caine Mutiny Court-Martial" from his own novel, entitled "The Caine Mutiny." Directed with decision and originality by Charles Laughton, it opened on January 19, 1954 and became one of the spectacular successes of the season. It is ingeniously underwritten. Although the story is sensational Mr. Wouk avoids heroics. From the casual tone of the opening scenes you have no indication that the ordeal of Captain Queeg is going to be so painful; nor are you prepared for the violence with which the defending attorney repudiates his courtroom methods in the last act. Mr. Wouk, a discriminating writer, never raises his voice. But the moral points at issue turn out to be explosive before the play is over.

From the technical point of view, the stage production was interesting because the director dispensed with scenery. The curtain was up, showing an empty stage, when the audience came into the theatre; the curtain was not lowered when the play was over. That is the sort of thing that would have been regarded as experimental a quarter of a century ago. In fact, it was when Ann Harding appeared in "The Trial of Mary Duggan" in 1927. But it is evidence of the enlightened attitude people have towards the theatre today that Mr. Laughton's style of production in "The Caine Mutiny Court-Martial" was accepted with little comment.

For there are no rules any more in dramatic construction or stage direction. There are only authors, actors, directors and scene designers with moral convictions and a passion for the theatre. The plays in this volume are evidence of the vitality that new dramatists consistently bring into our maturing theatre.

New Voices in the American Theatre

A Streetcar
Named
Desire

by **TENNESSEE WILLIAMS**

A STREETCAR NAMED DESIRE

was presented at the Barrymore Theatre in New York on December 3, 1947, by Irene Selznick. It was directed by Elia Kazan, with the following cast:

NEGRO WOMAN	Gee Gee James
EUNICE HUBBELL	Peg Hillias
STANLEY KOWALSKI	Marlon Brando
STELLA KOWALSKI	Kim Hunter
STEVE HUBBELL	Rudy Bond
HAROLD MITCHELL (MITCH)	Karl Malden
MEXICAN WOMAN	Edna Thomas
BLANCHE DUBOIS	Jessica Tandy
PABLO GONZALES	Nick Dennis
A YOUNG COLLECTOR	Vito Christi
NURSE	Ann Dere
DOCTOR	Richard Garrick

Scenery and lighting by Jo Meilziner, costumes by Lucinda Ballard. The action of the play takes place in the spring, summer, and early fall in New Orleans. It was performed with intermissions after Scene Four and Scene Six.

Assistant to the producer	Irving Schneider
Musical Advisor	Lehman Engel

And so it was I entered the broken world
To trace the visionary company of love, its voice
An instant in the wind (I know not whither hurled)
But not for long to hold each desperate choice.

"The Broken Tower" by Hart Crane

THE CHARACTERS

BLANCHE

STELLA

STANLEY

MITCH

EUNICE

STEVE

PABLO

A NEGRO WOMAN

A DOCTOR

A NURSE

A YOUNG COLLECTOR

A MEXICAN WOMAN

Scene
One

The exterior of a two-story corner building on a street in New Orleans which is named Elysian Fields and runs between the L & N tracks and the river. The section is poor but, unlike corresponding sections in other American cities, it has a raffish charm. The houses are mostly white frame, weathered grey, with rickety outside stairs and galleries and quaintly ornamented gables. This building contains two flats, upstairs and down. Faded white stairs ascend to the entrances of both.

It is first dark of an evening early in May. The sky that shows around the dim white building is a peculiarly tender blue, almost a turquoise, which invests the scene with a kind of lyricism and gracefully attenuates the atmosphere of decay. You can almost feel the warm breath of the brown river beyond the river warehouses with their faint redolences of bananas and coffee. A corresponding air is evoked by the music of Negro entertainers at a barroom around the corner. In this part of New Orleans you are practically always just around the corner, or a few doors down the street, from a tinny piano being played with the infatuated fluency of brown fingers. This "Blue Piano" expresses the spirit of the life which goes on here.

Two women, one white and one colored, are taking the air on the steps of the building. The white woman is EUNICE, who occupies the upstairs flat; the colored woman a neighbor, for New Orleans is a cosmopolitan city where there is a relatively warm and easy intermingling of races in the old part of town.

Above the music of the "Blue Piano" the voices of people on the street can be heard overlapping.

5

(*Two men come around the corner,* STANLEY KOWALSKI *and* MITCH. *They are about twenty-eight or thirty years old, roughly dressed in blue denim work clothes.* STANLEY *carries his bowling jacket and a red-stained package from a butcher's. They stop at the foot of the steps*)

STANLEY (*Bellowing*)   Hey, there! Stella, Baby!
(STELLA *comes out on the first floor landing, a gentle young woman, about twenty-five, and of a background obviously quite different from her husband's*)

STELLA (*Mildly*)   Don't holler at me like that. Hi, Mitch.

STANLEY   Catch!

STELLA   What?

STANLEY   Meat!
(*He heaves the package at her. She cries out in protest but manages to catch it: then she laughs breathlessly. Her husband and his companion have already started back around the corner*)

STELLA (*Calling after him*)   Stanley! Where are you going?

STANLEY   Bowling!

STELLA   Can I come watch?

STANLEY   Come on. (*He goes out*)

STELLA   Be over soon. (*To the white woman*) Hello, Eunice. How are you?

EUNICE   I'm all right. Tell Steve to get him a poor boy's sandwich 'cause nothing's left here.
(*They all laugh; the colored woman does not stop.* STELLA *goes out*)

COLORED WOMAN   What was that package he th'ew at 'er? (*She rises from steps, laughing louder*)

EUNICE   You hush, now!

NEGRO WOMAN   Catch *what*!
(*She continues to laugh.* BLANCHE *comes around the corner, carrying a valise. She looks at a slip of paper, then at the building, then again at the slip and again at the build-*

ing. Her expression is one of shocked disbelief. Her appearance is incongruous to this setting. She is daintily dressed in a white suit with a fluffy bodice, necklace and earrings of pearl, white gloves and hat, looking as if she were arriving at a summer tea or cocktail party in the garden district. She is about five years older than Stella. Her delicate beauty must avoid a strong light. There is something about her uncertain manner, as well as her white clothes, that suggests a moth)

EUNICE (*Finally*) What's the matter, honey? Are you lost?

BLANCHE (*With faintly hysterical humor*) They told me to take a street-car named Desire, and then transfer to one called Cemeteries and ride six blocks and get off at—Elysian Fields!

EUNICE That's where you are now.

BLANCHE At Elysian Fields?

EUNICE This here is Elysian Fields.

BLANCHE They mustn't have—understood—what number I wanted . . .

EUNICE What number you lookin' for?
(BLANCHE *wearily refers to the slip of paper*)

BLANCHE Six thirty-two.

EUNICE You don't have to look no further.

BLANCHE (*Uncomprehendingly*) I'm looking for my sister, Stella DuBois. I mean—Mrs. Stanley Kowalski.

EUNICE That's the party.—You just did miss her, though.

BLANCHE This—can this be—her home?

EUNICE She's got the downstairs here and I got the up.

BLANCHE Oh. She's—out?

EUNICE You noticed that bowling alley around the corner?

BLANCHE I'm—not sure I did.

EUNICE Well, that's where she's at, watchin' her husband bowl. (*There is a pause*) You want to leave your suitcase here an' go find her?

BLANCHE   No.

NEGRO WOMAN   I'll go tell her you come.

BLANCHE   Thanks.

NEGRO WOMAN   You welcome. (*She goes out*)

EUNICE   She wasn't expecting you?

BLANCHE   No. No, not tonight.

EUNICE   Well, why don't you just go in and make yourself at home till they get back.

BLANCHE   How could I—do that?

EUNICE   We own this place so I can let you in.
(*She gets up and opens the downstairs door. A light goes on behind the blind, turning it light blue.* BLANCHE *slowly follows her into the downstairs flat. The surrounding areas dim out as the interior is lighted*
(*Two rooms can be seen, not too clearly defined. The one first entered is primarily a kitchen but contains a folding bed to be used by* BLANCHE. *The room beyond this is a bedroom. Off this room is a narrow door to a bathroom*)

EUNICE   (*Defensively, noticing* BLANCHE's *look*)   It's sort of messed up right now but when it's clean it's real sweet.

BLANCHE   Is it?

EUNICE   Uh-huh, I think so. So you're Stella's sister?

BLANCHE   Yes. (*Wanting to get rid of her*)   Thanks for letting me in.

EUNICE   *Por nada,* as the Mexicans say, *por nada!* Stella spoke of you.

BLANCHE   Yes?

EUNICE   I think she said you taught school.

BLANCHE   Yes.

EUNICE   And you're from Mississippi, huh?

BLANCHE   Yes.

EUNICE   She showed me a picture of your home-place, the plantation.

BLANCHE   Belle Reve?

EUNICE   A great big place with white columns.

BLANCHE   Yes . . .

EUNICE   A place like that must be awful hard to keep up.

BLANCHE   If you will excuse me, I'm just about to drop.

EUNICE   Sure, honey. Why don't you set down?

BLANCHE   What I meant was I'd like to be left alone.

EUNICE   (*Offended*)   Aw. I'll make myself scarce, in that case.

BLANCHE   I didn't mean to be rude, but—

EUNICE   I'll drop by the bowling alley an' hustle her up. (*She goes out the door*)
   (BLANCHE *sits in a chair very stiffly with her shoulders slightly hunched and her legs pressed close together and her hands tightly clutching her purse as if she were quite cold. After a while the blind look goes out of her eyes and she begins to look slowly around. A cat screeches. She catches her breath with a startled gesture. Suddenly she notices something in a half opened closet. She springs up and crosses to it, and removes a whiskey bottle. She pours a half tumbler of whiskey and tosses it down. She carefully replaces the bottle and washes out the tumbler at the sink. Then she resumes her seat in front of the table*)

BLANCHE   (*Faintly to herself*)   I've got to keep hold of myself!
   (STELLA *comes quickly around the corner of the building and runs to the door of the downstairs flat*)

STELLA   (*Calling out joyfully*)   Blanche!
   (*For a moment they stare at each other. Then* BLANCHE *springs up and runs to her with a wild cry*)

BLANCHE   Stella, oh, Stella, Stella! Stella for Star!
   (*She begins to speak with feverish vivacity as if she feared*

for either of them to stop and think. They catch each other in a spasmodic embrace)

BLANCHE   Now, then, let me look at you. But don't you look at me, Stella, no, no, no, not till later, not till I've bathed and rested! And turn that over-light off! Turn that off! I won't be looked at in this merciless glare! (STELLA *laughs and complies*) Come back here now! Oh, my baby! Stella! Stella for Star! (*She embraces her again*) I thought you would never come back to this horrible place! What am I saying? I didn't mean to say that. I meant to be nice about it and say—Oh, what a convenient location and such—Ha-a-ha! Precious lamb! You haven't said a *word* to me.

STELLA   You haven't given me a chance to, honey! (*She laughs, but her glance at* BLANCHE *is a little anxious*)

BLANCHE   Well, now you talk. Open your pretty mouth and talk while I look around for some liquor! I know you must have some liquor on the place! Where could it be, I wonder? Oh, I spy, I spy!

(*She rushes to the closet and removes the bottle; she is shaking all over and panting for breath as she tries to laugh. The bottle nearly slips from her grasp*)

STELLA (*Noticing*)   Blanche, you sit down and let me pour the drinks. I don't know what we've got to mix with. Maybe a coke's in the icebox. Look'n see, honey, while I'm—

BLANCHE   No coke, honey, not with my nerves tonight! Where—where—where is—?

STELLA   Stanley? Bowling! He loves it. They're having a—found some soda!—tournament . . .

BLANCHE   Just water, baby, to chase it! Now don't get worried, your sister hasn't turned into a drunkard, she's just all shaken up and hot and tired and dirty! You sit down, now, and explain this place to me! What are you doing in a place like this?

STELLA   Now, Blanche—

BLANCHE   Oh, I'm not going to be hypocritical, I'm going to be honestly critical about it! Never, never, never in my worst dreams could I picture— Only Poe! Only Mr. Edgar Allan

Poe!—could do it justice! Out there I suppose is the ghoul-haunted woodland of Weir! (*She laughs*)

STELLA   No, honey, those are the L & N tracks.

BLANCHE   No, now seriously, putting joking aside. Why didn't you tell me, why didn't you write me, honey, why didn't you let me know?

STELLA (*Carefully, pouring herself a drink*)   Tell you what, Blanche?

BLANCHE   Why, that you had to live in these conditions!

STELLA   Aren't you being a little intense about it? It's not that bad at all! New Orleans isn't like other cities.

BLANCHE   This has got nothing to do with New Orleans. You might as well say—forgive me, blessed baby! (*She suddenly stops short*) The subject is closed!

STELLA (*A little drily*)   Thanks.
     (*During the pause,* BLANCHE *stares at her. She smiles at* BLANCHE)

BLANCHE (*Looking down at her glass, which shakes in her hand*)   You're all I've got in the world, and you're not glad to see me!

STELLA (*Sincerely*)   Why, Blanche, you know that's not true.

BLANCHE   No?—I'd forgotten how quiet you were.

STELLA   You never did give me a chance to say much, Blanche. So I just got in the habit of being quiet around you.

BLANCHE (*Vaguely*)   A good habit to get into . . . (*Then, abruptly*) You haven't asked me how I happened to get away from the school before the spring term ended.

STELLA   Well, I thought you'd volunteer that information—if you wanted to tell me.

BLANCHE   You thought I'd been fired?

STELLA   No, I—thought you might have—resigned . . .

BLANCHE   I was so exhausted by all I'd been through my—nerves broke. (*Nervously tamping cigarette*) I was on the

verge of—lunacy, almost! So Mr. Graves—Mr. Graves is the
high school superintendent—he suggested I take a leave of
absence. I couldn't put all of those details into the wire . . .
(*She drinks quickly*) Oh, this buzzes right through me and
feels so *good!*

STELLA   Won't you have another?

BLANCHE   No, one's my limit.

STELLA   Sure?

BLANCHE   You haven't said a word about my appearance.

STELLA   You look just fine.

BLANCHE   God love you for a liar! Daylight never exposed
so total a ruin! But you—you've put on some weight, yes,
you're just as plump as a little partridge! And it's so becoming to you!

STELLA   Now, Blanche—

BLANCHE   Yes, it is, it is or I wouldn't say it! You just have
to watch around the hips a little. Stand up.

STELLA   Not now.

BLANCHE   You hear me? I said stand up! (STELLA *complies
reluctantly*) You messy child, you, you've spilt something on
that pretty white lace collar! About your hair—you ought to
have it cut in a feather bob with your dainty features. Stella,
you have a maid, don't you?

STELLA   No. With only two rooms it's—

BLANCHE   What? *Two* rooms, did you say?

STELLA   This one and—(*She is embarrassed*)

BLANCHE   The other one? (*She laughs sharply. There is an
embarrassed silence*)

BLANCHE   I am going to take just one little tiny nip more,
sort of to put the stopper on, so to speak. . . . Then put the
bottle away so I won't be tempted. (*She rises*) I want you to
look at *my* figure! (*She turns around*) You know I haven't
put on one ounce in ten years, Stella? I weigh what I weighed

the summer you left Belle Reve. The summer Dad died and you left us . . .

STELLA (*A little wearily*) It's just incredible, Blanche, how well you're looking.

BLANCHE (*They both laugh uncomfortably*) But, Stella, there's only two rooms, I don't see where you're going to put me!

STELLA We're going to put you in here.

BLANCHE What kind of bed's this—one of those collapsible things? (*She sits on it*)

STELLA Does it feel all right?

BLANCHE (*Dubiously*) Wonderful, honey. I don't like a bed that gives much. But there's no door between the two rooms, and Stanley—will it be decent?

STELLA Stanley is Polish, you know.

BLANCHE Oh, yes. They're something like Irish, aren't they?

STELLA Well—

BLANCHE Only not so—highbrow? (*They both laugh again in the same way*) I brought some nice clothes to meet all your lovely friends in.

STELLA I'm afraid you won't think they are lovely.

BLANCHE What are they like?

STELLA They're Stanley's friends.

BLANCHE Polacks?

STELLA They're a mixed lot, Blanche.

BLANCHE Heterogeneous—types?

STELLA Oh, yes. Yes, types is right!

BLANCHE Well—anyhow—I brought nice clothes and I'll wear them. I guess you're hoping I'll say I'll put up at a hotel, but I'm not going to put up at a hotel. I want to be *near* you, got to be *with* somebody, I *can't* be *alone!* Because

—as you must have noticed—I'm—*not* very *well* . . . (*Her voice drops and her look is frightened*)

STELLA You seem a little bit nervous or overwrought or something.

BLANCHE Will Stanley like me, or will I be just a visiting in-law, Stella? I couldn't stand that.

STELLA You'll get along fine together, if you'll just try not to—well—compare him with men that we went out with at home.

BLANCHE Is he so—different?

STELLA Yes. A different species.

BLANCHE In what way; what's he like?

STELLA Oh, you can't describe someone you're in love with! Here's a picture of him! (*She hands a photograph to* BLANCHE)

BLANCHE An officer?

STELLA A Master Sergeant in the Engineers' Corps. Those are decorations!

BLANCHE He had those on when you met him?

STELLA I assure you I wasn't just blinded by all the brass.

BLANCHE That's not what I—

STELLA But of course there were things to adjust myself to later on.

BLANCHE Such as his civilian background! (STELLA *laughs uncertainly*) How did he take it when you said I was coming?

STELLA Oh, Stanley doesn't know yet.

BLANCHE (*Frightened*) You—haven't told him?

STELLA He's on the road a good deal.

BLANCHE Oh. Travels?

STELLA Yes.

BLANCHE Good. I mean—isn't it?

STELLA (*Half to herself*) I can hardly stand it when he is away for a night . . .

BLANCHE Why, Stella!

STELLA When he's away for a week I nearly go wild!

BLANCHE Gracious!

STELLA And when he comes back I cry on his lap like a baby . . . (*She smiles to herself*)

BLANCHE I guess that is what is meant by being in love . . . (STELLA *looks up with a radiant smile*) Stella—

STELLA What?

BLANCHE (*In an uneasy rush*) I haven't asked you the things you probably thought I was going to ask. And so I'll expect you to be understanding about what *I* have to tell *you*.

STELLA What, Blanche? (*Her face turns anxious*)

BLANCHE Well, Stella—you're going to reproach me, I know that you're bound to reproach me—but before you do—take into consideration—you left! I stayed and struggled! You came to New Orleans and looked out for yourself! *I* stayed at *Belle Reve* and tried to hold it together! I'm not meaning this in any reproachful way, but *all* the burden descended on *my* shoulders.

STELLA The best I could do was make my own living, Blanche.

(BLANCHE *begins to shake again with intensity*)

BLANCHE I know, I know. But you are the one that abandoned Belle Reve, not I! I stayed and fought for it, bled for it, almost died for it!

STELLA Stop this hysterical outburst and tell me what's happened? What do you mean fought and bled? What kind of—

BLANCHE I knew you would, Stella. I knew you would take this attitude about it!

STELLA About—what?—please!

BLANCHE (*Slowly*) The loss—the loss . . .

STELLA   Belle Reve? Lost, is it? No!

BLANCHE   Yes, Stella.
   (*They stare at each other across the yellow-checked lino-
   leum of the table.* BLANCHE *slowly nods her head and*
   STELLA *looks slowly down at her hands folded on the
   table. The music of the "blue piano" grows louder.*
   BLANCHE *touches her handkerchief to her forehead*)

STELLA   But how did it go? What happened?

BLANCHE   (*Springing up*)   You're a fine one to ask me how
it went!

STELLA   Blanche!

BLANCHE   You're a fine one to sit there *accusing me* of it!

STELLA   *Blanche!*

BLANCHE   I, I, *I* took the blows in my face and my body!
All of those deaths! The long parade to the graveyard! Father,
mother! Margaret, that dreadful way! So big with it, it
couldn't be put in a coffin! But had to be burned like rub-
bish! You just came home in time for the funerals, Stella.
And funerals are pretty compared to deaths. Funerals are
quiet, but deaths—not always. Sometimes their breathing is
hoarse, and sometimes it rattles, and sometimes they even
cry out to you, "Don't let me go!" Even the old, sometimes,
say, "Don't let me go." As if you were able to stop them!
But funerals are quiet, with pretty flowers. And, oh, what
gorgeous boxes they pack them away in! Unless you were
there at the bed when they cried out, "Hold me!" you'd
never suspect there was the struggle for breath and bleeding.
You didn't dream, but I saw! Saw! *Saw!* And now you sit
there telling me with your eyes that I let the place go! How
in hell do you think all that sickness and dying was paid for?
Death is expensive, Miss Stella! And old Cousin Jessie's right
after Margaret's, hers! Why, the Grim Reaper had put up his
tent on our doorstep! . . . Stella. Belle Reve was his head-
quarters! Honey—that's how it slipped through my fingers!
Which of them left us a fortune? Which of them left a cent
of insurance even? Only poor Jessie—one hundred to pay for
her coffin. That was all, Stella! And I with my pitiful salary
at the school. Yes, accuse me! Sit there and stare at me,

thinking I let the place go! *I* let the place go? Where were *you!* In bed with 'ur-.—Polack!

STELLA (*Springing*)   Blanche! You be still! That's enough!
(*She starts out*)

BLANCHE   Where are you going?

STELLA   I'm going into the bathroom to wash my face.

BLANCHE   Oh, Stella, Stella, you're crying!

STELLA   Does that surprise you?

BLANCHE   Forgive me—I didn't mean to—
(*The sound of men's voices is heard.* STELLA *goes into the bathroom, closing the door behind her. When the men appear, and* BLANCHE *realizes it must be* STANLEY *returning, she moves uncertainly from the bathroom door to the dressing table, looking apprehensively towards the front door.* STANLEY *enters, followed by* STEVE *and* MITCH. STANLEY *pauses near his door,* STEVE *by the foot of the Spiral stair, and* MITCH *is slightly above and to the right of them, about to go out. As the men enter, we hear some of the following dialogue.*)

STANLEY   Is that how he got it?

STEVE   Sure that's how he got it. He hit the old weather-bird for 300 bucks on a six-number-ticket.

MITCH   Don't tell him those things; he'll believe it.
(MITCH *starts out*)

STANLEY (*Restraining Mitch*)   Hey, Mitch—come back here.
(BLANCHE, *at the sound of voices, retires in the bedroom. She picks up* STANLEY'S *photo from dressing table, looks at it, puts it down. When* STANLEY *enters the apartment, she darts and hides behind the screen at the head of bed*)

STEVE (*To* STANLEY *and* MITCH)   Hey, are we playin' poker tomorrow?

STANLEY   Sure—at Mitch's.

MITCH (*Hearing this, returns quickly to the stair rail*)   No —not at my place. My mother's still sick!

STANLEY   Okay, at my place . . . (MITCH *starts out again*)
But you bring the beer!
  (MITCH *pretends not to hear,—calls out "Goodnight all,"
  and goes out, singing.* EUNICE'S *voice is heard, above*)

Break it up down there! I made the spaghetti dish and ate it
myself.

STEVE (*Going upstairs*)   I told you and phoned you we was
playing. (*To the men*) Jax beer!

EUNICE   You never phoned me once.

STEVE   I told you at breakfast—and phoned you at lunch . . .

EUNICE   Well, never mind about that. You just get yourself
home here once in a while.

STEVE   You want it in the papers?
  (*More laughter and shouts of parting come from the men.*
  STANLEY *throws the screen door of the kitchen open and
  comes in. He is of medium height, about five feet eight or
  nine, and strongly, compactly built. Animal joy in his being
  is implicit in all his movements and attitudes. Since earliest
  manhood the center of his life has been pleasure with
  women, the giving and taking of it, not with weak indul-
  gence, dependently, but with the power and pride of a
  richly feathered male bird among hens. Branching out from
  this complete and satisfying center are all the auxiliary
  channels of his life, such as his heartiness with men, his
  appreciation of rough humor, his love of good drink and
  food and games, his car, his radio, everything that is his,
  that bears his emblem of the gaudy seed-bearer. He sizes
  women up at a glance, with sexual classifications, crude
  images flashing into his mind and determining the way he
  smiles at them*)

BLANCHE (*Drawing involuntarily back from his stare*)   You
must be Stanley. I'm Blanche.

STANLEY   Stella's sister?

BLANCHE   Yes.

STANLEY   H'lo. Where's the little woman?

BLANCHE   In the bathroom.

STANLEY   Oh. Didn't know you were coming in town.

BLANCHE   I—uh—

STANLEY   Where you from, Blanche?

BLANCHE   Why, I—live in Laurel.
(*He has crossed to the closet and removed the whiskey bottle*)

STANLEY   In Laurel, huh? Oh, yeah. Yeah, in Laurel, that's right. Not in my territory. Liquor goes fast in hot weather. (*He holds the bottle to the light to observe its depletion*) Have a shot?

BLANCHE   No, I—rarely touch it.

STANLEY   Some people rarely touch it, but it touches them often.

BLANCHE (*Faintly*)   Ha-ha.

STANLEY   My clothes're stickin' to me. Do you mind if I make myself comfortable? (*He starts to remove his shirt*)

BLANCHE   Please, please do.

STANLEY   Be comfortable is my motto.

BLANCHE   It's mine, too. It's hard to stay looking fresh. I haven't washed or even powdered my face and—here you are!

STANLEY   You know you can catch cold sitting around in damp things, especially when you been exercising hard like bowling is. You're a teacher, aren't you?

BLANCHE   Yes.

STANLEY   What do you teach, Blanche?

BLANCHE   English.

STANLEY   I never was a very good English student. How long you here for, Blanche?

BLANCHE   I—don't know yet.

STANLEY   You going to shack up here?

BLANCHE   I thought I would if it's not inconvenient for you all.

STANLEY   Good.

BLANCHE   Traveling wears me out.

STANLEY   Well, take it easy.
    (*A cat screeches near the window.* BLANCHE *springs up*)

BLANCHE   What's that?

STANLEY   Cats . . . Hey, Stella!

STELLA   (*Faintly, from the bathroom*)   Yes, Stanley.

STANLEY   Haven't fallen in, have you? (*He grins at* BLANCHE. *She tries unsuccessfully to smile back. There is a silence*) I'm afraid I'll strike you as being the unrefined type. Stella's spoke of you a good deal. You were married once, weren't you?
    (*The music of the polka rises up, faint in the distance*)

BLANCHE   Yes. When I was quite young.

STANLEY   What happened?

BLANCHE   The boy—the boy died. (*She sinks back down*) I'm afraid I'm—going to be sick!
    (*Her head falls on her arms*)

Scene Two

It is six o'clock the following evening. BLANCHE *is bathing.* STELLA *is completing her toilette.* BLANCHE'S *dress, a flowered print, is laid out on* STELLA'S *bed.*

    STANLEY *enters the kitchen from outside, leaving the door open on the perpetual "blue piano" around the corner.*

STANLEY   What's all this monkey doings?

STELLA   Oh, Stan! (*She jumps up and kisses him which he accepts with lordly composure*) I'm taking Blanche to Galatoire's for supper and then to a show, because it's your poker night.

STANLEY   How about my supper, huh? I'm not going to no Galatoire's for supper!

STELLA   I put you a cold plate on ice.

STANLEY   Well, isn't that just dandy!

STELLA   I'm going to try to keep Blanche out till the party breaks up because I don't know how she would take it. So we'll go to one of the little places in the Quarter afterwards and you'd better give me some money.

STANLEY   Where is she?

STELLA   She's soaking in a hot tub to quiet her nerves. She's terribly upset.

STANLEY   Over what?

STELLA   She's been through such an ordeal.

STANLEY   Yeah?

STELLA   Stan, we've—lost Belle Reve!

STANLEY   The place in the country?

STELLA   Yes.

STANLEY   How?

STELLA (*Vaguely*)   Oh, it had to be—sacrificed or something. (*There is a pause while* STANLEY *considers.* STELLA *is changing into her dress*) When she comes in be sure to say something nice about her appearance. And, oh! Don't mention the baby. I haven't said anything yet, I'm waiting until she gets in a quieter condition.

STANLEY (*Ominously*)   So?

STELLA   And try to understand her and be nice to her, Stan.

BLANCHE (*Singing in the bathroom*)
"From the land of the sky blue water,
  They brought a captive maid!"

STELLA   She wasn't expecting to find us in such a small place. You see I'd tried to gloss things over a little in my letters.

STANLEY   So?

STELLA   And admire her dress and tell her she's looking wonderful. That's important with Blanche. Her little weakness!

STANLEY   Yeah. I get the idea. Now let's skip back a little to where you said the country place was disposed of.

STELLA   Oh!—yes . . .

STANLEY   How about that? Let's have a few more details on that subjeck.

STELLA   It's best not to talk much about it until she's calmed down.

STANLEY   So that's the deal, huh? Sister Blanche cannot be annoyed with business details right now!

STELLA   You saw how she was last night.

STANLEY   Uh-hum, I saw how she was. Now let's have a gander at the bill of sale.

STELLA   I haven't seen any.

STANLEY   She didn't show you no papers, no deed of sale or nothing like that, huh?

STELLA   It seems like it wasn't sold.

STANLEY   Well, what in hell was it then, give away? To charity?

STELLA   Shhh! She'll hear you.

STANLEY   I don't care if she hears me. Let's see the papers!

STELLA   There weren't any papers, she didn't show any papers, I don't care about papers.

STANLEY   Have you ever heard of the Napoleonic code?

STELLA   No, Stanley, I haven't heard of the Napoleonic code and if I have, I don't see what it—

STANLEY   Let me enlighten you on a point or two, baby.

STELLA   Yes?

STANLEY   In the state of Louisiana we have the Napoleonic code according to which what belongs to the wife belongs to the husband and vice versa. For instance if I had a piece of property, or you had a piece of property—

STELLA   My head is swimming!

STANLEY   All right. I'll wait till she gets through soaking in a hot tub and then I'll inquire if *she* is acquainted with the Napoleonic code. It looks to me like you have been swindled, baby, and when you're swindled under the Napoleonic code I'm swindled *too*. And I don't like to be *swindled*.

STELLA   There's plenty of time to ask her questions later but if you do now she'll go to pieces again. I don't understand what happened to Belle Reve but you don't know how ridiculous you are being when you suggest that my sister or I or anyone of our family could have perpetrated a swindle on anyone else.

STANLEY   Then where's the money if the place was sold?

STELLA   Not sold—*lost, lost!*
  (*He stalks into bedroom, and she follows him.*)
  Stanley! (*He pulls open the wardrobe trunk standing in middle of room and jerks out an armful of dresses*)

STANLEY   Open your eyes to this stuff! You think she got them out of a teacher's pay?

STELLA   Hush!

STANLEY   Look at these feathers and furs that she come here to preen herself in! What's this here? A solid-gold dress, I believe! And this one! What is these here? Fox-pieces! (*He blows on them*) Genuine fox fur-pieces, a half a mile long! Where are your fox-pieces, Stella? Bushy snow-white ones, no less! Where are your white fox-pieces?

STELLA   Those are inexpensive summer furs that Blanche has had a long time.

STANLEY   I got an acquaintance who deals in this sort of merchandise. I'll have him in here to appraise it. I'm willing to bet you there's thousands of dollars invested in this stuff here!

STELLA   Don't be such an idiot, Stanley!
(*He hurls the furs to the daybed. Then he jerks open small drawer in the trunk and pulls up a fist-full of costume jewelry*)

STANLEY   And what have we here? The treasure chest of a pirate!

STELLA   Oh, Stanley!

STANLEY   Pearls! Ropes of them! What is this sister of yours, a deep-sea diver? Bracelets of solid gold, too! Where are your pearls and gold bracelets?

STELLA   Shhh! Be still, Stanley!

STANLEY   And diamonds! A crown for an empress!

STELLA   A rhinestone tiara she wore to a costume ball.

STANLEY   What's rhinestone?

STELLA   Next door to glass.

STANLEY   Are you kidding? I have an acquaintance that works in a jewelry store. I'll have him in here to make an appraisal of this. Here's your plantation, or what was left of it, here!

STELLA   You have no idea how stupid and horrid you're being! Now close that trunk before she comes out of the bathroom!
(*He kicks the trunk partly closed and sits on the kitchen table*)

STANLEY   The Kowalskis and the DuBois have different notions.

STELLA   (*Angrily*)   Indeed they have, thank heavens!—*I'm* going outside. (*She snatches up her white hat and gloves and crosses to the outside door*) You come out with me while Blanche is getting dressed.

STANLEY   Since when do you give me orders?

STELLA   Are you going to stay here and insult her?

STANLEY   You're damn tootin' I'm going to stay here.
(STELLA *goes out to the porch.* BLANCHE *comes out of the bathroom in a red satin robe*)

BLANCHE (*Airily*) Hello, Stanley! Here I am, all freshly bathed and scented, and feeling like a brand new human being!
(*He lights a cigarette*)

STANLEY That's good.

BLANCHE (*Drawing the curtains at the windows*) Excuse me, while I slip on my pretty new dress!

STANLEY Go right ahead, Blanche.
(*She closes the drapes between the rooms*)

BLANCHE I understand there's to be a little card party to which we ladies are cordially *not* invited!

STANLEY (*Ominously*) Yeah?
(BLANCHE *throws off her robe and slips into a flowered print dress*)

BLANCHE Where's Stella?

STANLEY Out on the porch.

BLANCHE I'm going to ask a favor of you in a moment.

STANLEY What could that be, I wonder?

BLANCHE Some buttons in back! You may enter!
(*He crosses through drapes with a smoldering look*)
How do I look?

STANLEY You look all right.

BLANCHE Many thanks! Now the buttons!

STANLEY I can't do nothing with them.

BLANCHE You men with your big clumsy fingers. May I have a drag on your cig?

STANLEY Have one for yourself.

BLANCHE Why, thanks! . . . It looks like my trunk has exploded.

STANLEY Me an' Stella were helping you unpack.

BLANCHE Well, you certainly did a fast and thorough job of it.

STANLEY   It looks like you raided some stylish shops in Paris.

BLANCHE   Ha-ha! Yes—clothes are my passion!

STANLEY   What does it cost for a string of fur-pieces like that?

BLANCHE   Why, those were a tribute from an admirer of mine!

STANLEY   He must have had a lot of—admiration!

BLANCHE   Oh, in my youth I excited some admiration. But look at me now! (*She smiles at him radiantly*) Would you think it possible that I was once considered to be—attractive?

STANLEY   Your looks are okay.

BLANCHE   I was fishing for a compliment, Stanley.

STANLEY   I don't go in for that stuff.

BLANCHE   What—stuff?

STANLEY   Compliments to women about their looks. I never met a woman that didn't know if she was good-looking or not without being told, and some of them give themselves credit for more than they've got. I once went out with a doll who said to me, "I am the glamorous type, I am the glamorous type!" I said, "So what?"

BLANCHE   And what did she say then?

STANLEY   She didn't say nothing. That shut her up like a clam.

BLANCHE   Did it end the romance?

STANLEY   It ended the conversation—that was all. Some men are took in by this Hollywood glamor stuff and some men are not.

BLANCHE   I'm sure you belong in the second category.

STANLEY   That's right.

BLANCHE   I cannot imagine any witch of a woman casting a spell over you.

STANLEY   That's—right.

BLANCHE You're simple, straightforward and honest, a little bit on the primitive side I should think. To interest you a woman would have to— (*She pauses with an indefinite gesture*)

STANLEY (*Slowly*) Lay . . . her cards on the table.

BLANCHE (*Smiling*) Well, I never cared for wishy-washy people. That was why, when you walked in here last night, I said to myself—"My sister has married a man!"—Of course that was all that I could tell about you.

STANLEY (*Booming*) Now let's cut the re-bop!

BLANCHE (*Pressing hands to her ears*) Ouuuuu!

STELLA (*Calling from the steps*) Stanley! You come out here and let Blanche finish dressing!

BLANCHE I'm through dressing, honey.

STELLA Well, you come out, then.

STANLEY Your sister and I are having a little talk.

BLANCHE (*Lightly*) Honey, do me a favor. Run to the drugstore and get me a lemon-coke with plenty of chipped ice in it!—Will you do that for me, Sweetie?

STELLA (*Uncertainly*) Yes. (*She goes around the corner of the building*)

BLANCHE The poor little thing was out there listening to us, and I have an idea she doesn't understand you as well as I do. . . . All right; now, Mr. Kowalski, let us proceed without any more double-talk. I'm ready to answer all questions. I've nothing to hide. What is it?

STANLEY There is such a thing in this State of Louisiana as the Napoleonic code, according to which whatever belongs to my wife is also mine—and vice versa.

BLANCHE My, but you have an impressive judicial air!
(*She sprays herself with her atomizer; then playfully sprays him with it. He seizes the atomizer and slams it down on the dresser. She throws back her head and laughs*)

STANLEY If I didn't know that you was my wife's sister I'd get ideas about you!

BLANCHE   Such as what!

STANLEY   Don't play so dumb. You know what!

BLANCHE   (*She puts the atomizer on the table*)   All right.
Cards on the table. That suits me. (*She turns to* STANLEY) I
know I fib a good deal. After all, a woman's charm is fifty
per cent illusion, but when a thing is important I tell the
truth, and this is the truth: I haven't cheated my sister or you
or anyone else as long as I have lived.

STANLEY   Where's the papers? In the trunk?

BLANCHE   Everything that I own is in that trunk.
    (STANLEY *crosses to the trunk, shoves it roughly open and
    begins to open compartments*)

BLANCHE   What in the name of heaven are you thinking of!
What's in the back of that little boy's mind of yours? That I
am absconding with something, attempting some kind of
treachery on my sister?—Let me do that! It will be faster and
simpler . . . (*She crosses to the trunk and takes out a box*)
I keep my papers mostly in this tin box. (*She opens it*)

STANLEY   What's them underneath? (*He indicates another
sheaf of paper*)

BLANCHE   These are love-letters, yellowing with antiquity, all
from one boy. (*He snatches them up. She speaks fiercely*)
Give those back to me!

STANLEY   I'll have a look at them first!

BLANCHE   The touch of your hands insults them!

STANLEY   Don't pull that stuff!
    (*He rips off the ribbon and starts to examine them.*
    BLANCHE *snatches them from him, and they cascade to the
    floor*)

BLANCHE   Now that you've touched them I'll burn them!

STANLEY (*Staring, baffled*)   What in hell are they?

BLANCHE (*On the floor gathering them up*)   Poems a dead
boy wrote. I hurt him the way that you would like to hurt
me, but you can't! I'm not young and vulnerable any more.
But my young husband was and I—never mind about that!
Just give them back to me!

STANLEY What do you mean by saying you'll have to burn them?

BLANCHE I'm sorry, I must have lost my head for a moment. Everyone has something he won't let others touch because of their—intimate nature . . .

(*She now seems faint with exhaustion and she sits down with the strong box and puts on a pair of glasses and goes methodically through a large stack of papers*)

Ambler & Ambler. Hmmmmm. . . . Crabtree. . . . More Ambler & Ambler.

STANLEY What is Ambler & Ambler?

BLANCHE A firm that made loans on the place.

STANLEY Then it *was* lost on a mortgage?

BLANCHE (*Touching her forehead*) That must've been what happened.

STANLEY I don't want no ifs, ands or buts! What's all the rest of them papers?

(*She hands him the entire box. He carries it to the table and starts to examine the papers*)

BLANCHE (*Picking up a large envelope containing more papers*) There are thousands of papers, stretching back over hundreds of years, affecting Belle Reve as, piece by piece, our improvident grandfathers and father and uncles and brothers exchanged the land for their epic fornications—to put it plainly! (*She removes her glasses with an exhausted laugh*) The four-letter word deprived us of our plantation, till finally all that was left—and Stella can verify that!—was the house itself and about twenty acres of ground, including a graveyard, to which now all but Stella and I have retreated. (*She pours the contents of the envelope on the table*) Here all of them are, all papers! I hereby endow you with them! Take them, peruse them—commit them to memory, even! I think it's wonderfully fitting that Belle Reve should finally be this bunch of old papers in your big, capable hands! . . . I wonder if Stella's come back with my lemon-coke . . . (*She leans back and closes her eyes*)

STANLEY I have a lawyer acquaintance who will study these out.

BLANCHE   Present them to him with a box of aspirin tablets.

STANLEY (*Becoming somewhat sheepish*)   You see, under the Napoleonic code—a man has to take an interest in his wife's affairs—especially now that she's going to have a baby.
(BLANCHE *opens her eyes. The "blue piano" sounds louder*)

BLANCHE   Stella? Stella going to have a baby? (*Dreamily*) I didn't know she was going to have a baby!
(*She gets up and crosses to the outside door.* STELLA *appears around the corner with a carton from the drug-store.* (STANLEY *goes into the bedroom with the envelope and the box.*
(*The inner rooms fade to darkness and the outside wall of the house is visible.* BLANCHE *meets* STELLA *at the foot of the steps to the sidewalk*)

BLANCHE   Stella, Stella for Star! How lovely to have a baby! It's all right. Everything's all right.

STELLA   I'm sorry he did that to you.

BLANCHE   Oh, I guess he's just not the type that goes for jasmine perfume, but maybe he's what we need to mix with our blood now that we've lost Belle Reve. We thrashed it out. I feel a bit shaky, but I think I handled it nicely, I laughed and treated it all as a joke. (STEVE *and* PABLO *appear, carrying a case of beer*) I called him a little boy and laughed and flirted. Yes, I was flirting with your husband! (*As the men approach*) The guests are gathering for the poker party. (*The two men pass between them, and enter the house*) Which way do we go now, Stella—this way?

STELLA   No, this way. (*She leads* BLANCHE *away*)

BLANCHE (*Laughing*)   The blind are leading the blind!
(*A tamale Vendor is heard calling*)

VENDOR'S VOICE   Red-hot!

Scene Three

THE POKER NIGHT

There is a picture of Van Gogh's of a billiard-parlor at night. The kitchen now suggests that sort of lurid nocturnal brilliance, the raw colors of childhood's spectrum. Over the yellow linoleum of the kitchen table hangs an electric bulb with a vivid green glass shade. The poker players—STANLEY, STEVE, MITCH and PABLO—wear colored shirts, solid blues, a purple, a red-and-white check, a light green, and they are men at the peak of their physical manhood, as coarse and direct and powerful as the primary colors. There are vivid slices of watermelon on the table, whiskey bottles and glasses. The bedroom is relatively dim with only the light that spills between the portieres and through the wide window on the street.

For a moment, there is absorbed silence as a hand is dealt.

STEVE   Anything wild this deal?

PABLO   One-eyed jacks are wild.

STEVE   Give me two cards.

PABLO   You, Mitch?

MITCH   I'm out.

PABLO   One.

MITCH   Anyone want a shot?

STANLEY   Yeah. Me.

PABLO   Why don't somebody go to the Chinaman's and bring back a load of chop suey?

STANLEY   When I'm losing you want to eat! Ante up! Openers? Openers! Get y'r ass off the table, Mitch. Nothing belongs on a poker table but cards, chips and whiskey.
(*He lurches up and tosses some watermelon rinds to the floor.*)

MITCH   Kind of on your high horse, ain't you?

STANLEY   How many?

STEVE   Give me three.

STANLEY   One.

MITCH   I'm out again. I oughta go home pretty soon.

STANLEY   Shut up.

MITCH   I gotta sick mother. She don't go to sleep until I come in at night.

STANLEY   Then why don't you stay home with her?

MITCH   She says to go out, so I go, but I don't enjoy it. All the while I keep wondering how she is.

STANLEY   Aw, for the sake of Jesus, go home, then!

PABLO   What've you got?

STEVE   Spade flush.

MITCH   You all are married. But I'll be alone when she goes.—I'm going to the bathroom.

STANLEY   Hurry back and we'll fix you a sugar-tit.

MITCH   Aw, go rut. (*He crosses through the bedroom into the bathroom*)

STEVE (*Dealing a hand*)   Seven card stud. (*Telling his joke as he deals*) This ole farmer is out in back of his house sittin' down th'owing corn to the chickens when all at once he hears a loud cackle and this young hen comes lickety split around the side of the house with the rooster right behind her and gaining on her fast.

STANLEY (*Impatient with the story*) Deal!

STEVE But when the rooster catches sight of the farmer showing the corn he puts on the brakes and lets the hen get away and starts pecking corn. And the old farmer says, "Lord God, I hopes I never gits *that* hongry!"
(*Steve and Pablo laugh. The sisters appear around the corner of the building*)

STELLA The game is still going on.

BLANCHE How do I look?

STELLA Lovely, Blanche.

BLANCHE I feel so hot and frazzled. Wait till I powder before you open the door. Do I look done in?

STELLA Why no. You are as fresh as a daisy.

BLANCHE One that's been picked a few days.
(STELLA *opens the door and they enter*)

STELLA Well, well, well. I see you boys are still at it!

STANLEY Where you been?

STELLA Blanche and I took in a show. Blanche, this is Mr. Gonzales and Mr. Hubbell.

BLANCHE Please don't get up.

STANLEY Nobody's going to get up, so don't be worried.

STELLA How much longer is this game going to continue?

STANLEY Till we get ready to quit.

BLANCHE Poker is so fascinating. Could I kibitz?

STANLEY You could not. Why don't you women go up and sit with Eunice?

STELLA Because it is nearly two-thirty. (BLANCHE *crosses into the bedroom and partially closes the portieres*) Couldn't you call it quits after one more hand?
(*A chair scrapes.* STANLEY *gives a loud whack of his hand on her thigh*)

STELLA (*Sharply*) That's not fun, Stanley.
(*The men laugh.* STELLA *goes into the bedroom*)

STELLA   It makes me so mad when he does that in front of people.

BLANCHE   I think I will bathe.

STELLA   Again?

BLANCHE   My nerves are in knots. Is the bathroom occupied?

STELLA   I don't know.
   (BLANCHE *knocks.* MITCH *opens the door and comes out, still wiping his hands on a towel*)

BLANCHE   Oh!—good evening.

MITCH   Hello. (*He stares at her*)

STELLA   Blanche, this is Harold Mitchell. My sister, Blanche DuBois.

MITCH   (*With awkward courtesy*)   How do you do, Miss DuBois.

STELLA   How is your mother now, Mitch?

MITCH   About the same, thanks. She appreciated your sending over that custard.—Excuse me, please.
   (*He crosses slowly back into the kitchen, glancing back at* BLANCHE *and coughing a little shyly. He realizes he still has the towel in his hands and with an embarrassed laugh hands it to* STELLA. BLANCHE *looks after him with a certain interest*)

BLANCHE   That one seems—superior to the others.

STELLA   Yes, he is.

BLANCHE   I thought he had a sort of sensitive look.

STELLA   His mother is sick.

BLANCHE   Is he married?

STELLA   No.

BLANCHE   Is he a wolf?

STELLA   Why, Blanche! (BLANCHE *laughs*) I don't think he would be.

BLANCHE   What does—what does he do?
   (*She is unbuttoning her blouse*)

STELLA   He's on the precision bench in the spare parts department. At the plant Stanley travels for.

BLANCHE   Is that something much?

STELLA   No. Stanley's the only one of his crowd that's likely to get anywhere.

BLANCHE   What makes you think Stanley will?

STELLA   Look at him.

BLANCHE   I've looked at him.

STELLA   Then you should know.

BLANCHE   I'm sorry, but I haven't noticed the stamp of genius even on Stanley's forehead.
   (*She takes off the blouse and stands in her pink silk brassiere and white skirt in the light through the portieres. The game has continued in undertones*)

STELLA   It isn't on his forehead and it isn't genius.

BLANCHE   Oh. Well, what is it, and where? I would like to know.

STELLA   It's a drive that he has. You're standing in the light, Blanche!

BLANCHE   Oh, am I!
   (*She moves out of the yellow streak of light.* STELLA *has removed her dress and put on a light blue satin kimona*)

STELLA   (*With girlish laughter*)   You ought to see their wives.

BLANCHE   (*Laughingly*)   I can imagine. Big, beefy things, I suppose.

STELLA   You know that one upstairs? (*More laughter*) One time (*laughing*) the plaster—(*laughing*) cracked—

STANLEY   You hens cut out that conversation in there!

STELLA   You can't hear us.

STANLEY   Well, you can hear me and I said to hush up!

STELLA   This is my house and I'll talk as much as I want to!

BLANCHE   Stella, don't start a row.

STELLA   He's half drunk!—I'll be out in a minute.
(*She goes into the bathroom.* BLANCHE *rises and crosses leisurely to a small white radio and turns it on*)

STANLEY   Awright, Mitch, you in?

MITCH   What? Oh!—No, I'm out!
(BLANCHE *moves back into the streak of light. She raises her arms and stretches, as she moves indolently back to the chair.*
(*Rhumba music comes over the radio.* MITCH *rises at the table*)

STANLEY   Who turned that on in there?

BLANCHE   I did. Do you mind?

STANLEY   Turn it off!

STEVE   Aw, let the girls have their music.

PABLO   Sure, that's good, leave it on!

STEVE   Sounds like Xavier Cugat!
(STANLEY *jumps up and, crossing to the radio, turns it off. He stops short at the sight of* BLANCHE *in the chair. She returns his look without flinching. Then he sits again at the poker table.*
(*Two of the men have started arguing hotly*)

STEVE   I didn't hear you name it.

PABLO   Didn't I name it, Mitch?

MITCH   I wasn't listenin'.

PABLO   What were you doing, then?

STANLEY   He was looking through them drapes. (*He jumps up and jerks roughly at curtains to close them*) Now deal the hand over again and let's play cards or quit. Some people get ants when they win.

(MITCH *rises as* STANLEY *returns to his seat*)

STANLEY   (*Yelling*)   Sit down!

MITCH I'm going to the "head." Deal me out.

PABLO Sure he's got ants now. Seven five-dollar bills in his pants pocket folded up tight as spitballs.

STEVE Tomorrow you'll see him at the cashier's window getting them changed into quarters.

STANLEY And when he goes home he'll deposit them one by one in a piggy bank his mother give him for Christmas. (*Dealing*) This game is Spit in the Ocean.
  (MITCH *laughs uncomfortably and continues through the portieres. He stops just inside*)

BLANCHE (*Softly*) Hello! The Little Boys' Room is busy right now.

MITCH We've—been drinking beer.

BLANCHE I hate beer.

MITCH It's—a hot weather drink.

BLANCHE Oh, I don't think so; it always makes me warmer. Have you got any cigs? (*She has slipped on the dark red satin wrapper*)

MITCH Sure.

BLANCHE What kind are they?

MITCH Luckies.

BLANCHE Oh, good. What a pretty case. Silver?

MITCH Yes. Yes; read the inscription.

BLANCHE Oh, is there an inscription? I can't make it out. (*He strikes a match and moves closer*) Oh! (*Reading with feigned difficulty*):
"And if God choose,
 I shall but love thee better—after—death!"
Why, that's from my favorite sonnet by Mrs. Browning!

MITCH You know it?

BLANCHE Certainly I do!

MITCH There's a story connected with that inscription.

BLANCHE It sounds like a romance.

MITCH   A pretty sad one.

BLANCHE   Oh?

MITCH   The girl's dead now.

BLANCHE   (*In a tone of deep sympathy*)   *Oh!*

MITCH   She knew she was dying when she give me this. A very strange girl, very sweet—very!

BLANCHE   She must have been fond of you. Sick people have such deep, sincere attachments.

MITCH   That's right, they certainly do.

BLANCHE   Sorrow makes for sincerity, I think.

MITCH   It sure brings it out in people.

BLANCHE   The little there is belongs to people who have experienced some sorrow.

MITCH   I believe you are right about that.

BLANCHE   I'm positive that I am. Show me a person who hasn't known any sorrow and I'll show you a shuperficial— Listen to me! My tongue is a little—thick! You boys are responsible for it. The show let out at eleven and we couldn't come home on account of the poker game so we had to go somewhere and drink. I'm not accustomed to having more than one drink. Two is the limit—and *three!* (*She laughs*) Tonight I had three.

STANLEY   Mitch!

MITCH   Deal me out. I'm talking to Miss—

BLANCHE   DuBois.

MITCH   Miss DuBois?

BLANCHE   It's a French name. It means woods and Blanche means white, so the two together mean white woods. Like an orchard in spring! You can remember it by that.

MITCH   You're French?

BLANCHE   We are French by extraction. Our first American ancestors were French Huguenots.

MITCH   You are Stella's sister, are you not?

BLANCHE   Yes, Stella is my precious little sister. I call her little in spite of the fact she's somewhat older than I. Just slightly. Less than a year. Will you do something for me?

MITCH   Sure. What?

BLANCHE   I bought this adorable little colored paper lantern at a Chinese shop on Bourbon. Put it over the light bulb! Will you, please?

MITCH   Be glad to.

BLANCHE   I can't stand a naked light bulb, any more than I can a rude remark or a vulgar action.

MITCH   (*Adjusting the lantern*)   I guess we strike you as being a pretty rough bunch.

BLANCHE   I'm very adaptable—to circumstances.

MITCH   Well, that's a good thing to be. You are visiting Stanley and Stella?

BLANCHE   Stella hasn't been so well lately, and I came down to help her for a while. She's very run down.

MITCH   You're not—?

BLANCHE   Married? No, no. I'm an old maid schoolteacher!

MITCH   You may teach school but you're certainly not an old maid.

BLANCHE   Thank you, sir! I appreciate your gallantry!

MITCH   So you are in the teaching profession?

BLANCHE   Yes. Ah, yes . . .

MITCH   Grade school or high school or—

STANLEY   (*Bellowing*)   *Mitch!*

MITCH   *Coming!*

BLANCHE   Gracious, what lung-power! . . . I teach high school. In Laurel.

MITCH   What do you teach? What subject?

BLANCHE   Guess!

MITCH   I bet you teach art or music? (BLANCHE *laughs delicately*) Of course I could be wrong. You might teach arithmetic.

BLANCHE   Never arithmetic, sir; never arithmetic! (*With a laugh*) I don't even know my multiplication tables! No, I have the misfortune of being an English instructor. I attempt to instill a bunch of bobby-soxers and drug-store Romeos with reverence for Hawthorne and Whitman and Poe!

MITCH   I guess that some of them are more interested in other things.

BLANCHE   How very right you are! Their literary heritage is not what most of them treasure above all else! But they're sweet things! And in the spring, it's touching to notice them making their first discovery of love! As if nobody had ever known it before!
   (*The bathroom door opens and* STELLA *comes out.* BLANCHE *continues talking to* MITCH)
Oh! Have you finished? Wait—I'll turn on the radio.
   (*She turns the knobs on the radio and it begins to play "Wien, Wien, nur du allein."* BLANCHE *waltzes to the music with romantic gestures.* MITCH *is delighted and moves in awkward imitation like a dancing bear.*
   (STANLEY *stalks fiercely through the portieres into the bedroom. He crosses to the small white radio and snatches it off the table. With a shouted oath, he tosses the instrument out the window*)

STELLA   *Drunk—drunk—animal thing, you!* (*She rushes through to the poker table*) All of you—please go home! If any of you have one spark of decency in you—

BLANCHE (*Wildly*)   Stella, watch out, he's—
   (STANLEY *charges after* STELLA)

MEN (*Feebly*)   Take it easy, Stanley. Easy, fellow.—Let's all—

STELLA   You lay your hands on me and I'll—
   (*She backs out of sight. He advances and disappears. There is the sound of a blow.* STELLA *cries out.* BLANCHE *screams and runs into the kitchen. The men rush forward and there is grappling and cursing. Something is overturned with a crash*)

BLANCHE (*Shrilly*) My sister is going to have a baby!

MITCH This is terrible.

BLANCHE Lunacy, absolute lunacy!

MITCH Get him in here, men.
(STANLEY *is forced, pinioned by the two men, into the bedroom. He nearly throws them off. Then all at once he subsides and is limp in their grasp.*
(*They speak quietly and lovingly to him and he leans his face on one of their shoulders*)

STELLA (*In a high, unnatural voice, out of sight*) I want to go away, I want to go away!

MITCH Poker shouldn't be played in a house with women.
(BLANCHE *rushes into the bedroom*)

BLANCHE I want my sister's clothes! We'll go to that woman's upstairs!

MITCH Where is the clothes?

BLANCHE (*Opening the closet*) I've got them! (*She rushes through to* STELLA) Stella, Stella, precious! Dear, dear little sister, don't be afraid!
(*With her arms around* STELLA, BLANCHE *guides her to the outside door and upstairs*)

STANLEY (*Dully*) What's the matter; what's happened?

MITCH You just blew your top, Stan.

PABLO He's okay, now.

STEVE Sure, my boy's okay!

MITCH Put him on the bed and get a wet towel.

PABLO I think coffee would do him a world of good, now.

STANLEY (*Thickly*) I want water.

MITCH Put him under the shower!
(*The men talk quietly as they lead him to the bathroom*)

STANLEY Let the rut go of me, you sons of bitches!
(*Sounds of blows are heard. The water goes on full tilt*)

STEVE Let's get quick out of here!
(*They rush to the poker table and sweep up their winnings on their way out*)

MITCH (*Sadly but firmly*) Poker should not be played in a house with women.
(*The door closes on them and the place is still. The* NEGRO *entertainers in the bar around the corner play "Paper Doll" slow and blue. After a moment* STANLEY *comes out of the bathroom dripping water and still in his clinging wet polka dot drawers*)

STANLEY Stella! (*There is a pause*) My baby doll's left me!
(*He breaks into sobs. Then he goes to the phone and dials, still shuddering with sobs*)
Eunice? I want my baby! (*He waits a moment; then he hangs up and dials again*) Eunice! I'll keep on ringin' until I talk with my baby!
(*An indistinguishable shrill voice is heard. He hurls phone to floor. Dissonant brass and piano sounds as the rooms dim out to darkness and the outer walls appear in the night light. The "blue piano" plays for a brief interval.*
(*Finally,* STANLEY *stumbles half-dressed out to the porch and down the wooden steps to the pavement before the building. There he throws back his head like a baying hound and bellows his wife's name: "*STELLA! STELLA, sweetheart! STELLA!*"*)

STANLEY Stell-*lahhhhh!*

EUNICE (*Calling down from the door of her upper apartment*) Quit that howling out there an' go back to bed!

STANLEY I want my baby down here. Stella, Stella!

EUNICE She ain't comin' down so you quit! Or you'll git th' law on you!

STANLEY Stella!

EUNICE You can't beat on a woman an' then call 'er back! She won't come! And her goin' t' have a baby! . . . You stinker! You whelp of a Polack, you! I hope they do haul you in and turn the fire hose on you, same as the last time!

STANLEY (*Humbly*) Eunice, I want my girl to come down with me!

EUNICE   Hah! (*She slams her door*)

STANLEY   (*With heaven-splitting violence*) *STELL-LAHHHHH!*
(*The low-tone clarinet moans. The door upstairs opens again.* STELLA *slips down the rickety stairs in her robe. Her eyes are glistening with tears and her hair loose about her throat and shoulders. They stare at each other. Then they come together with low, animal moans. He falls to his knees on the steps and presses his face to her belly, curving a little with maternity. Her eyes go blind with tenderness as she catches his head and raises him level with her. He snatches the screen door open and lifts her off her feet and bears her into the dark flat.*
(BLANCHE *comes out on the upper landing in her robe and slips fearfully down the steps*)

BLANCHE   Where is my little sister? Stella? Stella?
(*She stops before the dark entrance of her sister's flat. Then catches her breath as if struck. She rushes down to the walk before the house. She looks right and left as if for a sanctuary.*
(*The music fades away.* MITCH *appears from around the corner*)

MITCH   Miss DuBois?

BLANCHE   Oh!

MITCH   All quiet on the Potomac now?

BLANCHE   She ran downstairs and went back in there with him.

MITCH   Sure she did.

BLANCHE   I'm terrified!

MITCH   Ho-ho! There's nothing to be scared of. They're crazy about each other.

BLANCHE   I'm not used to such—

MITCH   Naw, it's a shame this had to happen when you just got here. But don't take it serious.

BLANCHE   Violence! Is so—

MITCH   Set down on the steps and have a cigarette with me.

BLANCHE   I'm not properly dressed.

MITCH   That don't make no difference in the Quarter.

BLANCHE   Such a pretty silver case.

MITCH   I showed you the inscription, didn't I?

BLANCHE   Yes. (*During the pause, she looks up at the sky*)
There's so much—so much confusion in the world . . . (*He
coughs diffidently*) Thank you for being so kind! I need kindness now.

Scene Four

*It is early the following morning. There is a confusion
of street cries like a choral chant.*

  STELLA *is lying down in the bedroom. Her face is
serene in the early morning sunlight. One hand rests
on her belly, rounding slightly with new maternity.
From the other dangles a book of colored comics.
Her eyes and lips have that almost narcotized tran-
quility that is in the faces of Eastern idols.*

  *The table is sloppy with remains of breakfast and
the debris of the preceding night, and* STANLEY'S
*gaudy pyjamas lie across the threshold of the bath-
room. The outside door is slightly ajar on a sky of
summer brilliance.*

  BLANCHE *appears at this door. She has spent a
sleepless night and her appearance entirely contrasts
with* STELLA'S. *She presses her knuckles nervously to
her lips as she looks through the door, before entering.*

BLANCHE   Stella?

STELLA (*Stirring lazily*)   Hmmh?
 (BLANCHE *utters a moaning cry and runs into the bed-room, throwing herself down beside* STELLA *in a rush of hysterical tenderness*)

BLANCHE   Baby, my baby sister!

STELLA (*Drawing away from her*)   Blanche, what is the matter with you?
 (BLANCHE *straightens up slowly and stands beside the bed looking down at her sister with knuckles pressed to her lips*)

BLANCHE   He's left?

STELLA   Stan? Yes.

BLANCHE   Will he be back?

STELLA   He's gone to get the car greased. Why?

BLANCHE   Why! I've been half crazy, Stella! When I found out you'd been insane enough to come back in here after what happened—I started to rush in after you!

STELLA   I'm glad you didn't.

BLANCHE   What were you thinking of? (STELLA *makes an indefinite gesture*) Answer me! What? What?

STELLA   Please, Blanche! Sit down and stop yelling.

BLANCHE   All right, Stella. I will repeat the question quietly now. How could you come back in this place last night? Why, you must have slept with him!
 (STELLA *gets up in a calm and leisurely way*)

STELLA   Blanche, I'd forgotten how excitable you are. You're making much too much fuss about this.

BLANCHE   Am I?

STELLA   Yes, you are, Blanche. I know how it must have seemed to you and I'm awful sorry it had to happen, but it wasn't anything as serious as you seem to take it. In the first place, when men are drinking and playing poker anything can happen. It's always a powder-keg. He didn't know what he was doing. . . . He was as good as a lamb when I came back and he's really very, very ashamed of himself.

BLANCHE   And that—that makes it all right?

STELLA   No, it isn't all right for anybody to make such a terrible row, but—people do sometimes. Stanley's always smashed things. Why, on our wedding night—soon as we came in here—he snatched off one of my slippers and rushed about the place smashing the light-bulbs with it.

BLANCHE   He did—*what?*

STELLA   He smashed all the light-bulbs with the heel of my slipper! (*She laughs*)

BLANCHE   And you—you *let* him? Didn't *run,* didn't *scream?*

STELLA   I was—sort of—thrilled by it. (*She waits for a moment*) Eunice and you had breakfast?

BLANCHE   Do you suppose I wanted any breakfast?

STELLA   There's some coffee left on the stove.

BLANCHE   You're so—matter of fact about it, Stella.

STELLA   What other can I be? He's taken the radio to get it fixed. It didn't land on the pavement so only one tube was smashed.

BLANCHE   And you are standing there smiling!

STELLA   What do you want me to do?

BLANCHE   Pull yourself together and face the facts.

STELLA   What are they, in your opinion?

BLANCHE   In my opinion? You're married to a madman!

STELLA   No!

BLANCHE   Yes, you are, your fix is worse than mine is! Only you're not being sensible about it. I'm going to *do* something. Get hold of myself and make myself a new life!

STELLA   Yes?

BLANCHE   But you've given in. And that isn't right, you're not old! You can get out.

STELLA (*Slowly and emphatically*) I'm not in anything I
want to get out of.

BLANCHE (*Incredulously*) What—Stella?

STELLA I said I am not in anything that I have a desire to
get out of. Look at the mess in this room! And those empty
bottles! They went through two cases last night! He promised
this morning that he was going to quit having these poker
parties, but you know how long such a promise is going to
keep. Oh, well, it's his pleasure, like mine is movies and
bridge. People have got to tolerate each other's habits, I
guess.

BLANCHE I don't understand you. (STELLA *turns toward
her*) I don't understand your indifference. Is this a Chinese
philosophy you've—cultivated?

STELLA Is what—what?

BLANCHE This—shuffling about and mumbling—'One tube
smashed—beer-bottles—mess in the kitchen!'—as if nothing
out of the ordinary has happened! (STELLA *laughs uncertainly and picking up the broom, twirls it in her hands*)

BLANCHE Are you deliberately shaking that thing in my
face?

STELLA No.

BLANCHE Stop it. Let go of that broom. I won't have you
cleaning up for him!

STELLA Then who's going to do it? Are you?

BLANCHE I? I!

STELLA No, I didn't think so.

BLANCHE Oh, let me think, if only my mind would function! We've got to get hold of some money, that's the way
out!

STELLA I guess that money is always nice to get hold of.

BLANCHE Listen to me. I have an idea of some kind. (*Shakily she twists a cigarette into her holder*) Do you remember
Shep Huntleigh? (STELLA *shakes her head*) Of course you
remember Shep Huntleigh. I went out with him at college
and wore his pin for a while. Well—

STELLA   Well?

BLANCHE   I ran into him last winter. You know I went to Miami during the Christmas holidays?

STELLA   No.

BLANCHE   Well, I did. I took the trip as an investment, thinking I'd meet someone with a million dollars.

STELLA   Did you?

BLANCHE   Yes. I ran into Shep Huntleigh—I ran into him on Biscayne Boulevard, on Christmas Eve, about dusk . . . getting into his car—Cadillac convertible: must have been a block long!

STELLA   I should think it would have been—inconvenient in traffic!

BLANCHE   You've heard of oil-wells?

STELLA   Yes—remotely.

BLANCHE   He has them, all over Texas. Texas is literally spouting gold in his pockets.

STELLA   My, my.

BLANCHE   Y'know how indifferent I am to money. I think of money in terms of what it does for you. But he could do it, he could certainly do it!

STELLA   Do what, Blanche?

BLANCHE   Why—set us up in a—shop!

STELLA   What kind of a shop?

BLANCHE   Oh, a—shop of some kind! He could do it with half what his wife throws away at the races.

STELLA   He's married?

BLANCHE   Honey, would I be here if the man weren't married? (STELLA *laughs a little.* BLANCHE *suddenly springs up and crosses to phone. She speaks shrilly*) How do I get Western Union?—Operator! Western Union!

STELLA   That's a dial phone, honey.

BLANCHE   I can't dial, I'm too—

STELLA   Just dial O.

BLANCHE   O?

STELLA   Yes, "O" for Operator! (BLANCHE *considers a moment; then she puts the phone down*)

BLANCHE   Give me a pencil. Where is a slip of paper? I've got to write it down first—the message, I mean . . .
   (*She goes to the dressing table, and grabs up a sheet of Kleenex and an eyebrow pencil for writing equipment*)
Let me see now . . . (*She bites the pencil*) 'Darling Shep. Sister and I in desperate situation.'

STELLA   I beg your pardon!

BLANCHE   'Sister and I in desperate situation. Will explain details later. Would you be interested in—?' (*She bites the pencil again*) 'Would you be—interested—in . . .' (*She smashes the pencil on the table and springs up*) You never get anywhere with direct appeals!

STELLA (*With a laugh*)   Don't be so ridiculous, darling!

BLANCHE   But I'll think of something, I've *got* to think of—*some*thing! Don't, don't laugh at me, Stella! Please, please don't—I—I want you to look at the contents of my purse! Here's what's in it! (*She snatches her purse open*) Sixty-five measly cents in coin of the realm!

STELLA (*Crossing to bureau*)   Stanley doesn't give me a regular allowance, he likes to pay bills himself, but—this morning he gave me ten dollars to smooth things over. You take five of it, Blanche, and I'll keep the rest.

BLANCHE   Oh, no. No, Stella.

STELLA (*Insisting*)   I know how it helps your morale just having a little pocket-money on you.

BLANCHE   No, thank you—I'll take to the streets!

STELLA   Talk sense! How did you happen to get so low on funds?

BLANCHE   Money just goes—it goes places. (*She rubs her forehead*) Sometime today I've got to get hold of a bromo!

STELLA   I'll fix you one now.

BLANCHE   Not yet—I've got to keep thinking!

STELLA   I wish you'd just let things go, at least for a—while . . .

BLANCHE   Stella, I can't live with him! You can, he's your husband. But how could I stay here with him, after last night, with just those curtains between us?

STELLA   Blanche, you saw him at his worst last night.

BLANCHE   On the contrary, I saw him at his best! What such a man has to offer is animal force and he gave a wonderful exhibition of that! But the only way to live with such a man is to—go to bed with him! And that's your job—not mine!

STELLA   After you've rested a little, you'll see it's going to work out. You don't have to worry about anything while you're here. I mean—expenses . . .

BLANCHE   I have to plan for us both, to get us both—out!

STELLA   You take it for granted that I am in something that I want to get out of.

BLANCHE   I take it for granted that you still have sufficient memory of Belle Reve to find this place and these poker players impossible to live with.

STELLA   Well, you're taking entirely too much for granted.

BLANCHE   I can't believe you're in earnest.

STELLA   No?

BLANCHE   I understand how it happened—a little. You saw him in uniform, an officer, not here but—

STELLA   I'm not sure it would have made any difference where I saw him.

BLANCHE   Now don't say it was one of those mysterious electric things between people! If you do I'll laugh in your face.

STELLA   I am not going to say anything more at all about it!

BLANCHE   All right, then, don't!

STELLA   But there are things that happen between a man and a woman in the dark—that sort of make everything else seem—unimportant. (*Pause*)

BLANCHE   What you are talking about is brutal desire—just —Desire!—the name of that rattle-trap street-car that bangs through the Quarter, up one old narrow street and down another . . .

STELLA   Haven't you ever ridden on that street-car?

BLANCHE   It brought me here.—Where I'm not wanted and where I'm ashamed to be . . .

STELLA   Then don't you think your superior attitude is a bit out of place?

BLANCHE   I am not being or feeling at all superior, Stella. Believe me I'm not! It's just this. This is how I look at it. A man like that is someone to go out with—once—twice— three times when the devil is in you. But live with? Have a child by?

STELLA   I have told you I love him.

BLANCHE   Then I *tremble* for you! I just—*tremble* for you. . . .

STELLA   I can't help your trembling if you insist on trembling! (*There is a pause*)

BLANCHE   May I—speak—*plainly?*

STELLA   Yes, do. Go ahead. As plainly as you want to.
   (*Outside, a train approaches. They are silent till the noise subsides. They are both in the bedroom.*
   (*Under cover of the train's noise* STANLEY *enters from outside. He stands unseen by the women, holding some packages in his arms, and overhears their following conversation. He wears an undershirt and grease-stained seer-sucker pants*)

BLANCHE   Well—if you'll forgive me—he's *common!*

STELLA   Why, yes, I suppose he is.

BLANCHE   Suppose! You can't have forgotten that much of our bringing up, Stella, that you just *suppose* that any par⸱

of a gentleman's in his nature! *Not one particle, no!* Oh, if he was just—*ordinary!* Just *plain*—but good and wholesome, but—*no.* There's something downright—*bestial*—about him! You're hating me saying this, aren't you?

STELLA (*Coldly*)   Go on and say it all, Blanche.

BLANCHE   He acts like an animal, has an animal's habits! Eats like one, moves like one, talks like one! There's even something—sub-human—something not quite to the stage of humanity yet! Yes, something—ape-like about him, like one of those pictures I've seen in—anthropological studies! Thousands and thousands of years have passed him right by, and there he is—Stanley Kowalski—survivor of the stone age! Bearing the raw meat home from the kill in the jungle! And you—*you* here—*waiting* for him! Maybe he'll strike you or maybe grunt and kiss you! That is, if kisses have been discovered yet! Night falls and the other apes gather! There in the front of the cave, all grunting like him, and swilling and gnawing and hulking! His poker night!—you call it—this party of apes! Somebody growls—some creature snatches at something—the fight is on! *God!* Maybe we are a long way from being made in God's image, but Stella—my sister—there has been *some* progress since then! Such things as art—as poetry and music—such kinds of new light have come into the world since then! In some kinds of people some tenderer feelings have had some little beginning! That we have got to make *grow!* And *cling* to, and hold as our flag! In this dark march toward whatever it is we're approaching. . . . *Don't—don't hang back with the brutes!*
   (*Another train passes outside.* STANLEY *hesitates, licking his lips. Then suddenly he turns stealthily about and withdraws through front door. The women are still unaware of his presence. When the train has passed he calls through the closed front door*)

STANLEY   Hey! Hey, Stella!

STELLA (*Who has listened gravely to* BLANCHE)   Stanley!

BLANCHE   Stell, I—
   (*But* STELLA *has gone to the front door.* STANLEY *enters casually with his packages*)

STANLEY   Hiyuh, Stella. Blanche back?

STELLA   That's much more practical!
   (STEVE *comes down nursing a bruise on his forehead and looks in the door*)

STEVE   *She here?*

STANLEY   Naw, naw. At the Four Deuces.

STEVE   That rutting hunk! (*He looks around the corner a bit timidly, then turns with affected boldness and runs after her*)

BLANCHE   I must jot that down in my notebook. Ha-ha! I'm compiling a notebook of quaint little words and phrases I've picked up here.

STANLEY   You won't pick up nothing here you ain't heard before.

BLANCHE   Can I count on that?

STANLEY   You can count on it up to five hundred.

BLANCHE   That's a mighty high number. (*He jerks open the bureau drawer, slams it shut and throws shoes in a corner. At each noise* BLANCHE *winces slightly. Finally she speaks*) What sign were you born under?

STANLEY   (*While he is dressing*)   Sign?

BLANCHE   Astrological sign. I bet you were born under Aries. Aries people are forceful and dynamic. They dote on noise! They love to bang things around! You must have had lots of banging around in the army and now that you're out, you make up for it by treating inanimate objects with such a fury!
   (STELLA *has been going in and out of closet during this scene. Now she pops her head out of the closet*)

STELLA   Stanley was born just five minutes after Christmas.

BLANCHE   Capricorn—the Goat!

STANLEY   What sign were *you* born under?

BLANCHE   Oh, my birthday's next month, the fifteenth of September; that's under Virgo.

STANLEY   What's Virgo?

BLANCHE   Virgo is the Virgin.

STANLEY *(Contemptuously)*   *Hah!* *(He advances a little as he knots his tie)* Say, do you happen to know somebody named Shaw?

(Her face expresses a faint shock. She reaches for the cologne bottle and dampens her handkerchief as she answers carefully)

BLANCHE   Why, everybody knows somebody named Shaw!

STANLEY   Well, this somebody named Shaw is under the impression he met you in Laurel, but I figure he must have got you mixed up with some other party because this other party is someone he met at a hotel called the Flamingo.

(BLANCHE laughs breathlessly as she touches the cologne-dampened handkerchief to her temples)

BLANCHE   I'm afraid he does have me mixed up with this "other party." The Hotel Flamingo is not the sort of establishment I would dare to be seen in!

STANLEY   You know of it?

BLANCHE   Yes, I've seen it and smelled it.

STANLEY   You must've got pretty close if you could smell it.

BLANCHE   The odor of cheap perfume is penetrating.

STANLEY   That stuff you use is expensive?

BLANCHE   Twenty-five dollars an ounce! I'm nearly out. That's just a hint if you want to remember my birthday! *(She speaks lightly but her voice has a note of fear)*

STANLEY   Shaw must've got you mixed up. He goes in and out of Laurel all the time so he can check on it and clear up any mistake.

(He turns away and crosses to the portieres. BLANCHE closes her eyes as if faint. Her hand trembles as she lifts the handkerchief again to her forehead.

(STEVE and EUNICE come around corner. STEVE's arm is around EUNICE's shoulder and she is sobbing luxuriously and he is cooing love-words. There is a murmur of thunder as they go slowly upstairs in a tight embrace)

STANLEY *(To STELLA)*   I'll wait for you at the Four Deuces!

STELLA   Hey! Don't I rate one kiss?

STANLEY   Not in front of your sister.
  (*He goes out.* BLANCHE *rises from her chair. She seems
  faint; looks about her with an expression of almost panic*)

BLANCHE   Stella! What have you heard about me?

STELLA   Huh?

BLANCHE   What have people been telling you about me?

STELLA   Telling?

BLANCHE   You haven't heard any—unkind—gossip about
me?

STELLA   Why, no, Blanche, of course not!

BLANCHE   Honey, there was—a good deal of talk in Laurel

STELLA   About *you*, Blanche?

BLANCHE   I wasn't so good the last two years or so, after
Belle Reve had started to slip through my fingers.

STELLA   All of us do things we—

BLANCHE   I never was hard or self-sufficient enough. When
people are soft—soft people have got to shimmer and glow—
they've got to put on soft colors, the colors of butterfly wings,
and put a—paper lantern over the light. . . . It isn't enough
to be soft. You've got to be soft *and attractive*. And I—I'm
fading now! I don't know how much longer I can turn the
trick.
  (*The afternoon has faded to dusk.* STELLA *goes into the
  bedroom and turns on the light under the paper lantern.
  She holds a bottled soft drink in her hand*)

BLANCHE   Have you been listening to me?

STELLA   I don't listen to you when you are being morbid!
(*She advances with the bottled coke*)

BLANCHE (*With abrupt change to gaiety*)   Is that coke for
me?

STELLA   Not for anyone else!

BLANCHE   Why, you precious thing, you! Is it just coke?

STELLA (*Turning*)   You mean you want a shot in it!

BLANCHE   Well, honey, a shot never does a coke any harm! Let me! You mustn't wait on me!

STELLA   I like to wait on you, Blanche. It makes it seem more like home. (*She goes into the kitchen, finds a glass and pours a shot of whiskey into it*)

BLANCHE   I have to admit I love to be waited on . . .
(*She rushes into the bedroom.* STELLA *goes to her with the glass.* BLANCHE *suddenly clutches* STELLA'S *free hand with a moaning sound and presses the hand to her lips.* STELLA *is embarrassed by her show of emotion.* BLANCHE *speaks in a choked voice*)
You're—you're—so *good* to me! And I—

STELLA   Blanche.

BLANCHE   I know, I won't! You hate me to talk sentimental! But honey, *believe* I feel things more than I *tell* you! I *won't* stay long! I won't, I *promise* I—

STELLA   Blanche!

BLANCHE (*Hysterically*)   I won't, I promise, *I'll* go! Go *soon!* I will *really!* I *won't* hang around until he—throws me out . . .

STELLA   Now will you stop talking foolish?

BLANCHE   Yes, honey. Watch how you pour—that fizzy stuff foams over!
(BLANCHE *laughs shrilly and grabs the glass, but her hand shakes so it almost slips from her grasp.* STELLA *pours the coke into the glass. It foams over and spills.* BLANCHE *gives a piercing cry*)

STELLA (*Shocked by the cry*)   Heavens!

BLANCHE   Right on my pretty white skirt!

STELLA   Oh . . . Use my hanky. Blot gently.

BLANCHE (*Slowly recovering*)   I know—gently—gently . . .

STELLA   Did it stain?

BLANCHE Not a bit. Ha-ha! Isn't that lucky? (*She sits down shakily, taking a grateful drink. She holds the glass in both hands and continues to laugh a little*)

STELLA Why did you scream like that?

BLANCHE I don't know why I screamed! (*Continuing nervously*) Mitch—Mitch is coming at seven. I guess I am just feeling nervous about our relations. (*She begins to talk rapidly and breathlessly*) He hasn't gotten a thing but a goodnight kiss, that's all I have given him, Stella. I want his respect. And men don't want anything they get too easy. But on the other hand men lose interest quickly. Especially when the girl is over—thirty. They think a girl over thirty ought to—the vulgar term is—"put out." . . . And I—I'm not "putting out." Of course he—he doesn't know—I mean I haven't informed him—of my real age!

STELLA Why are you sensitive about your age?

BLANCHE Because of hard knocks my vanity's been given. What I mean is—he thinks I'm sort of—prim and proper, you know! (*She laughs out sharply*) I want to *deceive* him enough to make him—want me . . .

STELLA Blanche, do you want *him?*

BLANCHE I want to *rest!* I want to breathe quietly again! Yes—I *want* Mitch . . . *very badly!* Just think! If it happens! I can leave here and not be anyone's problem . . .
    (STANLEY *comes around the corner with a drink under his belt*)

STANLEY (*Bawling*) Hey, Steve! Hey, Eunice! Hey, Stella!
    (*There are joyous calls from above. Trumpet and drums are heard from around the corner*)

STELLA (*Kissing* BLANCHE *impulsively*) It *will* happen!

BLANCHE (*Doubtfully*) It will?

STELLA It *will!* (*She goes across into the kitchen, looking back at* BLANCHE) It will, honey, *it will.* . . . But don't take another drink! (*Her voice catches as she goes out the door to meet her husband.*

(BLANCHE *sinks faintly back in her chair with her drink.*
EUNICE *shrieks with laughter and runs down the steps.*
STEVE *bounds after her with goat-like screeches and chases
her around corner.* STANLEY *and* STELLA *twine arms as they
follow, laughing.*
(*Dusk settles deeper. The music from the Four Deuces is
slow and blue.*)

BLANCHE   Ah, me, ah, me, ah, me . . .
(*Her eyes fall shut and the palm leaf fan drops from her
fingers. She slaps her hand on the chair arm a couple of
times. There is a little glimmer of lightning about the
building*
(*A* YOUNG MAN *comes along the street and rings the bell*)

BLANCHE   Come in.
(*The* YOUNG MAN *appears through the portieres. She regards him with interest*)

BLANCHE   Well, well! What can I do for *you?*

YOUNG MAN   I'm collecting for *The Evening Star.*

BLANCHE   I didn't know that stars took up collections.

YOUNG MAN   It's the paper.

BLANCHE   I know, I was joking—feebly! Will you—have a
drink?

YOUNG MAN   No, ma'am. No, thank you. I can't drink on
the job.

BLANCHE   Oh, well, now, let's see. . . . No, I don't have a
dime! I'm not the lady of the house. I'm her sister from
Mississippi. I'm one of those poor relations you've heard
about.

YOUNG MAN   That's all right. I'll drop by later. (*He starts
to go out. She approaches a little*)

BLANCHE   Hey! (*He turns back shyly. She puts a cigarette
in a long holder*) Could you give me a light? (*She crosses
toward him. They meet at the door between the two rooms*)

YOUNG MAN   Sure. (*He takes out a lighter*) This doesn't
always work.

BLANCHE   It's temperamental? (*It flares*) Ah!—thank you.
(*He starts away again*) Hey! (*He turns again, still more
uncertainly. She goes close to him*) Uh—what time is it?

YOUNG MAN   Fifteen of seven, ma'am.

BLANCHE   So late? Don't you just love these long rainy
afternoons in New Orleans when an hour isn't just an hour
—but a little piece of eternity dropped into your hands—and
who knows what to do with it? (*She touches his shoulders*)
You—uh—didn't get wet in the rain?

YOUNG MAN   No, ma'am. I stepped inside.

BLANCHE   In a drug-store? And had a soda?

YOUNG MAN   Uh-huh.

BLANCHE   Chocolate?

YOUNG MAN   No, ma'am. Cherry.

BLANCHE (*Laughing*)   Cherry!

YOUNG MAN   A cherry soda.

BLANCHE   You make my mouth water. (*She touches his
cheek lightly, and smiles. Then she goes to the trunk*)

YOUNG MAN   Well, I'd better be going—

BLANCHE (*Stopping him*)   Young man!
   (*He turns. She takes a large, gossamer scarf from the
   trunk and drapes it about her shoulders
   (In the ensuing pause, the "blue piano" is heard. It continues through the rest of this scene and the opening of the
   next. The* YOUNG MAN *clears his throat and looks yearn-
   ingly at the door*)
Young man! Young, young, young man! Has anyone ever
told you that you look like a young Prince out of the
Arabian Nights?
   (*The* YOUNG MAN *laughs uncomfortably and stands like
   a bashful kid.* BLANCHE *speaks softly to him*)
Well, you do, honey lamb! Come here. I want to kiss you,
just once, softly and sweetly on your mouth!
   (*Without waiting for him to accept, she crosses quickly
   to him and presses her lips to his*)

Now run along, now, quickly! It would be nice to keep you, but I've got to be good—and keep my hands off children.
(*He stares at her a moment. She opens the door for him and blows a kiss at him as he goes down the steps with a dazed look. She stands there a little dreamily after he has disappeared. Then* MITCH *appears around the corner with a bunch of roses*)

BLANCHE (*Gaily*)   Look who's coming! My Rosenkavalier! Bow to me first . . . now present them! *Ahhhh—Merciiii!* (*She looks at him over them, coquettishly pressing them to her lips. He beams at her self-consciously*)

Scene Six

It is about two A.M. on the same evening. The outer wall of the building is visible. BLANCHE *and* MITCH *come in. The utter exhaustion which only a neurasthenic personality can know is evident in* BLANCHE'S *voice and manner.* MITCH *is stolid but depressed. They have probably been out to the amusement park on Lake Pontchartrain, for* MITCH *is bearing, upside down, a plaster statuette of Mae West, the sort of prize won at shooting-galleries and carnival games of chance.*

BLANCHE (*Stopping lifelessly at the steps*)   Well—
(MITCH *laughs uneasily*)
Well . . .

MITCH   I guess it must be pretty late—and you're tired.

BLANCHE   Even the hot tamale man has deserted the street, and he hangs on till the end. (MITCH *laughs uneasily again*) How will you get home?

MITCH   I'll walk over to Bourbon and catch an owl-car.

BLANCHE (*Laughing grimly*)   Is that street-car named Desire still grinding along the tracks at this hour?

MITCH (*Heavily*)   I'm afraid you haven't gotten much fun out of this evening, Blanche.

BLANCHE   I spoiled it for *you*.

MITCH   No, you didn't, but I felt all the time that I wasn't giving you much—entertainment.

BLANCHE   I simply couldn't rise to the occasion. That was all. I don't think I've ever tried so hard to be gay and made such a dismal mess of it. I get ten points for trying!—I *did* try.

MITCH   Why did you try if you didn't feel like it, Blanche?

BLANCHE   I was just obeying the law of nature.

MITCH   Which law is that?

BLANCHE   The one that says the lady must entertain the gentleman—or no dice! See if you can locate my door-key in this purse. When I'm so tired my fingers are all thumbs!

MITCH (*Rooting in her purse*)   This it?

BLANCHE   No, honey, that's the key to my trunk which I must soon be packing.

MITCH   You mean you are leaving here soon?

BLANCHE   I've overstayed my welcome.

MITCH   This it?
   (*The music fades away*)

BLANCHE   Eureka! Honey, you open the door while I take a last look at the sky. (*She leans on the porch rail. He opens the door and stands awkwardly behind her*) I'm looking for the Pleiades, the Seven Sisters, but these girls are not out tonight. Oh, yes, they are, there they are! God bless them! All in a bunch going home from their little bridge party. . . . Y' get the door open? Good boy! I guess you—want to go now . . .
   (*He shuffles and coughs a little*)

MITCH   Can I—uh—kiss you—goodnight?

BLANCHE   Why do you always ask me if you may?

MITCH   I don't know whether you want me to or not.

BLANCHE   Why should you be so doubtful?

MITCH   That night when we parked by the lake and I kissed you, you—

BLANCHE   Honey, it wasn't the kiss I objected to. I liked the kiss very much. It was the other little—familiarity—that I—felt obliged to—discourage. . . . I didn't resent it! Not a bit in the world! In fact, I was somewhat flattered that you—desired me! But, honey, you know as well as I do that a single girl, a girl alone in the world, has got to keep a firm hold on her emotions or she'll be lost!

MITCH (*Solemnly*)   Lost?

BLANCHE   I guess you are used to girls that like to be lost. The kind that get lost immediately, on the first date!

MITCH   I like you to be exactly the way that you are, because in all my—experience—I have never known anyone like you.
   (BLANCHE *looks at him gravely; then she bursts into laughter and then claps a hand to her mouth*)

MITCH   Are you laughing at me?

BLANCHE   No, honey. The lord and lady of the house have not yet returned, so come in. We'll have a night-cap. Let's leave the lights off. Shall we?

MITCH   You just—do what you want to.
   (BLANCHE *precedes him into the kitchen. The outer wall of the building disappears and the interiors of the two rooms can be dimly seen*)

BLANCHE (*Remaining in the first room*)   The other room's more comfortable—go on in. This crashing around in the dark is my search for some liquor.

MITCH   You want a drink?

BLANCHE   I want *you* to have a drink! You have been so anxious and solemn all evening, and so have I; we have both been anxious and solemn and now for these few last remaining moments of our lives together—I want to create—*joie de vivre!* I'm lighting a candle.

MITCH   That's good.

BLANCHE   We are going to be very Bohemian. We are going to pretend that we are sitting in a little artists' cafe on the Left Bank in Paris! (*She lights a candle stub and puts it in a bottle*) *Je suis la Dame aux Camellias! Vous êtes—Armand!* Understand French?

MITCH (*Heavily*)   Naw. Naw, I—

BLANCHE   *Voulez-vous couchez avec moi ce soir? Vous ne comprenez pas? Ah, quelle dommage!*—I mean it's a damned good thing. . . . I've found some liquor! Just enough for two shots without any dividends, honey . . .

MITCH (*Heavily*)   That's—good.
   (*She enters the bedroom with the drinks and the candle*)

BLANCHE   Sit down! Why don't you take off your coat and loosen your collar?

MITCH   I better leave it on.

BLANCHE   No. I want you to be comfortable.

MITCH   I am ashamed of the way I perspire. My shirt is sticking to me.

BLANCHE   Perspiration is healthy. If people didn't perspire they would die in five minutes. (*She takes his coat from him*) This is a nice coat. What kind of material is it?

MITCH   They call that stuff alpaca.

BLANCHE   Oh. Alpaca.

MITCH   It's very light weight alpaca.

BLANCHE   Oh. Light weight alpaca.

MITCH   I don't like to wear a wash-coat even in summer because I sweat through it.

BLANCHE   Oh.

MITCH   And it don't look neat on me. A man with a heavy build has got to be careful of what he puts on him so he don't look too clumsy.

BLANCHE   You are not too heavy.

MITCH   You don't think I am?

BLANCHE   You are not the delicate type. You have a massive bone-structure and a very imposing physique.

MITCH   Thank you. Last Christmas I was given a membership to the New Orleans Athletic Club.

BLANCHE   Oh, good.

MITCH   It was the finest present I ever was given. I work out there with the weights and I swim and I keep myself fit. When I started there, I was getting soft in the belly but now my belly is hard. It is so hard now that a man can punch me in the belly and it don't hurt me. Punch me! Go on! See? (*She pokes lightly at him*)

BLANCHE   Gracious. (*Her hand touches her chest*)

MITCH   Guess how much I weigh, Blanche?

BLANCHE   Oh, I'd say in the vicinity of—one hundred and eighty?

MITCH   Guess again.

BLANCHE   Not that much?

MITCH   No. More.

BLANCHE   Well, you're a tall man and you can carry a good deal of weight without looking awkward.

MITCH   I weigh two hundred and seven pounds and I'm six feet one and one half inches tall in my bare feet—without shoes on. And that is what I weigh stripped.

BLANCHE   Oh, my goodness, me! It's awe-inspiring.

MITCH (*Embarrassed*)   My weight is not a very interesting subject to talk about. (*He hesitates for a moment*) What's yours?

BLANCHE   My weight?

MITCH   Yes.

BLANCHE   Guess!

MITCH   Let me lift you.

BLANCHE   Samson! Go on, lift me. (*He comes behind her and puts his hands on her waist and raises her lightly off the ground*) Well?

MITCH   You are light as a feather.

BLANCHE   Ha-ha! (*He lowers her but keeps his hands on her waist.* BLANCHE *speaks with an affectation of demureness*) You may release me now.

MITCH   Huh?

BLANCHE (*Gaily*)   I said unhand me, sir. (*He fumblingly embraces her. Her voice sounds gently reproving*) Now, Mitch. Just because Stanley and Stella aren't at home is no reason why you shouldn't behave like a gentleman.

MITCH   Just give me a slap whenever I step out of bounds.

BLANCHE   That won't be necessary. You're a natural gentleman, one of the very few that are left in the world. I don't want you to think that I am severe and old maid schoolteacherish or anything like that. It's just—well—

MITCH   Huh?

BLANCHE   I guess it is just that I have—old-fashioned ideals! (*She rolls her eyes, knowing he cannot see her face.* MITCH *goes to the front door. There is a considerable silence between them.* BLANCHE *sighs and* MITCH *coughs self-consciously*)

MITCH (*Finally*)   Where's Stanley and Stella tonight?

BLANCHE   They have gone out. With Mr. and Mrs. Hubbell upstairs.

MITCH   Where did they go?

BLANCHE   I think they were planning to go to a midnight prevue at Loew's State.

MITCH   We should all go out together some night.

BLANCHE   No. That wouldn't be a good plan.

MITCH   Why not?

BLANCHE   You are an old friend of Stanley's?

MITCH   We was together in the Two-forty-first.

BLANCHE   I guess he talks to you frankly?

MITCH   Sure.

BLANCHE   Has he talked to you about me?

MITCH   Oh—not very much.

BLANCHE   The way you say that, I suspect that he has.

MITCH   No, he hasn't said much.

BLANCHE   But what he *has* said. What would you say his attitude toward me was?

MITCH   Why do you want to ask that?

BLANCHE   Well—

MITCH   Don't you get along with him?

BLANCHE   What do you think?

MITCH   I don't think he understands you.

BLANCHE   That is putting it mildly. If it weren't for Stella about to have a baby, I wouldn't be able to endure things here.

MITCH   He isn't—nice to you?

BLANCHE   He is insufferably rude. Goes out of his way to offend me.

MITCH   In what way, Blanche?

BLANCHE   Why, in every conceivable way.

MITCH   I'm surprised to hear that.

BLANCHE   Are you?

MITCH   Well, I—don't see how anybody could be rude to you.

BLANCHE   It's really a pretty frightful situation. You see, there's no privacy here. There's just these portieres between the two rooms at night. He stalks through the rooms in his underwear at night. And I have to ask him to close the bathroom door. That sort of commonness isn't necessary. You probably wonder why I don't move out. Well, I'll tell you frankly. A teacher's salary is barely sufficient for her

living-expenses. I didn't save a penny last year and so I had
to come here for the summer. That's why I have to put up
with my sister's husband. And he has to put up with me, apparently so much against his wishes. . . . Surely he must
have told you how much he hates me!

MITCH   I don't think he hates you.

BLANCHE   He hates me. Or why would he insult me? The
first time I laid eyes on him I thought to myself, that man is
my executioner! That man will destroy me, unless——

MITCH   Blanche—

BLANCHE   Yes, honey?

MITCH   Can I ask you a question?

BLANCHE   Yes. What?

MITCH   How old are you?
   (*She makes a nervous gesture*)

BLANCHE   Why do you want to know?

MITCH   I talked to my mother about you and she said, "How
old is Blanche?" And I wasn't able to tell her. (*There is
another pause*)

BLANCHE   You talked to your mother about me?

MITCH   Yes.

BLANCHE   Why?

MITCH   I told my mother how nice you were, and I liked
you.

BLANCHE   Were you sincere about that?

MITCH   You know I was.

BLANCHE   Why did your mother want to know my age?

MITCH   Mother is sick.

BLANCHE   I'm sorry to hear it. Badly?

MITCH   She won't live long. Maybe just a few months.

BLANCHE   Oh.

MITCH   She worries because I'm not settled.

BLANCHE   Oh.

MITCH   She wants me to be settled down before she— (*His voice is hoarse and he clears his throat twice, shuffling nervously around with his hands in and out of his pockets*)

BLANCHE   You love her very much, don't you?

MITCH   Yes.

BLANCHE   I think you have a great capacity for devotion. You will be lonely when she passes on, won't you? (MITCH *clears his throat and nods*) I understand what that is.

MITCH   To be lonely?

BLANCHE   I loved someone, too, and the person I loved I lost.

MITCH   Dead? (*She crosses to the window and sits on the sill, looking out. She pours herself another drink*) A man?

BLANCHE   He was a boy, just a boy, when I was a very young girl. When I was sixteen, I made the discovery—love. All at once and much, much too completely. It was like you suddenly turned a blinding light on something that had always been half in shadow, that's how it struck the world for me. But I was unlucky. Deluded. There was something different about the boy, a nervousness, a softness and tenderness which wasn't like a man's, although he wasn't the least bit effeminate looking—still—that thing was there. . . . He came to me for help. I didn't know that. I didn't find out anything till after our marriage when we'd run away and come back and all I knew was I'd failed him in some mysterious way and wasn't able to give the help he needed but couldn't speak of! He was in the quicksands and clutching at me—but I wasn't holding him out, I was slipping in with him! I didn't know that. I didn't know anything except I loved him unendurably but without being able to help him or help myself. Then I found out. In the worst of all possible ways. By coming suddenly into a room that I thought was empty—which wasn't empty, but had two people in it . . . the boy I had married and an older man who had been his friend for years . . .

  (*A locomotive is heard approaching outside. She claps her hands to her ears and crouches over. The headlight of the locomotive glares into the room as it thunders past. As the noise recedes she straightens slowly and continues speaking)*

Afterwards we pretended that nothing had been discovered. Yes, the three of us drove out to Moon Lake Casino, very drunk and laughing all the way.

(Polka music sounds, in a minor key faint with distance)

We danced the Varsouviana! Suddenly in the middle of the dance the boy I had married broke away from me and ran out of the casino. A few moments later—a shot!

(The Polka stops abruptly

(BLANCHE rises stiffly. Then, the Polka resumes in a major key)

I ran out—all did!—all ran and gathered about the terrible thing at the edge of the lake! I couldn't get near for the crowding. Then somebody caught my arm. "Don't go any closer! Come back! You don't want to see!" See? See what! Then I heard voices say—Allan! Allan! The Grey boy! He'd stuck the revolver into his mouth, and fired—so that the back of his head had been—blown away!

(She sways and covers her face)

It was because—on the dance-floor—unable to stop myself— I'd suddenly said—"I saw! I know! You disgust me . . ." And then the searchlight which had been turned on the world was turned off again and never for one moment since has there been any light that's stronger than this—kitchen— candle . . .

(MITCH gets up awkwardly and moves toward her a little. The Polka music increases. MITCH stands beside her)

MITCH *(Drawing her slowly into his arms)*   You need somebody. And I need somebody, too. Could it be—you and me, Blanche?

(She stares at him vacantly for a moment. Then with a soft cry huddles in his embrace. She makes a sobbing effort to speak but the words won't come. He kisses her forehead and her eyes and finally her lips. The Polka tune fades out. Her breath is drawn and released in long, grateful sobs)

BLANCHE   Sometimes—there's God—so quickly!

Scene Seven

It is late afternoon in mid-September.

The portieres are open and a table is set for a birthday supper, with cake and flowers.

STELLA _is completing the decorations as_ STANLEY _comes in._

STANLEY   What's all this stuff for?

STELLA   Honey, it's Blanche's birthday.

STANLEY   She here?

STELLA   In the bathroom.

STANLEY (_Mimicking_)   "Washing out some things"?

STELLA   I reckon so.

STANLEY   How long she been in there?

STELLA   All afternoon.

STANLEY (_Mimicking_)   "Soaking in a hot tub"?

STELLA   Yes.

STANLEY   Temperature 100 on the nose, and she soaks herself in a hot tub.

STELLA   She says it cools her off for the evening.

STANLEY   And you run out an' get her cokes, I suppose? And serve 'em to Her Majesty in the tub? (STELLA _shrugs_) Set down here a minute.

STELLA   Stanley, I've got things to do.

STANLEY   Set down! I've got th' dope on your big sister, Stella.

STELLA   Stanley, stop picking on Blanche.

STANLEY   That girl calls *me* common!

STELLA   Lately you been doing all you can think of to rub her the wrong way, Stanley, and Blanche is sensitive and you've got to realize that Blanche and I grew up under very different circumstances than you did.

STANLEY   So I been told. And told and told and told! You know she's been feeding us a pack of lies here?

STELLA   No, I don't, and—

STANLEY   Well, she has, however. But now the cat's out of the bag! I found out some things!

STELLA   What—things?

STANLEY   Things I already suspected. But now I got proof from the most reliable sources—which I have checked on! (BLANCHE *is singing in the bathroom a saccharine popular ballad which is used contrapuntally with* STANLEY's *speech*)

STELLA   (*To* STANLEY)   Lower your voice!

STANLEY   Some canary-bird, huh!

STELLA   Now please tell me quietly what you think you've found out about my sister.

STANLEY   Lie Number One: All this squeamishness she puts on! You should just know the line she's been feeding to Mitch. He thought she had never been more than kissed by a fellow! But Sister Blanche is no lily! Ha-ha! Some lily she is!

STELLA   What have you heard and who from?

STANLEY   Our supply-man down at the plant has been going through Laurel for years and he knows all about her and everybody else in the town of Laurel knows all about her. She is as famous in Laurel as if she was the President of the United States, only she is not respected by any party! This supply-man stops at a hotel called the Flamingo.

BLANCHE (*Singing blithely*)
"Say, it's only a paper moon, Sailing over a cardboard sea—
But it wouldn't be make-believe If you believed in me!"

STELLA   What about the—Flamingo?

STANLEY   She stayed there, too.

STELLA   My sister lived at Belle Reve.

STANLEY   This is after the home-place had slipped through
her lily-white fingers! She moved to the Flamingo! A second-
class hotel which has the advantage of not interfering in the
private social life of the personalities there! The Flamingo is
used to all kinds of goings-on. But even the management of
the Flamingo was impressed by Dame Blanche! In fact they
was so impressed by Dame Blanche that they requested her
to turn in her room-key—for permanently! This happened
a couple of weeks before she showed here.

BLANCHE (*Singing*)
"It's a Barnum and Bailey world, Just as phony as it can be—
But it wouldn't be make-believe If you believed in me!"

STELLA   What—contemptible—lies!

STANLEY   Sure, I can see how you would be upset by this.
She pulled the wool over your eyes as much as Mitch's!

STELLA   It's pure invention! There's not a word of truth in
it and if I were a man and this creature had dared to invent
such things in my presence—

BLANCHE (*Singing*)
"Without your love,
  It's a honky-tonk parade!
Without your love,
  It's a melody played In a penny arcade . . ."

STANLEY   Honey, I told you I thoroughly checked on these
stories! Now wait till I finished. The trouble with Dame
Blanche was that she couldn't put on her act any more in
Laurel! They got wised up after two or three dates with her
and then they quit, and she goes on to another, the same old
line, same old act, same old hooey! But the town was too
small for this to go on forever! And as time went by she

became a town character. Regarded as not just different but
downright loco—nuts.

(STELLA *draws back*)

And for the last year or two she has been washed up like
poison. That's why she's here this summer, visiting royalty,
putting on all this act—because she's practically told by the
mayor to get out of town! Yes, did you know there was an
army camp near Laurel and your sister's was one of the
places called "Out-of-Bounds"?

BLANCHE

"It's only a paper moon, Just as phony as it can be—
  But it wouldn't be make-believe If you believed in me!"

STANLEY   Well, so much for her being such a refined and
particular type of girl. Which brings us to Lie Number Two.

STELLA   I don't want to hear any more!

STANLEY   She's not going back to teach school! In fact I
am willing to bet you that she never had no idea of returning to Laurel! She didn't resign temporarily from the high
school because of her nerves! No, siree, Bob! She didn't.
They kicked her out of that high school before the spring
term ended—and I hate to tell you the reason that step was
taken! A seventeen-year-old boy—she'd gotten mixed up
with!

BLANCHE

"It's a Barnum and Bailey world, Just as phony as it can
be—"
  (*In the bathroom the water goes on loud; little breathless
  cries and peals of laughter are heard as if a child were
  frolicking in the tub*)

STELLA   This is making me—sick!

STANLEY   The boy's dad learned about it and got in touch
with the high school superintendent. Boy, oh, boy, I'd like
to have been in that office when Dame Blanche was called
on the carpet! I'd like to have seen her trying to squirm out
of that one! But they had her on the hook good and proper
that time and she knew that the jig was all up! They told
her she better move on to some fresh territory. Yep, it was
practickly a town ordinance passed against her!

(The bathroom door is opened and BLANCHE *thrusts her head out, holding a towel about her hair)*

BLANCHE   Stella!

STELLA *(Faintly)*   Yes, Blanche?

BLANCHE   Give me another bath-towel to dry my hair with. I've just washed it.

STELLA   Yes, Blanche. *(She crosses in a dazed way from the kitchen to the bathroom door with a towel)*

BLANCHE   What's the matter, honey?

STELLA   Matter? Why?

BLANCHE   You have such a strange expression on your face!

STELLA   Oh— *(She tries to laugh)* I guess I'm a little tired!

BLANCHE   Why don't you bathe, too, soon as I get out?

STANLEY *(Calling from the kitchen)*   How soon is that going to be?

BLANCHE   Not so terribly long! Possess your soul in patience!

STANLEY   It's not my soul, it's my kidneys I'm worried about!

*(*BLANCHE *slams the door.* STANLEY *laughs harshly.* STELLA *comes slowly back into the kitchen)*

STANLEY   Well, what do you think of it?

STELLA   I don't believe all of those stories and I think your supply-man was mean and rotten to tell them. It's possible that some of the things he said are partly true. There are things about my sister I don't approve of—things that caused sorrow at home. She was always—flighty!

STANLEY   Flighty!

STELLA   But when she was young, very young, she married a boy who wrote poetry. . . . He was extremely good-looking. I think Blanche didn't just love him but worshipped the ground he walked on! Adored him and thought him almost too fine to be human! But then she found out—

STANLEY   What?

STELLA   This beautiful and talented young man was a degenerate. Didn't your supply-man give you that information?

STANLEY   All we discussed was recent history. That must have been a pretty long time ago.

STELLA   Yes, it was—a pretty long time ago . . .
  (STANLEY *comes up and takes her by the shoulders rather gently. She gently withdraws from him. Automatically she starts sticking little pink candles in the birthday cake*)

STANLEY   How many candles you putting in that cake?

STELLA   I'll stop at twenty-five.

STANLEY   Is company expected?

STELLA   We asked Mitch to come over for cake and ice-cream.
  (STANLEY *looks a little uncomfortable. He lights a cigarette from the one he has just finished*)

STANLEY   I wouldn't be expecting Mitch over tonight.
  (STELLA *pauses in her occupation with candles and looks slowly around at* STANLEY)

STELLA   *Why?*

STANLEY   Mitch is a buddy of mine. We were in the same outfit together—Two-forty-first Engineers. We work in the same plant and now on the same bowling team. You think I could face him if—

STELLA   Stanley Kowalski, did you—did you repeat what that—?

STANLEY   You're goddam right I told him! I'd have that on my conscience the rest of my life if I knew all that stuff and let my best friend get caught!

STELLA   Is Mitch through with her?

STANLEY   Wouldn't you be if—?

STELLA   I said, *Is Mitch through with her?*
  (BLANCHE's *voice is lifted again, serenely as a bell. She sings "But it wouldn't be make believe if you believed in me."*)

STANLEY   No, I don't think he's necessarily through with her—just wised up!

STELLA Stanley, she thought Mitch was—going to—going to marry her. I was hoping so, too.

STANLEY Well, he's not going to marry her. Maybe he *was*, but he's not going to jump in a tank with a school of sharks —now! (*He rises*) Blanche! Oh, Blanche! Can I please get in my bathroom? (*There is a pause*)

BLANCHE Yes, indeed, sir! Can you wait one second while I dry?

STANLEY Having waited one hour I guess one second ought to pass in a hurry.

STELLA And she hasn't got her job? Well, what will she do!

STANLEY She's not stayin' here after Tuesday. You know that, don't you? Just to make sure I bought her ticket myself. A bus-ticket!

STELLA In the first place, Blanche wouldn't go on a bus.

STANLEY She'll go on a bus and like it.

STELLA No, she won't, no, she won't, Stanley!

STANLEY *She'll go!* Period. P.S. She'll go *Tuesday!*

STELLA (*Slowly*) What'll—she—do? What on earth will she —do!

STANLEY Her future is mapped out for her.

STELLA What do you mean?
  (BLANCHE *sings*)

STANLEY Hey, canary bird! Toots! Get *OUT* of the *BATH-ROOM!*
  (*The bathroom door flies open and* BLANCHE *emerges with a gay peal of laughter, but as* STANLEY *crosses past her, a frightened look appears in her face, almost a look of panic. He doesn't look at her but slams the bathroom door shut as he goes in*)

BLANCHE (*Snatching up a hair-brush*) Oh, I feel so good after my long, hot bath, I feel so good and cool and— rested!

STELLA (*Sadly and doubtfully from the kitchen*) Do you, Blanche?

BLANCHE (*Brushing her hair vigorously*) Yes, I do, so refreshed! (*She tinkles her highball glass*) A hot bath and a long, cold drink always give me a brand new outlook on life! (*She looks through the portieres at* STELLA, *standing between them, and slowly stops brushing*) Something has happened!—What is it?

STELLA (*Turning away quickly*) Why, nothing has happened, Blanche.

BLANCHE You're lying! Something has!
(*She stares fearfully at* STELLA, *who pretends to be busy at the table. The distant piano goes into a hectic breakdown*)

— Scene Eight

Three-quarters of an hour later.

The view through the big windows is fading gradually into a still-golden dusk. A torch of sunlight blazes on the side of a big water-tank or oil-drum across the empty lot toward the business district which is now pierced by pinpoints of lighted windows or windows reflecting the sunset.

The three people are completing a dismal birthday supper. STANLEY *looks sullen.* STELLA *is embarrassed and sad.*

BLANCHE *has a tight, artificial smile on her drawn face. There is a fourth place at the table which is left vacant.*

BLANCHE (*Suddenly*)   Stanley, tell us a joke, tell us a funny story to make us all laugh. I don't know what's the matter, we're all so solemn. Is it because I've been stood up by my beau?

(STELLA *laughs feebly*)

It's the first time in my entire experience with men, and I've had a good deal of all sorts, that I've actually been stood up by anybody! Ha-ha! I don't know how to take it. . . . Tell us a funny little story, Stanley! Something to help us out.

STANLEY   I didn't think you liked my stories, Blanche.

BLANCHE   I like them when they're amusing but not indecent.

STANLEY   I don't know any refined enough for your taste.

BLANCHE   Then let me tell one.

STELLA   Yes, you tell one, Blanche. You used to know lots of good stories.

(*The music fades*)

BLANCHE   Let me see, now. . . . I must run through my repertoire! Oh, yes—I love parrot stories! Do you all like parrot stories? Well, this one's about the old maid and the parrot. This old maid, she had a parrot that cursed a blue streak and knew more vulgar expressions than Mr. Kowalski!

STANLEY   Huh.

BLANCHE   And the only way to hush the parrot up was to put the cover back on its cage so it would think it was night and go back to sleep. Well, one morning the old maid had just uncovered the parrot for the day—when who should she see coming up the front walk but the preacher! Well, she rushed back to the parrot and slipped the cover back on the cage and then she let in the preacher. And the parrot was perfectly still, just as quiet as a mouse, but just as she was asking the preacher how much sugar he wanted in his coffee —the parrot broke the silence with a loud—(*She whistles*) —and said—"God *damn,* but that was a short day!"

(*She throws back her head and laughs.* STELLA *also makes an ineffectual effort to seem amused.* STANLEY *pays no attention to the story but reaches way over the table to spear his fork into the remaining chop which he eats with his fingers*)

BLANCHE   Apparently Mr. Kowalski was not amused.

STELLA   Mr. Kowalski is too busy making a pig of himself to think of anything else!

STANLEY   That's right, baby.

STELLA   Your face and your fingers are disgustingly greasy. Go and wash up and then help me clear the table.
   (*He hurls a plate to the floor*)

STANLEY   That's how I'll clear the table! (*He seizes her arm*) Don't ever talk that way to me! "Pig—Polack—disgusting—vulgar—greasy!"—them kind of words have been on your tongue and your sister's too much around here! What do you two think you are? A pair of queens? Remember what Huey Long said—"Every Man is a King!" And I am the king around here, so don't forget it! (*He hurls a cup and saucer to the floor*) My place is cleared! You want me to clear your places?
   (STELLA *begins to cry weakly.* STANLEY *stalks out on the porch and lights a cigarette*
   (*The Negro entertainers around the corner are heard*)

BLANCHE   What happened while I was bathing? What did he tell you, Stella?

STELLA   Nothing, nothing, nothing!

BLANCHE   I think he told you something about Mitch and me! You know why Mitch didn't come but you won't tell me! (STELLA *shakes her head helplessly*) I'm going to call him!

STELLA   I wouldn't call him, Blanche.

BLANCHE   I am, I'm going to call him on the phone.

STELLA   (*Miserably*)   I wish you wouldn't.

BLANCHE   I intend to be given some explanation from someone!
   (*She rushes to the phone in the bedroom.* STELLA *goes out on the porch and stares reproachfully at her husband. He grunts and turns away from her*)

STELLA   I hope you're pleased with your doings. I never had so much trouble swallowing food in my life, looking at that girl's face and the empty chair! (*She cries quietly*)

BLANCHE (*At the phone*) Hello. Mr. Mitchell, please. . . .
Oh. . . . I would like to leave a number if I may. Magnolia
9047. And say it's important to call. . . . Yes, very important. . . . Thank you. (*She remains by the phone with a
lost, frightened look*)

  (STANLEY *turns slowly back toward his wife and takes her
  clumsily in his arms*)

STANLEY Stell, it's gonna be all right after she goes and
after you've had the baby. It's gonna be all right again
between you and me the way that it was. You remember
that way that it was? Them nights we had together? God,
honey, it's gonna be sweet when we can make noise in the
night the way that we used to and get the colored lights
going with nobody's sister behind the curtains to hear us!

  (*Their upstairs neighbors are heard in bellowing laughter
  at something.* STANLEY *chuckles*)
Steve an' Eunice . . .

STELLA Come on back in. (*She returns to the kitchen and
starts lighting the candles on the white cake.*) Blanche?

BLANCHE Yes. (*She returns from the bedroom to the table
in the kitchen*) Oh, those pretty, pretty little candles! Oh,
don't burn them, Stella.

STELLA I certainly will.
  (STANLEY *comes back in*)

BLANCHE You ought to save them for baby's birthdays. Oh,
I hope candles are going to glow in his life and I hope that
his eyes are going to be like candles, like two blue candles
lighted in a white cake!

STANLEY (*Sitting down*) What poetry!

BLANCHE (*She pauses reflectively for a moment*) I shouldn't
have called him.

STELLA There's lots of things could have happened.

BLANCHE There's no excuse for it, Stella. I don't have to put
up with insults. I won't be taken for granted.

STANLEY Goddamn, it's hot in here with the steam from
the bathroom.

BLANCHE   I've said I was sorry three times. (*The piano fades out*) I take hot baths for my nerves. Hydro-therapy, they call it. You healthy Polack, without a nerve in your body, of course you don't know what anxiety feels like!

STANLEY   I am not a Polack. People from Poland are Poles, not Polacks. But what I am is a one hundred percent American, born and raised in the greatest country on earth and proud as hell of it, so don't ever call me a Polack.
   (*The phone rings.* BLANCHE *rises expectantly*)

BLANCHE   Oh, that's for me, I'm sure.

STANLEY   I'm not sure. Keep your seat. (*He crosses leisurely to phone*) H'lo. Aw, yeh, hello, Mac.
   (*He leans against wall, staring insultingly in at* BLANCHE. *She sinks back in her chair with a frightened look.* STELLA *leans over and touches her shoulder*)

BLANCHE   Oh, keep your hands off me, Stella. What is the matter with you? Why do you look at me with that pitying look?

STANLEY (*Bawling*)   QUIET IN THERE!—We've got a noisy woman on the place.—Go on, Mac. At Riley's? No, I don't wanta bowl at Riley's. I had a little trouble with Riley last week. I'm the team-captain, ain't I? All right, then, we're not gonna bowl at Riley's, we're gonna bowl at the West Side or the Gala! All right, Mac. See you!
   (*He hangs up and returns to the table.* BLANCHE *fiercely controls herself, drinking quickly from her tumbler of water. He doesn't look at her but reaches in a pocket. Then he speaks slowly and with false amiability*)
Sister Blanche, I've got a little birthday remembrance for you.

BLANCHE   Oh, have you, Stanley? I wasn't expecting any, I—I don't know why Stella wants to observe my birthday! I'd much rather forget it—when you—reach twenty-seven! Well—age is a subject that you'd prefer to—ignore!

STANLEY   Twenty-seven?

BLANCHE (*Quickly*)   What is it? Is it for *me*?
   (*He is holding a little envelope toward her*)

STANLEY   Yes, I hope you like it!

BLANCHE   Why, why— Why, it's a—

STANLEY   Ticket! Back to Laurel! On the Greyhound! Tuesday!

(*The Varsouviana music steals in softly and continues playing.* STELLA *rises abruptly and turns her back.* BLANCHE *tries to smile. Then she tries to laugh. Then she gives both up and springs from the table and runs into the next room. She clutches her throat and then runs into the bathroom. Coughing, gagging sounds are heard*)

Well!

STELLA   You didn't need to do that.

STANLEY   Don't forget all that I took off her.

STELLA   You needn't have been so cruel to someone alone as she is.

STANLEY   Delicate piece she is.

STELLA   She is. She was. You didn't know Blanche as a girl. Nobody, nobody, was tender and trusting as she was. But people like you abused her, and forced her to change.

(*He crosses into the bedroom, ripping off his shirt, and changes into a brilliant silk bowling shirt. She follows him*)

Do you think you're going bowling now?

STANLEY   Sure.

STELLA   You're not going bowling. (*She catches hold of his shirt*) Why did you do this to her?

STANLEY   I done nothing to no one. Let go of my shirt. You've torn it.

STELLA   I want to know why. Tell me why.

STANLEY   When we first met, me and you, you thought I was common. How right you was, baby. I was common as dirt. You showed me the snapshot of the place with the columns. I pulled you down off them columns and how you loved it, having them colored lights going! And wasn't we happy together, wasn't it all okay till she showed here?

(STELLA *makes a slight movement. Her look goes suddenly inward as if some interior voice had called her name. She begins a slow, shuffling progress from the bedroom to*

*the kitchen, leaning and resting on the back of the chair
and then on the edge of a table with a blind look and listening expression.* STANLEY, *finishing with his shirt, is
unaware of her reaction*)

And wasn't we happy together? Wasn't it all okay? Till she
showed here. Hoity-toity, describing me as an ape. (*He suddenly notices the change in* STELLA) Hey, what is it, Stell?
(*He crosses to her*)

STELLA (*Quietly*) Take me to the hospital.
(*He is with her now, supporting her with his arm, murmuring indistinguishably as they go outside*)

Scene
Nine

A while later that evening. BLANCHE *is seated in a
tense hunched position in a bedroom chair that she
has recovered with diagonal green and white stripes.
She has on her scarlet satin robe. On the table beside
chair is a bottle of liquor and a glass. The rapid, feverish polka tune, the "Varsouviana," is heard. The
music is in her mind; she is drinking to escape it and
the sense of disaster closing in on her, and she seems
to whisper the words of the song. An electric fan is
turning back and forth across her.*

    MITCH *comes around the corner in work clothes:
blue denim shirt and pants. He is unshaven. He climbs
the steps to the door and rings.* BLANCHE *is startled.*

BLANCHE Who is it, please?
MITCH (*Hoarsely*) Me. Mitch.
(*The polka tune stops*)

BLANCHE   Mitch!—Just a minute.
(*She rushes about frantically, hiding the bottle in a closet, crouching at the mirror and dabbing her face with cologne and powder. She is so excited that her breath is audible as she dashes about. At last she rushes to the door in the kitchen and lets him in*)
Mitch!—Y'know, I really shouldn't let you in after the treatment I have received from you this evening! So utterly uncavalier! But hello, beautiful!
(*She offers him her lips. He ignores it and pushes past her into the flat. She looks fearfully after him as he stalks into the bedroom*)
My, my, what a cold shoulder! And such uncouth apparel! Why, you haven't even shaved! The unforgivable insult to a lady! But I forgive you. I forgive you because it's such a relief to see you. You've stopped that polka tune that I had caught in my head. Have you ever had anything caught in your head? No, of course you haven't, you dumb angel-puss, you'd never get anything awful caught in your head!
(*He stares at her while she follows him while she talks. It is obvious that he has had a few drinks on the way over*)

MITCH   Do we have to have that fan on?

BLANCHE   No!

MITCH   I don't like fans.

BLANCHE   Then let's turn it off, honey. I'm not partial to them!
(*She presses the switch and the fan nods slowly off. She clears her throat uneasily as* MITCH *plumps himself down on the bed in the bedroom and lights a cigarette*)
I don't know what there is to drink. I—haven't investigated.

MITCH   I don't want Stan's liquor.

BLANCHE   It isn't Stan's. Everything here isn't Stan's. Some things on the premises are actually mine! How is your mother? Isn't your mother well?

MITCH   Why?

BLANCHE   Something's the matter tonight, but never mind. I won't cross-examine the witness. I'll just— (*She touches her forehead vaguely. The polka tune starts up again*)—pretend I don't notice anything different about you! That—music again . . .

MITCH   What music?

BLANCHE   The "Varsouviana"! The polka tune they were playing when Allan— Wait!
  (*A distant revolver shot is heard.* BLANCHE *seems relieved*)
There now, the shot! It always stops after that.
  (*The polka music dies out again*)
Yes, now it's stopped.

MITCH   Are you boxed out of your mind?

BLANCHE   I'll go and see what I can find in the way of—
(*She crosses into the closet, pretending to search for the bottle*) Oh, by the way, excuse me for not being dressed. But I'd practically given you up! Had you forgotten your invitation to supper?

MITCH   I wasn't going to see you any more.

BLANCHE   Wait a minute. I can't hear what you're saying and you talk so little that when you do say something, I don't want to miss a single syllable of it. . . . What am I looking around here for? Oh, yes—liquor! We've had so much excitement around here this evening that I *am* boxed out of my mind! (*She pretends suddenly to find the bottle. He draws his foot up on the bed and stares at her contemptuously*) Here's something. Southern Comfort! What is that, I wonder?

MITCH   If you don't know, it must belong to Stan.

BLANCHE   Take your foot off the bed. It has a light cover on it. Of course you boys don't notice things like that. I've done so much with this place since I've been here.

MITCH   I bet you have.

BLANCHE   You saw it before I came. Well, look at it now! This room is almost—dainty! I want to keep it that way. I wonder if this stuff ought to be mixed with something? Ummm, it's sweet, so sweet! It's terribly, terribly sweet! Why, it's a *liqueur,* I believe! Yes, that's what it *is,* a liqueur! (MITCH *grunts*) I'm afraid you won't like it, but try it, and maybe you will.

MITCH   I told you already I don't want none of his liquor and I mean it. You ought to lay off his liquor. He says you been lapping it up all summer like a wild-cat!

BLANCHE   What a fantastic statement! Fantastic of him to say it, fantastic of you to repeat it! I won't descend to the level of such cheap accusations to answer them, even!

MITCH   Huh.

BLANCHE   What's in your mind? I see something in your eyes!

MITCH   (*Getting up*)   It's dark in here.

BLANCHE   I like it dark. The dark is comforting to me.

MITCH   I don't think I ever seen you in the light. (BLANCHE *laughs breathlessly*) That's a fact!

BLANCHE   Is it?

MITCH   I've never seen you in the afternoon.

BLANCHE   Whose fault is that?

MITCH   You never want to go out in the afternoon.

BLANCHE   Why, Mitch, you're at the plant in the afternoon!

MITCH   Not Sunday afternoon. I've asked you to go out with me sometimes on Sundays but you always make an excuse. You never want to go out till after six and then it's always some place that's not lighted much.

BLANCHE   There is some obscure meaning in this but I fail to catch it.

MITCH   What it means is I've never had a real good look at you, Blanche. Let's turn the light on here.

BLANCHE   (*Fearfully*)   Light? Which light? What for?

MITCH   This one with the paper thing on it. (*He tears the paper lantern off the light bulb. She utters a frightened gasp*)

BLANCHE   What did you do that for?

MITCH   So I can take a look at you good and plain!

BLANCHE   Of course you don't really mean to be insulting!

MITCH   No, just realistic.

BLANCHE   I don't want realism. I want magic! (MITCH *laughs*) Yes, yes, magic! I try to give that to people. I misrepresent things to them. I don't tell truth, I tell what *ought* to be truth. And if that is sinful, then let me be damned for it!—*Don't turn the light on!*

(MITCH *crosses to the switch. He turns the light on and stares at her. She cries out and covers her face. He turns the light off again*)

MITCH (*Slowly and bitterly*)   I don't mind you being older than what I thought. But all the rest of it—Christ! That pitch about your ideals being so old-fashioned and all the malarkey that you've dished out all summer. Oh, I knew you weren't sixteen any more. But I was a fool enough to believe you was straight.

BLANCHE   Who told you I wasn't—'straight'? My loving brother-in-law. And you believed him.

MITCH   I called him a liar at first. And then I checked on the story. First I asked our supply-man who travels through Laurel. And then I talked directly over long-distance to this merchant.

BLANCHE   Who is this merchant?

MITCH   Kiefaber.

BLANCHE   The merchant Kiefaber of Laurel! I know the man. He whistled at me. I put him in his place. So now for revenge he makes up stories about me.

MITCH   Three people, Kiefaber, Stanley and Shaw, swore to them!

BLANCHE   Rub-a-dub-dub, three men in a tub! And such a filthy tub!

MITCH   Didn't you stay at a hotel called The Flamingo?

BLANCHE   Flamingo? No! Tartantula was the name of it! I stayed at a hotel called The Tarantula Arms!

MITCH (*Stupidly*)   Tarantula?

BLANCHE   Yes, a big spider! That's where I brought my victims. (*She pours herself another drink*) Yes, I had many intimacies with strangers. After the death of Allan—intimacies with strangers was all I seemed able to fill my empty heart with. . . . I think it was panic, just panic, that drove me from one to another, hunting for some protection—here and there, in the most—unlikely places—even, at last, in a seventeen-year-old boy but—somebody wrote the superintendent about it—"This woman is morally unfit for her position!"

(*She throws back her head with convulsive, sobbing laughter. Then she repeats the statement, gasps, and drinks*)

True? Yes, I suppose—unfit somehow—anyway. . . . So I came here. There was nowhere else I could go. I was played out. You know what played out is? My youth was suddenly gone up the water-spout, and—I met you. You said you needed somebody. Well, I needed somebody, too. I thanked God for you, because you seemed to be gentle—a cleft in the rock of the world that I could hide in! But I guess I was asking, hoping—too much! Kiefaber, Stanley and Shaw have tied an old tin can to the tail of the kite.

(*There is a pause.* MITCH *stares at her dumbly*)

MITCH   You lied to me, Blanche.

BLANCHE   Don't say I lied to you.

MITCH   Lies, lies, inside and out, all lies.

BLANCHE   Never inside, I didn't lie in my heart . . .
(*A* VENDOR *comes around the corner. She is a blind Mexican woman in a dark shawl, carrying bunches of those gaudy tin flowers that lower class Mexicans display at funerals and other festive occasions. She is calling barely audibly. Her figure is only faintly visible outside the building*)

MEXICAN WOMAN   Flores. Flores. Flores para los muertos. Flores. Flores.

BLANCHE   What? Oh! Somebody outside . . . (*She goes to the door, opens it and stares at the* MEXICAN WOMAN)

MEXICAN WOMAN   (*She is at the door and offers* BLANCHE *some of her flowers*)   Flores? Flores para los muertos?

BLANCHE   (*Frightened*)   No, no! Not now! Not now!
(*She darts back into the apartment, slamming the door*)

MEXICAN WOMAN (*She turns away and starts to move down the street*)   Flores para los muertos.
   (*The polka tune fades in*)

BLANCHE (*As if to herself*)   Crumble and fade and—regrets—recriminations . . . 'If you'd done this, it wouldn't've cost me that!'

MEXICAN WOMAN   Corones para los muertos. Corones . . .

BLANCHE   Legacies! Huh. . . . And other things such as bloodstained pillow-slips—'Her linen needs changing'—'Yes Mother. But couldn't we get a colored girl to do it?' No, we couldn't of course. Everything gone but the—

MEXICAN WOMAN   Flores.

BLANCHE   Death—I used to sit here and she used to sit over there and death was as close as you are. . . . We didn't dare even admit we had ever heard of it!

MEXICAN WOMAN   Flores para los muertos, flores—flores . . .

BLANCHE   The opposite is desire. So do you wonder? How could you possibly wonder! Not far from Belle Reve, before we had lost Belle Reve, was a camp where they trained young soldiers. On Saturday night they would go in town to get drunk—

MEXICAN WOMAN (*Softly*)   Corones . . .

BLANCHE   —and on the way back they would stagger onto my lawn and call—'Blanche! Blanche!'—The deaf old lady remaining suspected nothing. But sometimes I slipped outside to answer their calls. . . . Later the paddy-wagon would gather them up like daisies . . the long way home . . .
   (*The* MEXICAN WOMAN *turns slowly and drifts back off with her soft mournful cries.* BLANCHE *goes to the dresser and leans forward on it. After a moment,* MITCH *rises and follows her purposefully. The polka music fades away. He places his hands on her waist and tries to turn her about*)

BLANCHE   What do you want?

MITCH (*Fumbling to embrace her*)   What I been missing all summer.

BLANCHE   Then marry me, Mitch!

MITCH   I don't think I want to marry you any more.

BLANCHE   No?

MITCH (*Dropping his hands from her waist*)   You're not clean enough to bring in the house with my mother.

BLANCHE   Go away, then. (*He stares at her*) Get out of here quick before I start screaming fire! (*Her throat is tightening with hysteria*) Get out of here quick before I start screaming fire.
   (*He still remains staring. She suddenly rushes to the big window with its pale blue square of the soft summer light and cries wildly*)
Fire! Fire! Fire!
   (*With a startled gasp,* MITCH *turns and goes out the outer door, clatters awkwardly down the steps and around the corner of the building.* BLANCHE *staggers back from the window and falls to her knees. The distant piano is slow and blue*)

Scene Ten

It is a few hours later that night.
   BLANCHE *has been drinking fairly steadily since* MITCH *left. She has dragged her wardrobe trunk into the center of the bedroom. It hangs open with flowery dresses thrown across it. As the drinking and packing went on, a mood of hysterical exhilaration came into her and she has decked herself out in a somewhat soiled and crumpled white satin evening gown and a pair of scuffed silver slippers with brilliants set in their heels.*
   Now she is placing the rhinestone tiara on her head before the mirror of the dressing-table and murmuring excitedly as if to a group of special admirers.

BLANCHE   How about taking a swim, a moonlight swim at the old rock-quarry? If anyone's sober enough to drive a car! Ha-ha! Best way in the world to stop your head buzzing! Only you've got to be careful to dive where the deep pool is—if you hit a rock you don't come up till tomorrow . . .

(*Tremblingly she lifts the hand mirror for a closer inspection. She catches her breath and slams the mirror face down with such violence that the glass cracks. She moans a little and attempts to rise.*

(STANLEY *appears around the corner of the building. He still has on the vivid green silk bowling shirt. As he rounds the corner the honky-tonk music is heard. It continues softly throughout the scene.*

(*He enters the kitchen, slamming the door. As he peers in at* BLANCHE, *he gives a low whistle. He has had a few drinks on the way and has brought some quart beer bottles home with him*)

BLANCHE   How is my sister?

STANLEY   She is doing okay.

BLANCHE   And how is the baby?

STANLEY (*Grinning amiably*)   The baby won't come before morning so they told me to go home and get a little shut-eye.

BLANCHE   Does that mean we are to be alone in here?

STANLEY   Yep. Just me and you, Blanche. Unless you got somebody hid under the bed. What've you got on those fine feathers for?

BLANCHE   Oh, that's right. You left before my wire came.

STANLEY   You got a wire?

BLANCHE   I received a telegram from an old admirer of mine.

STANLEY   Anything good?

BLANCHE   I think so. An invitation.

STANLEY   What to? A fireman's ball?

BLANCHE (*Throwing back her head*)   A cruise of the Caribbean on a yacht!

STANLEY   Well, well. What do you know?

BLANCHE   I have never been so surprised in my life.

STANLEY   I guess not.

BLANCHE   It came like a bolt from the blue!

STANLEY   Who did you say it was from?

BLANCHE   An old beau of mine.

STANLEY   The one that give you the white fox-pieces?

BLANCHE   Mr. Shep Huntleigh. I wore his ATO pin my last year at college. I hadn't see him again until last Christmas. I ran in to him on Biscayne Boulevard. Then—just now—this wire—inviting me on a cruise of the Caribbean! The problem is clothes. I tore into my trunk to see what I have that's suitable for the tropics!

STANLEY   And come up with that—gorgeous—diamond—tiara?

BLANCHE   This old relic? Ha-ha! It's only rhinestones.

STANLEY   Gosh. I thought it was Tiffany diamonds. (*He unbuttons his shirt*)

BLANCHE   Well, anyhow, I shall be entertained in style.

STANLEY   Uh-huh. It goes to show, you never know what is coming.

BLANCHE   Just when I thought my luck had begun to fail me—

STANLEY   Into the picture pops this Miami millionaire.

BLANCHE   This man is not from Miami. This man is from Dallas.

STANLEY   This man is from Dallas?

BLANCHE   Yes, this man is from Dallas where gold spouts out of the ground!

STANLEY   Well, just so he's from somewhere! (*He starts removing his shirt*)

BLANCHE   Close the curtains before you undress any further.

STANLEY (*Amiably*) This is all I'm going to undress right now. (*He rips the sack off a quart beer-bottle*) Seen a bottle-opener?

  (*She moves slowly toward the dresser, where she stands with her hands knotted together*)

I used to have a cousin who could open a beer-bottle with his teeth. (*Pounding the bottle cap on the corner of table*) That was his only accomplishment, all he could do—he was just a human bottle-opener. And then one time, at a wedding party, he broke his front teeth off! After that he was so ashamed of himself he used t' sneak out of the house when company came . . .

  (*The bottle cap pops off and a geyser of foam shoots up. STANLEY laughs happily, holding up the bottle over his head*)

Ha-ha! Rain from heaven! (*He extends the bottle toward her*) Shall we bury the hatchet and make it a loving-cup? Huh?

BLANCHE No, thank you.

STANLEY Well, it's a red letter night for us both. You having an oil-millionaire and me having a baby.

  (*He goes to the bureau in the bedroom and crouches to remove something from the bottom drawer*)

BLANCHE (*Drawing back*) What are you doing in here?

STANLEY Here's something I always break out on special occasions like this. The silk pyjamas I wore on my wedding night!

BLANCHE Oh.

STANLEY When the telephone rings and they say, "You've got a son!" I'll tear this off and wave it like a flag! (*He shakes out a brilliant pyjama coat*) I guess we are both entitled to put on the dog. (*He goes back to the kitchen with the coat over his arm*)

BLANCHE When I think of how divine it is going to be to have such a thing as privacy once more—I could weep with joy!

STANLEY This millionaire from Dallas is not going to interfere with your privacy any?

BLANCHE It won't be the sort of thing you have in mind. This man is a gentleman and he respects me. (*Improvising feverishly*) What he wants is my companionship. Having great wealth sometimes makes people lonely! A cultivated woman, a woman of intelligence and breeding, can enrich a man's life—immeasurably! I have those things to offer, and this doesn't take them away. Physical beauty is passing. A transitory possession. But beauty of the mind and richness of the spirit and tenderness of the heart—and I have all of those things—aren't taken away, but grow! Increase with the years! How strange that I should be called a destitute woman! When I have all of these treasures locked in my heart. (*A choked sob comes from her*) I think of myself as a very, very rich woman! But I have been foolish—casting my pearls before swine!

STANLEY Swine, huh?

BLANCHE Yes, swine! Swine! And I'm thinking not only of you but of your friend, Mr. Mitchell. He came to see me tonight. He dared to come here in his work-clothes! And to repeat slander to me, vicious stories that he had gotten from you! I gave him his walking papers . . .

STANLEY You did, huh?

BLANCHE But then he came back. He returned with a box of roses to beg my forgiveness! He implored my forgiveness. But some things are not forgivable. Deliberate cruelty is not forgivable. It is the one unforgivable thing in my opinion and it is the one thing of which I have never, never been guilty. And so I told him, I said to him, "Thank you," but it was foolish of me to think that we could ever adapt ourselves to each other. Our ways of life are too different. Our attitudes and our backgrounds are incompatible. We have to be realistic about such things. So farewell, my friend! And let there be no hard feelings . . .

STANLEY Was this before or after the telegram came from the Texas oil millionaire?

BLANCHE What telegram? No! No, after! As a matter of fact, the wire came just as—

STANLEY   As a matter of fact there wasn't no wire at all!

BLANCHE   Oh, oh!

STANLEY   There isn't no millionaire! And Mitch didn't come back with roses 'cause I know where he is—

BLANCHE   Oh!

STANLEY   There isn't a goddam thing but imagination!

BLANCHE   Oh!

STANLEY   And lies and conceit and tricks!

BLANCHE   Oh!

STANLEY   And look at yourself! Take a look at yourself in that worn-out Mardi Gras outfit, rented for fifty cents from some rag-picker! And with the crazy crown on! What queen do you think you are?

BLANCHE   Oh—God . . .

STANLEY   I've been on to you from the start! Not once did you pull any wool over this boy's eyes! You come in here and sprinkle the place with powder and spray perfume and cover the light-bulb with a paper lantern, and lo and behold the place has turned into Egypt and you are the Queen of the Nile! Sitting on your throne and swilling down my liquor! I say—*Ha!—Ha!* Do you hear me? *Ha—ha—ha!* (*He walks into the bedroom*)

BLANCHE   Don't come in here!
    (*Lurid reflections appear on the walls around* BLANCHE. *The shadows are of a grotesque and menacing form. She catches her breath, crosses to the phone and jiggles the hook.* STANLEY *goes into the bathroom and closes the door*)
Operator, operator! Give me long-distance, please. . . . I want to get in touch with Mr. Shep Huntleigh of Dallas. He's so well-known he doesn't require any address. Just ask anybody who—Wait!!—No, I couldn't find it right now. . . . Please understand, I—No! No, wait! . . . One moment! Someone is—Nothing! Hold on, please!
    (*She sets the phone down and crosses warily into the*

*kitchen. The night is filled with inhuman voices like cries
in a jungle.*

*(The shadows and lurid reflections move sinuously as
flames along the wall spaces.*

*(Through the back wall of the rooms, which have become
transparent, can be seen the sidewalk. A prostitute has
rolled a drunkard. He pursues her along the walk, over-
takes her and there is a struggle. A policeman's whistle
breaks it up. The figures disappear.*

(Some moments later the NEGRO WOMAN *appears around
the corner with a sequined bag which the prostitute had
dropped on the walk. She is rooting excitedly through it.*

*(*BLANCHE *presses her knuckles to her lips and returns
slowly to the phone. She speaks in a hoarse whisper)*

BLANCHE Operator! Operator! Never mind long-distance.
Get Western Union. There isn't time to be—Western—Western Union!

(She waits anxiously)

Western Union? Yes! I—want to—Take down this message!
"In desperate, desperate circumstances! Help me! Caught in
a trap. Caught in—" *Oh!*

(The bathroom door is thrown open and STANLEY *comes
out in the brilliant silk pyjamas. He grins at her as he knots
the tasseled sash about his waist. She gasps and backs away
from the phone. He stares at her for a count of ten. Then
a clicking becomes audible from the telephone, steady and
rasping)*

STANLEY You left th' phone off th' hook.

*(He crosses to it deliberately and sets it back on the hook.
After he has replaced it, he stares at her again, his mouth
slowly curving into a grin, as he weaves between* BLANCHE
and the outer door.

*(The barely audible "blue piano" begins to drum up
louder. The sound of it turns into the roar of an approaching locomotive.* BLANCHE *crouches, pressing her fists to her
ears until it has gone by)*

BLANCHE *(Finally straightening)* Let me—let me get by
you!

STANLEY Get by me? Sure. Go ahead. *(He moves back a
pace in the doorway)*

BLANCHE   You—you stand over there! (*She indicates a further position*)

STANLEY (*Grinning*)   You got plenty of room to walk by me now.

BLANCHE   Not with you there! But I've got to get out somehow!

STANLEY   You think I'll interfere with you? Ha-ha!
(*The "blue piano" goes softly. She turns confusedly and makes a faint gesture. The inhuman jungle voices rise up. He takes a step toward her, biting his tongue which protrudes between his lips*)

STANLEY (*Softly*)   Come to think of it—maybe you wouldn't be bad to—interfere with . . .
(BLANCHE *moves backward through the door into the bedroom*)

BLANCHE   Stay back! Don't you come toward me another step or I'll—

STANLEY   What?

BLANCHE   Some awful thing will happen! It will!

STANLEY   What are you putting on now?
(*They are now both inside the bedroom*)

BLANCHE   I warn you, don't, I'm in danger!
(*He takes another step. She smashes a bottle on the table and faces him, clutching the broken top*)

STANLEY   What did you do that for?

BLANCHE   So I could twist the broken end in your face!

STANLEY   I bet you would do that!

BLANCHE   I would! I will if you—

STANLEY   Oh! So you want some rough-house! All right, let's have some rough-house!
(*He springs toward her, overturning the table. She cries out and strikes at him with the bottle top but he catches her wrist*)
Tiger—tiger! Drop the bottle-top! Drop it! We've had this date with each other from the beginning!

(She moans. The bottle-top falls. She sinks to her knees. He picks up her inert figure and carries her to the bed. The hot trumpet and drums from the Four Deuces sound loudly)

Scene Eleven

It is some weeks later. STELLA *is packing* BLANCHE'S *things. Sound of water can be heard running in the bathroom.*

    The portieres are partly open on the poker players —STANLEY, STEVE, MITCH *and* PABLO—*who sit around the table in the kitchen. The atmosphere of the kitchen is now the same raw, lurid one of the disastrous poker night.*

    The building is framed by the sky of turquoise. STELLA *has been crying as she arranges the flowery dresses in the open trunk.*

    EUNICE *comes down the steps from her flat above and enters the kitchen. There is an outburst from the poker table.*

STANLEY Drew to an inside straight and made it, by God.

PABLO *Maldita sea tu suerto!*

STANLEY Put it in English, greaseball.

PABLO I am cursing your rutting luck.

STANLEY (*Prodigiously elated*) You know what luck is? Luck is believing you're lucky. Take at Salerno. I believed I was lucky. I figured that 4 out of 5 would not come through but I would . . . and I did. I put that down as a rule. To hold front position in this rat-race you've got to believe you are lucky.

MITCH   You . . . you . . . you. . . . Brag . . . brag . . . bull . . . bull.

   (STELLA *goes into the bedroom and starts folding a dress*)

STANLEY   What's the matter with him?

EUNICE (*Walking past the table*)   I always did say that men are callous things with no feelings, but this does beat anything. Making pigs of yourselves. (*She comes through the portieres into the bedroom*)

STANLEY   What's the matter with her?

STELLA   How is my baby?

EUNICE   Sleeping like a little angel. Brought you some grapes. (*She puts them on a stool and lowers her voice*) Blanche?

STELLA   Bathing.

EUNICE   How is she?

STELLA   She wouldn't eat anything but asked for a drink.

EUNICE   What did you tell her?

STELLA   I—just told her that—we'd made arrangements for her to rest in the country. She's got it mixed in her mind with Shep Huntleigh.

   (BLANCHE *opens the bathroom door slightly*)

BLANCHE   Stella.

STELLA   Yes, Blanche?

BLANCHE   If anyone calls while I'm bathing take the number and tell them I'll call right back.

STELLA   Yes.

BLANCHE   That cool yellow silk—the bouclé. See if it's crushed. If it's not too crushed I'll wear it and on the lapel that silver and turquoise pin in the shape of a seahorse. You will find them in the heart-shaped box I keep my accessories in. And Stella . . . Try and locate a bunch of artificial violets in that box, too, to pin with the seahorse on the lapel of the jacket.

(*She closes the door.* STELLA *turns to* EUNICE)

STELLA   I don't know if I did the right thing.

EUNICE   What else could you do?

STELLA   I couldn't believe her story and go on living with Stanley.

EUNICE   Don't ever believe it. Life has got to go on. No matter what happens, you've got to keep on going.

(*The bathroom door opens a little*)

BLANCHE (*Looking out*)   Is the coast clear?

STELLA   Yes, Blanche. (*To* EUNICE) Tell her how well she's looking.

BLANCHE   Please close the curtains before I come out.

STELLA   They're closed.

STANLEY   —How many for you?

PABLO   —Two.

STEVE   —Three.

(BLANCHE *appears in the amber light of the door. She has a tragic radiance in her red satin robe following the sculptural lines of her body. The "Varsouviana" rises audibly as* BLANCHE *enters the bedroom*)

BLANCHE (*With faintly hysterical vivacity*)   I have just washed my hair.

STELLA   Did you?

BLANCHE   I'm not sure I got the soap out.

EUNICE   Such fine hair!

BLANCHE (*Accepting the compliment*)   It's a problem. Didn't I get a call?

STELLA   Who from, Blanche?

BLANCHE   Shep Huntleigh . . .

STELLA   Why, not yet, honey!

BLANCHE How strange! I—
(*At the sound of* BLANCHE'S *voice* MITCH'S *arm supporting his cards has sagged and his gaze is dissolved into space.* STANLEY *slaps him on the shoulder*)

STANLEY Hey, Mitch, come to!
(*The sound of this new voice shocks* BLANCHE. *She makes a shocked gesture, forming his name with her lips.* STELLA *nods and looks quickly away.* BLANCHE *stands quite still for some moments—the silverbacked mirror in her hand and a look of sorrowful perplexity as though all human experience shows on her face.* BLANCHE *finally speaks but with sudden hysteria*)

BLANCHE What's going on here?
(*She turns from* STELLA *to* EUNICE *and back to* STELLA. *Her rising voice penetrates the concentration of the game.* MITCH *ducks his head lower but* STANLEY *shoves back his chair as if about to rise.* STEVE *places a restraining hand on his arm*)

BLANCHE (*Continuing*) What's happened here? I want an explanation of what's happened here.

STELLA (*Agonizingly*) Hush! Hush!

EUNICE Hush! Hush! Honey.

STELLA Please, Blanche.

BLANCHE Why are you looking at me like that? Is something wrong with me?

EUNICE You look wonderful, Blanche. Don't she look wonderful?

STELLA Yes.

EUNICE I understand you are going on a trip.

STELLA Yes, Blanche *is*. She's going on a vacation.

EUNICE I'm green with envy.

BLANCHE Help me, help me get dressed!

STELLA (*Handing her dress*) Is this what you—

BLANCHE Yes, it will do! I'm anxious to get out of here—this place is a trap!

EUNICE   What a pretty blue jacket.

STELLA   It's lilac colored.

BLANCHE   You're both mistaken. It's Della Robbia blue. The blue of the robe in the old Madonna pictures. Are these grapes washed?
   (*She fingers the bunch of grapes which* EUNICE *had brought in*)

EUNICE   Huh?

BLANCHE   Washed, I said. Are they washed?

EUNICE   They're from the French Market.

BLANCHE   That doesn't mean they've been washed. (*The cathedral bells chime*) Those cathedral bells—they're the only clean thing in the Quarter. Well, I'm going now. I'm ready to go.

EUNICE (*Whispering*)   She's going to walk out before they get here.

STELLA   Wait, Blanche.

BLANCHE   I don't want to pass in front of those men.

EUNICE   Then wait'll the game breaks up.

STELLA   Sit down and . . .
   (BLANCHE *turns weakly, hesitantly about. She lets them push her into a chair*)

BLANCHE   I can smell the sea air. The rest of my time I'm going to spend on the sea. And when I die, I'm going to die on the sea. You know what I shall die of? (*She plucks a grape*) I shall die of eating an unwashed grape one day out on the ocean. I will die—with my hand in the hand of some nice-looking ship's doctor, a very young one with a small blond mustache and a big silver watch. "Poor lady," they'll say, "the quinine did her no good. That unwashed grape has transported her soul to heaven." (*The cathedral chimes are heard*) And I'll be buried at sea sewn up in a clean white sack and dropped overboard—at noon—in the blaze of summer—and into an ocean as blue as (*Chimes again*) my first lover's eyes!

(*A* DOCTOR *and a* MATRON *have appeared around the corner of the building and climbed the steps to the porch. The gravity of their profession is exaggerated—the unmistakable aura of the state institution with its cynical detachment. The* DOCTOR *rings the doorbell. The murmur of the game is interrupted*)

EUNICE (*Whispering to* STELLA)   That must be them.
(STELLA *presses her fists to her lips*)

BLANCHE (*Rising slowly*)   What is it?

EUNICE (*Affectedly casual*)   Excuse me while I see who's at the door.

STELLA   Yes.
(EUNICE *goes into the kitchen*)

BLANCHE (*Tensely*)   I wonder if it's for me.
(*A whispered colloquy takes place at the door*)

EUNICE (*Returning, brightly*)   Someone is calling for Blanche.

BLANCHE   It *is* for me, then! (*She looks fearfully from one to the other and then to the portieres. The "Varsouviana" faintly plays*) Is it the gentleman I was expecting from Dallas?

EUNICE   I think it is, Blanche.

BLANCHE   I'm not quite ready.

STELLA   Ask him to wait outside.

BLANCHE   I . . .
(EUNICE *goes back to the portieres. Drums sound very softly*)

STELLA   Everything packed?

BLANCHE   My silver toilet articles are still out.

STELLA   Ah!

EUNICE (*Returning*)   They're waiting in front of the house.

BLANCHE   They! Who's "they"?

EUNICE   There's a lady with him.

BLANCHE   I cannot imagine who this "lady" could be! How is she dressed?

EUNICE   Just—just a sort of a—plain-tailored outfit.

BLANCHE   Possibly she's—(*Her voice dies out nervously*)

STELLA   Shall we go, Blanche?

BLANCHE   Must we go through that room?

STELLA   I will go with you.

BLANCHE   How do I look?

STELLA   Lovely.

EUNICE (*Echoing*)   Lovely.
   (BLANCHE *moves fearfully to the portieres.* EUNICE *draws them open for her.* BLANCHE *goes into the kitchen*)

BLANCHE (*To the men*)   Please don't get up. I'm only passing through.
   (*She crosses quickly to outside door.* STELLA *and* EUNICE *follow. The poker players stand awkwardly at the table— all except* MITCH, *who remains seated, looking down at the table.* BLANCHE *steps out on a small porch at the side of the door. She stops short and catches her breath*)

DOCTOR   How do you do?

BLANCHE   You are not the gentleman I was expecting. (*She suddenly gasps and starts back up the steps. She stops by* STELLA, *who stands just outside the door, and speaks in a frightening whisper*) That man isn't Shep Huntleigh.
   (*The "Varsouviana" is playing distantly.*
   (STELLA *stares back at* BLANCHE. EUNICE *is holding* STELLA'S *arm. There is a moment of silence—no sound but that of* STANLEY *steadily shuffling the cards.*
   (BLANCHE *catches her breath again and slips back into the flat. She enters the flat with a peculiar smile, her eyes wide and brilliant. As soon as her sister goes past her,* STELLA *closes her eyes and clenches her hands.* EUNICE *throws her arms comfortingly about her. Then she starts up to her flat.* BLANCHE *stops just inside the door.* MITCH *keeps staring down at his hands on the table, but the other men look at her curiously. At last she starts around the table toward the bedroom. As she does,* STANLEY *suddenly*

pushes back his chair and rises as if to block her way. The
MATRON *follows her into the flat*)

STANLEY Did you forget something?

BLANCHE (*Shrilly*) Yes! Yes, I forgot something!
(*She rushes past him into the bedroom. Lurid reflections
appear on the walls in odd, sinuous shapes. The "Varsouviana" is filtered into a weird distortion, accompanied by
the cries and noises of the jungle.* BLANCHE *seizes the back
of a chair as if to defend herself*)

STANLEY (*Sotto voce*) Doc, you better go in.

DOCTOR (*Sotto voce, motioning to the* MATRON) Nurse,
bring her out.
(*The* MATRON *advances on one side,* STANLEY *on the other.
Divested of all the softer properties of womanhood, the*
MATRON *is a peculiarly sinister figure in her severe dress.
Her voice is bold and toneless as a firebell*)

MATRON Hello, Blanche.
(*The greeting is echoed and re-echoed by other mysterious
voices behind the walls, as if reverberated through a can-
yon of rock*)

STANLEY She says that she forgot something.
(*The echo sounds in threatening whispers*)

MATRON That's all right.

STANLEY What did you forget, Blanche?

BLANCHE I— I—

MATRON It don't matter. We can pick it up later.

STANLEY Sure. We can send it along with the trunk.

BLANCHE (*Retreating in panic*) I don't know you—I don't
know you. I want to be—left alone—please!

MATRON Now, Blanche!

ECHOES (*Rising and falling*) Now, Blanche—now, Blanche
—now, Blanche!

STANLEY You left nothing here but spilt talcum and old
empty perfume bottles—unless it's the paper lantern you
want to take with you. You want the lantern?

(He crosses to dressing table and seizes the paper lantern, tearing it off the light bulb, and extends it toward her. She cries out as if the lantern was herself. The MATRON *steps boldly toward her. She screams and tries to break past the* MATRON. *All the men spring to their feet.* STELLA *runs out to the porch, with* EUNICE *following to comfort her, simultaneously with the confused voices of the men in the kitchen.* STELLA *rushes into* EUNICE'S *embrace on the porch)*

STELLA   Oh, my God, Eunice help me! Don't let them do that to her, don't let them hurt her! Oh, God, oh, please God, don't hurt her! What are they doing to her? What are they doing? *(She tries to break from* EUNICE'S *arms)*

EUNICE   No, honey, no, no, honey. Stay here. Don't go back in there. Stay with me and don't look.

STELLA   What have I done to my sister? Oh, God, what have I done to my sister?

EUNICE   You done the right thing, the only thing you could do. She couldn't stay here; there wasn't no other place for her to go.
(While STELLA *and* EUNICE *are speaking on the porch the voices of the men in the kitchen overlap them.* MITCH *has started toward the bedroom.* STANLEY *crosses to block him.* STANLEY *pushes him aside.* MITCH *lunges and strikes at* STANLEY. STANLEY *pushes* MITCH *back.* MITCH *collapses at the table, sobbing.*
(During the preceding scenes, the MATRON *catches hold of* BLANCHE'S *arm and prevents her flight.* BLANCHE *turns wildly and scratches at the* MATRON. *The heavy woman pinions her arms.* BLANCHE *cries out hoarsely and slips to her knees)*

MATRON   These fingernails have to be trimmed. *(The* DOCTOR *comes into the room and she looks at him)* Jacket, Doctor?

DOCTOR   Not unless necessary.
(He takes off his hat and now he becomes personalized. The unhuman quality goes. His voice is gentle and reassur-

ing as he crosses to BLANCHE *and crouches in front of her. As he speaks her name, her terror subsides a little. The lurid reflections fade from the walls, the inhuman cries and noises die out and her own hoarse crying is calmed*)

DOCTOR   Miss DuBois.
(*She turns her face to him and stares at him with desperate pleading. He smiles; then he speaks to the* MATRON)
It won't be necessary.

BLANCHE (*Faintly*)   Ask her to let go of me.

DOCTOR (*To the* MATRON)   Let go.
(*The* MATRON *releases her.* BLANCHE *extends her hands toward the* DOCTOR. *He draws her up gently and supports her with his arm and leads her through the portieres*)

BLANCHE (*Holding tight to his arm*)   Whoever you are—I have always depended on the kindness of strangers.
(*The poker players stand back as* BLANCHE *and the* DOCTOR *cross the kitchen to the front door. She allows him to lead her as if she were blind. As they go out on the porch,* STELLA *cries out her sister's name from where she is crouched a few steps up on the stairs*)

STELLA   Blanche! Blanche, Blanche!
(BLANCHE *walks on without turning, followed by the* DOCTOR *and the* MATRON. *They go around the corner of the building.*
(EUNICE *descends to* STELLA *and places the child in her arms. It is wrapped in a pale blue blanket.* STELLA *accepts the child, sobbingly.* EUNICE *continues downstairs and enters the kitchen where the men, except for* STANLEY, *are returning silently to their places about the table.* STANLEY *has gone out on the porch and stands at the foot of the steps looking at* STELLA)

STANLEY (*A bit uncertainly*)   Stella?
(*She sobs with inhuman abandon. There is something luxurious in her complete surrender to crying now that her sister is gone*)

STANLEY (*Voluptuously, soothingly*)   Now, honey. Now, love. Now, now, love. (*He kneels beside her and his fingers find the opening of her blouse*) Now, now, love. Now, love. . . .

>   (*The luxurious sobbing, the sensual murmur fade away under the swelling music of the "blue piano" and the muted trumpet*)

STEVE This game is seven-card stud.

CURTAIN

Death
of a Salesman

Certain private conversations

in two acts and a requiem

by **ARTHUR MILLER**

DEATH OF A SALESMAN

A New Play by Arthur Miller

Staged by Elia Kazan

Cast (IN ORDER OF APPEARANCE)

WILLY LOMAN	Lee J. Cobb
LINDA	Mildred Dunnock
BIFF	Arthur Kennedy
HAPPY	Cameron Mitchell
BERNARD	Don Keefer
THE WOMAN	Winnifred Cushing
CHARLEY	Howard Smith
UNCLE BEN	Thomas Chalmers
HOWARD WAGNER	Alan Hewitt
JENNY	Ann Driscoll
STANLEY	Tom Pedi
MISS FORSYTHE	Constance Ford
LETTA	Hope Cameron

The setting and lighting were designed by Jo Mielziner.
The incidental music was composed by Alex North.
The costumes were designed by Julia Sze.
Presented by Kermit Bloomgarden and Walter Fried at the Morosco Theatre in New York on February 10, 1949.
The action takes place in Willy Loman's house and yard and in various places he visits in the New York and Boston of today.
Throughout the play, in the stage directions, left and right mean stage left and stage right.

Act One

A melody is heard, played upon a flute. It is small and fine, telling of grass and trees and the horizon. The curtain rises.

Before us is the Salesman's house. We are aware of towering, angular shapes behind it, surrounding it on all sides. Only the blue light of the sky falls upon the house and forestage; the surrounding area shows an angry glow of orange. As more light appears, we see a solid vault of apartment houses around the small, fragile-seeming home. An air of the dream clings to the place, a dream rising out of reality. The kitchen at center seems actual enough, for there is a kitchen table with three chairs, and a refrigerator. But no other fixtures are seen. At the back of the kitchen there is a draped entrance, which leads to the living-room. To the right of the kitchen, on a level raised two feet, is a bedroom furnished only with a brass bedstead and a straight chair. On a shelf over the bed a silver athletic trophy stands. A window opens onto the apartment house at the side.

Behind the kitchen, on a level raised six and a half feet, is the boys' bedroom, at present barely visible. Two beds are dimly seen, and at the back of the room a dormer window. (This bedroom is above the unseen living-room.) At the left a stairway curves up to it from the kitchen.

The entire setting is wholly or, in some places, partially transparent. The roof-line of the house is one-dimensional; under and over it we see the apartment buildings. Before the house lies an apron, curving beyond the forestage into the orchestra. This forward area serves as the back yard as well as the locale of

all WILLY'S *imaginings and of his city scenes. Whenever the action is in the present the actors observe the
imaginary wall-lines, entering the house only through
its door at the left. But in the scenes of the past these
boundaries are broken, and characters enter or leave
a room by stepping "through" a wall onto the forestage.*

From the right, WILLY LOMAN, *the Salesman, enters, carrying two large sample cases. The flute plays
on. He hears but is not aware of it. He is past sixty
years of age, dressed quietly. Even as he crosses the
stage to the doorway of the house, his exhaustion is
apparent. He unlocks the door, comes into the kitchen,
and thankfully lets his burden down, feeling the sore-
ness of his palms. A word-sigh escapes his lips—it
might be "Oh, boy, oh, boy." He closes the door,
then carries his cases out into the living-room, through
the draped kitchen doorway.*

*LINDA, his wife, has stirred in her bed at the right.
She gets out and puts on a robe, listening. Most often
jovial, she has developed an iron repression of her exceptions to* WILLY'S *behavior—she more than loves
him, she admires him, as though his mercurial nature,
his temper, his massive dreams and little cruelties,
served her only as sharp reminders of the turbulent
longings within him, longings which she shares but
lacks the temperament to utter and follow to their
end.*

LINDA (*Hearing* WILLY *outside the bedroom, calls with some
trepidation*)   Willy!

WILLY   It's all right. I came back.

LINDA   Why? What happened? (*Slight pause*) Did something
happen, Willy?

WILLY   No, nothing happened.

LINDA   You didn't smash the car, did you?

WILLY (*With casual irritation*)   I said nothing happened
Didn't you hear me?

LINDA Don't you feel well?

WILLY I'm tired to the death. (*The flute has faded away. He sits on the bed beside her, a little numb*) I couldn't make it. I just couldn't make it, Linda.

LINDA (*Very carefully, delicately*) Where were you all day? You look terrible.

WILLY I got as far as a little above Yonkers. I stopped for a cup of coffee. Maybe it was the coffee.

LINDA What?

WILLY (*After a pause*) I suddenly couldn't drive any more. The car kept going off onto the shoulder, y'know?

LINDA (*Helpfully*) Oh. Maybe it was the steering again. I don't think Angelo knows the Studebaker.

WILLY No, it's me, it's me. Suddenly I realize I'm goin' sixty miles an hour and I don't remember the last five minutes. I'm—I can't seem to—keep my mind to it.

LINDA Maybe it's your glasses. You never went for your new glasses.

WILLY No, I see everything. I came back ten miles an hour. It took me nearly four hours from Yonkers.

LINDA (*Resigned*) Well, you'll just have to take a rest, Willy, you can't continue this way.

WILLY I just got back from Florida.

LINDA But you didn't rest your mind. Your mind is over-active, and the mind is what counts, dear.

WILLY I'll start out in the morning. Maybe I'll feel better in the morning. (*She is taking off his shoes*) These goddam arch supports are killing me.

LINDA Take an aspirin. Should I get you an aspirin? It'll soothe you.

WILLY (*With wonder*) I was driving along, you understand? And I was fine. I was even observing the scenery. You can imagine, me looking at scenery, on the road every week of my life. But it's so beautiful up there, Linda, the trees are so thick, and the sun is warm. I opened the windshield and just

let the warm air bathe over me. And then all of a sudden
I'm goin' off the road! I'm tellin' ya, I absolutely forgot I
was driving. If I'd've gone the other way over the white line
I might've killed somebody. So I went on again—and five
minutes later I'm dreamin' again, and I nearly—(*He presses
two fingers against his eyes*) I have such thoughts, I have
such strange thoughts.

LINDA Willy, dear. Talk to them again. There's no reason
why you can't work in New York.

WILLY They don't need me in New York. I'm the New
England man. I'm vital in New England.

LINDA But you're sixty years old. They can't expect you to
keep traveling every week.

WILLY I'll have to send a wire to Portland. I'm supposed to
see Brown and Morrison tomorrow morning at ten o'clock to
show the line. Goddammit, I could sell them! (*He starts putting on his jacket*)

LINDA (*Taking the jacket from him*) Why don't you go
down to the place tomorrow and tell Howard you've simply
got to work in New York? You're too accommodating, dear.

WILLY If old man Wagner was alive I'd a been in charge of
New York now! That man was a prince, he was a masterful
man. But that boy of his, that Howard, he don't appreciate.
When I went north the first time, the Wagner Company
didn't know where New England was!

LINDA Why don't you tell those things to Howard, dear?

WILLY (*Encouraged*) I will, I definitely will. Is there any
cheese?

LINDA I'll make you a sandwich.

WILLY No, go to sleep. I'll take some milk. I'll be up right
away. The boys in?

LINDA They're sleeping. Happy took Biff on a date tonight.

WILLY (*Interested*) That so?

LINDA It was so nice to see them shaving together, one
behind the other, in the bathroom. And going out together.
You notice? The whole house smells of shaving lotion.

WILLY Figure it out. Work a lifetime to pay off a house. You finally own it, and there's nobody to live in it.

LINDA Well, dear, life is a casting off. It's always that way.

WILLY No, no, some people—some people accomplish something. Did Biff say anything after I went this morning?

LINDA You shouldn't have criticized him, Willy, especially after he just got off the train. You mustn't lose your temper with him.

WILLY When the hell did I lose my temper? I simply asked him if he was making any money. Is that a criticism?

LINDA But, dear, how could he make any money?

WILLY (*Worried and angered*) There's such an undercurrent in him. He became a moody man. Did he apologize when I left this morning?

LINDA He was crestfallen, Willy. You know how he admires you. I think if he finds himself, then you'll both be happier and not fight any more.

WILLY How can he find himself on a farm? Is that a life? A farmhand? In the beginning, when he was young, I thought, well, a young man, it's good for him to tramp around, take a lot of different jobs. But it's more than ten years now and he has yet to make thirty-five dollars a week!

LINDA He's finding himself, Willy.

WILLY Not finding yourself at the age of thirty-four is a disgrace!

LINDA Shh!

WILLY The trouble is he's lazy, goddammit!

LINDA Willy, please!

WILLY Biff is a lazy bum!

LINDA They're sleeping. Get something to eat. Go on down.

WILLY Why did he come home? I would like to know what brought him home.

LINDA I don't know. I think he's still lost, Willy. I think he's very lost.

WILLY   Biff Loman is lost. In the greatest country in the
world a young man with such—personal attractiveness, gets
lost. And such a hard worker. There's one thing about Biff—
he's not lazy.

LINDA   Never.

WILLY (*With pity and resolve*)   I'll see him in the morning;
I'll have a nice talk with him. I'll get him a job selling. He
could be big in no time. My God! Remember how they used
to follow him around in high school? When he smiled at
one of them their faces lit up. When he walked down the
street . . . (*He loses himself in reminiscences*)

LINDA (*Trying to bring him out of it*)   Willy, dear, I got a
new kind of American-type cheese today. It's whipped.

WILLY   Why do you get American when I like Swiss?

LINDA   I just thought you'd like a change—

WILLY   I don't want a change! I want Swiss cheese. Why
am I always being contradicted?

LINDA (*With a covering laugh*)   I thought it would be a surprise.

WILLY   Why don't you open a window in here, for God's
sake?

LINDA (*With infinite patience*)   They're all open, dear.

WILLY   The way they boxed us in here. Bricks and windows
windows and bricks.

LINDA   We should've bought the land next door.

WILLY   The street is lined with cars. There's not a breath
of fresh air in the neighborhood. The grass don't grow any
more, you can't raise a carrot in the back yard. They
should've had a law against apartment houses. Remember
those two beautiful elm trees out there? When I and Biff
hung the swing between them?

LINDA   Yeah, like being a million miles from the city.

WILLY   They should've arrested the builder for cutting those
down. They massacred the neighborhood. (*Lost*) More and

more I think of those days, Linda. This time of year it was
lilac and wisteria. And then the peonies would come out, and
the daffodils. What fragrance in this room!

LINDA   Well, after all, people had to move somewhere.

WILLY   No, there's more people now.

LINDA   I don't think there's more people. I think—

WILLY   There's more people! That's what's ruining this country! Population is getting out of control. The competition is
maddening! Smell the stink from that apartment house! And
another one on the other side . . . How can they whip
cheese?
  (*On* WILLY's *last line,* BIFF *and* HAPPY *raise themselves up
  in their beds, listening*)

LINDA   Go down, try it. And be quiet.

WILLY   (*Turning to* LINDA, *guiltily*)   You're not worried
about me, are you, sweetheart?

BIFF   What's the matter?

HAPPY   Listen!

LINDA   You've got too much on the ball to worry about.

WILLY   You're my foundation and my support, Linda.

LINDA   Just try to relax, dear. You make mountains out of
molehills.

WILLY   I won't fight with him any more. If he wants to go
back to Texas, let him go.

LINDA   He'll find his way.

WILLY   Sure. Certain men just don't get started till later in
life. Like Thomas Edison, I think. Or B. F. Goodrich. One
of them was deaf. (*He starts for the bedroom doorway*)
I'll put my money on Biff.

LINDA   And Willy—if it's warm Sunday, we'll drive in the
country. And we'll open the windshield, and take lunch.

WILLY   No, the windshields don't open on the new cars.

LINDA   But you opened it today.

WILLY Me? I didn't. (*He stops*) Now isn't that peculiar!
Isn't that a remarkable— (*He breaks off in amazement and
fright as the flute is heard distantly*)

LINDA What, darling?

WILLY That is the most remarkable thing.

LINDA What, dear?

WILLY I was thinking of the Chevvy. (*Slight pause*) Nine-
teen twenty-eight . . . when I had that red Chevvy—·
(*Breaks off*) That funny? I coulda sworn I was driving that
Chevvy today.

LINDA Well, that's nothing. Something must've reminded
you.

WILLY Remarkable. Ts. Remember those days? The way
Biff used to simonize that car? The dealer refused to believe
there was eighty thousand miles on it. (*He shakes his head*)
Heh! (*To* LINDA) Close your eyes, I'll be right up. (*He walks
out of the bedroom*)

HAPPY (*To* BIFF) Jesus, maybe he smashed up the car
again!

LINDA (*Calling after* WILLY) Be careful on the stairs, dear!
The cheese is on the middle shelf! (*She turns, goes over to
the bed, takes his jacket, and goes out of the bedroom*)
　　(*Light has risen on the boys' room. Unseen,* WILLY *is
　　heard talking to himself, "Eighty thousand miles," and
　　a little laugh.* BIFF *gets out of bed, comes downstage a bit,
　　and stands attentively.* BIFF *is two years older than his
　　brother* HAPPY, *well built, but in these days bears a worn
　　air and seems less self-assured. He has succeeded less, and
　　his dreams are stronger and less acceptable than* HAPPY's.
　　HAPPY *is tall, powerfully made. Sexuality is like a visible
　　color on him, or a scent that many women have dis-
　　covered. He, like his brother, is lost, but in a different
　　way, for he has never allowed himself to turn his face
　　toward defeat and is thus more confused and hard-skinned,
　　although seemingly more content*)

HAPPY (*Getting out of bed*) He's going to get his license
taken away if he keeps that up. I'm getting nervous about
him, y'know, Biff?

BIFF His eyes are going.

HAPPY No, I've driven with him. He sees all right. He just doesn't keep his mind on it. I drove into the city with him last week. He stops at a green light and then it turns red and he goes. (*He laughs*)

BIFF Maybe he's color-blind.

HAPPY Pop? Why he's got the finest eye for color in the business. You know that.

BIFF (*Sitting down on his bed*) I'm going to sleep.

HAPPY You're not still sour on Dad, are you, Biff?

BIFF He's all right, I guess.

WILLY (*Underneath them, in the living-room*) Yes, sir, eighty thousand miles—eighty-two thousand!

BIFF You smoking?

HAPPY (*Holding out a pack of cigarettes*) Want one?

BIFF (*Taking a cigarette*) I can never sleep when I smell it.

WILLY What a simonizing job, heh!

HAPPY (*With deep sentiment*) Funny, Biff, y'know? Us sleeping in here again? The old beds. (*He pats his bed affectionately*) All the talk that went across those two beds, huh? Our whole lives.

BIFF Yeah. Lotta dreams and plans.

HAPPY (*With a deep and masculine laugh*) About five hundred women would like to know what was said in this room.
    (*They share a soft laugh*)

BIFF Remember that big Betsy something—what the hell was her name—over on Bushwick Avenue?

HAPPY (*Combing his hair*) With the collie dog!

BIFF That's the one. I got you in there, remember?

HAPPY Yeah, that was my first time—I think. Boy, there was a pig! (*They laugh, almost crudely*) You taught me everything I know about women. Don't forget that.

BIFF   I bet you forgot how bashful you used to be. Especially with girls.

HAPPY   Oh, I still am, Biff.

BIFF   Oh, go on.

HAPPY   I just control it, that's all. I think I got less bashful and you got more so. What happened, Biff? Where's the old humor, the old confidence? (*He shakes* BIFF's *knee.* BIFF *gets up and moves restlessly about the room*) What's the matter?

BIFF   Why does Dad mock me all the time?

HAPPY   He's not mocking you, he—

BIFF   Everything I say there's a twist of mockery on his face. I can't get near him.

HAPPY   He just wants you to make good, that's all. I wanted to talk to you about Dad for a long time, Biff. Something's—happening to him. He—talks to himself.

BIFF   I noticed that this morning. But he always mumbled.

HAPPY   But not so noticeable. It got so embarrassing I sent him to Florida. And you know something? Most of the time he's talking to you.

BIFF   What's he say about me?

HAPPY   I can't make it out.

BIFF   What's he say about me?

HAPPY   I think the fact that you're not settled, that you're still kind of up in the air . . .

BIFF   There's one or two other things depressing him, Happy.

HAPPY   What do you mean?

BIFF   Never mind. Just don't lay it all to me.

HAPPY   But I think if you just got started—I mean—is there any future for you out there?

BIFF   I tell ya, Hap, I don't know what the future is. I don't know—what I'm supposed to want.

HAPPY   What do you mean?

BIFF Well, I spent six or seven years after high school trying to work myself up. Shipping clerk, salesman, business of one kind or another. And it's a measly manner of existence. To get on that subway on the hot mornings in summer. To devote your whole life to keeping stock, or making phone calls, or selling or buying. To suffer fifty weeks of the year for the sake of a two-week vacation, when all you really desire is to be outdoors, with your shirt off. And always to have to get ahead of the next fella. And still—that's how you build a future.

HAPPY Well, you really enjoy it on a farm? Are you content out there?

BIFF (*With rising agitation*) Hap, I've had twenty or thirty different kinds of jobs since I left home before the war, and it always turns out the same. I just realized it lately. In Nebraska when I herded cattle, and the Dakotas, and Arizona, and now in Texas. It's why I came home now, I guess, because I realized it. This farm I work on, it's spring there now, see? And they've got about fifteen new colts. There's nothing more inspiring or—beautiful than the sight of a mare and a new colt. And it's cool there now, see? Texas is cool now, and it's spring. And whenever spring comes to where I am, I suddenly get the feeling, my God, I'm not gettin' anywhere! What the hell am I doing, playing around with horses, twenty-eight dollars a week! I'm thirty-four years old, I oughta be makin' my future. That's when I come running home. And now, I get here, and I don't know what to do with myself. (*After a pause*) I've always made a point of not wasting my life, and every time I come back here I know that all I've done is to waste my life.

HAPPY You're a poet, you know that, Biff? You're a— you're an idealist!

BIFF No, I'm mixed up very bad. Maybe I oughta get married. Maybe I oughta get stuck into something. Maybe that's my trouble. I'm like a boy. I'm not married, I'm not in business, I just—I'm like a boy. Are you content, Hap? You're a success, aren't you? Are you content?

HAPPY Hell, no!

BIFF Why? You're making money, aren't you?

HAPPY (*Moving about with energy, expressiveness*)   All I can do now is wait for the merchandise manager to die. And suppose I get to be merchandise manager? He's a good friend of mine, and he just built a terrific estate on Long Island. And he lived there about two months and sold it, and now he's building another one. He can't enjoy it once it's finished. And I know that's just what I would do. I don't know what the hell I'm workin' for. Sometimes I sit in my apartment—all alone. And I think of the rent I'm paying. And it's crazy. But then, it's what I always wanted. My own apartment, a car, and plenty of women. And still, goddammit, I'm lonely.

BIFF (*With enthusiasm*)   Listen, why don't you come out West with me?

HAPPY   You and I, heh?

BIFF   Sure, maybe we could buy a ranch. Raise cattle, use our muscles. Men built like we are should be working out in the open.

HAPPY (*Avidly*)   The Loman Brothers, heh?

BIFF (*With vast affection*)   Sure, we'd be known all over the counties!

HAPPY (*Enthralled*)   That's what I dream about, Biff. Sometimes I want to just rip my clothes off in the middle of the store and outbox that goddam merchandise manager. I mean I can outbox, outrun, and outlift anybody in that store, and I have to take orders from those common, petty sons-of-bitches till I can't stand it any more.

BIFF   I'm tellin' you, kid, if you were with me I'd be happy out there.

HAPPY (*Enthused*)   See, Biff, everybody around me is so false that I'm constantly lowering my ideals . . .

BIFF   Baby, together we'd stand up for one another, we'd have someone to trust.

HAPPY   If I were around you—

BIFF   Hap, the trouble is we weren't brought up to grub for money. I don't know how to do it.

HAPPY Neither can I!

BIFF Then let's go!

HAPPY The only thing is—what can you make out there?

BIFF But look at your friend. Builds an estate and then hasn't the peace of mind to live in it.

HAPPY Yeah, but when he walks into the store the waves part in front of him. That's fifty-two thousand dollars a year coming through the revolving door, and I got more in my pinky finger than he's got in his head.

BIFF Yeah, but you just said—

HAPPY I gotta show some of those pompous, self-important executives over there that Hap Loman can make the grade. I want to walk into the store the way he walks in. Then I'll go with you, Biff. We'll be together yet, I swear. But take those two we had tonight. Now weren't they gorgeous creatures?

BIFF Yeah, yeah, most gorgeous I've had in years.

HAPPY I get that any time I want, Biff. Whenever I feel disgusted. The only trouble is, it gets like bowling or something. I just keep knockin' them over and it doesn't mean anything. You still run around a lot?

BIFF Naa. I'd like to find a girl—steady, somebody with substance.

HAPPY That's what I long for.

BIFF Go on! You'd never come home.

HAPPY I would! Somebody with character, with resistance! Like Mom, y'know? You're gonna call me a bastard when I tell you this. That girl Charlotte I was with tonight is engaged to be married in five weeks. (*He tries on his new hat*)

BIFF No kiddin'!

HAPPY Sure, the guy's in line for the vice-presidency of the store. I don't know what gets into me, maybe I just have an overdeveloped sense of competition or something, but I went and ruined her, and furthermore I can't get rid of her. And he's the third executive I've done that to. Isn't that a crummy characteristic? And to top it all, I go to their weddings! (*Indignantly, but laughing*) Like I'm not supposed to take bribes. Manufacturers offer me a hundred-dollar bill now and then to throw an order their way. You know how honest I am, but it's like this girl, see. I hate myself for it. Because I don't want the girl, and, still, I take it and—I love it!

BIFF   Let's go to sleep.

HAPPY   I guess we didn't settle anything, heh?

BIFF   I just got one idea that I think I'm going to try.

HAPPY   What's that?

BIFF   Remember Bill Oliver?

HAPPY   Sure, Oliver is very big now. You want to work for him again?

BIFF   No, but when I quit he said something to me. He put his arm on my shoulder, and he said, "Biff, if you ever need anything, come to me."

HAPPY   I remember that. That sounds good.

BIFF   I think I'll go to see him. If I could get ten thousand or even seven or eight thousand dollars I could buy a beautiful ranch.

HAPPY   I bet he'd back you. 'Cause he thought highly of you, Biff. I mean, they all do. You're well liked, Biff. That's why I say to come back here, and we both have the apartment. And I'm tellin' you, Biff, any babe you want . . .

BIFF   No, with a ranch I could do the work I like and still be something. I just wonder though. I wonder if Oliver still thinks I stole that carton of basketballs.

HAPPY   Oh, he probably forgot that long ago. It's almost ten years. You're too sensitive. Anyway, he didn't really fire you.

BIFF   Well, I think he was going to. I think that's why I quit. I was never sure whether he knew or not. I know he thought the world of me, though. I was the only one he'd let lock up the place.

WILLY (*Below*)   You gonna wash the engine, Biff?

HAPPY   Shh!
   (BIFF *looks at* HAPPY, *who is gazing down, listening.* WILLY *is mumbling in the parlor*)

HAPPY   You hear that?
   (*They listen.* WILLY *laughs warmly*)

BIFF (*Growing angry*)   Doesn't he know Mom can hear that?

WILLY   Don't get your sweater dirty, Biff!
   (*A look of pain crosses* BIFF's *face*)

HAPPY   Isn't that terrible? Don't leave again, will you? You'll find a job here. You gotta stick around. I don't know what to do about him, it's getting embarrassing.

WILLY   What a simonizing job!

BIFF   Mom's hearing that!

WILLY   No kiddin', Biff, you got a date? Wonderful!

HAPPY   Go on to sleep. But talk to him in the morning, will you?

BIFF (*Reluctantly getting into bed*)   With her in the house. Brother!

HAPPY (*Getting into bed*)   I wish you'd have a good talk with him.
   (*The light on their room begins to fade*)

BIFF (*To himself in bed*)   That selfish, stupid . . .

HAPPY   Sh . . . Sleep, Biff.
   (*Their light is out. Well before they have finished speaking,* WILLY's *form is dimly seen below in the darkened kitchen. He opens the refrigerator, searches in there, and takes out a bottle of milk. The apartment houses are fading out, and the entire house and surroundings become covered with leaves. Music insinuates itself as the leaves appear.*)

WILLY   Just wanna be careful with those girls, Biff, that's all. Don't make any promises. No promises of any kind. Because a girl, y'know, they always believe what you tell 'em,

and you're very young, Biff, you're too young to be talking
seriously to girls.

(*Light rises on the kitchen.* WILLY, *talking, shuts the
refrigerator door and comes downstage to the kitchen table. He pours milk into a glass. He is totally immersed in
himself, smiling faintly*)

WILLY Too young entirely, Biff. You want to watch your
schooling first. Then when you're all set, there'll be plenty
of girls for a boy like you. (*He smiles broadly at a kitchen
chair*) That so? The girls pay for you? (*He laughs*) Boy,
you must really be makin' a hit.

(WILLY *is gradually addressing—physically—a point offstage, speaking through the wall of the kitchen, and his
voice has been rising in volume to that of a normal conversation*)

WILLY I been wondering why you polish the car so careful.
Ha! Don't leave the hubcaps, boys. Get the chamois to the
hubcaps. Happy, use newspaper on the windows, it's the easiest thing. Show him how to do it, Biff! You see, Happy?
Pad it up, use it like a pad. That's it, that's it, good work.
You're doin' all right, Hap. (*He pauses, then nods in appro-
bation for a few seconds, then looks upward*) Biff, first thing
we gotta do when we get time is clip that big branch over
the house. Afraid it's gonna fall in a storm and hit the roof.
Tell you what. We get a rope and sling her around, and then
we climb up there with a couple of saws and take her down.
Soon as you finish the car, boys, I wanna see ya. I got a
surprise for you, boys.

BIFF (*Offstage*) Whatta ya got, Dad?

WILLY No, you finish first. Never leave a job till you're
finished—remember that. (*Looking toward the "big trees"*)
Biff, up in Albany I saw a beautiful hammock. I think I'll
buy it next trip, and we'll hang it right between those two
elms. Wouldn't that be something? Just swingin' there under
those branches. Boy, that would be . . .

(YOUNG BIFF *and* YOUNG HAPPY *appear from the direction
WILLY was addressing.* HAPPY *carries rags and a pail of
water.* BIFF, *wearing a sweater with a block "S," carries a
football.*)

BIFF (*Pointing in the direction of the car offstage*) How's that, Pop, professional?

WILLY Terrific. Terrific job, boys. Good work, Biff.

HAPPY Where's the surprise, Pop?

WILLY In the back seat of the car.

HAPPY Boy! (*He runs off*)

BIFF What is it, Dad? Tell me, what'd you buy?

WILLY (*Laughing, cuffs him*) Never mind, something I want you to have.

BIFF (*Turns and starts off*) What is it, Hap?

HAPPY (*Offstage*) It's a punching bag!

BIFF Oh, Pop!

WILLY It's got Gene Tunney's signature on it!
(HAPPY *runs onstage with a punching bag*)

BIFF Gee, how'd you know we wanted a punching bag?

WILLY Well, it's the finest thing for the timing.

HAPPY (*Lies down on his back and pedals with his feet*) I'm losing weight, you notice, Pop?

WILLY (*To* HAPPY) Jumping rope is good too.

BIFF Did you see the new football I got?

WILLY (*Examining the ball*) Where'd you get a new ball?

BIFF The coach told me to practice my passing.

WILLY That so? And he gave you the ball, heh?

BIFF Well, I borrowed it from the locker room. (*He laughs confidentially*)

WILLY (*Laughing with him at the theft*) I want you to return that.

HAPPY I told you he wouldn't like it!

BIFF (*Angrily*) Well, I'm bringing it back!

WILLY (*Stopping the incipient argument, to* HAPPY) Sure, he's gotta practice with a regulation ball, doesn't he? (*To* BIFF) Coach'll probably congratulate you on your initiative!

BIFF Oh, he keeps congratulating my initiative all the time, Pop.

WILLY That's because he likes you. If somebody else took that ball there'd be an uproar. So what's the report, boys, what's the report?

BIFF Where'd you go this time, Dad? Gee we were lonesome for you.

WILLY (*Pleased, puts an arm around each boy and they come down to the apron*) Lonesome, heh?

BIFF Missed you every minute.

WILLY Don't say? Tell you a secret, boys. Don't breathe it to a soul. Someday I'll have my own business, and I'll never have to leave home any more.

HAPPY Like Uncle Charley, heh?

WILLY Bigger than Uncle Charley! Because Charley is not— liked. He's liked, but he's not—well liked.

BIFF Where'd you go this time, Dad?

WILLY Well, I got on the road, and I went north to Providence. Met the Mayor.

BIFF The Mayor of Providence!

WILLY He was sitting in the hotel lobby.

BIFF What'd he say?

WILLY He said, "Morning!" And I said, "You got a fine city here, Mayor." And then he had coffee with me. And then I went to Waterbury. Waterbury is a fine city. Big clock city, the famous Waterbury clock. Sold a nice bill there. And then Boston—Boston is the cradle of the Revolution. A fine city. And a couple of other towns in Mass., and on to Portland and Bangor and straight home!

BIFF Gee, I'd love to go with you sometime, Dad.

WILLY Soon as summer comes.

HAPPY   Promise?

WILLY   You and Hap and I, and I'll show you all the towns. America is full of beautiful towns and fine, upstanding people. And they know me, boys, they know me up and down New England. The finest people. And when I bring you fellas up, there'll be open sesame for all of us, 'cause one thing, boys: I have friends. I can park my car in any street in New England, and the cops protect it like their own. This summer, heh?

BIFF *and* HAPPY, *together:* Yeah! You bet!

WILLY   We'll take our bathing suits.

HAPPY   We'll carry your bags, Pop!

WILLY   Oh, won't that be something! Me comin' into the Boston stores with you boys carryin' my bags. What a sensation!
(BIFF *is prancing around, practicing passing the ball.*)

WILLY   You nervous, Biff, about the game?

BIFF   Not if you're gonna be there.

WILLY   What do they say about you in school, now that they made you captain?

HAPPY   There's a crowd of girls behind him every time the classes change.

BIFF (*Taking* WILLY's *hand*)   This Saturday, Pop, this Saturday—just for you, I'm going to break through for a touchdown.

HAPPY   You're supposed to pass.

BIFF   I'm takin' one play for Pop. You watch me, Pop, and when I take off my helmet, that means I'm breakin' out. Then you watch me crash through that line!

WILLY (*Kisses* BIFF)   Oh, wait'll I tell this in Boston!
(BERNARD *enters in knickers. He is younger than* BIFF, *earnest and loyal, a worried boy*)

BERNARD   Biff, where are you? You're supposed to study with me today.

WILLY Hey, looka Bernard. What're you lookin' so anemic about, Bernard?

BERNARD He's gotta study, Uncle Willy. He's got Regents next week.

HAPPY (*Tauntingly, spinning* BERNARD *around*) Let's box, Bernard!

BERNARD Biff! (*He gets away from* HAPPY) Listen, Biff, I heard Mr. Birnbaum say that if you don't start studyin' math he's gonna flunk you, and you won't graduate. I heard him!

WILLY You better study with him, Biff. Go ahead now.

BERNARD I heard him!

BIFF Oh, Pop, you didn't see my sneakers! (*He holds up a foot for* WILLY *to look at*)

WILLY Hey, that's a beautiful job of printing!

BERNARD (*Wiping his glasses*) Just because he printed University of Virginia on his sneakers doesn't mean they've got to graduate him, Uncle Willy!

WILLY (*Angrily*) What're you talking about? With scholarships to three universities they're gonna flunk him?

BERNARD But I heard Mr. Birnbaum say—

WILLY Don't be a pest, Bernard! (*To his boys*) What an anemic!

BERNARD Okay, I'm waiting for you in my house, Biff.
  (BERNARD *goes off. The Lomans laugh*)

WILLY Bernard is not well liked, is he?

BIFF He's liked, but he's not well liked.

HAPPY That's right, Pop.

WILLY That's just what I mean. Bernard can get the best marks in school, y'understand, but when he gets out in the business world, y'understand, you are going to be five times ahead of him. That's why I thank Almighty God you're both built like Adonises. Because the man who makes an appearance in the business world, the man who creates personal interest, is the man who gets ahead. Be liked and you will

never want. You take me, for instance. I never have to wait
in line to see a buyer. "Willy Loman is here!" That's all they
have to know, and I go right through.

BIFF   Did you knock them dead, Pop?

WILLY   Knocked 'em cold in Providence, slaughtered 'em in
Boston.

HAPPY (*On his back, pedaling again*)   I'm losing weight, you
notice, Pop?
  (LINDA *enters, as of old, a ribbon in her hair, carrying a
  basket of washing*)

LINDA (*With youthful energy*)   Hello, dear!

WILLY   Sweetheart!

LINDA   How'd the Chevvy run?

WILLY   Chevrolet, Linda, is the greatest car ever built. (*To
the boys*) Since when do you let your mother carry wash up
the stairs?

BIFF   Grab hold there, boy!

HAPPY   Where to, Mom?

LINDA   Hang them up on the line. And you better go down
to your friends, Biff. The cellar is full of boys. They don't
know what to do with themselves.

BIFF   Ah, when Pop comes home they can wait!

WILLY (*Laughs appreciatively*)   You better go down and tell
them what to do, Biff.

BIFF   I think I'll have them sweep out the furnace room.

WILLY   Good work, Biff.

BIFF (*Goes through wall-line of kitchen to doorway at back
and calls down*)   Fellas! Everybody sweep out the furnace
room! I'll be right down!

VOICES   All right! Okay, Biff.

BIFF   George and Sam and Frank, come out back! We're
hangin' up the wash! Come on, Hap, on the double! (*He
and* HAPPY *carry out the basket*)

LINDA   The way they obey him!

WILLY   Well, that's training, the training. I'm tellin' you, I was sellin' thousands and thousands, but I had to come home.

LINDA   Oh, the whole block'll be at that game. Did you sell anything?

WILLY   I did five hundred gross in Providence and seven hundred gross in Boston.

LINDA   No! Wait a minute, I've got a pencil. (*She pulls pencil and paper out of her apron pocket*) That makes your commission . . . Two hundred—my God! Two hundred and twelve dollars!

WILLY   Well, I didn't figure it yet, but . . .

LINDA   How much did you do?

WILLY   Well, I—I did—about a hundred and eighty gross in Providence. Well, no—it came to—roughly two hundred gross on the whole trip.

LINDA   (*Without hesitation*)   Two hundred gross. That's . . . (*She figures*)

WILLY   The trouble was that three of the stores were half closed for inventory in Boston. Otherwise I woulda broke records.

LINDA   Well, it makes seventy dollars and some pennies. That's very good.

WILLY   What do we owe?

LINDA   Well, on the first there's sxiteen dollars on the refrigerator—

WILLY   Why sixteen?

LINDA   Well, the fan belt broke, so it was a dollar eighty.

WILLY   But it's brand new.

LINDA   Well, the man said that's the way it is. Till they work themselves in, y'know.
   (*They move through the wall-line into the kitchen*)

WILLY   I hope we didn't get stuck on that machine.

LINDA   They got the biggest ads of any of them!

WILLY   I know, it's a fine machine. What else?

LINDA   Well, there's nine-sixty for the washing machine. And for the vacuum cleaner there's three and a half due on the fifteenth. Then the roof, you got twenty-one dollars remaining.

WILLY   It don't leak, does it?

LINDA   No, they did a wonderful job. Then you owe Frank for the carburetor.

WILLY   I'm not going to pay that man! That goddam Chevrolet, they ought to prohibit the manufacture of that car!

LINDA   Well, you owe him three and a half. And odds and ends, comes to around a hundred and twenty dollars by the fifteenth.

WILLY   A hundred and twenty dollars! My God, if business don't pick up I don't know what I'm gonna do!

LINDA   Well, next week you'll do better.

WILLY   Oh, I'll knock 'em dead next week. I'll go to Hartford. I'm very well liked in Hartford. You know, the trouble is, Linda, people don't seem to take to me.
(They move onto the forestage)

LINDA   Oh, don't be foolish.

WILLY   I know it when I walk in. They seem to laugh at me.

LINDA   Why? Why would they laugh at you? Don't talk that way, Willy.
(WILLY moves to the edge of the stage. LINDA goes into the kitchen and starts to darn stockings)

WILLY   I don't know the reason for it, but they just pass me by. I'm not noticed.

LINDA   But you're doing wonderful, dear. You're making seventy to a hundred dollars a week.

WILLY   But I gotta be at it ten, twelve hours a day. Other men—I don't know—they do it easier. I don't know why—

I can't stop myself—I talk too much. A man oughta come in with a few words. One thing about Charley. He's a man of few words, and they respect him.

LINDA   You don't talk too much, you're just lively.

WILLY (*Smiling*)   Well, I figure, what the hell, life is short, a couple of jokes. (*To himself*) I joke too much! (*The smile goes*)

LINDA   Why? You're—

WILLY   I'm fat. I'm very—foolish to look at, Linda. I didn't tell you, but Christmas time I happened to be calling on F. H. Stewarts, and a salesman I know, as I was going in to see the buyer I heard him say something about—walrus. And I—I cracked him right across the face. I won't take that. I simply will not take that. But they do laugh at me. I know that.

LINDA   Darling . . .

WILLY   I gotta overcome it. I know I gotta overcome it. I'm not dressing to advantage, maybe.

LINDA   Willy, darling, you're the handsomest man in the world—

WILLY   Oh, no, Linda.

LINDA   To me you are. (*Slight pause*) The handsomest.
   (*From the darkness is heard the laughter of a woman.* WILLY *doesn't turn to it, but it continues through* LINDA's *lines*)

LINDA   And the boys, Willy. Few men are idolized by their children the way you are.
   (*Music is heard as behind a scrim, to the left of the house,* THE WOMAN, *dimly seen, is dressing*)

WILLY (*With great feeling*)   You're the best there is, Linda, you're a pal, you know that? On the road—on the road I want to grab you sometimes and just kiss the life outa you.
   (*The laughter is loud now, and he moves into a brightening area at the left, where* THE WOMAN *has come from behind the scrim and is standing, putting on her hat, looking into a "mirror" and laughing*)

WILLY 'Cause I get so lonely—especially when business is bad and there's nobody to talk to. I get the feeling that I'll never sell anything again, that I won't make a living for you, or a business, a business for the boys. (*He talks through* THE WOMAN's *subsiding laughter;* THE WOMAN *primps at the "mirror"*) There's so much I want to make for—

THE WOMAN Me? You didn't make me, Willy. I picked you.

WILLY (*Pleased*) You picked me?

THE WOMAN (*Who is quite proper-looking,* WILLY's *age*) I did. I've been sitting at that desk watching all the salesmen go by, day in, day out. But you've got such a sense of humor, and we do have such a good time together, don't we?

WILLY Sure, sure. (*He takes her in his arms*) Why do you have to go now?

THE WOMAN It's two o'clock . . .

WILLY No, come on in! (*He pulls her*)

THE WOMAN . . . my sisters'll be scandalized. When'll you be back?

WILLY Oh, two weeks about. Will you come up again?

THE WOMAN Sure thing. You do make me laugh. It's good for me. (*She squeezes his arm, kisses him*) And I think you're a wonderful man.

WILLY You picked me, heh?

THE WOMAN Sure. Because you're so sweet. And such a kidder.

WILLY Well, I'll see you next time I'm in Boston.

THE WOMAN I'll put you right through to the buyers.

WILLY (*Slapping her bottom*) Right. Well, bottoms up!

THE WOMAN (*Slaps him gently and laughs*) You just kill me, Willy. (*He suddenly grabs her and kisses her roughly*) You kill me. And thanks for the stockings. I love a lot of stockings. Well, good night.

WILLY Good night. And keep your pores open!

THE WOMAN Oh, Willy!
(THE WOMAN *bursts out laughing, and* LINDA'S *laughter blends in.* THE WOMAN *disappears into the dark. Now the area at the kitchen table brightens.* LINDA *is sitting where she was at the kitchen table, but now is mending a pair of her silk stockings*)

LINDA You are, Willy. The handsomest man. You've got no reason to feel that—

WILLY (*Coming out of* THE WOMAN'S *dimming area and going over to* LINDA) I'll make it all up to you, Linda, I'll—

LINDA There's nothing to make up, dear. You're doing fine, better than—

WILLY (*Noticing her mending*) What's that?

LINDA Just mending my stockings. They're so expensive—

WILLY (*Angrily, taking them from her*) I won't have you mending stockings in this house! Now throw them out!
(LINDA *puts the stockings in her pocket*)

BERNARD (*Entering on the run*) Where is he? If he doesn't study!

WILLY (*Moving to the forestage, with great agitation*) You'll give him the answers!

BERNARD I do, but I can't on a Regents! That's a state exam! They're liable to arrest me!

WILLY Where is he? I'll whip him, I'll whip him!

LINDA And he'd better give back that football, Willy, it's not nice.

WILLY Biff! Where is he? Why is he taking everything?

LINDA He's too rough with the girls, Willy. All the mothers are afraid of him!

WILLY I'll whip him!

BERNARD He's driving the car without a license!
(THE WOMAN'S *laugh is heard*)

WILLY Shut up!

LINDA   All the mothers—

WILLY   Shut up!

BERNARD   (*Backing quietly away and out*)   Mr. Birnbaum says he's stuck up.

WILLY   Get outa here!

BERNARD   If he doesn't buckle down he'll flunk math! (*He goes off*)

LINDA   He's right, Willy, you've gotta—

WILLY (*Exploding at her*)   There's nothing the matter with him! You want him to be a worm like Bernard? He's got spirit, personality . . .
  (*As he speaks, LINDA, almost in tears, exits into the living-room. WILLY is alone in the kitchen, wilting and staring. The leaves are gone. It is night again, and the apartment houses look down from behind*)

WILLY   Loaded with it. Loaded! What is he stealing? He's giving it back, isn't he? Why is he stealing? What did I tell him? I never in my life told him anything but decent things.
  (*HAPPY in pajamas has come down the stairs; WILLY suddenly becomes aware of HAPPY's presence*)

HAPPY   Let's go now, come on.

WILLY (*Sitting down at the kitchen table*)   Huh! Why did she have to wax the floors herself? Every time she waxes the floors she keels over. She knows that!

HAPPY   Shh! Take it easy. What brought you back tonight?

WILLY   I got an awful scare. Nearly hit a kid in Yonkers. God! Why didn't I go to Alaska with my brother Ben that time! Ben! That man was a genius, that man was success incarnate! What a mistake! He begged me to go.

HAPPY   Well, there's no use in—

WILLY   You guys! There was a man started with the clothes on his back and ended up with diamond mines!

HAPPY   Boy, someday I'd like to know how he did it.

WILLY   What's the mystery? The man knew what he wanted and went out and got it! Walked into a jungle, and comes

out, the age of twenty-one, and he's rich! The world is an
oyster, but you don't crack it open on a mattress!

HAPPY   Pop, I told you I'm gonna retire you for life.

WILLY   You'll retire me for life on seventy goddam dollars
a week? And your women and your car and your apartment,
and you'll retire me for life! Christ's sake, I couldn't get past
Yonkers today! Where are you guys, where are you? The
woods are burning! I can't drive a car!
   (CHARLEY *has appeared in the doorway. He is a large man,
   slow of speech, laconic, immovable. In all he says, despite
   what he says, there is pity, and, now, trepidation. He has
   a robe over pajamas, slippers on his feet. He enters the
   kitchen*)

CHARLEY   Everything all right?

HAPPY   Yeah, Charley, everything's . . .

WILLY   What's the matter?

CHARLEY   I heard some noise. I thought something happened. Can't we do something about the walls? You sneeze
in here, and in my house hats blow off.

HAPPY   Let's go to bed, Dad. Come on.
   (CHARLEY *signals to* HAPPY *to go*)

WILLY   You go ahead, I'm not tired at the moment.

HAPPY (*To* WILLY)   Take it easy, huh? (*He exits*)

WILLY   What're you doin' up?

CHARLEY (*Sitting down at the kitchen table opposite* WILLY)
Couldn't sleep good. I had a heartburn.

WILLY   Well, you don't know how to eat.

CHARLEY   I eat with my mouth.

WILLY   No, you're ignorant. You gotta know about vitamins
and things like that.

CHARLEY   Come on, let's shoot. Tire you out a little.

WILLY (*Hesitantly*)   All right. You got cards?

CHARLEY (*Taking a deck from his pocket*)   Yeah, I got
them. Someplace. What is it with those vitamins?

WILLY (*Dealing*)   They build up your bones. Chemistry.

CHARLEY   Yeah, but there's no bones in a heartburn.

WILLY   What are you talkin' about? Do you know the first thing about it?

CHARLEY   Don't get insulted.

WILLY   Don't talk about something you don't know anything about.

(*They are playing. Pause*)

CHARLEY   What're you doin' home?

WILLY   A little trouble with the car.

CHARLEY   Oh. (*Pause*) I'd like to take a trip to California.

WILLY   Don't say.

CHARLEY   You want a job?

WILLY   I got a job, I told you that. (*After a slight pause*) What the hell are you offering me a job for?

CHARLEY   Don't get insulted.

WILLY   Don't insult me.

CHARLEY   I don't see no sense in it. You don't have to go on this way.

WILLY   I got a good job. (*Slight pause*) What do you keep comin' in here for?

CHARLEY   You want me to go?

WILLY (*After a pause, withering*)   I can't understand it. He's going back to Texas again. What the hell is that?

CHARLEY   Let him go.

WILLY   I got nothin' to give him, Charley, I'm clean, I'm clean.

CHARLEY   He won't starve. None a them starve. Forget about him.

WILLY   Then what have I got to remember?

CHARLEY   You take it too hard. To hell with it. When a deposit bottle is broken you don't get your nickel back.

WILLY   That's easy enough for you to say.

CHARLEY   That ain't easy for me to say.

WILLY   Did you see the ceiling I put up in the living-room?

CHARLEY   Yeah, that's a piece of work. To put up a ceiling is a mystery to me. How do you do it?

WILLY   What's the difference?

CHARLEY   Well, talk about it.

WILLY   You gonna put up a ceiling?

CHARLEY   How could I put up a ceiling?

WILLY   Then what the hell are you bothering me for?

CHARLEY   You're insulted again.

WILLY   A man who can't handle tools is not a man. You're disgusting.

CHARLEY   Don't call me disgusting, Willy.
(UNCLE BEN, *carrying a valise and an umbrella, enters the forestage from around the right corner of the house. He is a stolid man, in his sixties, with a mustache and an authoritative air. He is utterly certain of his destiny, and there is an aura of far places about him. He enters exactly as* WILLY *speaks*)

WILLY   I'm getting awfully tired, Ben.
(BEN'S *music is heard*. BEN *looks around at everything*)

CHARLEY   Good, keep playing; you'll sleep better. Did you call me Ben?
(BEN *looks at his watch*)

WILLY   That's funny. For a second there you reminded me of my brother Ben.

BEN   I only have a few minutes. (*He strolls, inspecting the place*. WILLY *and* CHARLEY *continue playing*)

CHARLEY   You never heard from him again, heh? Since that time?

WILLY   Didn't Linda tell you? Couple of weeks ago we got a letter from his wife in Africa. He died.

CHARLEY   That so.

BEN (*Chuckling*)   So this is Brooklyn, eh?

CHARLEY   Maybe you're in for some of his money.

WILLY   Naa, he had seven sons. There's just one opportunity I had with that man . . .

BEN   I must make a train, William. There are several properties I'm looking at in Alaska.

WILLY   Sure, sure! If I'd gone with him to Alaska that time, everything would've been totally different.

CHARLEY   Go on, you'd froze to death up there.

WILLY   What're you talking about?

BEN   Opportunity is tremendous in Alaska, William. Surprised you're not up there.

WILLY   Sure, tremendous.

CHARLEY   Heh?

WILLY   There was the only man I ever met who knew the answers.

CHARLEY   Who?

BEN   How are you all?

WILLY (*Taking a pot, smiling*)   Fine, fine.

CHARLEY   Pretty sharp tonight.

BEN   Is Mother living with you?

WILLY   No, she died a long time ago.

CHARLEY   Who?

BEN   That's too bad. Fine specimen of a lady, Mother.

WILLY (*To* CHARLEY)   Heh?

BEN   I'd hoped to see the old girl.

CHARLEY   Who died?

BEN   Heard anything from Father, have you?

WILLY (*Unnerved*)   What do you mean, who died?

CHARLEY (*Taking a pot*)   What're you talkin' about?

BEN (*Looking at his watch*)   William, it's half-past eight!

WILLY (*As though to dispel his confusion he angrily stops
CHARLEY's hand*)   That's my build!

CHARLEY   I put the ace—

WILLY   If you don't know how to play the game I'm not
gonna throw my money away on you!

CHARLEY (*Rising*)   It was my ace, for God's sake!

WILLY   I'm through, I'm through!

BEN   When did Mother die?

WILLY   Long ago. Since the beginning you never knew how
to play cards.

CHARLEY (*Picks up the cards and goes to the door*)   All
right! Next time I'll bring a deck with five aces.

WILLY   I don't play that kind of game!

CHARLEY (*Turning to him*)   You ought to be ashamed of
yourself!

WILLY   Yeah?

CHARLEY   Yeah! (*He goes out*)

WILLY (*Slamming the door after him*)   Ignoramus!

BEN (*As WILLY comes toward him through the wall-line of
the kitchen*)   So you're William.

WILLY (*Shaking BEN's hand*)   Ben! I've been waiting for
you so long! What's the answer? How did you do it?

BEN   Oh, there's a story in that.
    (LINDA *enters the forestage, as of old, carrying the wash
    basket*)

LINDA   Is this Ben?

BEN (*Gallantly*)   How do you do, my dear.

LINDA   Where've you been all these years? Willy's always
wondered why you—

WILLY (*Pulling* BEN *away from her impatiently*) Where is
Dad? Didn't you follow him? How did you get started?

BEN   Well, I don't know how much you remember.

WILLY   Well, I was just a baby, of course, only three or four
years old—

BEN   Three years and eleven months.

WILLY   What a memory, Ben!

BEN   I have many enterprises, William, and I have never
kept books.

WILLY   I remember I was sitting under the wagon in—was it
Nebraska?

BEN   It was South Dakota, and I gave you a bunch of wild
flowers.

WILLY   I remember you walking away down some open
road.

BEN (*Laughing*)   I was going to find Father in Alaska.

WILLY   Where is he?

BEN   At that age I had a very faulty view of geography,
William. I discovered after a few days that I was heading due
south, so instead of Alaska, I ended up in Africa.

LINDA   Africa!

WILLY   The Gold Coast!

BEN   Principally diamond mines.

LINDA   Diamond mines!

BEN   Yes, my dear. But I've only a few minutes—

WILLY   No! Boys! Boys! (YOUNG BIFF *and* HAPPY *appear*)
Listen to this. This is your Uncle Ben, a great man! Tell my
boys, Ben!

BEN   Why, boys, when I was seventeen I walked into the
jungle, and when I was twenty-one I walked out. (*He laughs*)
And by God I was rich.

WILLY (*To the boys*)   You see what I been talking about?
The greatest things can happen!

BEN (*Glancing at his watch*) I have an appointment in Ketchikan Tuesday week.

WILLY No, Ben! Please tell about Dad. I want my boys to hear. I want them to know the kind of stock they spring from. All I remember is a man with a big beard, and I was in Mamma's lap, sitting around a fire, and some kind of high music.

BEN His flute. He played the flute.

WILLY Sure, the flute, that's right!
  (*New music is heard, a high, rollicking tune*)

BEN Father was a very great and a very wild-hearted man. We would start in Boston, and he'd toss the whole family into the wagon, and then he'd drive the team right across the country; through Ohio, and Indiana, Michigan, Illinois, and all the Western states. And we'd stop in the towns and sell the flutes that he'd made on the way. Great inventor, Father. With one gadget he made more in a week than a man like you could make in a lifetime.

WILLY That's just the way I'm bringing them up, Ben— rugged, well liked, all-around.

BEN Yeah? (*To* BIFF) Hit that, boy—hard as you can. (*He pounds his stomach*)

BIFF Oh, no, sir!

BEN (*Taking boxing stance*) Come on, get to me! (*He laughs*)

WILLY Go to it, Biff! Go ahead, show him!

BIFF Okay! (*He cocks his fists and starts in*)

LINDA (*To* WILLY) Why must he fight, dear?

BEN (*Sparring with* BIFF) Good boy! Good boy!

WILLY How's that, Ben, heh?

HAPPY Give him the left, Biff!

LINDA Why are you fighting?

BEN Good boy! (*Suddenly comes in, trips* BIFF, *and stands over him, the point of his umbrella poised over* BIFF'S *eye*)

LINDA   Look out, Biff!

BIFF   Gee!

BEN (*Patting* BIFF's *knee*)   Never fight fair with a stranger, boy. You'll never get out of the jungle that way. (*Taking* LINDA's *hand and bowing*) It was an honor and a pleasure to meet you, Linda.

LINDA (*Withdrawing her hand coldly, frightened*)   Have a nice—trip.

BEN (*To* WILLY)   And good luck with your—what do you do?

WILLY   Selling.

BEN   Yes. Well . . . (*He raises his hand in farewell to all*)

WILLY   No, Ben, I don't want you to think . . . (*He takes* BEN's *arm to show him*) It's Brooklyn, I know, but we hunt too.

BEN   Really, now.

WILLY   Oh, sure, there's snakes and rabbits and—that's why I moved out here. Why, Biff can fell any one of these trees in no time! Boys! Go right over to where they're building the apartment house and get some sand. We're gonna rebuild the entire front stoop right now! Watch this, Ben!

BIFF   Yes, sir! On the double, Hap!

HAPPY (*As he and* BIFF *run off*)   I lost weight, Pop, you notice?
  (CHARLEY *enters in knickers, even before the boys are gone*)

CHARLEY   Listen, if they steal any more from that building the watchman'll put the cops on them!

LINDA (*To* WILLY)   Don't let Biff . . .
  (BEN *laughs lustily*)

WILLY   You shoulda seen the lumber they brought home last week. At least a dozen six-by-tens worth all kinds a money.

CHARLEY   Listen, if that watchman—

WILLY I gave them hell, understand. But I got a couple of fearless characters there.

CHARLEY Willy, the jails are full of fearless characters.

BEN (*Clapping* WILLY *on the back, with a laugh at* CHARLEY) And the stock exchange, friend!

WILLY (*Joining in* BEN'S *laughter*) Where are the rest of your pants?

CHARLEY My wife bought them.

WILLY Now all you need is a golf club and you can go upstairs and go to sleep. (*To* BEN) Great athlete! Between him and his son Bernard they can't hammer a nail!

BERNARD (*Rushing in*) The watchman's chasing Biff!

WILLY (*Angrily*) Shut up! He's not stealing anything!

LINDA (*Alarmed, hurrying off left*) Where is he? Biff, dear! (*She exits*)

WILLY (*Moving toward the left, away from* BEN) There's nothing wrong. What's the matter with you?

BEN Nervy boy. Good!

WILLY (*Laughing*) Oh, nerves of iron, that Biff!

CHARLEY Don't know what it is. My New England man comes back and he's bleedin', they murdered him up there.

WILLY It's contacts, Charley, I got important contacts!

CHARLEY (*Sarcastically*) Glad to hear it, Willy. Come in later, we'll shoot a little casino. I'll take some of your Portland money. (*He laughs at* WILLY *and exits*)

WILLY (*Turning to* BEN) Business is bad, it's murderous. But not for me, of course.

BEN I'll stop by on my way back to Africa.

WILLY (*Longingly*) Can't you stay a few days? You're just what I need, Ben, because I—I have a fine position here, but I—well, Dad left when I was such a baby and I never had a chance to talk to him and I still feel—kind of temporary about myself.

BEN   I'll be late for my train.
  (*They are at opposite ends of the stage*)

WILLY   Ben, my boys—can't we talk? They'd go into the jaws of hell for me, see, but I—

BEN   William, you're being first-rate with your boys. Outstanding, manly chaps!

WILLY   (*Hanging on to his words*)   Oh, Ben, that's good to hear! Because sometimes I'm afraid that I'm not teaching them the right kind of— Ben, how should I teach them?

BEN   (*Giving great weight to each word, and with a certain vicious audacity*)   William, when I walked into the jungle, I was seventeen. When I walked out I was twenty-one. And, by God, I was rich! (*He goes off into darkness around the right corner of the house*)

WILLY   . . . was rich! That's just the spirit I want to imbue them with! To walk into a jungle! I was right! I was right! I was right!
  (BEN *is gone, but* WILLY *is still speaking to him as* LINDA, *in nightgown and robe, enters the kitchen, glances around for* WILLY, *then goes to the door of the house, looks out and sees him. Comes down to his left. He looks at her*)

LINDA   Willy, dear? Willy?

WILLY   I was right!

LINDA   Did you have some cheese? (*He can't answer*) It's very late, darling. Come to bed, heh?

WILLY   (*Looking straight up*)   Gotta break your neck to see a star in this yard.

LINDA   You coming in?

WILLY   Whatever happened to that diamond watch fob? Remember? When Ben came from Africa that time? Didn't he give me a watch fob with a diamond in it?

LINDA   You pawned it, dear. Twelve, thirteen years ago. For Biff's radio correspondence course.

WILLY   Gee, that was a beautiful thing. I'll take a walk.

LINDA   But you're in your slippers.

WILLY (*Starting to go around the house at the left*)   I was right! I was! (*Half to* LINDA, *as he goes, shaking his head*) What a man! There was a man worth talking to. I was right!

LINDA (*Calling after* WILLY)   But in your slippers, Willy!
(WILLY *is almost gone when* BIFF, *in his pajamas, comes down the stairs and enters the kitchen*)

BIFF   What is he doing out there?

LINDA   Sh!

BIFF   God Almighty, Mom, how long has he been doing this?

LINDA   Don't, he'll hear you.

BIFF   What the hell is the matter with him?

LINDA   It'll pass by morning.

BIFF   Shouldn't we do anything?

LINDA   Oh, my dear, you should do a lot of things, but there's nothing to do, so go to sleep.
(HAPPY *comes down the stair and sits on the steps*)

HAPPY   I never heard him so loud, Mom.

LINDA   Well, come around more often; you'll hear him. (*She sits down at the table and mends the lining of* WILLY'S *jacket*)

BIFF   Why didn't you ever write me about this, Mom?

LINDA   How would I write to you? For over three months you had no address.

BIFF   I was on the move. But you know I thought of you all the time. You know that, don't you, pal?

LINDA   I know, dear, I know. But he likes to have a letter. Just to know that there's still a possibility for better things.

BIFF   He's not like this all the time, is he?

LINDA   It's when you come home he's always the worst.

BIFF   When I come home?

LINDA   When you write you're coming, he's all smiles, and talks about the future, and—he's just wonderful. And then the closer you seem to come, the more shaky he gets, and then, by the time you get here, he's arguing, and he seems angry at you. I think it's just that maybe he can't bring himself to—to open up to you. Why are you so hateful to each other? Why is that?

BIFF (*Evasively*) I'm not hateful, Mom.

LINDA But you no sooner come in the door than you're fighting!

BIFF I don't know why. I mean to change. I'm tryin', Mom, you understand?

LINDA Are you home to stay now?

BIFF I don't know. I want to look around, see what's doin'.

LINDA Biff, you can't look around all your life, can you?

BIFF I just can't take hold, Mom. I can't take hold of some kind of a life.

LINDA Biff, a man is not a bird, to come and go with the springtime.

BIFF Your hair . . . (*He touches her hair*) Your hair got so gray.

LINDA Oh, it's been gray since you were in high school. I just stopped dyeing it, that's all.

BIFF Dye it again, will ya? I don't want my pal looking old. (*He smiles*)

LINDA You're such a boy! You think you can go away for a year and . . . You've got to get it into your head now that one day you'll knock on this door and there'll be strange people here—

BIFF What are you talking about? You're not even sixty, Mom.

LINDA But what about your father?

BIFF (*Lamely*) Well, I meant him too.

HAPPY He admires Pop.

LINDA Biff, dear, if you don't have any feeling for him, then you can't have any feeling for me.

BIFF   Sure I can, Mom.

LINDA   No. You can't just come to see me, because I love him. (*With a threat, but only a threat, of tears*) He's the dearest man in the world to me, and I won't have anyone making him feel unwanted and low and blue. You've got to make up your mind now, darling, there's no leeway any more. Either he's your father and you pay him that respect, or else you're not to come here. I know he's not easy to get along with—nobody knows that better than me—but . . .

WILLY   (*From the left, with a laugh*)   Hey, hey, Biffo!

BIFF   (*Starting to go out after* WILLY)   What the hell is the matter with him? (HAPPY *stops him*)

LINDA   Don't—don't go near him!

BIFF   Stop making excuses for him! He always, always wiped the floor with you. Never had an ounce of respect for you.

HAPPY   He's always had respect for—

BIFF   What the hell do you know about it?

HAPPY   (*Surlily*)   Just don't call him crazy!

BIFF   He's got no character— Charley wouldn't do this. Not in his own house—spewing out that vomit from his mind.

HAPPY   Charley never had to cope with what he's got to.

BIFF   People are worse off than Willy Loman. Believe me, I've seen them!

LINDA   Then make Charley your father, Biff. You can't do that, can you? I don't say he's a great man. Willy Loman never made a lot of money. His name was never in the paper. He's not the finest character that ever lived. But he's a human being, and a terrible thing is happening to him. So attention must be paid. He's not to be allowed to fall into his grave like an old dog. Attention, attention must be finally paid to such a person. You called him crazy—

BIFF   I didn't mean—

LINDA   No, a lot of people think he's lost his—balance. But you don't have to be very smart to know what his trouble is. The man is exhausted.

HAPPY   Sure!

LINDA   A small man can be just as exhausted as a great man. He works for a company thirty-six years this March, opens up unheard-of territories to their trademark, and now in his old age they take his salary away.

HAPPY (*Indignantly*)   I didn't know that, Mom.

LINDA   You never asked, my dear! Now that you get your spending money someplace else you don't trouble your mind with him.

HAPPY   But I gave you money last—

LINDA   Christmas time, fifty dollars! To fix the hot water it cost ninety-seven fifty! For five weeks he's been on straight commission, like a beginner, an unknown!

BIFF   Those ungrateful bastards!

LINDA   Are they any worse than his sons? When he brought them business, when he was young, they were glad to see him. But now his old friends, the old buyers that loved him so and always found some order to hand him in a pinch— they're all dead, retired. He used to be able to make six, seven calls a day in Boston. Now he takes his valises out of the car and puts them back and takes them out again and he's exhausted. Instead of walking he talks now. He drives seven hundred miles, and when he gets there no one knows him any more, no one welcomes him. And what goes through a man's mind, driving seven hundred miles home without having earned a cent? Why shouldn't he talk to himself? Why? When he has to go to Charley and borrow fifty dollars a week and pretend to me that it's his pay? How long can that go on? How long? You see what I'm sitting here and waiting for? And you tell me he has no character? The man who never worked a day but for your benefit? When does he get the medal for that? Is this his reward—to turn around at the age of sixty-three and find his sons, who he loved better than his life, one a philandering bum—

HAPPY   Mom!

LINDA   That's all you are, my baby! (*To* BIFF) And you! What happened to the love you had for him? You were such pals! How you used to talk to him on the phone every night! How lonely he was till he could come home to you!

BIFF   All right, Mom. I'll live here in my room, and I'll get a job. I'll keep away from him, that's all.

LINDA   No, Biff. You can't stay here and fight all the time.

BIFF   He threw me out of this house, remember that.

LINDA   Why did he do that? I never knew why.

BIFF   Because I know he's a fake and he doesn't like anybody around who knows!

LINDA   Why a fake? In what way? What do you mean?

BIFF   Just don't lay it all at my feet. It's between me and him—that's all I have to say. I'll chip in from now on. He'll settle for half my pay check. He'll be all right. I'm going to bed. (*He starts for the stairs*)

LINDA   He won't be all right.

BIFF   (*Turning on the stairs, furiously*)   I hate this city and I'll stay here. Now what do you want?

LINDA   He's dying, Biff.
        (HAPPY *turns quickly to her, shocked*)

BIFF   (*After a pause*)   Why is he dying?

LINDA   He's been trying to kill himself.

BIFF   (*With great horror*)   How?

LINDA   I live from day to day.

BIFF   What're you talking about?

LINDA   Remember I wrote you that he smashed up the car again? In February?

BIFF   Well?

LINDA   The insurance inspector came. He said that they have evidence. That all these accidents in the last year—weren't—weren't—accidents.

HAPPY   How can they tell that? That's a lie.

LINDA   It seems there's a woman . . . (*She takes a breath as*

{ BIFF (*Sharply but contained*)   What woman?

{ LINDA (*Simultaneously*)   . . . and this woman . . .

LINDA   What?

BIFF   Nothing. Go ahead.

LINDA   What did you say?

BIFF   Nothing. I just said what woman?

HAPPY   What about her?

LINDA   Well, it seems she was walking down the road and saw his car. She says that he wasn't driving fast at all, and that he didn't skid. She says he came to that little bridge, and then deliberately smashed into the railing, and it was only the shallowness of the water that saved him.

BIFF   Oh, no, he probably just fell asleep again.

LINDA   I don't think he fell asleep.

BIFF   Why not?

LINDA   Last month . . . (*With great difficulty*) Oh, boys, it's so hard to say a thing like this! He's just a big stupid man to you, but I tell you there's more good in him than in many other people. (*She chokes, wipes her eyes*) I was looking for a fuse. The lights blew out, and I went down the cellar. And behind the fuse box—it happened to fall out—was a length of rubber pipe—just short.

HAPPY   No kidding?

LINDA   There's a little attachment on the end of it. I knew right away. And sure enough, on the bottom of the water heater there's a new little nipple on the gas pipe.

HAPPY (*Angrily*)   That—jerk.

BIFF   Did you have it taken off?

LINDA   I'm—I'm ashamed to. How can I mention it to him? Every day I go down and take away that little rubber pipe. But, when he comes home, I put it back where it was. How can I insult him that way? I don't know what to do. I live from day to day, boys. I tell you, I know every thought in his mind. It sounds so old-fashioned and silly, but I tell you he put his whole life into you and you've turned your backs on him. (*She is bent over in the chair, weeping, her face in her hands*) Biff, I swear to God! Biff, his life is in your hands!

HAPPY (*To* BIFF)   How do you like that damned fool!

BIFF (*Kissing her*)   All right, pal, all right. It's all settled now. I've been remiss. I know that, Mom. But now I'll stay, and I swear to you, I'll apply myself. (*Kneeling in front of her, in a fever of self-reproach*) It's just—you see, Mom, I don't fit in business. Not that I won't try. I'll try, and I'll make good.

HAPPY   Sure you will. The trouble with you in business was you never tried to please people.

BIFF   I know, I—

HAPPY   Like when you worked for Harrison's. Bob Harrison said you were tops, and then you go and do some damn fool thing like whistling whole songs in the elevator like a comedian.

BIFF (*Against* HAPPY)   So what? I like to whistle sometimes.

HAPPY   You don't raise a guy to a responsible job who whistles in the elevator!

LINDA   Well, don't argue about it now.

HAPPY   Like when you'd go off and swim in the middle of the day instead of taking the line around.

BIFF (*His resentment rising*)   Well, don't you run off? You take off sometimes, don't you? On a nice summer day?

HAPPY   Yeah, but I cover myself!

LINDA   Boys!

HAPPY   If I'm going to take a fade the boss can call any number where I'm supposed to be and they'll swear to him that I just left. I'll tell you something that I hate to say, Biff, but in the business world some of them think you're crazy.

BIFF (*Angered*)   Screw the business world!

HAPPY   All right, screw it! Great, but cover yourself!

LINDA   Hap, Hap!

BIFF   I don't care what they think! They've laughed at Dad
for years, and you know why? Because we don't belong in
this nuthouse of a city! We should be mixing cement on some
open plain, or—or carpenters. A carpenter is allowed to
whistle!

(WILLY *walks in from the entrance of the house, at left*)

WILLY   Even your grandfather was better than a carpenter.
(*Pause. They watch him*) You never grew up. Bernard does
not whistle in the elevator, I assure you.

BIFF (*As though to laugh* WILLY *out of it*)   Yeah, but you
do, Pop.

WILLY   I never in my life whistled in an elevator! And who
in the business world thinks I'm crazy?

BIFF   I didn't mean it like that, Pop. Now don't make a
whole thing out of it, will ya?

WILLY   Go back to the West! Be a carpenter, a cowboy,
enjoy yourself!

LINDA   Willy, he was just saying—

WILLY   I heard what he said!

HAPPY (*Trying to quiet* WILLY)   Hey, Pop, come on
now . . .

WILLY (*Continuing over* HAPPY's *line*)   They laugh at me,
heh? Go to Filene's, go to the Hub, go to Slattery's, Boston.
Call out the name Willy Loman and see what happens! Big
shot!

BIFF   All right, Pop.

WILLY   Big!

BIFF   All right!

WILLY   Why do you always insult me?

BIFF   I didn't say a word. (*To* LINDA) Did I say a word?

LINDA   He didn't say anything, Willy.

WILLY (*Going to the doorway of the living-room*)   All right,
good night, good night.

LINDA   Willy, dear, he just decided . . .

WILLY (*To* BIFF)   If you get tired hanging around tomorrow, paint the ceiling I put up in the living-room.

BIFF   I'm leaving early tomorrow.

HAPPY   He's going to see Bill Oliver, Pop.

WILLY (*Interestedly*)   Oliver? For what?

BIFF (*With reserve, but trying, trying*)   He always said he'd stake me. I'd like to go into business, so maybe I can take him up on it.

LINDA   Isn't that wonderful?

WILLY   Don't interrupt. What's wonderful about it? There's fifty men in the City of New York who'd stake him. (*To* BIFF) Sporting goods?

BIFF   I guess so. I know something about it and—

WILLY   He knows something about it! You know sporting goods better than Spalding, for God's sake! How much is he giving you?

BIFF   I don't know, I didn't even see him, yet, but—

WILLY   Then what're you talkin' about?

BIFF (*Getting angry*)   Well, all I said was I'm gonna see him, that's all!

WILLY (*Turning away*)   Ah, you're counting your chickens again.

BIFF (*Starting left for the stairs*)   Oh, Jesus, I'm going to sleep!

WILLY (*Calling after him*)   Don't curse in this house!

BIFF (*Turning*)   Since when did you get so clean?

HAPPY (*Trying to stop them*)   Wait a . . .

WILLY   Don't use that language to me! I won't have it!

HAPPY (*Grabbing* BIFF, *shouts*)   Wait a minute! I got an idea. I got a feasible idea. Come here, Biff, let's talk this over now, let's talk some sense here. When I was down in Florida last time, I thought of a great idea to sell sporting goods. It just came back to me. You and I, Biff—we have a line, the Loman Line. We train a couple of weeks, and put on a couple of exhibitions, see?

WILLY   That's an idea!

HAPPY   Wait! We form two basketball teams, see? Two waterpolo teams. We play each other. It's a million dollars' worth of publicity. Two brothers, see? The Loman Brothers. Displays in the Royal Palms—all the hotels. And banners over the ring and the basketball court: "Loman Brothers." Baby, we could sell sporting goods!

WILLY   That is a one-million-dollar idea!

LINDA   Marvelous!

BIFF   I'm in great shape as far as that's concerned.

HAPPY   And the beauty of it is, Biff, it wouldn't be like a business. We'd be out playin' ball again . . .

BIFF   (*Enthused*)   Yeah, that's . . .

WILLY   Million-dollar . . .

HAPPY   And you wouldn't get fed up with it, Biff. It'd be the family again. There'd be the old honor, and comradeship, and if you wanted to go off for a swim or somethin'—well, you'd do it! Without some smart cooky gettin' up ahead of you!

WILLY   Lick the world! You guys together could absolutely lick the civilized world.

BIFF   I'll see Oliver tomorrow. Hap, if we could work that out . . .

LINDA   Maybe things are beginning to—

WILLY   (*Wildly enthused, to* LINDA)   Stop interrupting! (*To* BIFF)   But don't wear sport jacket and slacks when you see Oliver.

BIFF   No, I'll—

WILLY   A business suit, and talk as little as possible, and don't crack any jokes.

BIFF   He did like me. Always liked me.

LINDA   He loved you!

WILLY (*To* LINDA) Will you stop! (*To* BIFF) Walk in very serious. You are not applying for a boy's job. Money is to pass. Be quiet, fine, and serious. Everybody likes a kidder, but nobody lends him money.

HAPPY   I'll try to get some myself, Biff. I'm sure I can.

WILLY   I see great things for you kids, I think your troubles are over. But remember, start big and you'll end big. Ask for fifteen. How much you gonna ask for?

BIFF   Gee, I don't know—

WILLY   And don't say "Gee." "Gee" is a boy's word. A man walking in for fifteen thousand dollars does not say "Gee!"

BIFF   Ten, I think, would be top though.

WILLY   Don't be so modest. You always started too low. Walk in with a big laugh. Don't look worried. Start off with a couple of your good stories to lighten things up. It's not what you say, it's how you say it—because personality always wins the day.

LINDA   Oliver always thought the highest of him—

WILLY   Will you let me talk?

BIFF   Don't yell at her, Pop, will ya?

WILLY (*Angrily*) I was talking, wasn't I?

BIFF   I don't like you yelling at her all the time, and I'm tellin' you, that's all.

WILLY   What're you, takin' over this house?

LINDA   Willy—

WILLY (*Turning on her*) Don't take his side all the time, goddammit!

BIFF (*Furiously*) Stop yelling at her!

WILLY (*Suddenly pulling on his cheek, beaten down, guilt ridden*) Give my best to Bill Oliver—he may remember me. (*He exits through the living-room doorway*)

LINDA (*Her voice subdued*)   What'd you have to start that
for? (BIFF *turns away*) You see how sweet he was as soon as
you talked hopefully? (*She goes over to* BIFF) Come up and
say good night to him. Don't let him go to bed that way.

HAPPY   Come on, Biff, let's buck him up.

LINDA   Please, dear. Just say good night. It takes so little to
make him happy. Come. (*She goes through the living-room
doorway, calling upstairs from within the living-room*) Your
pajamas are hanging in the bathroom, Willy!

HAPPY (*Looking toward where* LINDA *went out*)   What a
woman! They broke the mold when they made her. You
know that, Biff?

BIFF   He's off salary. My God, working on commission!

HAPPY   Well, let's face it: he's no hot-shot selling man. Except that sometimes, you have to admit, he's a sweet personality.

BIFF (*Deciding*)   Lend me ten bucks, will ya? I want to buy
some new ties.

HAPPY   I'll take you to a place I know. Beautiful stuff. Wear
one of my striped shirts tomorrow.

BIFF   She got gray. Mom got awful old. Gee, I'm gonna go
in to Oliver tomorrow and knock him for a—

HAPPY   Come on up. Tell that to Dad. Let's give him a
whirl. Come on.

BIFF (*Steamed up*)   You know, with ten thousand bucks,
boy!

HAPPY (*As they go into the living-room*)   That's the talk,
Biff, that's the first time I've heard the old confidence out of
you! (*From within the living-room, fading off*) You're gonna
live with me, kid, and any babe you want just say the word
. . . (*The last lines are hardly heard. They are mounting
the stairs to their parents' bedroom*)

LINDA (*Entering her bedroom and addressing* WILLY, *who is
in the bathroom. She is straightening the bed for him*)   Can
you do anything about the shower? It drips.

WILLY (*From the bathroom*) All of a sudden everything falls to pieces! Goddam plumbing, oughta be sued, those people. I hardly finished putting it in and the thing . . . (*His words rumble off*)

LINDA I'm just wondering if Oliver will remember him. You think he might?

WILLY (*Coming out of the bathroom in his pajamas*) Remember him? What's the matter with you, you crazy? If he'd've stayed with Oliver he'd be on top by now! Wait'll Oliver gets a look at him. You don't know the average caliber any more. The average young man today—(*He is getting into bed*)—is got a caliber of zero. Greatest thing in the world for him was to bum around.

(BIFF *and* HAPPY *enter the bedroom. Slight pause*)

WILLY (*Stops short, looking at* BIFF) Glad to hear it, boy.

HAPPY He wanted to say good night to you, sport.

WILLY (*To* BIFF) Yeah. Knock him dead, boy. What'd you want to tell me?

BIFF Just take it easy, Pop. Good night. (*He turns to go*)

WILLY (*Unable to resist*) And if anything falls off the desk while you're talking to him—like a package or something—don't you pick it up. They have office boys for that.

LINDA I'll make a big breakfast—

WILLY Will you let me finish? (*To* BIFF) Tell him you were in the business in the West. Not farm work.

BIFF All right, Dad.

LINDA I think everything—

WILLY (*Going right through her speech*) And don't undersell yourself. No less than fifteen thousand dollars.

BIFF (*Unable to bear him*) Okay. Good night, Mom. (*He starts moving*)

WILLY Because you got a greatness in you, Biff, remember that. You got all kinds a greatness . . . (*He lies back, exhausted.* BIFF *walks out*)

LINDA (*Calling after* BIFF) Sleep well, darling!

HAPPY I'm gonna get married, Mom. I wanted to tell you.

LINDA   Go to sleep, dear.

HAPPY (*Going*)   I just wanted to tell you.

WILLY   Keep up the good work. (HAPPY *exits*) God . . . remember that Ebbets Field game? The championship of the city?

LINDA   Just rest. Should I sing to you?

WILLY   Yeah. Sing to me. (LINDA *hums a soft lullaby*) When that team came out—he was the tallest, remember?

LINDA   Oh, yes. And in gold.
(BIFF *enters the darkened kitchen, takes a cigarette, and leaves the house. He comes downstage into a golden pool of light. He smokes, staring at the night*)

WILLY   Like a young god. Hercules—something like that. And the sun, the sun all around him. Remember how he waved to me? Right up from the field, with the representatives of three colleges standing by? And the buyers I brought, and the cheers when he came out—Loman, Loman, Loman! God Almighty, he'll be great yet. A star like that, magnificent, can never really fade away!
(*The light on* WILLY *is fading. The gas heater begins to glow through the kitchen wall, near the stairs, a blue flame beneath red coils*)

LINDA (*Timidly*)   Willy dear, what has he got against you?

WILLY   I'm so tired. Don't talk any more.
(BIFF *slowly returns to the kitchen. He stops, stares toward the heater*)

LINDA   Will you ask Howard to let you work in New York?

WILLY   First thing in the morning. Everything'll be all right.
(BIFF *reaches behind the heater and draws out a length of rubber tubing. He is horrified and turns his head toward* WILLY'S *room, still dimly lit, from which the strains of* LINDA'S *desperate but monotonous humming rise*)

WILLY (*Staring through the window into the moonlight*) Gee, look at the moon moving between the buildings!
(BIFF *wraps the tubing around his hand and quickly goes up the stairs*)

CURTAIN

Act
Two

Music is heard, gay and bright. The curtain rises as the music fades away. WILLY, *in shirt sleeves, is sitting at the kitchen table, sipping coffee, his hat in his lap.* LINDA *is filling his cup when she can.*

WILLY   Wonderful coffee. Meal in itself.

LINDA   Can I make you some eggs?

WILLY   No. Take a breath.

LINDA   You look so rested, dear.

WILLY   I slept like a dead one. First time in months. Imagine, sleeping till ten on a Tuesday morning. Boys left nice and early, heh?

LINDA   They were out of here by eight o'clock.

WILLY   Good work!

LINDA   It was so thrilling to see them leaving together. I can't get over the shaving lotion in this house!

WILLY (*Smiling*)   Mmm—

LINDA   Biff was very changed this morning. His whole attitude seemed to be hopeful. He couldn't wait to get downtown to see Oliver.

WILLY   He's heading for a change. There's no question, there simply are certain men that take longer to get—solidified. How did he dress?

LINDA   His blue suit. He's so handsome in that suit. **He** could be a—anything in that suit!
   (WILLY *gets up from the table.* LINDA *holds his jacket for him*)

WILLY   There's no question, no question at all. Gee, on the way home tonight I'd like to buy some seeds.

LINDA   (*Laughing*)   That'd be wonderful. But not enough sun gets back there. Nothing'll grow any more.

WILLY   You wait, kid, before it's all over we're gonna get a little place out in the country, and I'll raise some vegetables, a couple of chickens . . .

LINDA   You'll do it yet, dear.
   (WILLY *walks out of his jacket.* LINDA *follows him*)

WILLY   And they'll get married, and come for a weekend. I'd build a little guest house. 'Cause I got so many fine tools, all I'd need would be a little lumber and some peace of mind.

LINDA   (*Joyfully*)   I sewed the lining . . .

WILLY   I could build two guest houses, so they'd both come. Did he decide how much he's going to ask Oliver for?

LINDA   (*Getting him into the jacket*)   He didn't mention it, but I imagine ten or fifteen thousand. You going to talk to Howard today?

WILLY   Yeah. I'll put it to him straight and simple. He'll just have to take me off the road.

LINDA   And Willy, don't forget to ask for a little advance, because we've got the insurance premium. It's the grace period now.

WILLY   That's a hundred . . . ?

LINDA   A hundred and eight, sixty-eight. Because we're a little short again.

WILLY   Why are we short?

LINDA   Well, you had the motor job on the car . . .

WILLY   That goddam Studebaker!

LINDA   And you got one more payment on the refrigerator . . .

WILLY   But it just broke again!

LINDA   Well, it's old, dear.

WILLY   I told you we should've bought a well-advertised machine. Charley bought a General Electric and it's twenty years old and it's still good, that son-of-a-bitch.

LINDA   But, Willy—

WILLY   Whoever heard of a Hastings refrigerator? Once in my life I would like to own something outright before it's broken! I'm always in a race with the junkyard! I just finished paying for the car and it's on its last legs. The refrigerator consumes belts like a goddam maniac. They time those things. They time them so when you finally paid for them, they're used up.

LINDA   (*Buttoning up his jacket as he unbuttons it*)   All told, about two hundred dollars would carry us, dear. But that includes the last payment on the mortgage. After this payment, Willy, the house belongs to us.

WILLY   It's twenty-five years!

LINDA   Biff was nine years old when we bought it.

WILLY   Well, that's a great thing. To weather a twenty-five year mortgage is—

LINDA   It's an accomplishment.

WILLY   All the cement, the lumber, the reconstruction I put in this house! There ain't a crack to be found in it any more.

LINDA   Well, it served its purpose.

WILLY   What purpose? Some stranger'll come along, move in, and that's that. If only Biff would take this house, and raise a family . . . (*He starts to go*) Good-by, I'm late.

LINDA   (*Suddenly remembering*)   Oh, I forgot! You're supposed to meet them for dinner.

WILLY   Me?

LINDA   At Frank's Chop House on Forty-eighth near Sixth Avenue.

WILLY   Is that so! How about you?

LINDA   No, just the three of you. They're gonna blow you to a big meal!

WILLY   Don't say! Who thought of that?

LINDA   Biff came to me this morning, Willy, and he said, "Tell Dad, we want to blow him to a big meal." Be there six o'clock. You and your two boys are going to have dinner.

WILLY   Gee whiz! That's really somethin'. I'm gonna knock Howard for a loop, kid. I'll get an advance, and I'll come home with a New York job. Goddammit, now I'm gonna do it!

LINDA   Oh, that's the spirit, Willy!

WILLY   I will never get behind a wheel the rest of my life!

LINDA   It's changing, Willy, I can feel it changing!

WILLY   Beyond a question. G'by, I'm late. (*He starts to go again*)

LINDA (*Calling after him as she runs to the kitchen table for a handkerchief*)   You got your glasses?

WILLY (*Feels for them, then comes back in*)   Yeah, yeah, got my glasses.

LINDA (*Giving him the handkerchief*)   And a handkerchief.

WILLY   Yeah, handkerchief.

LINDA   And your saccharine?

WILLY   Yeah, my saccharine.

LINDA   Be careful on the subway stairs.
(*She kisses him, and a silk stocking is seen hanging from her hand.* WILLY *notices it*)

WILLY   Will you stop mending stockings? At least while I'm in the house. It gets me nervous. I can't tell you. Please.
(LINDA *hides the stocking in her hand as she follows* WILLY *across the forestage in front of the house*)

LINDA   Remember, Frank's Chop House.

WILLY (*Passing the apron*)   Maybe beets would grow out there.

LINDA (*Laughing*)   But you tried so many times.

WILLY   Yeah. Well, don't work hard today. (*He disappears around the right corner of the house*)

LINDA   Be careful!
(*As* WILLY *vanishes,* LINDA *waves to him. Suddenly the phone rings. She runs across the stage and into the kitchen and lifts it*)

LINDA   Hello? Oh, Biff! I'm so glad you called, I just . . . Yes, sure, I just told him. Yes, he'll be there for dinner at six o'clock, I didn't forget. Listen, I was just dying to tell you. You know that little rubber pipe I told you about? That he connected to the gas heater? I finally decided to go down the cellar this morning and take it away and destroy it. But it's gone! Imagine? He took it away himself, it isn't there! (*She listens*) When? Oh, then you took it. Oh—nothing, it's just that I'd hoped he'd taken it away himself. Oh, I'm not worried, darling, because this morning he left in such high spirits, it was like the old days! I'm not afraid any more. Did Mr. Oliver see you? . . . Well, you wait there then. And make a nice impression on him, darling. Just don't perspire too much before you see him. And have a nice time with Dad. He may have big news too! . . . That's right, a New York job. And be sweet to him tonight, dear. Be loving to him. Because he's only a little boat looking for a harbor. (*She is trembling with sorrow and joy*) Oh, that's wonderful, Biff, you'll save his life. Thanks, darling. Just put your arm around him when he comes into the restaurant. Give him a smile. That's the boy . . . Good-by, dear. . . . You got your comb? . . . That's fine. Good-by, Biff dear.

(*In the middle of her speech, Howard Wagner, thirty-six, wheels on a small typewriter table on which is a wire-recording machine and proceeds to plug it in. This is on the left forestage. Light slowly fades on Linda as it rises on Howard. Howard is intent on threading the machine and only glances over his shoulder as Willy appears*)

WILLY   Pst! Pst!

HOWARD   Hello, Willy, come in.

WILLY   Like to have a little talk with you, Howard.

HOWARD   Sorry to keep you waiting. I'll be with you in a
minute.

WILLY   What's that, Howard?

HOWARD   Didn't you ever see one of these? Wire recorder.

WILLY   Oh. Can we talk a minute?

HOWARD   Records things. Just got delivery yesterday. Been
driving me crazy, the most terrific machine I ever saw in my
life. I was up all night with it.

WILLY   What do you do with it?

HOWARD   I bought it for dictation, but you can do anything
with it. Listen to this. I had it home last night. Listen to what
I picked up. The first one is my daughter. Get this. (*He flicks
the switch and "Roll out the Barrel" is heard being whistled*)
Listen to that kid whistle.

WILLY   That is lifelike, isn't it?

HOWARD   Seven years old. Get that tone.

WILLY   Ts, ts, Like to ask a little favor if you . . .
(*The whistling breaks off, and the voice of* HOWARD'S
daughter is heard)

HIS DAUGHTER   "Now you, Daddy."

HOWARD   She's crazy for me! (*Again the same song is whistled*) That's me! Ha! (*He winks*)

WILLY   You're very good!
(*The whistling breaks off again. The machine runs silent
for a moment*)

HOWARD   Sh! Get this now, this is my son.

HIS SON   "The capital of Alabama is Montgomery; the
capital of Arizona is Phoenix; the capital of Arkansas is
Little Rock; the capital of California is Sacramento . . ."
(*And on, and on*)

HOWARD (*Holding up five fingers*)   Five years old, Willy!

WILLY   He'll make an announcer some day!

HIS SON (*Continuing*)   "The capital . . ."

HOWARD   Get that —alphabetical order! (*The machine breaks off suddenly*) Wait a minute. The maid kicked the plug out.

WILLY   It certainly is a—

HOWARD   Sh, for God's· sake!

HIS SON   "It's nine o'clock, Bulova watch time. So I have to go to sleep."

WILLY   That really is—

HOWARD   Wait a minute! The next is my wife.
   (*They wait*)

HOWARD'S VOICE   "Go on, say something." (*Pause*) "Well, you gonna talk?"

HIS WIFE   "I can't think of anything."

HOWARD'S VOICE   "Well, talk—it's turning."

HIS WIFE (*Shyly, beaten*)   "Hello." (*Silence*) "Oh, Howard, I can't talk into this . . ."

HOWARD (*Snapping the machine off*) That was my wife.

WILLY   That is a wonderful machine. Can we—

HOWARD   I tell you, Willy, I'm gonna take my camera, and my bandsaw, and all my hobbies, and out they go. This is the most fascinating relaxation I ever found.

WILLY   I think I'll get one myself.

HOWARD   Sure, they're only a hundred and a half. You can't do without it. Supposing you wanna hear Jack Benny, see? But you can't be at home at that hour. So you tell the maid to turn the radio on when Jack Benny comes on, and this automatically goes on with the radio . . .

WILLY   And when you come home you . . .

HOWARD   You can come home twelve o'clock, one o'clock, any time you like, and you get yourself a Coke and sit yourself down, throw the switch, and there's Jack Benny's program in the middle of the night!

WILLY   I'm definitely going to get one. Because lots of time I'm on the road, and I think to myself, what I must be missing on the radio!

HOWARD   Don't you have a radio in the car?

WILLY   Well, yeah, but who ever thinks of turning it on?

HOWARD   Say, aren't you supposed to be in Boston?

WILLY   That's what I want to talk to you about, Howard. You got a minute? (*He draws a chair in from the wing*)

HOWARD   What happened? What're you doing here?

WILLY   Well . . .

HOWARD   You didn't crack up again, did you?

WILLY   Oh, no. No . . .

HOWARD   Geez, you had me worried there for a minute. What's the trouble?

WILLY   Well, tell you the truth, Howard. I've come to the decision that I'd rather not travel any more.

HOWARD   Not travel! Well, what'll you do?

WILLY   Remember, Christmas time, when you had the party here? You said you'd try to think of some spot for me here in town.

HOWARD   With us?

WILLY   Well, sure.

HOWARD   Oh, yeah, yeah. I remember. Well, I couldn't think of anything for you, Willy.

WILLY   I tell ya, Howard. The kids are all grown up, y'know. I don't need much any more. If I could take home—well, sixty-five dollars a week, I could swing it.

HOWARD   Yeah, but Willy, see I—

WILLY   I tell ya why, Howard. Speaking frankly and between the two of us, y'know—I'm just a little tired.

HOWARD   Oh, I could understand that, Willy. But you're a road man, Willy, and we do a road business. We've only got a half-dozen salesmen on the floor here.

WILLY   God knows, Howard, I never asked a favor of any
man. But I was with the firm when your father used to carry
you in here in his arms.

HOWARD   I know that, Willy, but—

WILLY   Your father came to me the day you were born and
asked me what I thought of the name of Howard, may he
rest in peace.

HOWARD   I appreciate that, Willy, but there just is no spot
here for you. If I had a spot I'd slam you right in, but I just
don't have a single solitary spot.
    (*He looks for his lighter.* WILLY *has picked it up and gives
    it to him. Pause*)

WILLY   (*With increasing anger*)   Howard, all I need to set
my table is fifty dollars a week.

HOWARD   But where am I going to put you, kid?

WILLY   Look, it isn't a question of whether I can sell merchandise, is it?

HOWARD   No, but it's business, kid, and everybody's gotta
pull his own weight.

WILLY   (*Desperately*)   Just let me tell you a story, Howard—

HOWARD   'Cause you gotta admit, business is business.

WILLY   (*angrily*)   Business is definitely business, but just
listen for a minute. You don't understand this. When I was a
boy—eighteen, nineteen—I was already on the road. And
there was a question in my mind as to whether selling had a
future for me. Because in those days I had a yearning to go
to Alaska. See, there were three gold strikes in one month
in Alaska, and I felt like going out. Just for the ride, you
might say.

HOWARD   (*Barely interested*)   Don't say.

WILLY   Oh, yeah, my father lived many years in Alaska. He
was an adventurous man. We've got quite a little streak of
self-reliance in our family. I thought I'd go out with my
older brother and try to locate him, and maybe settle in the
North with the old man. And I was almost decided to go,
when I met a salesman in the Parker House. His name was

Dave Singleman. And he was eighty-four years old, and he'd drummed merchandise in thirty-one states. And old Dave, he'd go up to his room, y'understand, put on his green velvet slippers—I'll never forget—and pick up his phone and call the buyers, and without ever leaving his room, at the age of eighty-four, he made his living. And when I saw that, I realized that selling was the greatest career a man could want. 'Cause what could be more satisfying than to be able to go, at the age of eighty-four, into twenty or thirty different cities, and pick up a phone, and be remembered and loved and helped by so many different people? Do you know? when he died—and by the way he died the death of a salesman, in his green velvet slippers in the smoker of the New York, New Haven and Hartford, going into Boston—when he died, hundreds of salesmen and buyers were at his funeral. Things were sad on a lotta trains for months after that. (*He stands up.* HOWARD *has not looked at him*) In those days there was personality in it, Howard. There was respect, and comradeship, and gratitude in it. Today, it's all cut and dried, and there's no chance for bringing friendship to bear—or personality. Yet see what I mean? They don't know me any more.

HOWARD (*Moving away, to the right*) That's just the thing, Willy.

WILLY If I had forty dollars a week—that's all I'd need. Forty dollars, Howard.

HOWARD Kid, I can't take blood from a stone, I—

WILLY (*Desperation is on him now*) Howard, the year Al Smith was nominated, your father came to me and—

HOWARD (*Starting to go off*) I've got to see some people, kid.

WILLY (*Stopping him*) I'm talking about your father! There were promises made across this desk! You mustn't tell me you've got people to see—I put thirty-four years into this firm, Howard, and now I can't pay my insurance! You can't eat the orange and throw the peel away—a man is not a piece of fruit! (*After a pause*) Now pay attention. Your father —in 1928 I had a big year. I averaged a hundred and seventy dollars a week in commissions.

HOWARD (*Impatiently*) Now, Willy, you never averaged—

WILLY (*Banging his hand on the desk*)   I averaged a hundred and seventy dollars a week in the year of 1928! And your father came to me—or rather, I was in the office here—it was right over this desk—and he put his hand on my shoulder—

HOWARD (*Getting up*)   You'll have to excuse me, Willy, I gotta see some people. Pull yourself together. (*Going out*) I'll be back in a little while.

(*On* HOWARD'S *exit, the light on his chair grows very bright and strange*)

WILLY   Pull myself together! What the hell did I say to him? My God, I was yelling at him! How could I! (WILLY *breaks off, staring at the light, which occupies the chair, animating it. He approaches this chair, standing across the desk from it*) Frank, Frank, don't you remember what you told me that time? How you put your hand on my shoulder, and Frank . . . (*He leans on the desk and as he speaks the dead man's name he accidentally switches on the recorder, and instantly*)

HOWARD'S SON   ". . . of New York is Albany. The capital of Ohio is Cincinnati, the capital of Rhode Island is . . ." (*The recitation continues*)

WILLY (*Leaping away with fright, shouting*)   Ha! Howard! Howard! Howard!

HOWARD (*Rushing in*)   What happened?

WILLY (*Pointing at the machine, which continues nasally, childishly, with the capital cities*)   Shut it off! Shut it off!

HOWARD (*Pulling the plug out*)   Look, Willy . . .

WILLY (*Pressing his hands to his eyes*)   I gotta get myself some coffee. I'll get some coffee . . .

(WILLY *starts to walk out.* HOWARD *stops him*)

HOWARD (*Rolling up the cord*)   Willy, look . . .

WILLY   I'll go to Boston.

HOWARD   Willy, you can't go to Boston for us.

WILLY   Why can't I go?

HOWARD I don't want you to represent us. I've been meaning to tell you for a long time now.

WILLY Howard, are you firing me?

HOWARD I think you need a good long rest, Willy.

WILLY Howard—

HOWARD And when you feel better, come back, and we'll see if we can work something out.

WILLY But I gotta earn money, Howard. I'm in no position to—

HOWARD Where are your sons? Why don't your sons give you a hand?

WILLY They're working on a very big deal.

HOWARD This is no time for false pride, Willy. You go to your sons and you tell them that you're tired. You've got two great boys, haven't you?

WILLY Oh, no question, no question, but in the meantime . . .

HOWARD Then that's that, heh?

WILLY All right, I'll go to Boston tomorrow.

HOWARD No, no.

WILLY I can't throw myself on my sons. I'm not a cripple!

HOWARD Look, kid, I'm busy this morning.

WILLY (*Grasping* HOWARD's *arm*) Howard, you've got to let me go to Boston!

HOWARD (*Hard, keeping himself under control*) I've got a line of people to see this morning. Sit down, take five minutes, and pull yourself together, and then go home, will ya? I need the office, Willy. (*He starts to go, turns, remembering the recorder, starts to push off the table holding the recorder*) Oh, yeah. Whenever you can this week, stop by and drop off the samples. You'll feel better, Willy, and then come back and we'll talk. Pull yourself together, kid, there's people outside.

(HOWARD *exits, pushing the table off left.* WILLY *stares into space, exhausted. Now the music is heard—*BEN'S *music— first distantly, then closer, closer. As* WILLY *speaks,* BEN *enters from the right. He carries valise and umbrella*)

WILLY   Oh, Ben, how did you do it? What is the answer? Did you wind up the Alaska deal already?

BEN   Doesn't take much time if you know what you're doing. Just a short business trip. Boarding ship in an hour. Wanted to say good-by.

WILLY   Ben, I've got to talk to you.

BEN (*Glancing at his watch*)   Haven't the time, William.

WILLY (*Crossing the apron to* BEN)   Ben, nothing's working out. I don't know what to do.

BEN   Now, look here, William. I've bought timberland in Alaska and I need a man to look after things for me.

WILLY   God, timberland! Me and my boys in those grand outdoors!

BEN   You've a new continent at your doorstep, William. Get out of these cities, they're full of talk and time payments and courts of law. Screw on your fists and you can fight for a fortune up there.

WILLY   Yes, yes! Linda, Linda!
    (LINDA *enters as of old, with the wash*)

LINDA   Oh, you're back?

BEN   I haven't much time.

WILLY   No, wait! Linda, he's got a proposition for me in Alaska.

LINDA   But you've got— (*To* BEN) He's got a beautiful job here.

WILLY   But in Alaska, kid, I could—

LINDA   You're doing well enough, Willy!

BEN (*To* LINDA)   Enough for what, my dear?

LINDA (*Frightened of* BEN *and angry at him*)   Don't say those things to him! Enough to be happy right here, right now. (*To* WILLY, *while* BEN *laughs*) Why must everybody conquer the world? You're well liked, and the boys love you, and someday— (*To* BEN)—why, old man Wagner told him just the other day that if he keeps it up he'll be a member of the firm, didn't he, Willy?

WILLY Sure, sure. I am building something with this firm, Ben, and if a man is building something he must be on the right track, mustn't he?

BEN What are you building? Lay your hand on it. Where is it?

WILLY (*Hesitantly*) That's true, Linda, there's nothing.

LINDA Why? (*To* BEN) There's a man eighty-four years old—

WILLY That's right, Ben, that's right. When I look at that man I say, what is there to worry about?

BEN Bah!

WILLY It's true, Ben. All he has to do is go into any city, pick up the phone, and he's making his living and you know why?

BEN (*Picking up his valise*) I'v got to go.

WILLY (*Holding* BEN *back*) Look at this boy!
  (BIFF, *in his high school sweater, enters carrying suitcase.* HAPPY *carries* BIFF'S *shoulder guards, gold helmet, and football pants*)

WILLY Without a penny to his name, three great universities are begging for him, and from there the sky's the limit, because it's not what you do, Ben. It's who you know and the smile on your face! It's contacts, Ben, contacts! The whole wealth of Alaska passes over the lunch table at the Commodore Hotel, and that's the wonder, the wonder of this country, that a man can end with diamonds here on the basis of being liked! (*He turns to* BIFF) And that's why when you get out on that field today it's important. Because thousands of people will be rooting for you and loving you. (*To* BEN, *who has again begun to leave*) And Ben! when he walks into a business office his name will sound out like a bell and all the doors will open to him! I've seen it, Ben, I've seen it a thousand times! You can't feel it with your hand like timber, but it's there!

BEN   Good-by, William.

WILLY   Ben, am I right? Don't you think I'm right? I value your advice.

BEN   There's a new continent at your doorstep, William. You could walk out rich. Rich! (*He is gone*)

WILLY   We'll do it here, Ben! You hear me? We're gonna do it here!
  (*Young* BERNARD *rushes in. The gay music of the* BOYS *is heard*)

BERNARD   Oh, gee, I was afraid you left already!

WILLY   Why? What time is it?

BERNARD   It's half-past one!

WILLY   Well, come on, everybody! Ebbets Field next stop! Where's the pennants? (*He rushes through the wall-line of the kitchen and out into the living-room*)

LINDA (*To* BIFF)   Did you pack fresh underwear?

BIFF (*Who has been limbering up*)   I want to go!

BERNARD   Biff, I'm carrying your helmet, ain't I?

HAPPY   No, I'm carrying the helmet.

BERNARD   Oh, Biff, you promised me.

HAPPY   I'm carrying the helmet.

BERNARD   How am I going to get in the locker room?

LINDA   Let him carry the shoulder guards. (*She puts her coat and hat on in the kitchen*)

BERNARD   Can I, Biff? 'Cause I told everybody I'm going to be in the locker room.

HAPPY   In Ebbets Field it's the clubhouse.

BERNARD   I meant the clubhouse. Biff!

HAPPY   Biff!

BIFF (*Grandly, after a slight pause*) Let him carry the shoulder guards.

HAPPY (*As he gives* BERNARD *the shoulder guards*) Stay close to us now.
(WILLY *rushes in with the pennants*)

WILLY (*Handing them out*) Everybody wave when Biff comes out on the field. (HAPPY *and* BERNARD *run off*) You set now, boy?
(*The music has died away*)

BIFF Ready to go, Pop. Every muscle is ready.

WILLY (*At the edge of the apron*) You realize what this means?

BIFF That's right, Pop.

WILLY (*Feeling* BIFF'S *muscles*) You're comin' home this afternoon captain of the All-Scholastic Championship Team of the City of New York.

BIFF I got it, Pop. And remember, pal, when I take off my helmet, that touchdown is for you.

WILLY Let's go! (*He is starting out, with his arm around* BIFF, *when* CHARLEY *enters, as of old, in knickers*) I got no room for you, Charley.

CHARLEY Room? For what?

WILLY In the car.

CHARLEY You goin' for a ride? I wanted to shoot some casino.

WILLY (*Furiously*) Casino! (*Incredulously*) Don't you realize what today is?

LINDA Oh, he knows, Willy. He's just kidding you.

WILLY That's nothing to kid about!

CHARLEY No, Linda, what's goin' on?

LINDA He's playing in Ebbets Field.

CHARLEY Baseball in this weather?

WILLY Don't talk to him. Come on, come on! (*He is pushing them out*)

CHARLEY Wait a minute, didn't you hear the news?

WILLY What?

CHARLEY Don't you listen to the radio? Ebbets Field just blew up.

WILLY You go to hell! (CHARLEY *laughs. Pushing them out*) Come on, come on! We're late.

CHARLEY (*As they go*) Knock a homer, Biff, knock a homer!

WILLY (*The last to leave, turning to* CHARLEY) I don't think that was funny, Charley. This is the greatest day of his life.

CHARLEY Willy, when are you going to grow up?

WILLY Yeah, heh? When this game is over, Charley, you'll be laughing out of the other side of your face. They'll be calling him another Red Grange. Twenty-five thousand a year.

CHARLEY (*Kidding*) Is that so?

WILLY Yeah, that's so.

CHARLEY Well, then, I'm sorry, Willy. But tell me something.

WILLY What?

CHARLEY Who is Red Grange?

WILLY Put up your hands. Goddam you, put up your hands!
(CHARLEY, *chuckling, shakes his head and walks away, around the left corner of the stage.* WILLY *follows him. The music rises to a mocking frenzy*)

WILLY Who the hell do you think you are, better than everybody else? You don't know everything, you big, ignorant, stupid . . . Put up your hands!
(*Light rises, on the right side of the forestage, on a small table in the reception room of* CHARLEY'S *office. Traffic sounds are heard.* BERNARD, *now mature, sits whistling to himself. A pair of tennis rackets and an overnight bag are on the floor beside him*)

WILLY (*Offstage*) What are you walking away for? Don't walk away! If you're going to say something say it to my face! I know you laugh at me behind my back. You'll laugh out of the other side of your goddam face after this game. Touchdown! Touchdown! Eighty thousand people! Touchdown! Right between the goal posts.

(BERNARD *is a quiet, earnest, but self-assured young man.* WILLY'S *voice is coming from right upstage now.* BERNARD *lowers his feet off the table and listens.* JENNY, *his father's secretary, enters*)

JENNY (*Distressed*) Say, Bernard, will you go out in the hall?

BERNARD What is that noise? Who is it?

JENNY Mr. Loman. He just got off the elevator.

BERNARD (*Getting up*) Who's he arguing with?

JENNY Nobody. There's nobody with him. I can't deal with him any more, and your father gets all upset everytime he comes. I've got a lot of typing to do, and your father's waiting to sign it. Will you see him?

WILLY (*Entering*) Touchdown! Touch— (*He sees* JENNY) Jenny, Jenny, good to see you. How're ya? Workin'? Or still honest?

JENNY Fine. How've you been feeling?

WILLY Not much any more, Jenny. Ha, ha! (*He is surprised to see the rackets*)

BERNARD Hello, Uncle Willy.

WILLY (*Almost shocked*) Bernard! Well, look who's here! (*He comes quickly, guiltily, to* BERNARD *and warmly shakes his hand*)

BERNARD How are you? Good to see you.

WILLY What are you doing here?

BERNARD Oh, just stopped by to see Pop. Get off my feet till my train leaves. I'm going to Washington in a few minutes.

WILLY   Is he in?

BERNARD   Yes, he's in his office with the accountant. Sit down.

WILLY (*Sitting down*)   What're you going to do in Washington?

BERNARD   Oh, just a case I've got there, Willy.

WILLY   That so? (*Indicating the rackets*) You going to play tennis there?

BERNARD   I'm staying with a friend who's got a court.

WILLY   Don't say. His own tennis court. Must be fine people, I bet.

BERNARD   They are, very nice. Dad tells me Biff's in town.

WILLY (*With a big smile*)   Yeah, Biff's in. Working on a very big deal, Bernard.

BERNARD   What's Biff doing?

WILLY   Well, he's been doing very big things in the West. But he decided to establish himself here. Very big. We're having dinner. Did I hear your wife had a boy?

BERNARD   That's right. Our second.

WILLY   Two boys! What do you know!

BERNARD   What kind of a deal has Biff got?

WILLY   Well, Bill Oliver—very big sporting-goods man—he wants Biff very badly. Called him in from the West. Long distance, carte blanche, special deliveries. Your friends have their own private tennis court?

BERNARD   You still with the old firm, Willy?

WILLY (*After a pause*)   I'm—I'm overjoyed to see how you made the grade, Bernard, overjoyed. It's an encouraging thing to see a young man really—really— Looks very good for Biff—very— (*He breaks off, then*) Bernard— (*He is so full of emotion, he breaks off again*)

BERNARD   What is it, Willy?

WILLY (*Small and alone*)   What—what's the secret?

BERNARD   What secret?

WILLY   How—how did you? Why didn't he ever catch on?

BERNARD   I wouldn't know that, Willy.

WILLY (*Confidentially, desperately*)   You were his friend, his boyhood friend. There's something I don't understand about it. His life ended after that Ebbets Field game. From the age of seventeen nothing good ever happened to him.

BERNARD   He never trained himself for anything.

WILLY   But he did, he did. After high school he took so many correspondence courses. Radio mechanics; television; God knows what, and never made the slightest mark.

BERNARD (*Taking off his glasses*)   Willy, do you want to talk candidly?

WILLY (*Rising, faces* BERNARD)   I regard you as a very brilliant man, Bernard. I value your advice.

BERNARD   Oh, the hell with the advice, Willy. I couldn't advise you. There's just one thing I've always wanted to ask you. When he was supposed to graduate, and the math teacher flunked him—

WILLY   Oh, that son-of-a-bitch ruined his life.

BERNARD   Yeah, but, Willy, all he had to do was go to summer school and make up that subject.

WILLY   That's right, that's right.

BERNARD   Did you tell him not to go to summer school?

WILLY   Me? I begged him to go. I ordered him to go!

BERNARD   Then why wouldn't he go?

WILLY   Why? Why! Bernard, that question has been trailing me like a ghost for the last fifteen years. He flunked the subject, and laid down and died like a hammer hit him!

BERNARD   Take it easy, kid.

WILLY   Let me talk to you—I got nobody to talk to. Bernard, Bernard, was it my fault? Y'see? It keeps going around in my mind, maybe I did something to him. I got nothing to give him.

BERNARD   Don't take it so hard.

WILLY   Why did he lay down? What is the story there? You were his friend!

BERNARD   Willy, I remember, it was June, and our grades came out. And he'd flunked math.

WILLY   That son-of-a-bitch!

BERNARD   No, it wasn't right then. Biff just got very angry, I remember, and he was ready to enroll in summer school.

WILLY (*Surprised*)   He was?

BERNARD   He wasn't beaten by it at all. But then, Willy, he disappeared from the block for almost a month. And I got the idea that he'd gone up to New England to see you. Did he have a talk with you then?
  (WILLY *stares in silence*)

BERNARD   Willy?

WILLY (*With a strong edge of resentment in his voice*)   Yeah, he came to Boston. What about it?

BERNARD   Well, just that when he came back—I'll never forget this, it always mystifies me. Because I'd thought so well of Biff, even though he'd always taken advantage of me. I loved him, Willy, y'know? And he came back after that month and took his sneakers—remember those sneakers with "University of Virginia" printed on them? He was so proud of those, wore them every day. And he took them down in the cellar, and burned them up in the furnace. We had a fist fight. It lasted at least half an hour. Just the two of us, punching each other down the cellar, and crying right through it. I've often thought of how strange it was that I knew he'd given up his life. What happened in Boston, Willy?
  (WILLY *looks at him as at an intruder*)

BERNARD   I just bring it up because you asked me.

WILLY (*Angrily*)   Nothing. What do you mean, "What happened?" What's that got to do with anything?

BERNARD   Well, don't get sore.

WILLY   What are you trying to do, blame it on me? If a boy lays down is that my fault?

BERNARD   Now, Willy, don't get—

WILLY   Well, don't—don't talk to me that way! What does that mean, "What happened?"
   (CHARLEY *enters. He is in his vest, and he carries a bottle of bourbon*)

CHARLEY   Hey, you're going to miss that train. (*He waves the bottle*)

BERNARD   Yeah, I'm going. (*He takes the bottle*) Thanks, Pop. (*He picks up his rackets and bag*) Good-by, Willy, and don't worry about it. You know, "If at first you don't succeed . . ."

WILLY   Yes, I believe in that.

BERNARD   But sometimes, Willy, it's better for a man just to walk away.

WILLY   Walk away?

BERNARD   That's right.

WILLY   But if you can't walk away?

BERNARD   (*After a slight pause*)   I guess that's when it's tough. (*Extending his hand*) Good-by, Willy.

WILLY   (*Shaking* BERNARD'S *hand*)   Good-by, boy.

CHARLEY   (*An arm on* BERNARD'S *shoulder*)   How do you like this kid? Gonna argue a case in front of the Supreme Court.

BERNARD   (*Protesting*)   Pop!

WILLY   (*Genuinely shocked, pained, and happy*)   No! The Supreme Court!

BERNARD   I gotta run. 'By, Dad!

CHARLEY   Knock 'em dead, Bernard!
   (BERNARD *goes off*)

WILLY   (*As* CHARLEY *takes out his wallet*)   The Supreme Court! And he didn't even mention it!

CHARLEY   (*Counting out money on the desk*)   He don't have to—he's gonna do it.

WILLY   And you never told him what to do, did you? You never took any interest in him.

CHARLEY   My salvation is that I never took any interest in anything. There's some money—fifty dollars. I got an accountant inside.

WILLY   Charley, look . . . (*With difficulty*) I got my insurance to pay. If you can manage it—I need a hundred and ten dollars.

   (CHARLEY *doesn't reply for a moment; merely stops moving*)

WILLY   I'd draw it from my bank but Linda would know, and I . . .

CHARLEY   Sit down, Willy.

WILLY   (*Moving toward the chair*) I'm keeping an account of everything, remember. I'll pay every penny back. (*He sits*)

CHARLEY   Now listen to me, Willy.

WILLY   I want you to know I appreciate . . .

CHARLEY   (*Sitting down on the table*)   Willy, what're you doin'? What the hell is goin' on in your head?

WILLY   Why? I'm simply . . .

CHARLEY   I offered you a job. You can make fifty dollars a week. And I won't send you on the road.

WILLY   I've got a job.

CHARLEY   Without pay? What kind of a job is a job without pay? (*He rises*) Now, look, kid, enough is enough. I'm no genius but I know when I'm being insulted.

WILLY   Insulted!

CHARLEY   Why don't you want to work for me?

WILLY   What's the matter with you? I've got a job.

CHARLEY   Then what're you walkin' in here every week for?

WILLY   (*Getting up*)   Well, if you don't want me to walk in here—

CHARLEY I am offering you a job.

WILLY I don't want your goddam job!

CHARLEY When the hell are you going to grow up?

WILLY (*Furiously*) You big ignoramus, if you say that to me again I'll rap you one! I don't care how big you are! (*He's ready to fight*)
(*Pause*)

CHARLEY (*Kindly, going to him*) How much do you need, Willy?

WILLY Charley, I'm strapped, I'm strapped. I don't know what to do. I was just fired.

CHARLEY Howard fired you?

WILLY That snotnose. Imagine that? I named him. I named him Howard.

CHARLEY Willy, when're you gonna realize that them things don't mean anything? You named him Howard, but you can't sell that. The only thing you got in this world is what you can sell. And the funny thing is that you're a salesman, and you don't know that.

WILLY I've always tried to think otherwise, I guess. I always felt that if a man was impressive, and well liked, that nothing—

CHARLEY Why must everybody like you? Who liked J. P. Morgan? Was he impressive? In a Turkish bath he'd look like a butcher. But with his pockets on he was very well liked. Now listen, Willy, I know you don't like me, and nobody can say I'm in love with you, but I'll give you a job because— just for the hell of it, put it that way. Now what do you say?

WILLY I—I just can't work for you, Charley.

CHARLEY What're you, jealous of me?

WILLY I can't work for you, that's all, don't ask me why.

CHARLEY (*Angered, takes out more bills*) You been jealous of me all your life, you damned fool! Here, pay your insurance. (*He puts the money in* WILLY's *hand*)

WILLY I'm keeping strict accounts.

CHARLEY   I've got some work to do. Take care of yourself. And pay your insurance.

WILLY (*Moving to the right*)   Funny, y'know? After all the highways, and the trains, and the appointments, and the years, you end up worth more dead than alive.

CHARLEY   Willy, nobody's worth nothin' dead. (*After a slight pause*) Did you hear what I said?
   (WILLY *stands still, dreaming*)

CHARLEY   Willy!

WILLY   Apologize to Bernard for me when you see him. I didn't mean to argue with him. He's a fine boy. They're all fine boys, and they'll end up big—all of them. Someday they'll all play tennis together. Wish me luck, Charley, He saw Bill Oliver today.

CHARLEY   Good luck.

WILLY (*On the verge of tears*)   Charley, you're the only friend I got. Isn't that a remarkable thing? (*He goes out*)

CHARLEY   Jesus!
   (CHARLEY *stares after him a moment and follows. All light blacks out. Suddenly raucous music is heard, and a red glow rises behind the screen at right.* STANLEY, *a young waiter, appears, carrying a table, followed by* HAPPY, *who is carrying two chairs*)

STANLEY (*Putting the table down*)   That's all right, Mr. Loman, I can handle it myself. (*He turns and takes the chairs from* HAPPY *and places them at the table*)

HAPPY (*Glancing around*)   Oh, this is better.

STANLEY   Sure, in the front there you're in the middle of all kinds a noise. Whenever you got a party, Mr. Loman, you just tell me and I'll put you back here. Y'know, there's a lotta people they don't like it private, because when they go out they like to see a lotta action around them because they're sick and tired to stay in the house by theirself. But I know you, you ain't from Hackensack. You know what I mean?

HAPPY (*Sitting down*)   So how's it coming, Stanley?

STANLEY   Ah, it's a dog's life. I only wish during the war they'd a took me in the Army. I coulda been dead by now.

HAPPY   My brother's back, Stanley.

STANLEY   Oh, he come back, heh? From the Far West.

HAPPY   Yeah, big cattle man, my brother, so treat him right. And my father's coming too.

STANLEY   Oh, your father too!

HAPPY   You got a couple of nice lobsters?

STANLEY   Hundred per cent, big.

HAPPY   I want them with the claws.

STANLEY   Don't worry, I don't give you no mice. (HAPPY *laughs*) How about some wine? It'll put a head on the meal.

HAPPY   No. You remember, Stanley, that recipe I brought you from overseas? With the champagne in it?

STANLEY   Oh, yeah, sure. I still got it tacked up yet in the kitchen. But that'll have to cost a buck apiece anyways.

HAPPY   That's all right.

STANLEY   What'd you, hit a number or somethin'?

HAPPY   No, it's a little celebration. My brother is—I think he pulled off a big deal today. I think we're going into business together.

STANLEY   Great! That's the best for you. Because a family business, you know what I mean?—that's the best.

HAPPY   That's what I think.

STANLEY   'Cause what's the difference? Somebody steals? It's in the family. Know what I mean? (*Sotto voce*) Like this bartender here. The boss is goin' crazy what kinda leak he's got in the cash register. You put it in but it don't come out.

HAPPY (*Raising his head*)   Sh!

STANLEY   What?

HAPPY   You notice I wasn't lookin' right or left, was I?

STANLEY   No.

HAPPY   And my eyes are closed.

STANLEY   So what's the—?

HAPPY   Strudel's comin'.

STANLEY (*Catching on, looks around*)   Ah, no, there's no—
(*He breaks off as a furred, lavishly dressed girl enters and
sits at the next table. Both follow her with their eyes*)

STANLEY   Geez, how'd ya know?

HAPPY   I got radar or something. (*Staring directly at her profile*) Oooooooo . . . Stanley.

STANLEY   I think that's for you, Mr. Loman.

HAPPY   Look at that mouth. Oh, God. And the binoculars.

STANLEY   Geez, you got a life, Mr. Loman.

HAPPY   Wait on her.

STANLEY (*Going to the* GIRL'S *table*)   Would you like a menu,
ma'am?

GIRL   I'm expecting someone, but I'd like a—

HAPPY   Why don't you bring her—excuse me, miss, do you
mind? I sell champagne, and I'd like you to try my brand.
Bring her a champagne, Stanley.

GIRL   That's awfully nice of you.

HAPPY   Don't mention it. It's all company money. (*He
laughs*)

GIRL   That's a charming product to be selling, isn't it?

HAPPY   Oh, gets to be like everything else. Selling is selling,
y'know.

GIRL   I suppose.

HAPPY   You don't happen to sell, do you?

GIRL   No, I don't sell.

HAPPY   Would you object to a compliment from a stranger?
You ought to be on a magazine cover.

GIRL (*Looking at him a little archly*) I have been.
 (STANLEY *comes in with a glass of champagne*)

HAPPY What'd I say before, Stanley? You see? She's a cover girl.

STANLEY Oh, I could see, I could see.

HAPPY (*To the* GIRL) What magazine?

GIRL Oh, a lot of them. (*She takes the drink*) Thank you.

HAPPY You know what they say in France, don't you? "Champagne is the drink of the complexion"—Hya, Biff!
 (BIFF *has entered and sits with* HAPPY)

BIFF Hello, kid. Sorry I'm late.

HAPPY I just got here. Uh, Miss—?

GIRL Forsythe.

HAPPY Miss Forsythe, this is my brother.

BIFF Is Dad here?

HAPPY His name is Biff. You might've heard of him. Great football player.

GIRL Really? What team?

HAPPY Are you familiar with football?

GIRL No, I'm afraid I'm not.

HAPPY Biff is quarterback with the New York Giants.

GIRL Well, that is nice, isn't it? (*She drinks*)

HAPPY Good health.

GIRL I'm happy to meet you.

HAPPY That's my name. Hap. It's really Harold, but at West Point they called me Happy.

GIRL (*Now really impressed*) Oh, I see. How do you do? (*She turns her profile*)

BIFF Isn't Dad coming?

HAPPY You want her?

BIFF Oh, I could never make that.

HAPPY   I remember the time that idea would never come into your head. Where's the old confidence, Biff?

BIFF   I just saw Oliver—

HAPPY   Wait a minute. I've got to see that old confidence again. Do you want her? She's on call.

BIFF   Oh, no. (*He turns to look at the* GIRL)

HAPPY   I'm telling you. Watch this. (*Turning to the* GIRL) Honey? (*She turns to him*) Are you busy?

GIRL   Well, I am . . . but I could make a phone call.

HAPPY   Do that, will you, honey? And see if you can get a friend. We'll be here for a while. Biff is one of the greatest football players in the country.

GIRL (*Standing up*)   Well, I'm certainly happy to meet you.

HAPPY   Come back soon.

GIRL   I'll try.

HAPPY   Don't try, honey, try hard.
   (*The* GIRL *exits.* STANLEY *follows, shaking his head in bewildered admiration*)

HAPPY   Isn't that a shame now? A beautiful girl like that? That's why I can't get married. There's not a good woman in a thousand. New York is loaded with them, kid!

BIFF   Hap, look—

HAPPY   I told you she was on call!

BIFF (*Strangely unnerved*)   Cut it out, will ya? I want to say something to you.

HAPPY   Did you see Oliver?

BIFF   I saw him all right. Now look, I want to tell Dad a couple of things and I want you to help me.

HAPPY   What? Is he going to back you?

BIFF   Are you crazy? You're out of your goddam head, you know that?

HAPPY   Why? What happened?

BIFF (*Breathlessly*) I did a terrible thing today, Hap. It's been the strangest day I ever went through. I'm all numb, I swear.

HAPPY You mean he wouldn't see you?

BIFF Well, I waited six hours for him, see? All day. Kept sending my name in. Even tried to date his secretary so she'd get me to him, but no soap.

HAPPY Because you're not showin' the old confidence, Biff. He remembered you, didn't he?

BIFF (*Stopping* HAPPY *with a gesture*) Finally, about five o'clock, he comes out. Didn't remember who I was or anything. I felt like such an idiot, Hap.

HAPPY Did you tell him my Florida idea?

BIFF He walked away. I saw him for one minute. I got so mad I could've torn the walls down! How the hell did I ever get the idea I was a salesman there? I even believed myself that I'd been a salesman for him! And then he gave me one look and—I realized what a ridiculous lie my whole life has been! We've been talking in a dream for fifteen years. I was a shipping clerk.

HAPPY What'd you do?

BIFF (*With great tension and wonder*) Well, he left, see. And the secretary went out. I was all alone in the waiting-room. I don't know what came over me, Hap. The next thing I know I'm in his office—paneled walls, everything. I can't explain it. I—Hap, I took his fountain pen.

HAPPY Geez, did he catch you?

BIFF I ran out. I ran down all eleven flights. I ran and ran and ran.

HAPPY That was an awful dumb—what'd you do that for?

BIFF (*Agonized*) I don't know, I just—wanted to take something, I don't know. You gotta help me, Hap, I'm gonna tell Pop.

HAPPY You crazy? What for?

BIFF Hap, he's got to understand that I'm not the man somebody lends that kind of money to. He thinks I've been spiting him all these years and it's eating him up.

HAPPY That's just it. You tell him something nice.

BIFF I can't.

HAPPY Say you got a lunch date with Oliver tomorrow.

BIFF So what do I do tomorrow?

HAPPY You leave the house tomorrow and come back at night and say Oliver is thinking it over. And he thinks it over for a couple of weeks, and gradually it fades away and nobody's the worse.

BIFF But it'll go on forever!

HAPPY Dad is never so happy as when he's looking forward to something!
      (WILLY *enters*)

HAPPY Hello, scout!

WILLY Gee, I haven't been here in years!
      (STANLEY *has followed* WILLY *in and sets a chair for him.*
      STANLEY *starts off but* HAPPY *stops him*)

HAPPY Stanley!
      (STANLEY *stands by, waiting for an order*)

BIFF (*Going to* WILLY *with guilt, as to an invalid*) Sit down, Pop. You want a drink?

WILLY Sure, I don't mind.

BIFF Let's get a load on.

WILLY You look worried.

BIFF N-no. (*To* STANLEY) Scotch all around. Make it doubles.

STANLEY Doubles, right. (*He goes*)

WILLY You had a couple already, didn't you?

BIFF Just a couple, yeah.

WILLY Well, what happened, boy? (*Nodding affirmatively, with a smile*) Everything go all right?

BIFF (*Takes a breath, then reaches out and grasps* WILLY'S *hand*) Pal . . . (*He is smiling bravely, and* WILLY *is smiling too*) I had an experience today.

HAPPY Terrific, Pop.

WILLY That so? What happened?

BIFF (*High, slightly alcoholic, above the earth*) I'm going to tell you everything from first to last. It's been a strange day. (*Silence. He looks around, composes himself as best he can, but his breath keeps breaking the rhythm of his voice*) I had to wait quite a while for him, and—

WILLY Oliver?

BIFF Yeah, Oliver. All day, as a matter of cold fact. And a lot of—instances—facts, Pop, facts about my life came back to me. Who was it, Pop? Who ever said I was a salesman with Oliver?

WILLY Well, you were.

BIFF No, Dad, I was a shipping clerk.

WILLY But you were practically—

BIFF (*With determination*) Dad, I don't know who said it first, but I was never a salesman for Bill Oliver.

WILLY What're you talking about?

BIFF Let's hold on to the facts tonight, Pop. We're not going to get anywhere bullin' around. I was a shipping clerk.

WILLY (*Angrily*) All right, now listen to me—

BIFF Why don't you let me finish?

WILLY I'm not interested in stories about the past or any crap of that kind because the woods are burning, boys, you understand? There's a big blaze going on all around. I was fired today.

BIFF (*Shocked*) How could you be?

WILLY I was fired, and I'm looking for a little good news to tell your mother, because the woman has waited and the woman has suffered. The gist of it is that I haven't got a story left in my head, Biff. So don't give me a lecture about facts and aspects. I am not interested. Now what've you got to say to me?

(STANLEY *enters with three drinks. They wait until he leaves*)

WILLY   Did you see Oliver?

BIFF   Jesus, Dad!

WILLY   You mean you didn't go up there?

HAPPY   Sure he went up there.

BIFF   I did. I—saw him. How could they fire you?

WILLY (*On the edge of his chair*)   What kind of a welcome did he give you?

BIFF   He won't even let you work on commission?

WILLY   I'm out! (*Driving*) So tell me, he gave you a warm welcome?

HAPPY   Sure, Pop, sure!

BIFF (*Driven*)   Well, it was kind of—

WILLY   I was wondering if he'd remember you. (*To* HAPPY) Imagine, man doesn't see him for ten, twelve years and gives him that kind of a welcome!

HAPPY   Damn right!

BIFF (*Trying to return to the offensive*)   Pop, look—

WILLY   You know why he remembered you, don't you? Because you impressed him in those days.

BIFF   Let's talk quietly and get this down to the facts, huh?

WILLY (*As though* BIFF *had been interrupting*)   Well, what happened? It's great news, Biff. Did he take you into his office or'd you talk in the waiting-room?

BIFF   Well, he came in, see, and—

WILLY (*With a big smile*)   What'd he say? Betcha he threw his arm around you.

BIFF   Well, he kinda—

WILLY He's a fine man. (*To* HAPPY) Very hard man to see, y'know.

HAPPY (*Agreeing*) Oh, I know.

WILLY (*To* BIFF) Is that where you had the drinks?

BIFF Yeah, he gave me a couple of—no, no!

HAPPY (*Cutting in*) He told him my Florida idea.

WILLY Don't interrupt. (*To* BIFF) How'd he react to the Florida idea?

BIFF Dad, will you give me a minute to explain?

WILLY I've been waiting for you to explain since I sat down here! What happened? He took you into his office and what?

BIFF Well—I talked. And—and he listened, see.

WILLY Famous for the way he listens, y'know. What was his answer?

BIFF His answer was— (*He breaks off, suddenly angry*) Dad, you're not letting me tell you what I want to tell you!

WILLY (*Accusing, angered*) You didn't see him, did you?

BIFF I did see him!

WILLY What'd you insult him or something? You insulted him, didn't you?

BIFF Listen, will you let me out of it, will you just let me out of it!

HAPPY What the hell!

WILLY Tell me what happened!

BIFF (*To* HAPPY) I can't talk to him!
(*A single trumpet note jars the ear. The light of green leaves stains the house, which holds the air of night and a dream.* YOUNG BERNARD *enters and knocks on the door of the house*)

YOUNG BERNARD (*Frantically*) Mrs. Loman, Mrs. Loman!

HAPPY Tell him what happened!

BIFF (*To* HAPPY)   Shut up and leave me alone!

WILLY   No, no! You had to go and flunk math!

BIFF   What math? What're you talking about?

YOUNG BERNARD   Mrs. Loman, Mrs. Loman!
  (LINDA *appears in the house, as of old*)

WILLY (*Wildly*)   Math, math, math!

BIFF   Take it easy, Pop!

YOUNG BERNARD   Mrs. Loman!

WILLY (*Furiously*)   If you hadn't flunked you'd've been set
by now!

BIFF   Now, look, I'm gonna tell you what happened, and
you're going to listen to me.

YOUNG BERNARD   Mrs. Loman!

BIFF   I waited six hours—

HAPPY   What the hell are you saying?

BIFF   I kept sending in my name but he wouldn't see me.
So finally he . . . (*He continues unheard as light fades low
on the restaurant*)

YOUNG BERNARD   Biff flunked math!

LINDA   No!

YOUNG BERNARD   Birnbaum flunked him! They won't graduate him!

LINDA   But they have to. He's gotta go to the university.
Where is he? Biff! Biff!

YOUNG BERNARD   No, he left. He went to Grand Central.

LINDA   Grand— You mean he went to Boston!

YOUNG BERNARD   Is Uncle Willy in Boston?

LINDA   Oh, maybe Willy can talk to the teacher. Oh, the
poor, poor boy!
  (*Light on house area snaps out*)

BIFF (*At the table, now audible, holding up a gold fountain pen*) . . . so I'm washed up with Oliver, you understand? Are you listening to me?

WILLY (*At a loss*)   Yeah, sure. If you hadn't flunked—

BIFF   Flunked what? What're you talking about?

WILLY   Don't blame everything on me! I didn't flunk math— you did! What pen?

HAPPY   That was awful dumb, Biff, a pen like that is worth—

WILLY (*Seeing the pen for the first time*)   You took Oliver's pen?

BIFF (*Weakening*)   Dad, I just explained it to you.

WILLY   You stole Bill Oliver's fountain pen!

BIFF   I didn't exactly steal it! That's just what I've been explaining to you!

HAPPY   He had it in his hand and just then Oliver walked in, so he got nervous and stuck it in his pocket!

WILLY   My God, Biff!

BIFF   I never intended to do it, Dad!

OPERATOR'S VOICE   Standish Arms, good evening!

WILLY (*Shouting*)   I'm not in my room!

BIFF (*Frightened*)   Dad, what's the matter? (*He and* HAPPY *stand up*)

OPERATOR   Ringing Mr. Loman for you!

WILLY   I'm not there, stop it!

BIFF (*Horrified, gets down on one knee before* WILLY)   Dad, I'll make good, I'll make good. (WILLY *tries to get to his feet,* BIFF *holds him down*) Sit down now.

WILLY   No, you're no good, you're no good for anything.

BIFF   I am, Dad, I'll find something else, you understand? Now don't worry about anything. (*He holds up* WILLY's *face*) Talk to me, Dad.

OPERATOR Mr. Loman does not answer. Shall I page him?

WILLY (*Attempting to stand, as though to rush and silence the* OPERATOR) No, no, no!

HAPPY He'll strike something, Pop.

WILLY No, no . . .

BIFF (*Desperately, standing over* WILLY) Pop, listen! Listen to me! I'm telling you something good. Oliver talked to his partner about the Florida idea. You listening? He—he talked to his partner, and he came to me . . . I'm going to be all right, you hear? Dad, listen to me, he said it was just a question of the amount!

WILLY Then you . . . got it?

HAPPY He's gonna be terrific, Pop!

WILLY (*Trying to stand*) Then you got it, haven't you? You got it! You got it!

BIFF (*Agonized, holds* WILLY *down*) No, no. Look, Pop. I'm supposed to have lunch with them tomorrow. I'm just telling you this so you'll know that I can still make an impression, Pop. And I'll make good somewhere, but I can't go tomorrow, see?

WILLY Why not? You simply—

BIFF But the pen, Pop!

WILLY You give it to him and tell him it was an oversight!

HAPPY Sure, have lunch tomorrow!

BIFF I can't say that—

WILLY You were doing a crossword puzzle and accidentally used his pen!

BIFF Listen, kid, I took those balls years ago, now I walk in with his fountain pen? That clinches it, don't you see? I can't face him like that! I'll try elsewhere.

PAGE'S VOICE Paging Mr. Loman!

WILLY Don't you want to be anything?

BIFF Pop, how can I go back?

WILLY You don't want to be anything, is that what's behind it?

BIFF (*Now angry at* WILLY *for not crediting his sympathy*) Don't take it that way! You think it was easy walking into that office after what I'd done to him? A team of horses couldn't have dragged me back to Bill Oliver!

WILLY Then why'd you go?

BIFF Why did I go? Why did I go! Look at you! Look at what's become of you!
    (*Off left,* THE WOMAN *laughs*)

WILLY Biff, you're going to go to that lunch tomorrow, or—

BIFF I can't go. I've got no appointment!

HAPPY Biff, for . . . !

WILLY Are you spiting me?

BIFF Don't take it that way! Goddammit!

WILLY (*Strikes* BIFF *and falters away from the table*) You rotten little louse! Are you spiting me?

THE WOMAN Someone's at the door, Willy!

BIFF I'm no good, can't you see what I am?

HAPPY (*Separating them*) Hey, you're in a restaurant! Now cut it out, both of you! (*The girls enter*) Hello, girls, sit down.
    (THE WOMAN *laughs, off left*)

MISS FORSYTHE I guess we might as well. This is Letta.

THE WOMAN Willy, are you going to wake up?

BIFF (*Ignoring* WILLY) How're ya, miss, sit down. What do you drink?

MISS FORSYTHE Letta might not be able to stay long.

LETTA I gotta get up very early tomorrow. I got jury duty I'm so excited! Were you fellows ever on a jury?

BIFF No, but I been in front of them! (*The girls laugh*) This is my father.

LETTA Isn't he cute? Sit down with us, Pop.

HAPPY   Sit him down, Biff!

BIFF   (*Going to him*)   Come on, slugger, drink us under the table. To hell with it! Come on, sit down, pal.
(*on* BIFF'S *last insistence,* WILLY *is about to sit*)

THE WOMAN   (*Now urgently*)   Willy, are you going to answer the door!
(THE WOMAN'S *call pulls* WILLY *back. He starts right, befuddled*)

BIFF   Hey, where are you going?

WILLY   Open the door.

BIFF   The door?

WILLY   The washroom . . . the door . . . where's the door?

BIFF   (*Leading* WILLY *to the left*)   Just go straight down.
(WILLY *moves left*)

THE WOMAN   Willy, Willy, are you going to get up, get up, get up, get up?
(WILLY *exits left*)

LETTA   I think it's sweet you bring your daddy along.

MISS FORSYTHE   Oh, he isn't really your father!

BIFF   (*At left, turning to her resentfully*)   Miss Forsythe, you've just seen a prince walk by. A fine, troubled prince. A hard-working, unappreciated prince. A pal, you understand? A good companion. Always for his boys.

LETTA   That's so sweet.

HAPPY   Well, girls, what's the program? We're wasting time. Come on, Biff. Gather round. Where would you like to go?

BIFF   Why don't you do something for him?

HAPPY   Me!

BIFF   Don't you give a damn for him, Hap?

HAPPY   What're you talking about? I'm the one who—

BIFF   I sense it, you don't give a good goddam about him.
(*He takes the rolled-up hose from his pocket and puts it on*

the table in front of HAPPY) Look what I found in the cellar, for Christ's sake. How can you bear to let it go on?

HAPPY   Me? Who goes away? Who runs off and—

BIFF   Yeah, but he doesn't mean anything to you. You could help him—I can't! Don't you understand what I'm talking about? He's going to kill himself, don't you know that?

HAPPY   Don't I know it! Me!

BIFF   Hap, help him! Jesus . . . help him . . . Help me, help me, I can't bear to look at his face! (*Ready to weep, he hurries out, up right*)

HAPPY (*Starting after him*)   Where are you going?

MISS FORSYTHE   What's he so mad about?

HAPPY   Come on, girls, we'll catch up with him.

MISS FORSYTHE (*As* HAPPY *pushes her out*)   Say, I don't like that temper of his!

HAPPY   He's just a little overstrung, he'll be all right!

WILLY (*Off left, as* THE WOMAN *laughs*)   Don't answer! Don't answer!

LETTA   Don't you want to tell your father—

HAPPY   No, that's not my father. He's just a guy. Come on, we'll catch Biff, and, honey, we're going to paint this town! Stanley, where's the check! Hey, Stanley!
   (*They exit.* STANLEY *looks toward left*)

STANLEY (*Calling to* HAPPY *indignantly*)   Mr. Loman! Mr. Loman!
   (STANLEY *picks up a chair and follows them off. Knocking is heard off left.* THE WOMAN *enters, laughing.* WILLY *follows her. She is in a black slip; he is buttoning his shirt. Raw, sensuous music accompanies their speech*)

WILLY   Will you stop laughing? Will you stop?

THE WOMAN   Aren't you going to answer the door? He'll wake the whole hotel.

WILLY   I'm not expecting anybody.

THE WOMAN   Whyn't you have another drink, honey, and stop being so damn self-centered?

WILLY   I'm so lonely.

THE WOMAN   You know you ruined me, Willy? From now on, whenever you come to the office, I'll see that you go right through to the buyers. No waiting at my desk any more, Willy. You ruined me.

WILLY   That's nice of you to say that.

THE WOMAN   Gee, you are self-centered! Why so sad? You are the saddest, self-centeredest soul I ever did see-saw. (*She laughs. He kisses her*) Come on inside, drummer boy. It's silly to be dressing in the middle of the night. (*As knocking is heard*) Aren't you going to answer the door?

WILLY   They're knocking on the wrong door.

THE WOMAN   But I felt the knocking. And he heard us talking in here. Maybe the hotel's on fire!

WILLY (*His terror rising*)   It's a mistake.

THE WOMAN   Then tell him to go away!

WILLY   There's nobody there.

THE WOMAN   It's getting on my nerves, Willy. There's somebody standing out there and it's getting on my nerves!

WILLY (*Pushing her away from him*)   All right, stay in the bathroom here, and don't come out. I think there's a law in Massachusetts about it, so don't come out. It may be that new room clerk. He looked very mean. So don't come out. It's a mistake, there's no fire.

(*The knocking is heard again. He takes a few steps away from her, and she vanishes into the wing. The light follows him, and now he is facing* YOUNG BIFF, *who carries a suitcase.* BIFF *steps toward him. The music is gone*)

BIFF   Why didn't you answer?

WILLY   Biff! What are you doing in Boston?

BIFF   Why didn't you answer? I've been knocking for five minutes, I called you on the phone—

WILLY   I just heard you. I was in the bathroom and had the door shut. Did anything happen home?

BIFF   Dad—I let you down.

WILLY   What do you mean?

BIFF   Dad . . .

WILLY   Biffo, what's this about? (*Putting his arm around* BIFF) Come on, let's go downstairs and get you a malted.

BIFF   Dad, I flunked math.

WILLY   Not for the term?

BIFF   The term. I haven't got enough credits to graduate.

WILLY   You mean to say Bernard wouldn't give you the answers?

BIFF   He did, he tried, but I only got a sixty-one.

WILLY   And they wouldn't give you four points?

BIFF   Birnbaum refused absolutely. I begged him, Pop, but he won't give me those points. You gotta talk to him before they close the school. Because if he saw the kind of man you are, and you just talked to him in your way, I'm sure he'd come through for me. The class came right before practice, see, and I didn't go enough. Would you talk to him? He'd like you, Pop. You know the way you could talk.

WILLY   You're on. We'll drive right back.

BIFF   Oh, Dad, good work! I'm sure he'll change it for you!

WILLY   Go downstairs and tell the clerk I'm checkin' out. Go right down.

BIFF   Yes, sir! See, the reason he hates me, Pop—one day he was late for class so I got up at the blackboard and imitated him. I crossed my eyes and talked with a lithp.

WILLY (*Laughing*)   You did? The kids like it?

BIFF   They nearly died laughing!

WILLY   Yeah! What'd you do?

BIFF   The thquare root of thixthy twee is . . . (WILLY *bursts out laughing;* BIFF *joins him*) And in the middle of it he walked in!
  (WILLY *laughs and* THE WOMAN *joins in offstage*)

WILLY (*Without hesitation*)   Hurry downstairs and—

BIFF   Somebody in there?

WILLY   No, that was next door.
  (THE WOMAN *laughs offstage*)

BIFF   Somebody got in your bathroom!

WILLY   No, it's the next room, there's a party—

THE WOMAN (*Enters, laughing. She lisps this*)   Can I come in? There's something in the bathtub, Willy, and it's moving!
  (WILLY *looks at* BIFF, *who is staring open-mouthed and horrified at* THE WOMAN)

WILLY   Ah—you better go back to your room. They must be finished painting by now. They're painting her room so I let her take a shower here. Go back, go back . . . (*He pushes her*)

THE WOMAN (*Resisting*)   But I've got to get dressed, Willy, I can't—

WILLY   Get out of here! Go back, go back . . . (*Suddenly striving for the ordinary*) This is Miss Francis, Biff, she's a buyer. They're painting her room. Go back, Miss Francis, go back . . .

THE WOMAN   But my clothes, I can't go out naked in the hall!

WILLY (*Pushing her offstage*)   Get outa here! Go back, go back!
  (BIFF *slowly sits down on his suitcase as the argument continues offstage*)

THE WOMAN   Where's my stockings? You promised me stockings, Willy!

WILLY   I have no stockings here!

THE WOMAN   You had two boxes of size nine sheers for me, and I want them!

WILLY   Here, for God's sake, will you get outa here!

THE WOMAN (*Enters holding a box of stockings*)   I just hope there's nobody in the hall. That's all I hope. (*To* BIFF) Are you football or baseball?

BIFF   Football.

THE WOMAN (*Angry, humiliated*)   That's me too. G'night. (*She snatches her clothes from* WILLY, *and walks out*)

WILLY (*After a pause*)   Well, better get going. I want to get to the school first thing in the morning. Get my suits out of the closet. I'll get my valise. (BIFF *doesn't move*) What's the matter? (BIFF *remains motionless, tears falling*) She's a buyer. Buys for J. H. Simmons. She lives down the hall—they're painting. You don't imagine— (*He breaks off. After a pause*) Now listen, pal, she's just a buyer. She sees merchandise in her room and they have to keep it looking just so . . . (*Pause. Assuming command*) All right, get my suits. (BIFF *doesn't move*) Now stop crying and do as I say. I gave you an order. Biff, I gave you an order! Is that what you do when I give you an order? How dare you cry! (*Putting his arm around* BIFF) Now look, Biff, when you grow up you'll understand about these things. You mustn't—you mustn't overemphasize a thing like this. I'll see Birnbaum first thing in the morning.

BIFF   Never mind.

WILLY (*Getting down beside* BIFF)   Never mind! He's going to give you those points. I'll see to it.

BIFF   He wouldn't listen to you.

WILLY   He certainly will listen to me. You need those points for the U. of Virginia.

BIFF   I'm not going there.

WILLY   Heh? If I can't get him to change that mark you'll make it up in summer school. You've got all summer to—

BIFF (*His weeping breaking from him*)   Dad . . .

WILLY (*Infected by it*)   Oh, my boy . . .

BIFF   Dad . . .

WILLY   She's nothing to me, Biff. I was lonely, I was terribly lonely.

BIFF   You—you gave her Mama's stockings! (*His tears break through and he rises to go*)

WILLY (*Grabbing for* BIFF)   I gave you an order!

BIFF   Don't touch me, you—liar!

WILLY   Apologize for that!

BIFF   You fake! You phony little fake! You fake! (*Overcome, he turns quickly and weeping fully goes out with his suitcase.* WILLY *is left on the floor on his knees*)

WILLY   I gave you an order! Biff, come back here or I'll beat you! Come back here! I'll whip you!
  (STANLEY *comes quickly in from the right and stands in front of* WILLY)

WILLY (*Shouts at* STANLEY)   I gave you an order . . .

STANLEY   Hey, let's pick it up, pick it up, Mr. Loman. (*He helps* WILLY *to his feet*) Your boys left with the chippies. They said they'll see you home.
  (*A second waiter watches some distance away*)

WILLY   But we were supposed to have dinner together.
  (*Music is heard,* WILLY'S *theme*)

STANLEY   Can you make it?

WILLY   I'll—sure, I can make it. (*Suddenly concerned about his clothes*) Do I—I look all right?

STANLEY   Sure, you look all right. (*He flicks a speck off* WILLY'S *lapel*)

WILLY   Here—here's a dollar.

STANLEY   Oh, your son paid me. It's all right.

WILLY (*Putting it in* STANLEY'S *hand*)   No, take it. You're a good boy.

STANLEY   Oh, no, you don't have to . . .

WILLY   Here—here's some more, I don't need it any more. (*After a slight pause*) Tell me—is there a seed store in the neighborhood?

STANLEY   Seeds? You mean like to plant?
   (*As* WILLY *turns,* STANLEY *slips the money back into his jacket pocket*)

WILLY   Yes. Carrots, peas . . .

STANLEY   Well, there's hardware stores on Sixth Avenue, but it may be too late now.

WILLY (*Anxiously*)   Oh, I'd better hurry. I've got to get some seeds. (*He starts off to the right*) I've got to get some seeds, right away. Nothing's planted. I don't have a thing in the ground.
   (WILLY *hurries out as the light goes down.* STANLEY *moves over to the right after him, watches him off. The other waiter has been staring at* WILLY)

STANLEY (*To the waiter*)   Well, whatta you looking at?
   (*The waiter picks up the chairs and moves off right.* STANLEY *takes the table and follows him. The light fades on this area. There is a long pause, the sound of the flute coming over. The light gradually rises on the kitchen, which is empty.* HAPPY *appears at the door of the house, followed by* BIFF. HAPPY *is carrying a large bunch of long-stemmed roses. He enters the kitchen, looks around for* LINDA. *Not seeing her, he turns to* BIFF, *who is just outside the house door, and makes a gesture with his hands, indicating "Not here, I guess." He looks into the living-room and freezes. Inside,* LINDA, *unseen, is seated,* WILLY'S *coat on her lap. She rises ominously and quietly and moves toward* HAPPY, *who backs up into the kitchen, afraid*)

HAPPY   Hey, what're you doing up? (LINDA *says nothing but moves toward him implacably*) Where's Pop? (*He keeps backing to the right, and now* LINDA *is in full view in the doorway to the living-room*) Is he sleeping?

LINDA   Where were you?

HAPPY (*Trying to laugh it off*)   We met two girls, Mom, very fine types. Here, we brought you some flowers. (*Offering them to her*) Put them in your room, Ma.
   (*She knocks them to the floor at* BIFF'S *feet. He has now come inside and closed the door behind him. She stares at* BIFF, *silent*)

HAPPY   Now what'd you do that for? Mom, I want you to
have some flowers—

LINDA (*Cutting* HAPPY *off, violently to* BIFF)   Don't you care
whether he lives or dies?

HAPPY (*Going to the stairs*)   Come upstairs, Biff.

BIFF (*With a flare of disgust, to* HAPPY)   Go away from me!
(*To* LINDA) What do you mean, lives or dies? Nobody's dying
around here, pal.

LINDA   Get out of my sight! Get out of here!

BIFF   I wanna see the boss.

LINDA   You're not going near him!

BIFF   Where is he? (*He moves into the living-room and*
LINDA *follows*)

LINDA (*Shouting after* BIFF)   You invite him for dinner. He
looks forward to it all day—(BIFF *appears in his parents' bedroom, looks around, and exits*)—and then you desert him
there. There's no stranger you'd do that to!

HAPPY   Why? He had a swell time with us. Listen, when I—
(LINDA *comes back into the kitchen*)—desert him I hope I
don't outlive the day!

LINDA   Get out of here!

HAPPY   Now look, Mom . . .

LINDA   Did you have to go to women tonight? You and your
lousy rotten whores!
    (BIFF *re-enters the kitchen*)

HAPPY   Mom, all we did was follow Biff around trying to
cheer him up! (*To* BIFF) Boy, what a night you gave me!

LINDA   Get out of here, both of you, and don't come back!
I don't want you tormenting him any more. Go on now, get
your things together! (*To* BIFF) You can sleep in his apartment. (*She starts to pick up the flowers and stops herself*)
Pick up this stuff, I'm not your maid any more. Pick it up,
you bum, you!
    (HAPPY *turns his back to her in refusal.* BIFF *slowly moves
    over and gets down on his knees, picking up the flowers*)

LINDA   You're a pair of animals! Not one, not another living soul would have had the cruelty to walk out on that man in a restaurant!

BIFF (*Not looking at her*)   Is that what he said?

LINDA   He didn't have to say anything. He was so humiliated he nearly limped when he came in.

HAPPY   But, Mom, he had a great time with us—

BIFF (*Cutting him off violently*)   Shut up!
  (*Without another word,* HAPPY *goes upstairs*)

LINDA   You! You didn't even go in to see if he was all right!

BIFF (*Still on the floor in front of* LINDA, *the flowers in his hand; with self-loathing*)   No. Didn't. Didn't do a damned thing. How do you like that, heh? Left him babbling in a toilet.

LINDA   You louse. You . . .

BIFF   Now you hit it on the nose! (*He gets up, throws the flowers in the wastebasket*) The scum of the earth, and you're looking at him!

LINDA   Get out of here!

BIFF   I gotta talk to the boss, Mom. Where is he?

LINDA   You're not going near him. Get out of this house!

BIFF (*With absolute assurance, determination*)   No. We're gonna have an abrupt conversation, him and me.

LINDA   You're not talking to him!
  (*Hammering is heard from outside the house, off right.* BIFF *turns toward the noise*)

LINDA (*Suddenly pleading*)   Will you please leave him alone?

BIFF   What's he doing out there?

LINDA   He's planting the garden!

BIFF (*Quietly*)   Now? Oh, my God!
  (BIFF *moves outside,* LINDA *following. The light dies down on them and comes up on the center of the apron as* WILLY *walks into it. He is carrying a flashlight, a hoe, and a handful of seed packets. He raps the top of the hoe*

sharply to fix it firmly, and then moves to the left, measur-
ing off the distance with his foot. He holds the flashlight
to look at the seed packets, reading off the instructions. He
is in the blue of night)

WILLY   Carrots . . . quarter-inch apart. Rows . . . one-foot
rows. (*He measures it off*) One foot. (*He puts down a pack-*
age and measures off) Beets. (*He puts down another package*
and measures again) Lettuce. (*He reads the package, puts it*
down) One foot— (*He breaks off as* BEN *appears at the right*
and moves slowly down to him) What a proposition, ts, ts.
Terrific, terrific. 'Cause she's suffered, Ben, the woman has
suffered. You understand me? A man can't go out the way
he came in, Ben, a man has got to add up to something. You
can't, you can't   (BEN *moves toward him as though to inter-*
rupt) You gotta consider, now. Don't answer so quick. Remember, it's a guaranteed twenty-thousand-dollar proposition.
Now look, Ben, I want you to go through the ins and outs of
this thing with me. I've got nobody to talk to, Ben, and the
woman has suffered, you hear me?

BEN (*Standing still, considering*)   What's the proposition?

WILLY   It's twenty thousand dollars on the barrelhead. Guaranteed, gilt-edged, you understand?

BEN   You don't want to make a fool of yourself. They might
not honor the policy.

WILLY   How can they dare refuse? Didn't I work like a
coolie to meet every premium on the nose? And now they
don't pay off? Impossible!

BEN   It's called a cowardly thing, William.

WILLY   Why? Does it take more guts to stand here the rest
of my life ringing up a zero?

BEN (*Yielding*)   That's a point, William. (*He moves, think-*
ing, turns) And twenty thousand—that *is* something one can
feel with the hand, it is there.

WILLY (*Now assured, with rising power*)   Oh, Ben, that's
the whole beauty of it! I see it like a diamond, shining in the
dark, hard and rough, that I can pick up and touch in my
hand. Not like—like an appointment! This would not be
another damned-fool appointment, Ben, and it changes all

the aspects. Because he thinks I'm nothing, see, and so he spites me. But the funeral— (*Straightening up*) Ben, *that* funeral will be massive! They'll come from Maine, Massachusetts, Vermont, New Hampshire! All the old-timers with the strange license plates—that boy will be thunder-struck, Ben, because he never realized—I am known! Rhode Island, New York, New Jersey—I am known, Ben, and he'll see it with his eyes once and for all. He'll see what I am, Ben! He's in for a shock, that boy!

BEN (*Coming down to the edge of the garden*)   He'll call you a coward.

WILLY (*Suddenly fearful*)   No, that would be terrible.

BEN   Yes. And a damned fool.

WILLY   No, no, he mustn't, I won't have that! (*He is broken and desperate*)

BEN   He'll hate you, William.
   (*The gay music of the* BOYS *is heard*)

WILLY   Oh, Ben, how do we get back to all the great times? Used to be so full of light, and comradeship, the sleigh-riding in winter, and the ruddiness on his cheeks. And always some kind of good news coming up, always something nice coming up ahead. And never even let me carry the valises in the house, and simonizing, simonizing that little red car! Why, why can't I give him something and not have him hate me?

BEN   Let me think about it. (*He glances at his watch*) I still have a little time. Remarkable proposition, but you've got to be sure you're not making a fool of yourself.
   (BEN *drifts off upstage and goes out of sight.* BIFF *comes down from the left*)

WILLY (*Suddenly conscious of* BIFF, *turns and looks up at him, then begins picking up the packages of seeds in confusion*)   Where the hell is that seed? (*Indignantly*) You can't see nothing out here! They boxed in the whole goddam neighborhood!

BIFF   There are people all around here. Don't you realize that?

'VILLY   I'm busy. Don't bother me.

BIFF (*Taking the hoe from* WILLY) I'm saying good-by to
you, Pop. (WILLY *looks at him, silent, unable to move*) I'm
not coming back any more.

WILLY You're not going to see Oliver tomorrow?

BIFF I've got no appointment, Dad.

WILLY He put his arm around you, and you've got no appointment?

BIFF Pop, get this now, will you? Everytime I've left it's
been a fight that sent me out of here. Today I realized something about myself and I tried to explain it to you and I—I
think I'm just not smart enough to make any sense out of it
for you. To hell with whose fault it is or anything like that.
(*He takes* WILLY's *arm*) Let's just wrap it up, heh? Come on
in, we'll tell Mom. (*He gently tries to pull* WILLY *to left*)

WILLY (*Frozen, immobile, with guilt in his voice*) No, I
don't want to see her.

BIFF Come on! (*He pulls again, and* WILLY *tries to pull
away*)

WILLY (*Highly nervous*) No, no, I don't want to see her.

BIFF (*Tries to look into* WILLY's *face, as if to find the answer
there*) Why don't you want to see her?

WILLY (*More harshly now*) Don't bother me, will you?

BIFF What do you mean, you don't want to see her? You
don't want them calling you yellow, do you? This isn't your
fault; it's me, I'm a bum. Now come inside! (WILLY *strains
to get away*) Did you hear what I said to you?
  (WILLY *pulls away and quickly goes by himself into the
  house.* BIFF *follows*)

LINDA (*To* WILLY) Did you plant, dear?

BIFF (*At the door, to* LINDA) All right, we had it out. I'm
going and I'm not writing any more.

LINDA (*Going to* WILLY *in the kitchen*) I think that's the
best way, dear. 'Cause there's no use drawing it out, you'll
just never get along.
  (WILLY *doesn't respond*)

BIFF People ask where I am and what I'm doing, you don't know, and you don't care. That way it'll be off your mind and you can start brightening up again. All right? That clears it, doesn't it? (WILLY *is silent, and* BIFF *goes to him*) You gonna wish me luck, scout? (*He extends his hand*) What do you say?

LINDA Shake his hand, Willy.

WILLY (*Turning to her, seething with hurt*) There's no necessity to mention the pen at all, y'know

BIFF (*Gently*) I've got no appointment, Dad.

WILLY (*Erupting fiercely*) He put his arm around . . . ?

BIFF Dad, you're never going to see what I am, so what's the use of arguing? If I strike oil I'll send you a check. Meantime forget I'm alive.

WILLY (*To* LINDA) Spite, see?

BIFF Shake hands, Dad.

WILLY Not my hand.

BIFF I was hoping not to go this way.

WILLY Well, this is the way you're going. Good-by.
  (BIFF *looks at him a moment, then turns sharply and goes to the stairs*)

WILLY (*Stops him with*) May you rot in hell if you leave this house!

BIFF (*Turning*) Exactly what is it that you want from me?

WILLY I want you to know, on the train, in the mountains, in the valleys, wherever you go, that you cut down your life for spite!

BIFF No, no.

WILLY Spite, spite, is the word of your undoing! And when you're down and out, remember what did it. When you're rotting somewhere beside the railroad tracks, remember, and don't you dare blame it on me!

BIFF I'm not blaming it on you!

WILLY   I won't take the rap for this, you hear?
(HAPPY *comes down the stairs and stands on the bottom step, watching*)

BIFF   That's just what I'm telling you!

WILLY (*Sinking into a chair at the table, with full accusation*)
You're trying to put a knife in me—don't think I don't know what you're doing!

BIFF   All right, phony! Then let's lay it on the line. (*He whips the rubber tube out of his pocket and puts it on the table*)

HAPPY   You crazy—

LINDA   Biff! (*She moves to grab the hose, but* BIFF *holds it down with his hand*)

BIFF   Leave it there! Don't move it!

WILLY (*Not looking at it*)   What is that?

BIFF   You know goddam well what that is.

WILLY (*Caged, wanting to escape*)   I never saw that.

BIFF   You saw it. The mice didn't bring it into the cellar! What is this supposed to do, make a hero out of you? This supposed to make me sorry for you?

WILLY   Never heard of it.

BIFF   There'll be no pity for you, you hear it? No pity!

WILLY (*To* LINDA)   You hear the spite!

BIFF   No, you're going to hear the truth—what you are and what I am!

LINDA   Stop it!

WILLY   Spite!

HAPPY (*Coming down toward* BIFF)   You cut it now!

BIFF (*To* HAPPY)   The man don't know who we are! The man is gonna know! (*To* WILLY) We never told the truth for ten minutes in this house!

HAPPY   We always told the truth!

BIFF (*Turning on him*) You big blow, are you the assistant buyer? You're one of the two assistants to the assistant, aren't you?

HAPPY Well, I'm practically—

BIFF You're practically full of it! We all are! And I'm through with it. (*To* WILLY) Now hear this, Willy, this is me.

WILLY I know you!

BIFF You know why I had no address for three months? I stole a suit in Kansas City and I was in jail. (*To* LINDA, *who is sobbing*) Stop crying. I'm through with it.

(LINDA *turns away from them, her hands covering her face*)

WILLY I suppose that's my fault!

BIFF I stole myself out of every good job since high school!

WILLY And whose fault is that?

BIFF And I never got anywhere because you blew me so full of hot air I could never stand taking orders from anybody! That's whose fault it is!

WILLY I hear that!

LINDA Don't, Biff!

BIFF It's goddam time you heard that! I had to be boss big shot in two weeks, and I'm through with it!

WILLY Then hang yourself! For spite, hang yourself!

BIFF No! Nobody's hanging himself, Willy! I ran down eleven flights with a pen in my hand today. And suddenly I stopped, you hear me? And in the middle of that office building, do you hear this? I stopped in the middle of that building and I saw—the sky. I saw the things that I love in this world. The work and the food and time to sit and smoke. And I looked at the pen and said to myself, what the hell am I grabbing this for? Why am I trying to become what I don't want to be? What am I doing in an office, making a contemptuous, begging fool of myself, when all I want is out there, waiting for me the minute I say I know who I am! Why can't I say that, Willy? (*He tries to make* WILLY *face him, but* WILLY *pulls away and moves to the left*)

WILLY (*With hatred, threateningly*)   The door of your life is wide open!

BIFF   Pop! I'm a dime a dozen, and so are you!

WILLY (*Turning on him now in an uncontrolled outburst*)   I am not a dime a dozen! I am Willy Loman, and you are Biff Loman!
  (BIFF *starts for* WILLY, *but is blocked by* HAPPY. *In his fury,* BIFF *seems on the verge of attacking his father*)

BIFF   I am not a leader of men, Willy, and neither are you. You were never anything but a hard-working drummer who landed in the ash can like all the rest of them! I'm one dollar an hour, Willy! I tried seven states and couldn't raise it. A buck an hour! Do you gather my meaning? I'm not bringing home any prizes any more, and you're going to stop waiting for me to bring them home!

WILLY (*Directly to* BIFF)   You vengeful, spiteful mut!
  (BIFF *breaks from* HAPPY. WILLY, *in fright, starts up the stairs.* BIFF *grabs him*)

BIFF (*At the peak of his fury*)   Pop, I'm nothing! I'm nothing, Pop. Can't you understand that? There's no spite in it any more. I'm just what I am, that's all.
  (BIFF'S *fury has spent itself, and he breaks down, sobbing, holding on to* WILLY, *who dumbly fumbles for* BIFF'S *face*)

WILLY (*Astonished*)   What're you doing? What're you doing? (*To* LINDA) Why is he crying?

BIFF (*Crying, broken*)   Will you let me go, for Christ's sake? Will you take that phony dream and burn it before something happens? (*Struggling to contain himself, he pulls away and moves to the stairs*) I'll go in the morning. Put him— put him to bed. (*Exhausted,* BIFF *moves up the stairs to his room*)

WILLY (*After a long pause, astonished, elevated*)   Isn't that— isn't that remarkable? Biff—he likes me!

LINDA   He loves you, Willy!

HAPPY (*Deeply moved*)   Always did, Pop.

WILLY Oh, Biff! (*Staring wildly*) He cried! Cried to me. (*He is choking with his love, and now cries out his promise*) That boy—that boy is going to be magnificent!

(BEN *appears in the light just outside the kitchen*)

BEN Yes, outstanding, with twenty thousand behind him.

LINDA (*Sensing the racing of his mind, fearfully, carefully*) Now come to bed, Willy. It's all settled now.

WILLY (*Finding it difficult not to rush out of the house*) Yes, we'll sleep. Come on. Go to sleep, Hap.

BEN And it does take a great kind of a man to crack the jungle.

(*In accents of dread,* BEN'S *idyllic music starts up*)

HAPPY (*His arm around* LINDA) I'm getting married, Pop, don't forget it. I'm changing everything. I'm gonna run that department before the year is up. You'll see, Mom. (*He kisses her*)

BEN The jungle is dark but full of diamonds, Willy.

(WILLY *turns, moves, listening to* BEN)

LINDA Be good. You're both good boys, just act that way, that's all.

HAPPY 'Night, Pop. (*He goes upstairs*)

LINDA (*To* WILLY) Come, dear.

BEN (*With greater force*) One must go in to fetch a diamond out.

WILLY (*To* LINDA, *as he moves slowly along the edge of the kitchen, toward the door*) I just want to get settled down, Linda. Let me sit alone for a little.

LINDA (*Almost uttering her fear*) I want you upstairs.

WILLY (*Taking her in his arms*) In a few minutes, Linda. I couldn't sleep right now. Go on, you look awful tired. (*He kisses her*)

BEN Not like an appointment at all. A diamond is rough and hard to the touch.

WILLY Go on now. I'll be right up.

LINDA   I think this is the only way, Willy.

WILLY   Sure, it's the best thing.

BEN   Best thing!

WILLY   The only way. Everything is gonna be—go on, kid, get to bed. You look so tired.

LINDA   Come right up.

WILLY   Two minutes.

(LINDA *goes into the living-room, then reappears in her bedroom.* WILLY *moves just outside the kitchen door*)

WILLY   Loves me. (*Wonderingly*) Always loved me. Isn't that a remarkable thing? Ben, he'll worship me for it!

BEN (*With promise*)   It's dark there, but full of diamonds.

WILLY   Can you imagine that magnificence with twenty thousand dollars in his pocket?

LINDA (*Calling from her room*)   Willy! Come up!

WILLY (*Calling into the kitchen*)   Yes! Yes. Coming! It's very smart, you realize that, don't you, sweetheart? Even Ben sees it. I gotta go, baby. 'By! 'By! (*Going over to* BEN, *almost dancing*) Imagine? When the mail comes he'll be ahead of Bernard again!

BEN   A perfect proposition all around.

WILLY   Did you see how he cried to me? Oh, if I could kiss him, Ben!

BEN   Time, William, time!

WILLY   Oh, Ben, I always knew one way or another we were gonna make it, Biff and I!

BEN (*Looking at his watch*)   The boat. We'll be late. (*He moves slowly off into the darkness*)

WILLY (*Elegiacally, turning to the house*)   Now when you kick off, boy, I want a seventy-yard boot, and get right down the field under the ball, and when you hit, hit low and hit hard, because it's important, boy. (*He swings around and faces the audience*) There's all kinds of important people in the stands, and the first thing you know . . . (*Suddenly realizing he is alone*) Ben! Ben, where do I . . . ? (*He makes a sudden movement of search*) Ben, how do I . . . ?

LINDA (*Calling*)   Willy, you coming up?

WILLY (*Uttering a gasp of fear, whirling about as if to quiet her*)   Sh! (*He turns around as if to find his way; sounds, faces, voices, seem to be swarming in upon him and he flicks at them, crying*) Sh! Sh! (*Suddenly music, faint and high, stops him. It rises in intensity, almost to an unbearable scream. He goes up and down on his toes, and rushes off around the house*) Shhh!

LINDA   Willy?
(*There is no answer. LINDA waits. BIFF gets up off his bed. He is still in his clothes. HAPPY sits up. BIFF stands listening*)

LINDA (*With real fear*)   Willy, answer me! Willy!
(*There is the sound of a car starting and moving away at full speed*)

LINDA   No!

BIFF (*Rushing down the stairs*)   Pop!
(*As the car speeds off, the music crashes down in a frenzy of sound, which becomes the soft pulsation of a single cello string. BIFF slowly returns to his bedroom. He and HAPPY gravely don their jackets. LINDA slowly walks out of her room. The music has developed into a dead march. The leaves of day are appearing over everything. CHARLEY and BERNARD, somberly dressed, appear and knock on the kitchen door. BIFF and HAPPY slowly descend the stairs to the kitchen as CHARLEY and BERNARD enter. All stop a moment when LINDA, in clothes of mourning, bearing a little bunch of roses, comes through the draped doorway into the kitchen. She goes to CHARLEY and takes his arm. Now all move toward the audience, through the wall-line of the kitchen. At the limit of the apron, LINDA lays down the flowers, kneels, and sits back on her heels. All stare down at the grave*)

━ *Requiem*

CHARLEY   It's getting dark, Linda.
   (LINDA *doesn't react. She stares at the grave*)

BIFF   How about it, Mom? Better get some rest, heh? They'll
be closing the gate soon.
   (LINDA *makes no move. Pause*)

HAPPY (*Deeply angered*)   He had no right to do that. There
was no necessity for it. We would've helped him.

CHARLEY (*Grunting*)   Hmmm.

BIFF   Come along, Mom.

LINDA   Why didn't anybody come?

CHARLEY   It was a very nice funeral.

LINDA   But where are all the people he knew? Maybe they
blame him.

CHARLEY   Naa. It's a rough world, Linda. They wouldn't
blame him.

LINDA   I can't understand it. At this time especially. First
time in thirty-five years we were just about free and clear.
He only needed a little salary. He was even finished with the
dentist.

CHARLEY   No man only needs a little salary.

LINDA   I can't understand it.

BIFF   There were a lot of nice days. When he'd come home
from a trip; or on Sundays, making the stoop; finishing the
cellar; putting on the new porch; when he built the extra
bathroom; and put up the garage. You know something,
Charley, there's more of him in that front stoop than in all
the sales he ever made.

CHARLEY   Yeah. He was a happy man with a batch of cement.

LINDA   He was so wonderful with his hands.

BIFF   He had the wrong dreams. All, all, wrong.

HAPPY (*Almost ready to fight* BIFF)   Don't say that!

BIFF   He never knew who he was.

CHARLEY (*Stopping* HAPPY'S *movement and reply. To* BIFF)
Nobody dast blame this man. You don't understand: Willy
was a salesman. And for a salesman, there is no rock bottom
to the life. He don't put a bolt to a nut, he don't tell you
the law or give you medicine. He's a man way out there in
the blue, riding on a smile and a shoeshine. And when they
start not smiling back—that's an earthquake. And then you
get yourself a couple of spots on your hat, and you're finished.
Nobody dast blame this man. A salesman is got to dream,
boy. It comes with the territory.

BIFF   Charley, the man didn't know who he was.

HAPPY (*Infuriated*)   Don't say that!

BIFF   Why don't you come with me, Happy?

HAPPY   I'm not licked that easily. I'm staying right in this
city, and I'm gonna beat this racket! (*He looks at* BIFF, *his
chin set*) The Loman Brothers!

BIFF   I know who I am, kid.

HAPPY   All right, boy. I'm gonna show you and everybody
else that Willy Loman did not die in vain. He had a good
dream. It's the only dream you can have—to come out
number-one man. He fought it out here, and this is where
I'm gonna win it for him.

BIFF (*With a hopeless glance at* HAPPY, *bends toward his
mother*)   Let's go, Mom.

LINDA   I'll be with you in a minute. Go on, Charley. (*He hesitates*) I want to, just for a minute. I never had a chance to
say good-by.

   (CHARLEY *moves away, followed by* HAPPY. BIFF *remains
   a slight distance up and left of* LINDA. *She sits there, sum-
   moning herself. The flute begins, not far away, playing
   behind her speech*)

LINDA Forgive me, dear. I can't cry. I don't know what it is, but I can't cry. I don't understand it. Why did you ever do that? Help me, Willy, I can't cry. It seems to me that you're just on another trip. I keep expecting you. Willy, dear, I can't cry. Why did you do it? I search and search and I search, and I can't understand it, Willy. I made the last payment on the house today. Today, dear. And there'll be nobody home. (*A sob rises in her throat*) We're free and clear. (*Sobbing more fully, released*) We're free. (BIFF *comes slowly toward her*) We're free . . . We're free . . .

(BIFF *lifts her to her feet and moves out up right with her in his arms.* LINDA *sobs quietly.* BERNARD *and* CHARLEY *come together and follow them, followed by* HAPPY. *Only the music of the flute is left on the darkening stage as over the house the hard towers of the apartment buildings rise into sharp focus, and*

THE CURTAIN FALLS)

Come Back, Little Sheba

by WILLIAM INGE

FOR *Phyllis Anderson*

COME BACK, LITTLE SHEBA

was first presented by The Theatre Guild at the Booth Theatre, New York City, on February 15, 1950, with the following cast:

IN ORDER OF APPEARANCE

DOC	Sidney Blackmer
MARIE	Joan Lorring
LOLA	Shirley Booth
TURK	Lonny Chapman
POSTMAN	Daniel Reed
MRS. COFFMAN	Olga Fabian
MILKMAN	John Randolph
MESSENGER	Arnold Schulman
BRUCE	Robert Cunningham
ED ANDERSON	Wilson Brooks
ELMO HUSTON	Paul Krauss

Directed by Daniel Mann

Setting and lighting designed by Howard Bay

Costumes by Lucille Little

Production under the supervision of Lawrence Langner and Theresa Helburn

Associate Producer, Phyllis Anderson

SCENE

An old house in a run-down neighborhood of a Midwestern city.

Act One

SCENE I Morning in late spring.

SCENE II The same evening, after supper.

Act Two

SCENE I The following morning.

SCENE II Late afternoon the same day.

SCENE III 5:30 the next morning.

SCENE IV Morning, a week later.

Act One

SCENE I

The stage is empty.

It is the downstairs of an old house in one of those semi-respectable neighborhoods in a Midwestern city. The stage is divided into two rooms, the living room at right and the kitchen at left, with a stairway and a door between. At the foot of the stairway is a small table with a telephone on it. The time is about 8:00 A.M., a morning in the late spring.

At rise of curtain the sun hasn't come out in full force and outside the atmosphere is a little gray. The house is extremely cluttered and even dirty. The living room somehow manages to convey the atmosphere of the twenties, decorated with cheap pretense at niceness and respectability. The general effect is one of fussy awkwardness. The furniture is all heavy and rounded-looking, the chairs and davenport being covered with a shiny mohair. The davenport is littered and there are lace antimacassars on all the chairs. In such areas, houses are so close together, they hide each other from the sunlight. What sun could come through the window, at right, is dimmed by the smoky glass curtains. In the kitchen there is a table, center. On it are piled dirty dishes from supper the night before. Woodwork in the kitchen is dark and grimy. No industry whatsoever has been spent in making it one of those white, cheerful rooms that we commonly think kitchens should be. There is no action on stage for several seconds.

DOC *comes downstairs and turns into the kitchen, looking rather regretful at the disarray he always finds there. He hangs his suit coat on the back of a chair*

*and then puts the water on the stove for coffee. Time
is his own now, and he kneels reverently before the
kitchen table and says a prayer, mumbling the words
inaudibly but with deep feeling and humility. When
the prayer is finished, he can smile, and set about
getting his breakfast with a light heart.*

A young college student, MARIE, *rents a bedroom
just off the living room downstairs. She pops out of
the door suddenly, wearing a dainty but respectable
negligee, and skips into the kitchen with the ebul-
lience that only youth can feel in the morning. She
speaks to* DOC *as though he were someone she took
pleasantly for granted, and he appears happy to see her.*

MARIE (*Goes to chair, opens pocketbook there*) Hi!

DOC Well, well, how is our star boarder this morning?

MARIE Fine.

DOC Want your breakfast now?

MARIE Just my fruit juice. I'll drink it while I dress and
have my breakfast later.

DOC (*Places two glasses on table*) Up a little early, aren't
you?

MARIE I have to get to the library and check out some books
before anyone else gets them.

DOC Yes, you want to study hard, Marie, learn to be a fine
artist some day. Paint lots of beautiful pictures. I remember
a picture my mother had over the mantelpiece at home, a
picture of a cathedral in a sunset, one of those big cathedrals
in Europe somewhere. Made you feel religious just to look at
it.

MARIE These books aren't for art, they're for biology. I have
an exam.

DOC Biology? Why do they make you take biology?

MARIE (*Laughs*) It's required. Didn't you have to take
biology when you were in college?

DOC   Well . . . yes, but I was preparing to study medicine, so of course I *had* to take biology and things like that. You see—I was going to be a real doctor then—only I left college my third year.

MARIE   What's the matter? Didn't you like the pre-med course?

DOC   Yes, of course . . . I had to give it up.

MARIE   Why?

DOC   (*Goes to stove with roll on plate—evasive*)   I'll put your sweet roll in now, Marie, so it will be nice and warm for you when you want it.

MARIE   Dr. Delaney, I hope my husband is as nice as you are. Most husbands would never think of getting their own breakfast.

DOC   (*Accepting it as a compliment*)   . . . uh . . . you might as well sit down now and . . . yes, sit here and I'll serve you your breakfast now, Marie, and we can eat it together, the two of us.

MARIE   (*A light little laugh as she dances away from him*) No, I like to bathe first and feel that I'm all fresh and clean to start the day. I'm going to hop into the tub now. See you later. (*She goes upstairs*)

DOC   (*The words appeal to him*)   Yes, fresh and clean— (DOC *now goes on in businesslike way setting his breakfast on the table*)

MARIE   (*Offstage*)   Mrs. Delaney.

LOLA   (*Offstage*)   'Mornin', honey.
(LOLA *comes downstairs. She is a contrast to* DOC'S *neat cleanliness, and* MARIE'S *scrubbed youthfulness. Over a nightdress she wears a lumpy kimono. Her eyes are dim with a morning expression of disillusionment, as though she had had a beautiful dream during the night and found on waking none of it was true. On her feet are worn dirty comfies*)

LOLA   (*With some self-pity*)   I can't sleep late like I used to. It used to be I could sleep till noon if I wanted to, but I can't any more. I don't know why.

DOC   Habits change. Here's your fruit juice.

LOLA (*Taking it*)   I oughta be gettin' your breakfast, Doc, instead of you gettin' mine.

DOC   I have to get up anyway, Baby.

LOLA (*Sadly*)   I had another dream last night.

DOC (*Pours coffee*)   About Little Sheba?

LOLA (*With sudden animation*)   It was just as real. I dreamt I put her on a leash and we walked downtown—to do some shopping. All the people on the street turned around to admire her, and I felt so proud. Then we started to walk, and the blocks started going by so fast that Little Sheba couldn't keep up with me. Suddenly, I looked around and Little Sheba was gone. Isn't that funny? I looked everywhere for her but I couldn't find her. And I stood there feeling sort of afraid. (*Pause*) Do you suppose that means anything?

DOC   Dreams are funny.

LOLA   Do you suppose it means Little Sheba is going to come back?

DOC   I don't know, Baby.

LOLA (*Petulant*)   I miss her so, Doc. She was such a cute little puppy. Wasn't she cute?

DOC (*Smiles with the reminiscence*)   Yes, she was cute.

LOLA   Remember how white and fluffy she used to be after I gave her a bath? And how her little hind-end wagged from side to side when she walked?

DOC (*An appealing memory*)   I remember.

LOLA   She was such a cute little puppy. I hated to see her grow old, didn't you, Doc?

DOC   Yah. Little Sheba should have stayed young forever. Some things should never grow old. That's what it amounts to, I guess.

LOLA   She's been gone for such a long time. What do you suppose ever happened to her?

DOC   You can't ever tell.

LOLA (*With anxiety*) Do you suppose she got run over by a car? Or do you think that old Mrs. Coffman next door poisoned her? I wouldn't be a bit surprised.

DOC No, Baby. She just disappeared. That's all we know.

LOLA (*Redundantly*) Just vanished one day . . . vanished into thin air.
  (*As though in a dream*)

DOC I told you I'd find you another one, Baby.

LOLA (*Pessimistically*) You couldn't ever find another puppy as cute as Little Sheba.

DOC (*Back to reality*) Want an egg?

LOLA No. Just this coffee. (*He pours coffee and sits down to breakfast.* LOLA, *suddenly*) Have you said your prayer, Doc?

DOC Yes, Baby.

LOLA And did you ask God to be with you—all through the day, and keep you strong?

DOC Yes, Baby.

LOLA Then God will be with you, Docky. He's been with you almost a year now and I'm so proud of you.

DOC (*Preening a little*) Sometimes I feel sorta proud of my-self.

LOLA Say your prayer, Doc. I like to hear it.

DOC (*Matter-of-factly*) God grant me the serenity to accept the things I cannot change, courage to change the things I can, and wisdom always to tell the difference.

LOLA That's nice. That's so pretty. When I think of the way you used to drink, always getting into fights, we had so much trouble. I was so scared! I never knew what was going to happen.

DOC That was a long time ago, Baby.

LOLA I know it, Daddy. I know how you're going to be when you come home now.
  (*She kisses him lightly*)

DOC   *I* don't know what I would have done without you.

LOLA   And now you've been sober almost a year.

DOC   Yep. A year next month.
      (*He rises and goes to the sink with coffee cup and two glasses, rinsing them*)

LOLA   Do you have to go to the meeting tonight?

DOC   No. No meeting tonight.

LOLA   Oh, good! Then you can take me to a movie.

DOC   Sorry, Baby. I'm going out on some Twelfth Step work with Ed Anderson.

LOLA   What's that?

DOC   (*Drying the glasses*)   I showed you that list of twelve steps the Alcoholics Anonymous have to follow. This is the final one. After you learn to stay dry yourself, then you go out and help other guys that need it.

LOLA   Oh!

DOC   When we help others, we help ourselves.

LOLA   I know what you mean. Whenever I help Marie in some way, it makes me feel good.

DOC   Yes. (LOLA *takes her cup to* DOC *and he washes it*) Yes, but this is a lot different, Baby. When I go out to help some poor drunk, I have to give him courage—to stay sober like I've stayed sober. Most alcoholics are disappointed men . . . . They need courage . . .

LOLA   You weren't ever disappointed, were you, Daddy?

DOC   (*After another evasive pause*)   The important thing is to forget the past and live for the present. And stay sober doing it.

LOLA   Who do you have to help tonight?

DOC   Some guy they picked up on Skid Row last night. (*Gets his coat from back of chair*) They got him at the City Hospital. I kinda dread it.

LOLA   I thought you said it helped you.

DOC (*Puts on coat*) It does, if you can stand it. I did some Twelfth Step work down there once before. They put alcoholics right in with the crazy people. It's horrible—these men all twisted and shaking—eyes all foggy and full of pain. Some guy there with his fists clamped together, so he couldn't kill anyone. There was a young man, just a *young* man, had scratched his eyes out.

LOLA (*Cringing*) Don't, Daddy. Seems a shame to take a man there just 'cause he got drunk.

DOC Well, they'll sober a man up. That's the important thing. Let's not talk about it any more.

LOLA (*With relief*) Rita Hayworth's on tonight, out at the Plaza. Don't you want to see it?

DOC Maybe Marie will go with you.

LOLA Oh, no. She's probably going out with Turk tonight.

DOC She's too nice a girl to be going out with a guy like Turk.

LOLA I don't know why, Daddy. Turk's nice.

DOC A guy like that doesn't have any respect for *nice* young girls. You can tell that by looking at him.

LOLA I never saw Marie object to any of the love-making.

DOC A big, brawny bozo like Turk, he probably forces her to kiss him.

LOLA Daddy, that's not so at all. I came in the back way once when they were in the living room, and she was kissing him like he was Rudolph Valentino.

DOC (*An angry denial*) Marie is a nice girl.

LOLA I know she's nice. I just said she and Turk were doing some tall spooning. It wouldn't surprise me any if . . .

DOC Honey, I don't want to hear any more about it.

LOLA You try to make out like every young girl is Jennifer Jones in the *Song of Bernadette*.

DOC I do not. I just like to believe that young people like her are clean and decent. . . .

(MARIE *comes downstairs*)

MARIE Hi!
(*Gets cup and saucer from drainboard*)

LOLA (*At stove*) There's an extra sweet roll for you this
morning, honey. I didn't want mine.

MARIE One's plenty, thank you.

DOC How soon do you leave this morning?
(LOLA *brings coffee*)

MARIE (*Eating*) As soon as I finish my breakfast.

DOC Well, I'll wait and we can walk to the corner together.

MARIE Oh, I'm sorry, Doc. Turk's coming by. He has to go
to the library, too.

DOC Oh, well, I'm not going to be competition with a football player. (*To* LOLA) It's a nice spring morning. Wanta
walk to the office with me?

LOLA I look too terrible, Daddy. I ain't even dressed.

DOC Kiss Daddy good-bye.

LOLA (*Gets up and kisses him softly*) Bye, bye, Daddy. If
you get hungry, come home and I'll have something for you.

MARIE (*Joking*) Aren't you going to kiss *me*, Dr. Delaney?

DOC (*Startled, hesitates, forces himself to realize she is only
joking and manages to answer*) Can't spend my time kissing
all the girls.
    (MARIE *laughs.* DOC *goes into living room while* LOLA *and*
    MARIE *continue talking.* MARIE'S *scarf is tossed over his
    hat on chair, so he picks it up, then looks at it fondly,
    holding it in the air gazing through its transparent loveli-
    ness. Suddenly, he drops it back on chair and starts out*)

MARIE I think Dr. Delaney is so nice.

LOLA (*She is by the closet now, where she keeps a few personal articles. She is getting into a more becoming smock*)
When did you say Turk was coming by?

MARIE Said he'd be here about 9:30. (DOC *exits, hearing the
line about* TURK) That's a pretty smock.

LOLA (*Goes to table, sits in chair and changes shoes*)   It'll be better to work around the house in.

MARIE (*Not sounding exactly cheerful*)   Mrs. Delaney, I'm expecting a telegram this morning. Would you leave it on my dresser for me when it comes?

LOLA   Sure, honey. No bad news, I hope.

MARIE   Oh, no! It's from Bruce.

LOLA (MARIE'S *boy friends are one of her liveliest interests*) Oh, your boy friend in Cincinnati. Is he coming to see you?

MARIE   I guess so.

LOLA   I'm just dying to meet him.

MARIE (*Changing the subject*)   Really, Mrs. Delaney, you and Doc have been so nice to me. I just want you to know I appreciate it.

LOLA   Thanks, honey.

MARIE   You've been like a father and mother to me. I appreciate it.

LOLA   Thanks, honey.

MARIE   Turk was saying just the other night what good sports you both are.

LOLA (*Brushing hair*)   That so?

MARIE   Honest. He said it was just as much fun being with you as with kids our own age.

LOLA (*Couldn't be more flattered*)   Oh, I like that Turk. He reminds me of a boy I used to know in high school, Dutch McCoy. Where did you ever meet him?

MARIE   In art class.

LOLA   Turk take art?

MARIE (*Laughs*)   No. It was in a life class. He was modeling. Lots of the athletes do that. It pays them a dollar an hour.

LOLA   That's nice.

MARIE   Mrs. Delaney? I've got some corrections to make in some of my drawings. Is it all right if I bring Turk home this morning to pose for me? It'll just take a few minutes.

LOLA   Sure, honey.

MARIE   There's a contest on now. They're giving a prize for the best drawing to use for advertising the Spring Relays.

LOLA   And you're going to do a picture of Turk? That's nice. (*A sudden thought*) Doc's gonna be gone tonight. You and Turk can have the living room if you want to. (*A little secretively*)

MARIE (*This is a temptation*)   O.K. Thanks.
   (*Exits to bedroom*)

LOLA   Tell me more about Bruce.
   (*Follows her to bedroom door*)

MARIE (*Offstage in bedroom*)   Well, he comes from one of the best families in Cincinnati. And they have a great big house. And they have a maid, too. And he's got a wonderful personality. He makes $300 a month.

LOLA   That so?

MARIE   And he stays at the best hotels. His company insists on it.
   (*Returns to living room*)

LOLA   Do you like him as well as Turk?

MARIE (*Evasive*)   Bruce is so dependable, and . . . he's a gentleman, too.

LOLA   Are you goin' to marry him, honey?

MARIE   Maybe, after I graduate from college and he feels he can support a wife and children. I'm going to have lots and lots of children.

LOLA   I wanted children, too. When I lost my baby and found out I couldn't have any more, I didn't know what to do with myself. I wanted to get a job, but Doc wouldn't hear of it.

MARIE   Bruce is going to come into a lot of money some day. His uncle made a fortune in men's garters.

LOLA   Doc was a rich boy when I married him. His mother left him $25,000 when she died. (*Disillusioned*) It took him a lot to get his office started and everything . . . then, he got sick. (*She makes a futile gesture*) But Doc's always good to me . . . *now*.

MARIE (*Re-enters*)   O, Doc's a peach.

LOLA   I used to be pretty, something like you. (*She gets her picture from table*) I was Beauty Queen of the senior class in high school. My dad was awful strict, though. Once he caught me holding hands with that good-looking Dutch McCoy. Dad sent Dutch home, and wouldn't let me go out after supper for a whole month. Daddy would never let me go out with boys much. Just because I was pretty. He was afraid all the boys would get the wrong idea—*you* know. I never had any fun at all until I met Doc.

MARIE   Sometimes I'm glad I didn't know my father. Mom always let me do pretty much as I please.

LOLA   Doc was the first boy my dad ever let me go out with. We got married that spring.
   (*Replaces picture.* MARIE *sits on couch, puts on shoes and socks*)

MARIE   What did your father think of that?

LOLA   We came right to the city then. And, well, Doc gave up his pre-med course and went to Chiropractor School instead.

MARIE   You must have been married awful young.

LOLA   Oh, yes. Eighteen.

MARIE   That must have made your father really mad.

LOLA   Yes, it did. I never went home after that, but my mother comes down here from Green Valley to visit me sometimes.

TURK (*Bursts into the front room from outside. He is a young, good-looking boy, nineteen or twenty. He has the openness, vigor and health of youth. He wears faded dungarees and a T-shirt. He always enters unannounced*)   Hey, Marie! Ready?

MARIE (*Calling. Runs and exits into bedroom, closing door*) Just a minute, Turk.

LOLA (*Confidentially*) I'll entertain him until you're ready. (*She is by nature coy and kittenish with any attractive man. Picks up papers—stuffs them under table*) The house is such a mess, Turk! I bet you think I'm an awful housekeeper. Some day I'll surprise you. But you're like one of the family now. (*Pause*) My, you're an early caller.

TURK   Gotta get to the library. Haven't cracked a book for a biology exam and Marie's gotta help me.

LOLA (*Unconsciously admiring his stature*) My, I'd think you'd be chilly running around in just that thin little shirt.

TURK   Me? I go like this in the middle of winter.

LOLA   Well, you're a big husky man.

TURK (*Laughs*)   Oh, I'm a brute, *I* am.

LOLA   You should be out in Hollywood making those Tarzan movies.

TURK (*Calling*)   Hey, Marie, hurry up.

MARIE   Oh, be patient, Turk.

TURK (*To* LOLA)   She doesn't realize how busy I am. I'll only have a half hour to study at most. I gotta report to the coach at 10:30.

LOLA   What are you in training for now?

TURK   Spring track. They got me throwing the javelin.

LOLA   The javelin? What's that?

TURK (*Laughs at her ignorance*)   It's a big, long lance. (*Assumes the stance*) You hold it like this, erect—then you let go and it goes singing through the air, and lands yards away, if you're any good at it, and sticks in the ground, quivering like an arrow. I won the State championship last year.

LOLA (*She has watched as though fascinated*)   My!

TURK (*Very generous*)   Get Marie to take you to the track field some afternoon, and you can watch me.

LOLA   That would be thrilling.

MARIE (*Comes dancing in*) Hi, Turk.

TURK   Hi, juicy.

LOLA (*As the young couple move to the doorway*) Remember, Marie, you and Turk can have the front room tonight. All to yourselves. You can play the radio and dance and make a plate of fudge, or anything you want.

MARIE (*To* TURK) O.K.?

TURK   Sure.

MARIE Let's go. (*Exits*)

LOLA   'Bye, kids.

TURK   'Bye, Mrs. Delaney. (*Gives her a chuck under the chin*) You're a swell skirt.
(LOLA *couldn't be more flattered. For a moment she is breathless. They speed out the door and* LOLA *stands, sadly watching them depart. Then a sad, vacant look comes over her face. Her arms drop in a gesture of futility. Slowly she walks out on the front porch and calls*)

LOLA   Little Sheba! Come, Little She-ba. Come back . . . come back, Little Sheba! (*She waits for a few moments, then comes wearily back into the house, closing the door behind her. Now the morning has caught up with her. She goes to the kitchen, kicks off her pumps and gets back into comfies. The sight of the dishes on the drainboard depresses her. Clearly she is bored to death. Then the telephone rings with the promise of relieving her. She answers it*) Hello— Oh, no, you've got the wrong number— Oh, that's all right. (*Again it looks hopeless. She hears the* POSTMAN. *Now her spirits are lifted. She runs to the door, opens it and awaits him. When he's within distance, she lets loose a barrage of welcome*) 'Morning, Mr. Postman.

POSTMAN 'Morning, ma'am.

LOLA   You better have something for me today. Sometimes I think you don't even know I live here. You haven't left me anything for two whole weeks. If you can't do better than that, I'll just have to get a new postman.

POSTMAN (*On the porch*)   You'll have to get someone to write you some letters, lady. Nope, nothing for you.

LOLA   Well, I was only joking. You knew I was joking, didn't you? I bet you're thirsty. You come right in here and I'll bring you a glass of cold water. Come in and sit down for a few minutes and rest your feet awhile.

POSTMAN   I'll take you up on that, lady. I've worked up quite a thirst. (*Coming in*)

LOLA   You sit down. I'll be back in just a minute.
   (*Goes to kitchen, gets pitcher out of refrigerator and brings it back*)

POSTMAN   Spring is turnin' into summer awful soon.

LOLA   You feel free to stop here and ask me for a drink of water any time you want to. (*Pouring drink*) That's what we're all here for, isn't it? To make each other comfortable?

POSTMAN   Thank you, ma'am.

LOLA (*Clinging, not wanting to be left alone so soon; she hurries her conversation to hold him*)   You haven't been our postman very long, have you?

POSTMAN (*She pours him a glass of water, stands holding pitcher as he drinks*)   No.

LOLA   You postmen have things pretty nice, don't you? I hear you get nice pensions after you been working for the government twenty years. I think that's dandy. It's a *good* job, too. (*Pours him a second glass*) You may get tired but I think it's good for a man to be outside and get a lot of exercise. Keeps him strong and healthy. My husband, he's a doctor, a *chiro*practor; he has to stay inside his office all day long. The only exercise he gets is rubbin' people's backbones. (*They laugh*) It makes his hands strong, but he's got a poor digestion. I keep tellin' him he oughta get some fresh air once in a while and some exercise. (POSTMAN *rises as if to go, and this hurries her into a more absorbing monologue*) You know what? My husband is an Alcoholics Anonymous. He doesn't care if I tell you that 'cause he's proud of it. He hasn't touched a drop in almost a year. All that time we've had a quart of whiskey in the pantry for company and he hasn't even gone near it. Doesn't even want to. You know, alcoholics can't drink like ordinary people; they're *allergic* to it. It affects them different. They get started drinking and can't stop. Liquor transforms them. Sometimes they get mean and violent and wanta fight, but if they let liquor alone, they're perfectly all right, just like you and me. (POSTMAN *tries to leave*) You should have seen Doc before he gave it up. He lost all his patients, wouldn't even go to the office; just wanted to stay drunk all day long and he'd come home at night and . . . (*Decides against saying more*) You just wouldn't believe it if you saw him now. He's got his patients all back, and he's just doing fine.

POSTMAN   Sure, I know Dr. Delaney. I deliver his office mail. He's a fine man.

LOLA   Oh, thanks. You don't ever drink, do you?

POSTMAN   Oh, a few beers once in a while. (*He is ready to go*)

LOLA   Well, I guess that stuff doesn't do any of us any good.

POSTMAN   No. (*Crosses down for mail on floor center*) Well, good day, ma'am.

LOLA   Say, you got any kids?

POSTMAN   Three grandchildren.

LOLA (*Getting it from console table*)   We don't have any kids, and we got this toy in a box of breakfast food. Why don't you take it home to them?

POSTMAN   Why, that's very kind of you, ma'am. (*He takes it, and goes*)

LOLA   Good-bye, Mr. Postman.

POSTMAN (*On porch*)   Good-bye, ma'am.

LOLA (*Left alone, she turns on radio. Then she goes to kitchen to start dishes, showing her boredom in the half-hearted way she washes them. She spies* MRS. COFFMAN *hanging baby clothes on lines just outside kitchen door. She calls*)   My, you're a busy woman this morning, Mrs. Coffman.

MRS. COFFMAN (*A German woman, she speaks with a little accent, appearing briefly at the window*) Being busy is being happy.

LOLA I guess so.

MRS. COFFMAN I don't have it as easy as you. When you got seven kids to look after, you got no time to sit around the house, Mrs. Delaney.

LOLA I s'pose not.

MRS. COFFMAN But you don't hear me complain.

LOLA Oh, no. You never complain. (*Pause*) I guess my little doggie's gone for good, Mrs. Coffman. I sure miss her.

MRS. COFFMAN The only way to keep from missing one dog is to get another.

LOLA (*Goes to sink, turns off water*) Oh, I never could find another doggie as cute as Little Sheba.

MRS. COFFMAN Did you put an ad in the paper?

LOLA For two whole weeks. No one answered it. It's just like she vanished—into thin air. (*She likes this metaphor*) Every day, though, I go out on the porch and call her. You can't tell; she might be around. Don't you think?

MRS. COFFMAN You should get busy and forget her. You should get busy, Mrs. Delaney.

LOLA Yes, I'm going to. I'm going to start my spring house-cleaning one of these days real soon. Why don't you come in and have a cup of coffee with me, Mrs. Coffman, and we can chat awhile?

MRS. COFFMAN I got work to do, Mrs. Delaney. I got work. (*Exit*)

(LOLA *turns from the window, annoyed at her rejection. She is about to start on the dishes again when the* MILK-MAN *arrives. She opens the back door and detains him*)

MILKMAN 'Morning, Mrs. Coffman.

MRS. COFFMAN 'Morning.

LOLA (*Brightly*) Hello there, Mr. Milkman. How are you today?

MILKMAN 'Morning, Lady.

LOLA I think I'm going to want a few specials today. Can you come in a minute?
(Goes to icebox)

MILKMAN *(Coming in)* What'll it be?
(He probably is used to her. He is not a handsome man but husky and attractive in his uniform)

LOLA *(At refrigerator)* Well, now, let's see. You got any cottage cheese?

MILKMAN We always got cottage cheese, Lady. *(Showing her card)* All you gotta do is check the items on the card and we leave 'em. Now I gotta go back to the truck.

LOLA Now, don't scold me. I always mean to do that but you're always here before I think of it. Now, I guess I'll need some coffee cream, too—half a pint.

MILKMAN Coffee cream. O.K.

LOLA Now let me see . . . Oh, yes, I want a quart of buttermilk. My husband has liked buttermilk ever since he stopped drinking. My husband's an alcoholic. Had to give it up. Did I ever tell you? *(Starts out. Stops at sink)*

MILKMAN Yes, Lady. *(Starts to go. She follows)*

LOLA Now he can't get enough to eat. Eats six times a day. He comes home in the middle of the morning, and I fix him a snack. In the middle of the afternoon he has a malted milk with an egg in it. And then another snack before he goes to bed.

MILKMAN What'd ya know?

LOLA Keeps his energy up.

MILKMAN I'll bet. Anything else, Lady?

LOLA No, I guess not.

MILKMAN *(Going out)* Be back in a jiffy. *(Gives her slip)*

LOLA I'm just so sorry I put you to so much extra work.
(He goes. Returns shortly with dairy products)
After this I'm going to do my best to remember to check the

card. I don't think it's right to put people to extra work. (*Goes to icebox, puts things away*)

MILKMAN (*Smiles, is willing to forget*) That's all right, Lady.

LOLA Maybe you'd like a piece of cake or a sandwich. Got some awfully good cold cuts in the icebox.

MILKMAN No, thanks, Lady.

LOLA Or maybe you'd like a cup of coffee.

MILKMAN No, thanks.
(*He's checking the items, putting them on the bill*)

LOLA You're just a young man. You oughta be going to college. I think everyone should have an education. Do you like your job?

MILKMAN It's O.K. (*Looks at* LOLA)

LOLA You're a husky young man. You oughta be out in Hollywood making those Tarzan movies.

MILKMAN (*Steps back. Feels a little flattered*) When I first began on this job I didn't get enough exercise, so I started working out on the bar-bell.

LOLA Bar-bells?

MILKMAN Keeps you in trim.

LOLA (*Fascinated*) Yes, I imagine.

MILKMAN I sent my picture in to *Strength and Health* last month. (*Proudly*) It's a physique study! If they print it, I'll bring you a copy.

LOLA Oh, will you? I think we should all take better care of ourselves, don't you?

MILKMAN If you ask me, Lady, that's what's wrong with the world today. We're not taking care of ourselves.

LOLA I wouldn't be surprised.

MILKMAN Every morning, I do forty push-ups before I eat my breakfast.

LOLA Push-ups?

MILKMAN   Like this.
   (*He spreads himself on the floor and demonstrates, doing three rapid push-ups. LOLA couldn't be more fascinated. Then he springs to his feet*)
That's good for shoulder development. Wanta feel my shoulders?

LOLA   Why . . . why, yes. (*He makes one arm tense and puts her hand on his shoulder*) Why, it's just like a rock.

MILKMAN   I can do seventy-nine without stopping.

LOLA   Seventy-nine!

MILKMAN   Now feel my arm.

LOLA (*Does so*)   Goodness!

MILKMAN   You wouldn't believe what a puny kid I was. Sickly, no appetite.

LOLA   Is that a fact? And, my! Look at you now.

MILKMAN (*Very proud*)   Shucks, any man could do the same . . . if he just takes care of himself.

LOLA   Oh, sure, sure.
   (*A horn is heard offstage*)

MILKMAN   There's my partner. I gotta beat it. (*Picks up his things, shakes hands, leaves hurriedly*) See you tomorrow, Lady.

LOLA   'Bye.
   (*She watches him from kitchen window until he gets out of sight. There is a look of some wonder on her face, an emptiness, as though she were unable to understand anything that ever happened to her. She looks at clock, runs into living room, turns on radio. A pulsating tom-tom is heard as a theme introduction. Then the ANNOUNCER*)

ANNOUNCER (*In dramatic voice*)   TA-BOOoooo!
   (*Now in a very soft, highly personalized voice. LOLA sits on couch, eats candy*)
It's Ta-boo, radio listeners, your fifteen minutes of temptation. (*An alluring voice*) Won't you join me?
   (*LOLA swings feet up*)
Won't you leave behind your routine, the dull cares that

make up your day-to-day existence, the little worries, the
uncertainties, the confusions of the work-a-day world, and
follow *me* where pagan spirits hold sway, where lithe natives
dance on a moon-enchanted isle, where palm trees sway with
the restless ocean tide, restless surging on the white shore?
Won't you come along?

> (*More tom-tom*)
> (*Now in an oily voice*)

But remember, it's TA-BOOOOOooooo-OOO!

> (*Now the tom-tom again, going into a sensual, primitive
> rhythm melody.* LOLA *has been transfixed from the begin-
> ning of the program. She lies down on the davenport, lis-
> tening, then slowly, growing more and more comfortable*)

WESTERN UNION BOY (*Appears suddenly in the open door*)
Telegram for Miss Marie Buckholder.

LOLA (*Startled*) Oh! She's not here.

WESTERN UNION BOY   Sign here.

> (LOLA *signs, then she closes the door and brings the en-
> velope into the house, looking at it wonderingly. This is a
> major temptation for her. She puts the envelope on the
> table but can't resist looking at it. Finally she gives in and
> takes it to the kitchen to steam it open. Then* MARIE *and*
> TURK *burst into the room.* LOLA, *confused, wonders what
> to do with the telegram*)

MARIE   Mrs. Delaney!

> (*Turns off radio.* LOLA *embarrassedly slips the message into
> her apron pocket and runs in to greet them*)

Mind if we turn your parlor into an art studio?

LOLA   Sure, go right ahead. Hi, Turk.

> (TURK *gives a wave of his arm*)

MARIE (*To* TURK, *indicating her bedroom*)   You can change
in there, Turk. (*Exit to bedroom*)

LOLA (*Puzzled*)   Change?

MARIE   He's gotta take off his clothes.

LOLA   Huh?

> (*Closes door*)

MARIE   These drawings are for my life class.

LOLA (*Consoled but still mystified*) Oh.

MARIE (*Sits on couch*) Turk's the best male model we've had all year. Lotsa athletes pose for us 'cause they've all got muscles.

LOLA You mean . . . he's gonna pose *naked?*

MARIE (*Laughs*) No. The women do, but the men are always more proper. Turk's going to pose in his track suit.

LOLA Oh. (*Almost to herself*) The women pose naked but the men don't. (*This strikes her as a startling inconsistency*) If it's all right for a woman, it oughta be for a man.

MARIE (*Businesslike*) The man always keeps covered. (*Calling to* TURK) Hurry up, Turk.

TURK (*With all his muscles in place, he comes out. He is not at all self-conscious about his semi-nudity. His body is something he takes very much for granted.* LOLA *is a little dazed by the spectacle of flesh*) How do you want this lovely body? Same pose I took in Art Class?

MARIE Yah. Over there where I can get more light on you.

TURK (*Opens door. Starts pose*) Anything in the house I can use for a javelin?

MARIE Is there, Mrs. Delaney?

LOLA How about the broom?

TURK O.K.
  (LOLA *runs out to get it.* TURK *goes to her in kitchen, takes it, returns to living room and resumes pose*)

MARIE (*From her sofa, studying* TURK *in relation to her sketch-pad*) Your left foot a little more this way. (*Studying it*) O.K., hold it.
  (*Starts sketching rapidly and industriously*)

LOLA (*Starts unwillingly into the kitchen, changes her mind and returns to the scene of action.* MARIE *and* TURK *are too busy to comment.* LOLA *looks at sketch, inspecting it*) Well . . . that's real pretty, Marie.
  (MARIE *is intent.* LOLA *moves closer to look at the drawing*)
It . . . it's real artistic. (*Pause*) I wish *I* was artistic.

TURK   Baby, I can't hold this pose very long at a time.

MARIE   Rest whenever you feel like it.

TURK   O.K.

MARIE   (*To* LOLA) If I make a good drawing, they'll use it for the posters for the Spring Relays.

LOLA   Ya. You told me.

MARIE   (*To* TURK) After I'm finished with these sketches I won't have to bother you any more.

TURK   No bother. (*Rubs his shoulder—he poses*) Hard pose, though. Gets me in the shoulder.
   (MARIE *pays no attention.* LOLA *peers at him so closely, he becomes a little self-conscious and breaks pose. This also breaks* LOLA'S *concentration*)

LOLA   I'll heat you up some coffee.
   (*A little embarrassed, she goes to kitchen*)

TURK   (*Softly to* MARIE) Hey, can't you keep her out of here? She makes me feel naked.

MARIE   (*Laughs*) I can't keep her out of her own house, can I?

TURK   Didn't she ever see a man before?

MARIE   Not a big, beautiful man like you, Turky.
   (TURK *smiles, is flattered by any recognition of his physical worth, takes it as an immediate invitation to lovemaking. Pulling her up, he kisses her as* DOC *comes up on porch.* MARIE *pushes* TURK *away*)
Turk, get back in your corner.
   (DOC *comes in from outside*)

DOC   (*Cheerily*) Hi, everyone.

MARIE   Hi.

TURK   Hi, Doc. (DOC *then sees* TURK, *feels immediate resentment. Goes into kitchen to* LOLA) What's goin' on here?

LOLA   (*Getting cups*) Oh, hello, Daddy. Marie's doin' a drawin'.

DOC (*Trying to size up the situation.* MARIE *and* TURK *are too busy to speak*) Oh.

LOLA I've just heated up the coffee, want some?

DOC Yeah. What happened to Turk's clothes?

LOLA Marie's doing some drawings for her *life* class, Doc.

DOC Can't she draw him with his clothes on?

LOLA (*Very professional now*) No, Doc, it's not the same. See, it's a *life* class. They draw bodies. They all do it, right in the classroom.

DOC Why, Marie's just a young girl; she shouldn't be drawing things like that. I don't care if they do teach it at college. It's not right.

LOLA (*Disclaiming responsibility*) I don't know, Doc.

TURK (*Turns*) I'm tired.

MARIE (*Squats at his feet*) Just let me finish the foot.

DOC Why doesn't she draw something else, a bowl of flowers or a cathedral . . . or a sunset?

LOLA All she told me, Doc, was if she made a good drawing of Turk, they'd use it for the posters for the Spring Relay. (*Pause*) So I guess they don't want sunsets.

DOC What if someone walked into the house now? What would they think?

LOLA Daddy, Marie just asked me if it was all right if Turk came and posed for her. Now that's all she said, and I said O.K. But if you think it's wrong I won't let them do it again.

DOC I just don't like it.

MARIE Hold it a minute more.

TURK O.K.

LOLA Well, then you speak to Marie about it if . . .

DOC (*He'd never mention anything disapprovingly to* MARIE) No. Baby. I couldn't do that.

LOLA Well, then . . .

DOC Besides, it's not her fault. If those college people make her do drawings like that, I suppose she has to do them. I just don't think it's right she should have to, that's all.

LOLA Well, if you think it's wrong . . .

DOC (*Ready to dismiss it*) Never mind.

LOLA I don't see any harm in it, Daddy.

DOC Forget it.

LOLA (*Goes to icebox*) Would you like some buttermilk?

DOC Thanks.
  (MARIE *finishes sketch*)

MARIE O.K. That's all I can do for today.

TURK Is there anything I can do for *you?*

MARIE Yes—get your clothes on.

TURK O.K., coach.
  (TURK *exits*)

LOLA You know what Marie said, Doc? She said that the women pose naked, but the men don't.

DOC Why, of course, honey.

LOLA Why is that?

DOC (*Stumped*) Well . . .

LOLA If it's all right for a woman it oughta be for a man. But the man always keeps covered. That's what she said.

DOC Well, that's the way it should be, honey. A man, after all, is a man, and he . . . well, he has to protect himself.

LOLA And a woman doesn't?

DOC It's different, honey.

LOLA Is it? (*She doesn't understand, so she changes the subject*) I've got a secret, Doc, Bruce is coming.

DOC Is that so?

LOLA (*After a glum silence*) You know, Marie's boy friend from Cincinnati. I promised Marie a long time ago, when her fiancé came to town, dinner was on me. So I'm getting out the best china and cooking the best meal you ever sat down to.

DOC When did she get the news?

LOLA The telegram came this morning.

DOC That's fine. That Bruce sounds to me like just the fellow for her. I think I'll go in and congratulate her.

LOLA (*Nervous*) Not now, Doc.

DOC Why not?

LOLA Well, Turk's there. It might make him feel embarrassed.

DOC Well, why doesn't Turk clear out now that Bruce is coming? What's he hanging around for? She's engaged to marry Bruce, isn't she?
  (TURK *enters from bedroom and goes to* MARIE, *starting to make advances*)

LOLA Marie's just doing a picture of him, Doc.

DOC You always stick up for him. You encourage him.

LOLA Shhh, Daddy. Don't get upset.

DOC (*Angrily*) Who says I'm upset?

LOLA (*Cautiously*) Well . . . you are, Doc. Just a little.

DOC (*Angry and embarrassed*) Why *should* I be? Why should I?

LOLA I don't know, Doc, but . . .

DOC (*Stamping out of kitchen*) You imagine things. (*He hurries upstairs as though to avoid further disclosure of his feelings.* LOLA *remains in kitchen almost in tears, she is so dismayed.* TURK, *knowing he is unobserved, grabs* MARIE *in his arms and she is ready to let him kiss her. They are unobserved*)

CURTAIN

SCENE II

*The same evening, after supper. Outside it is dark.
There has been an almost miraculous transformation
of the entire house. LOLA, apparently, has been working hard and fast all day. The rooms are spotlessly
clean and there are such additions as new lampshades,
fresh curtains, etc. In the kitchen all the enamel sur-
faces glisten, and piles of junk that have lain around
for months have been disposed of. LOLA and DOC are
in the kitchen, he washing up the dishes and she put-
tering around putting the finishing touches on her
housecleaning.*

LOLA (*At stove*)   There's still some beans left. Do you want
them, Doc?

DOC   I had enough.

LOLA   I hope you got enough to eat tonight, Daddy. I been
so busy cleaning I didn't have time to fix you much.

DOC   I wasn't very hungry.

LOLA (*At table, cleaning up*)   You know what? Mrs. Coffman said I could come over and pick all the lilacs I wanted
for my centerpiece tomorrow. Isn't that nice? I don't think
she poisoned Little Sheba, do you?

DOC   I never did think so, Baby. Where'd you get the new
curtains?

LOLA   I went out and bought them this afternoon. Aren't
they pretty? Be careful of the woodwork, it's been varnished.

DOC   How come, honey?

LOLA (*Gets broom and dustpan from closet*)   Bruce is
comin'. I figured I had to do my spring housecleaning *some*
time.

DOC   You got all this done in one day? The house hasn't
looked like this in years.

LOLA   I can be a good housekeeper when I want to be, can't I, Doc?

DOC   (*Holding dustpan for* LOLA)   I never had any complaints. Where's Marie now?

LOLA   I don't know, Doc. I haven't seen her since she left here this morning with Turk.

DOC   Well! I'm not going to say anything more about that.

LOLA   Daddy, Marie can take care of herself. Don't worry.
      (*Returns broom to closet*)

DOC   (*Goes into living room*)   'Bout time for Fibber McGee and Molly.

LOLA   (*At the back door, before going out*)   Daddy, I'm gonna run over to Mrs. Coffman's and see if she's got any silver polish. I'll be right back.
      (*At the radio* DOC *starts twisting the dial. He rejects one noisy program after another, then very unexpectedly he comes across a rendition of Shubert's famous "Ave Maria," sung in a high soprano voice. Probably he has encountered the piece before somewhere, but it is now making its first impression on him. Gradually he is transported into a world of ethereal beauty which he never knew existed. He listens intently. The music has expressed some ideal of beauty he never fully realized. Then* LOLA *returns through the back door, letting it slam, breaking the spell, and announcing in a loud, energetic voice*)
Isn't it funny? I'm not a bit tired tonight. You'd think after working so hard all day I'd be pooped.

DOC   (*In the living room; he cringes*)   Baby, don't use that word.

LOLA   (*Sets silver polish on kitchen table and joins* DOC)   I'm sorry, Doc. I hear Marie and Turk say it all the time, and I thought it was kinda cute.

DOC   It . . . it sounds vulgar.

LOLA   (*Kisses* DOC)   I won't say it again, Daddy. Where's Fibber McGee?

DOC   Not quite time yet.

LOLA   Let's get some peppy music.

DOC   (*Tuning in a sentimental dance band*)   That what you want?

LOLA   That's O.K. (DOC *takes a pack of cards off radio and starts shuffling them, very deftly*) I love to watch you shuffle cards, Daddy. You use your hands so gracefully. (*She watches closely*) Do me one of your card tricks.

DOC   Baby, you've seen them all.

LOLA   But I never get tired of them.

DOC   O.K. Take a card. (LOLA *does*) Keep it now. Don't tell me what it is.

LOLA   I won't.

DOC   (*Shuffling cards again*)   Now put it back in the deck. I won't look. (*He closes his eyes*)

LOLA   (*With childish delight*)   All right.

DOC   Put it back.

LOLA   Uh-huh.

DOC   O.K. (*Shuffles cards again, cutting them, taking top half off, exposing* LOLA'S *card to her astonishment*) That your card?

LOLA   (*Unbelievingly*)   Daddy, how did you do it?

DOC   Baby, I've pulled that trick on you dozens of times.

LOLA   But I never understand how you do it.

DOC   Very simple.

LOLA   Docky, show me how you do that.

DOC   (*You can forgive him a harmless feeling of superiority*) Try it for yourself.

LOLA   Doc, you're clever. I never could do it.

DOC   Nothing to it.

LOLA   There is *too*. Show me how you do it, Doc.

DOC   And give away all my secrets? It's a gift, honey. A magic gift.

LOLA   Can't you give it to me?

DOC (*Picks up newspaper*)   A man has to keep some things to himself.

LOLA   It's not a gift at all, it's just some trick you *learned*.

DOC   O.K., Baby, any way you want to look at it.

LOLA   Let's have some music. How soon do you have to meet Ed Anderson?
   (DOC *turns on radio*)

DOC   I still got a little time. (*Pleased*)

LOLA   We'll have a real party for Marie and Bruce, won't we, Doc? And maybe you'll do your card tricks.

DOC   Sure.

LOLA   And then we'll make sure they get a chance to be alone a while, won't we, Doc?

DOC   I . . . I suppose. After all, they're engaged.

LOLA   There were times when *we* wanted to be alone. Remember, Doc?

DOC   . . . Yes.

LOLA   And we wouldn't wanta act like *my* folks used to. We had to *steal* all the good times we used to have, didn't we, Doc? Remember the dances we used to go to, without ever telling Mama and Daddy?

DOC   Yes, Baby.

LOLA   Remember the homecoming dance, when Charlie Kettlekamp and I won the Charleston contest?

DOC (*He'd like to forget it*)   Please, honey, I'm trying to read.

LOLA   And you got mad at him 'cause he thought he should take me home afterwards.

DOC   I did not.

LOLA   Yes, you did— Charlie was all right, Doc, really he was. You were just jealous.

DOC   I *wasn't* jealous.

LOLA (*She has become very coy and flirtatious now, an old dog playing old tricks*)   You got jealous every time we went out any place and I even looked at another boy. There was never anything between Charlie and me; there never was.

DOC   That was a long time ago . . .

LOLA   Lots of other boys called me up for dates . . Sammy Knight . . . Hank Biderman . . . Dutch McCoy.

DOC   Sure, Baby. You were the "it" girl.

LOLA (*Pleading for his attention now*)   But I saved all my dates for *you*, didn't I, Doc?

DOC (*Trying to joke*)   As far as *I* know, Baby.

LOLA (*Hurt*)   Daddy, I did. You *got* to believe that. I never took a date with any other boy but you.

DOC (*A little weary and impatient*)   That's all forgotten now. (*Turns off radio*)

LOLA   How can you talk that way, Doc? That was the happiest time of our lives. I'll never forget it.

DOC (*Disapprovingly*)   Honey!

LOLA (*At the window*)   That was a lovely spring. The trees were so heavy and green and the air smelled so sweet. Remember the walks we used to take, down to the old chapel, where it was so quiet and still? (*Sits on couch*)

DOC   In the spring a young man's fancy turns . . . pretty fancy.

LOLA (*In the same tone of reverie*)   I was pretty then, wasn't I, Doc? Remember the first time you kissed me? You were scared as a young girl, I believe, Doc; you trembled so. (*She is being very soft and delicate. Caught in the reverie, he chokes a little and cannot answer*)   We'd been going together all year and you were always so shy. Then for the first time you grabbed me and kissed me. Tears came to your eyes, Doc, and you said you'd love me forever and ever. Remember? You said . . . if I didn't marry you, you wanted to die . . . I remember 'cause it scared me for anyone to say a thing like that.

DOC (*In a repressed tone*)   Yes, Baby.

LOLA   And when the evening came on, we stretched out on the cool grass and you kissed me all night long.

DOC (*Opens doors*)   Baby, you've got to forget those things. That was twenty years ago.

LOLA   I'll soon be forty. Those years have just vanished— vanished into thin air.

DOC   Yes.

LOLA   Just disappeared—like Little Sheba. (*Pause*) Maybe you're sorry you married me now. You didn't know I was going to get old and fat and sloppy . . .

DOC   Oh, Baby!

LOLA   It's the truth. That's what I am. But I didn't know it, either. Are you sorry you married me, Doc?

DOC   Of course not.

LOLA   I mean, are you sorry you *had* to marry me?

DOC (*Goes to porch*)   We were never going to talk about that, Baby.

LOLA (*Following* DOC *out*)   You *were* the first one, Daddy, the *only* one. I'd just die if you didn't believe that.

DOC (*Tenderly*)   I know, Baby.

LOLA   You were so nice and so proper, Doc; I thought nothing we could do together could ever be wrong—or make us unhappy. Do you think we did wrong, Doc?

DOC (*Consoling*)   No, Baby, of course I don't.

LOLA   I don't think anyone knows about it except my folks, do you?

DOC   Of course not, Baby.

LOLA (*Follows him in*)   I wish the baby had lived, Doc. I don't think that woman knew her business, do you, Doc?

DOC   I guess not.

LOLA If we'd gone to a doctor, she would have lived, don't you think?

DOC Perhaps.

LOLA A doctor wouldn't have known we'd just got married, would he? Why were we so afraid?

DOC (*Sits on couch*) We were just kids. Kids don't know how to look after things.

LOLA (*Sits on couch*) If we'd had the baby she'd be a young girl now; then maybe you'd have *saved* your money, Doc, and she could be going to college—like Marie.

DOC Baby, what's done is done.

LOLA It must make you feel bad at times to think you had to give up being a doctor and to think you don't have any money like you used to.

DOC No . . . no, Baby. We should never feel bad about what's past. What's in the past can't be helped. You . . . you've got to forget it and live for the present. If you can't forget the past, you stay in it and never get out. I might be a big M.D. today, instead of a chiropractor; we might have had a family to raise and be with us now; I might still have a lot of money if I'd used my head and invested it carefully, instead of gettin' drunk every night. We might have a nice house, and comforts, and friends. But we don't have any of those things. So what! We gotta keep on living, don't we? I can't stop just 'cause I made a few mistakes. I gotta keep goin' . . . somehow.

LOLA Sure, Daddy.

DOC (*Sighs and wipes brow*) I . . . I wish you wouldn't ask me questions like that, Baby. Let's not talk about it any more. I gotta keep goin', and not let things upset me, or . . . or . . .

LOLA I'm sorry, Doc. I didn't mean to upset you.

DOC I'm not upset.

LOLA What time'll you be home tonight?

DOC 'Bout eleven o'clock.

LOLA I wish you didn't have to go tonight. I feel kinda lonesome.

DOC Some time soon, we'll go *out* together. I kinda hate to go to those night clubs and places since I stopped drinking, but some night I'll take you out to dinner.

LOLA Oh, will you, Daddy?

DOC We'll get dressed up and go to the Windermere and have a fine dinner and dance between courses.

LOLA (*Eagerly*) Let's do, Daddy. I got a little money saved up. I got about forty dollars out in the kitchen. We can take that if you need it.

DOC I'll have plenty of money the first of the month.

LOLA (*She has made a quick response to the change of mood, seeing a future evening of carefree fun*) What are we sitting round here so serious for? (*Turns to radio*) Let's have some music. (LOLA *gets a lively foxtrot on the radio, dances with* DOC. *They begin dancing vigorously as though to dispense with the sadness of the preceding dialogue, but slowly it winds them and leaves* LOLA *panting*) We oughta go dancing . . . all the time, Docky . . . It'd be good for us. Maybe if I danced more often, I'd lose . . . some of . . . this fat. I remember . . . I used to be able to dance like this . . . all night . . . and not even notice . . . it. (LOLA *breaks into a Charleston routine as of yore*) Remember the Charleston, Daddy?
    (DOC *is clapping his hands in rhythm. Then* MARIE *bursts in through the front door, the personification of the youth that* LOLA *is trying to recapture*)

DOC Hi, Marie.

MARIE What are you trying to do, a jig, Mrs. Delaney?
    (MARIE *doesn't intend her remark to be cruel, but it wounds* LOLA. LOLA *stops abruptly in her dancing, losing all the fun she has been able to create for herself. She feels she might cry; so to hide her feelings she hurries quietly out to kitchen, but* DOC *and* MARIE *do not notice.* MARIE *notices the change in atmosphere*)
Hey, what's been happening around here?

DOC Lola got to feeling industrious. You oughta see the kitchen.

MARIE (*Running to kitchen, where she is too observant of the changes to notice* LOLA *weeping in corner.* LOLA, *of course, straightens up as soon as* MARIE *enters*) What got into you, Mrs. Delaney? You've done wonders with the house. It looks marvelous.

LOLA (*Quietly*) Thanks, Marie.

MARIE (*Darting back into living room*) I can hardly believe I'm in the same place.

DOC Think your boy friend'll like it? (*Meaning* BRUCE)

MARIE (*Thinking of* TURK) You know how men are. Turk never notices things like that.
  (*Starts into her room blowing a kiss to* DOC *on her way.* LOLA *comes back in, dabbing at her eyes*)

DOC Turk? (MARIE *is gone*)

LOLA I didn't want her to see me dancing that way. I feel sorta silly.

DOC Does she know we're having *Bruce* to dinner? Not Turk!

LOLA (*Nervous*) Let's not argue any more, Daddy.

MARIE (*Jumps back into the room with her telegram*) My telegram's here. When did it come?

LOLA It came about an hour ago, honey.
  (LOLA *looks nervously at* DOC. DOC *looks puzzled and a little sore*)

MARIE Bruce is coming! "Arriving tomorrow 5:00 P.M. CST, Flight 22, Love, Bruce." When did the telegram come?

DOC (*Looking hopelessly at* LOLA) So it came an hour ago.

LOLA (*Nervously*) Isn't it nice I got the house all cleaned? Marie, you bring Bruce to dinner with us tomorrow night. It'll be a sort of wedding present.

MARIE That would be wonderful, Mrs. Delaney, but I don't want you to go to any trouble.

LOLA   No trouble at all. Now I insist. (*Front doorbell rings*) That must be Turk.

MARIE   (*Whisper*) Don't tell *him*. (*Goes to door.* LOLA *scampers to kitchen*) Hi, Turk. Come on in.

TURK   (*Entering. Stalks her*)   Hi.
   (*Looks around to see if anyone is present, then takes her in his arms and starts to kiss her*)

LOLA   I'm sorry, Doc. I'm sorry about the telegram.

DOC   Baby, people don't do things like that. Don't you understand? *Nice* people don't.

MARIE   Stop it!

TURK   What's the matter?

MARIE   They're in the kitchen.
   (TURK *sits with book*)

DOC   Why didn't you give it to her when it came?

LOLA   Turk was posing for Marie this morning and I couldn't give it to her while he was here.
   (TURK *listens at door*)

DOC   Well, it just isn't nice to open other people's mail.
   (TURK *goes to* MARIE'S *door*)

LOLA   I guess I'm not nice then. That what you mean?

MARIE   Turk, will you get away from that door?

DOC   No, Baby, but . . .

LOLA   I don't see any harm in it, Doc. I steamed it open and sealed it back. (TURK *at switch in living room*) She'll never know the difference. I don't see any harm in that, Doc.

DOC   (*Gives up*)   O.K., Baby, if you don't see any harm in it, I guess I can't explain it.
   (*Starts getting ready to go*)

LOLA   I'm sorry, Doc. Honest, I'll never do it again. Will you forgive me?

DOC   (*Giving her a peck of a kiss*)   I forgive you.

MARIE (*Comes back with book*)   Let's look like we're studying.

TURK   Biology? Hot dog!

LOLA (*After* MARIE *leaves her room*)   Now I feel better. Do you have to go now?
   (TURK *sits by* MARIE *on the couch*)

DOC   Yah.

LOLA   Before you go, why don't you show your tricks to Marie?

DOC (*Reluctantly*)   Not now.

LOLA   Oh, please do. They'd be crazy about them.

DOC (*With pride*)   O.K. (*Preens himself a little*) If you think they'd enjoy them . . .
   (LOLA, *starting to living room, stops suddenly upon seeing* MARIE *and* TURK *spooning behind a book. A broad, pleased smile breaks on her face and she stands silently watching.* DOC *is at sink*)
Well . . . what's the matter, Baby?

LOLA (*In a soft voice*)   Oh . . . nothing . . . nothing . . . Doc.

DOC   Well, do you want me to show 'em my tricks or don't you?

LOLA (*Coming back to center kitchen; in a secretive voice with a little giggle*)   I guess they wouldn't be interested now.

DOC (*With injured pride. A little sore*)   Oh, very well.

LOLA   Come and look, Daddy.

DOC (*Shocked and angry*)   No!

LOLA   Just one little look. They're just kids, Daddy. It's sweet.
   (*Drags him by arm*)

DOC (*Jerking loose*)   Stop it, Baby. I won't do it. It's not decent to snoop around spying on people like that. It's cheap and mischievous and n

LOLA (*This had never occurred to her*)   Is it?

DOC   Of course it is.

LOLA   I don't spy on Marie and Turk to be mischievous and mean.

DOC   Then why *do* you do it?

LOLA   You watch young people make love in the movies, don't you, Doc? There's nothing wrong with that. And I *know* Marie and I like her, and Turk's nice, too. They're both so young and pretty. Why shouldn't I watch them?

DOC   I give up.

LOLA   Well, why shouldn't I?

DOC   I don't know, Baby, but it's not nice.
    (TURK *kisses* MARIE'S *ear*)

LOLA (*Plaintive*)   I think it's one of the nicest things I know.

DOC   It's not right for Marie to do that, particularly since Bruce is coming. We shouldn't allow it.

LOLA   Oh, they don't do any harm, Doc. I think it's all right.

DOC   It's not all right. I don't know why you encourage that sort of thing.

LOLA   I don't encourage it.

DOC   You do, too. You like that fellow Turk. You said so. And I say he's no good. Marie's sweet and innocent; she doesn't understand guys like him. I think I oughta run him outa the house.

LOLA   Daddy, you wouldn't do that.

DOC (*Very heated*)   Then you talk to her and tell her how we feel.

LOLA   Hush, Daddy. They'll hear you.

DOC   I don't care if they do hear me.

LOLA (*To* DOC *at stove*)   Don't get upset, Daddy. Bruce is coming and Turk won't be around any longer. I promise you.

DOC   All right. I better go.

268 William Inge

LOLA I'll go with you, Doc. Just let me run up and get a sweater. Now wait for me.

DOC Hurry, Baby.

(LOLA *hurries upstairs.* DOC *stands in the center of the kitchen where he can hear, from the living room, the cautious murmur of intimate laughter shared by* MARIE *and* TURK. *To* DOC, *the laughter suggests something a little obscene and he bristles with indignation. But when he hears* LOLA'S *voice, he finds composure again*)

LOLA I'm coming, Doc. (*She hurries downstairs.* DOC *turns out kitchen lights and joins her at foot of stairs.* LOLA *speaks to* TURK *and* MARIE.) I'm walking Doc to the bus. (TURK *has been studying a youthful picture of* LOLA *which* DOC, *rather rudely, takes from his hands. Eager to prevent any possible conflict,* LOLA *hurries* DOC *out the front door. When he is outside, she turns back to* MARIE *and speaks very privately.*) Then I'm going for a long, long walk in the moonlight. You kids have a good time. (*She goes out*)

MARIE 'Bye, Mrs. Delaney. (*Exits*)

TURK He hates my guts. (*Goes to front door*)

MARIE Oh, he does not. (*Follows* TURK, *blocks his exit in door*)

TURK Yes, he does. If you ask me, he's jealous.

MARIE Jealous?

TURK I've always thought he had a crush on you.

MARIE Now, Turk, don't be silly. Doc is nice to me. It's just in a few little things he does, like fixing my breakfast, but he's nice to everyone.

TURK He ever make a pass?

MARIE No.

TURK He better not.

MARIE Turk, don't be ridiculous. Doc's such a nice, quiet man; if he gets any fun out of being nice to me, why not?

TURK He's got a wife of his own, hasn't he? Why doesn't he make a few passes at her?

MARIE Things like that are none of our business.

TURK O.K. How about a snuggle, lovely?

MARIE (*A little prim*) No more for tonight, Turk.

TURK Why's tonight different from any other night?

MARIE I think we should make it a rule, every once in a while, just to sit and talk.
  (*Starts to sit on couch, but goes to chair*)

TURK (*Restless, sits on couch*) O.K. What'll we talk about?

MARIE Well . . . there's lotsa things.

TURK O.K. Start in.

MARIE A person doesn't start a conversation that way.

TURK Start it any way you want to.

MARIE Two people should have something to talk about, like politics or psychology or religion.

TURK How 'bout sex?

MARIE Turk!

TURK Have you read the Kinsey Report, Miss Buckholder?

MARIE I should say not.

TURK How old were you when you had your first affair, Miss Buckholder? And did you ever have relations with your grandfather?

MARIE Turk, stop it.

TURK You wanted to talk about something; I was only trying to please. Let's have a kiss.

MARIE Not tonight.

TURK Who you savin' it up for?

MARIE Don't talk that way.

TURK (*Gets up, yawns*) Well, thanks, Miss Buckholder, for a nice evening. It's been a most enjoyable talk.

MARIE (*Anxious*) Turk, where are you going?

TURK I guess I'm a man of action, Baby.

MARIE   Turk, don't go.

TURK   Why not? I'm not doin' any good here.

MARIE   Don't go.

TURK   (*Returns and she touches him. They sit on couch*)
Now why didn't you think of this before? C'mon, let's get to
work.

MARIE   Oh, Turk, this is all we ever do.

TURK   Are you complaining?

MARIE   (*Weakly*) No.

TURK   Then what do you want to put on such a front for?

MARIE   It's not a front.

TURK   What else is it? (*Mimicking*) Oh, no, Turk. Not tonight, Turk. I want to talk about philosophy, Turk. (*Himself
again*) When all the time you know that if I went outa here
without givin' you a good lovin' up you'd be sore as hell
. . . Wouldn't you?

MARIE   (*She has to admit to herself it's true; she chuckles*)
Oh . . . Turk . . .

TURK   It's true, isn't it?

MARIE   Maybe.

TURK   How about tonight, lovely; going to be lonesome?

MARIE   Turk, you're in training.

TURK   What of it? I can throw that old javelin any old
time, *any* old time. C'mon, Baby, we've got by with it before,
haven't we?

MARIE   I'm not so sure.

TURK   What do you mean?

MARIE   Sometimes I think Mrs. Delaney knows.

TURK   Well, bring her along. I'll take care of her, too, if it'll
keep her quiet.

MARIE   (*A pretense of being shocked*) Turk!

TURK   What makes you think so?

MARIE   Women just sense those things. She asks so many questions.

TURK   She ever *say* anything?

MARIE   No.

TURK   Now *you're* imagining things.

MARIE   Maybe.

TURK   Well, stop it.

MARIE   O.K.
(*Now they engage in a little rough-house, he cuffing her like an affectionate bear, she responding with "Stop it," "Turk, that hurt," etc. And she slaps him playfully. Then they laugh together at their own pretense. Now* LOLA *enters the back way very quietly, tiptoeing through the dark kitchen, standing by the doorway where she can peek at them. There is a quiet, satisfied smile on her face. She watches every move they make, alertly*)

TURK   Now, Miss Buckholder, what is your opinion of the psychodynamic pressure of living in the atomic age?

MARIE   (*Playfully*)   Turk, don't make fun of me.

TURK   Tonight?

MARIE   (*Her eyes dance as she puts him off just a little longer*)   Well.

TURK   Tonight will never come again. (*This is true. She smiles*) O.K.?

MARIE   (*They embrace and start to dance*)   Let's go out somewhere first and have a few beers. We can't come back till they're asleep.

TURK   O.K.
(*They dance slowly out the door. Then* LOLA *moves quietly into the living room and out onto the porch. There she can be heard calling plaintively in a lost voice*)

LOLA   Little Sheba . . . Come back . . . Come back, Little Sheba. Come back.

CURTAIN

Act Two

SCENE I

The next morning. LOLA _and_ DOC _are at breakfast again._ LOLA _is rambling on while_ DOC _sits meditatively, his head down, his face in his hands._

LOLA (_In a light, humorous way, as though the faults of youth were as blameless as the uncontrollable actions of a puppy. Chuckles_) Then they danced for a while and went out together, arm in arm. . . .

DOC (_Sitting at table, very nervous and tense_) I don't wanta hear any more about it, Baby.

LOLA What's the matter, Docky?

DOC Nothing.

LOLA You look like you didn't feel very good.

DOC I didn't sleep well last night.

LOLA You didn't take any of those sleeping pills, did you?

DOC No.

LOLA Well, don't. The doctors say they're terrible for you.

DOC I'll feel better after a while.

LOLA Of course you will.

DOC What time did Marie come in last night?

LOLA I don't know, Doc. I went to bed early and went right to sleep. Why?

DOC   Oh . . . nothing.

LOLA   You musta slept if you didn't hear her.

DOC   I heard her; it was after midnight.

LOLA   Then what did you ask me for?

DOC   I wasn't sure it was her.

LOLA   What do you mean?

DOC   I thought I heard a man's voice.

LOLA   Turk probably brought her inside the door.

DOC (*Troubled*)   I thought I heard someone laughing. A man's laugh . . . I guess I was just hearing things.

LOLA   Say your prayer?

DOC (*Gets up*)   Yes.

LOLA   Kiss me 'bye. (*He leans over and kisses her, then puts on his coat and starts to leave*) Do you think you could get home a little early? I want you to help me entertain Bruce. Marie said he'd be here about 5:30. I'm going to have a lovely dinner: stuffed pork chops, twice-baked potatoes, and asparagus, and for dessert a big chocolate cake and maybe ice cream . . .

DOC   Sounds fine.

LOLA   So you get home and help me.

DOC   O.K.

(DOC *leaves kitchen and goes into living room. Again on the chair is* MARIE'S *scarf. He picks it up as before and fondles it. Then there is the sound of* TURK'S *laughter, soft and barely audible. It sounds like the laugh of a sated Bacchus.* DOC'S *body stiffens. It is a sickening fact he must face and it has been revealed to him in its ugliest light. The lyrical grace, the spiritual ideal of Ave Maria is shattered. He has been fighting the truth, maybe suspecting all along that he was deceiving himself. Now he looks sick, with all his blind confusion inside him. With an immobile expression of blankness on his face, he stumbles into the table above the sofa*)

LOLA (*Still in kitchen*)   Haven't you gone yet, Docky?

DOC (*Dazed*) No . . . no, Baby.

LOLA (*In doorway*) Anything the matter?

DOC No . . . no. I'm all right now. (*Drops scarf, takes hat, exits. He has managed to sound perfectly natural. He braces himself and goes out.* LOLA *stands a moment, looking after him with a little curiosity. Then* MRS. COFFMAN *sticks her head in back door*)

MRS. COFFMAN Anybody home?

LOLA (*Turning*) 'Morning, Mrs. Coffman.

MRS. COFFMAN (*Inspecting the kitchen's new look*) So this is what you've been up to, Mrs. Delaney.

LOLA (*Proud*) Yes, I been busy.
(MARIE'S *door opens and closes.* MARIE *sticks her head out of her bedroom door to see if the coast is clear, then sticks her head back in again to whisper to* TURK *that he can leave without being observed*)

MRS. COFFMAN Busy? Good Lord, I never seen such activity. What got into you, Lady?

LOLA Company tonight. I thought I'd fix things up a little.

MRS. COFFMAN You mean you done all this in one day?

LOLA (*With simple pride*) I said I been busy.

MRS. COFFMAN Dear God, you done your spring house-cleaning all in one day.
(TURK *appears in living room*)

LOLA (*Appreciating this*) I fixed up the living room a little, too.

MRS. COFFMAN I must see it. (*Goes into living room.* TURK *overhears her and ducks back into* MARIE'S *room, shutting the door behind himself and* MARIE) I declare! Overnight you turn the place into something really swanky.

LOLA Yes, and I bought a few new things, too.

MRS. COFFMAN Neat as a pin, and so warm and cozy. I take my hat off to you, Mrs. Delaney. I didn't know you had it in you. All these years, now, I been sayin' to myself, "That Mrs. Delaney is a good for nothing, sits around the house all day, and never so much as shakes a dust mop." I guess it just shows, we never really know what people are like.

LOLA I still got some coffee.

MRS. COFFMAN Not now, Mrs. Delaney. Seeing your house so clean makes me feel ashamed. I gotta get home and get to work. (*Goes to kitchen*)

LOLA (*Follows*) I hafta get busy, too. I got to get out all the silver and china. I like to set the table early, so I can spend the rest of the day looking at it.
   (*Both laugh*)

MRS. COFFMAN Good day, Mrs. Delaney. (*Exits*)
   (*Hearing the screen door slam, MARIE guards the kitchen door and TURK slips out the front. But neither has counted on DOC's reappearance. After seeing that TURK is safe, MARIE blows a good-bye kiss to him and joins LOLA in the kitchen. But DOC is coming in the front door just as TURK starts to go out. There is a moment of blind embarrassment, during which DOC only looks stupefied and TURK, after mumbling an unintelligible apology, runs out. First DOC is mystified, trying to figure it all out. His face looks more and more troubled. Meanwhile, MARIE and LOLA are talking in the kitchen*)

MARIE Boo! (*Sneaking up behind LOLA at back porch*)

LOLA (*Jumping around*) Heavens! You scared me, Marie. You up already?

MARIE Yah.

LOLA This is Saturday. You could sleep as late as you wanted.

MARIE (*Pouring a cup of coffee*) I thought I'd get up early and help you.

LOLA Honey, I'd sure appreciate it. You can put up the table in the living room, after you've had your breakfast. That's where we'll eat. Then you can help me set it.
   (*DOC closes door*)

MARIE O.K.

LOLA Want a sweet roll?

MARIE   I don't think so. Turk and I had so much beer last
night. He got kinda tight.

LOLA   He shouldn't do that, Marie.

MARIE (*Starts for living room*)   Just keep the coffee hot for
me. I'll want another cup in a minute. (*Stops on seeing* DOC)
Why, Dr. Delaney! I thought you'd gone.

DOC (*Trying to sustain his usual manner*)   Good morning,
Marie. (*But not looking at her*)

MARIE (*She immediately wonders*)   Why . . . why . . .
how long have you been here, Doc?

DOC   Just got here, just this minute.

LOLA (*Comes in*)   That you, Daddy?

DOC   It's me.

LOLA   What are you doing back?

DOC   I . . . I just thought maybe I'd feel better . . . if I
took a glass of soda water . . .

LOLA   I'm afraid you're not well, Daddy.

DOC   I'm all right. (*Starts for kitchen*)

LOLA (*Helping* MARIE *with table*)   The soda's on the drainboard.
    (DOC *goes to kitchen, fixes some soda, and stands a mo-
    ment, just thinking. Then he sits sipping the soda, as
    though he were trying to make up his mind about some-
    thing*)
Marie, would you help me move the table? It'd be nice now
if we had a dining room, wouldn't it? But if we had a dining
room, I guess we wouldn't have you, Marie. It was my idea
to turn the dining room into a bedroom and rent it. I thought
of lots of things to do for extra money . . . a few years ago
. . . when Doc was so . . . so sick.
    (*They set up table*—LOLA *gets cloth from cabinet*)

MARIE   This is a lovely tablecloth.

LOLA   Irish linen. Doc's mother gave it to us when we got
married. She gave us all our silver and china, too. The china's
Havelin. I'm so proud of it. It's the most valuable possession

we own. I just washed it. . . . Will you help me bring it in?
(*Getting china from kitchen*) Doc was sortuva Mama's boy.
He was an only child and his mother thought the sun rose
and set in him. Didn't she, Docky? She brought Doc up like
a real gentleman.

MARIE   Where are the napkins?

LOLA   Oh, I forgot them. They're so nice I keep them in my
bureau drawer with my handkerchiefs. Come upstairs and
we'll get them.

(LOLA *and* MARIE *go upstairs. Then* DOC *listens to be sure*
LOLA *and* MARIE *are upstairs, looks cautiously at the whis-*
key bottle on pantry shelf but manages to resist several
times. Finally he gives in to temptation, grabs bottle off
shelf, then starts wondering how to get past LOLA *with it.*
Finally, it occurs to him to wrap it inside his trench coat
which he gets from pantry and carries over his arm. LOLA
and MARIE *are heard upstairs. They return to the living*
room and continue setting table as DOC *enters from kitchen*
on his way out)

LOLA (*Coming downstairs*)   Did you ever notice how nice
he keeps his fingernails? Not many men think of things like
that. And he used to take his mother to church every Sunday.

MARIE (*At table*)   Oh, Doc's a real gentleman.

LOLA   Treats women like they were all beautiful angels. We
went together a whole year before he even kissed me. (DOC
comes through the living room with coat and bottle, going to
front door) On your way back to the office now, Docky?

DOC (*His back to them*)   Yes.

LOLA   Aren't you going to kiss me good-bye before you go,
Daddy? (*She goes to him and kisses him.* MARIE *catches*
DOC'S *eye and smiles. Then she exits to her room, leaving*
door open) Get home early as you can. I'll need you. We
gotta give Bruce a royal welcome.

DOC   Yes, Baby.

LOLA   Feeling all right?

DOC   Yes.

LOLA (*In doorway,* DOC *is on porch*)   Take care of yourself.

DOC (*In a toneless voice*) Good-bye. (*He goes*)

LOLA (*Coming back to table with pleased expression, which changes to a puzzled look, calls to* MARIE) Now that's funny. Why did Doc take his raincoat? It's a beautiful day. There isn't a cloud in sight.

CURTAIN

SCENE II

It is now 5:30. The scene is the same as the preceding except that more finishing touches have been added and the two women, still primping the table, lighting the tapers, are dressed in their best. LOLA *is arranging the centerpiece.*

LOLA (*Above table, fixing flowers*) I just love lilacs, don't you, Marie? (*Takes one and studies it*) Mrs. Coffman was nice; she let me have all I wanted. (*Looks at it very closely*) Aren't they pretty? And they smell so sweet. I think they're the nicest flower there is.

MARIE They don't last long.

LOLA (*Respectfully*) No. Just a few days. Mrs. Coffman's started blooming just day before yesterday.

MARIE By the first of the week they'll all be gone.

LOLA Vanish . . . they'll vanish into thin air. (*Gayer now*) Here, honey, we have them to spare *now*. Put this in your hair. There. (MARIE *does*) Mrs. Coffman's been so nice lately. I didn't use to like her. Now where could Doc be? He promised he'd get here early. He didn't even come home for lunch.

MARIE (*Gets two chairs from bedroom*) Mrs. Delaney, you're a peach to go to all this trouble.

LOLA (*Gets salt and pepper*) Shoot, I'm gettin' more fun out of it than you are. Do you think Bruce is going to like us?

MARIE If he doesn't, I'll never speak to him again.

LOLA (*Eagerly*) I'm just dying to meet him. But I feel sorta bad I never got to do anything nice for Turk.

MARIE (*Carefully prying*) Did . . . Doc ever say anything to you about Turk . . . and me?

LOLA About Turk and you? No, honey. Why?

MARIE (*She seems to feel a little guilty*) I just wondered.

LOLA What if Bruce finds out that you've been going with someone else?

MARIE Bruce and I had a very businesslike understanding before I left for school that we weren't going to sit around lonely just because we were separated.

LOLA Aren't you being kind of mean to Turk?

MARIE I don't think so.

LOLA How's he going to feel when Bruce comes?

MARIE He may be sore for a little while, but he'll get over it.

LOLA Won't he feel bad?

MARIE He's had his eye on a pretty little Spanish girl in his history class for a long time. I like Turk, but I wouldn't think of marrying him.

LOLA No! Really?
(LOLA, *with a look of sad wonder on her face, sits on arm of couch. It's been a serious disillusionment*)

MARIE What's the matter?

LOLA I . . . I don't know.

MARIE Did I say anything that upset you?

LOLA Well . . . I guess I thought you and Turk kind of *cared* for each other. You know what I mean. (MARIE *gives an irresponsible little laugh*)

MARIE You're a sentimentalist, Mrs. Delaney.

LOLA (*With sad realization*) Yes . . . I suppose I am.
(*The doorbell rings and* MARIE *jumps to answer it*)

MARIE That must be Bruce. (*Opens the door and greets him*) Bruce!

BRUCE (*Steps inside, taking* MARIE *in his arms*) How are you, sweetheart?

(*He is an efficient-looking young businessman*)

MARIE Wonderful.

BRUCE Did you get my wire?

MARIE Sure.

BRUCE You're looking swell.

MARIE Thanks. What took you so long to get here?

BRUCE Well, honey, I had to go to my hotel and take a shower.

MARIE Bruce, this is Mrs. Delaney.

BRUCE (*Now he gets the cozy quality out of his voice*) How do you do, ma'am?

LOLA How d'ya do?

BRUCE Marie has said some very nice things about you in her letters.

MARIE Mrs. Delaney has fixed the grandest dinner for us.

BRUCE Now that was to be my treat. I have a big expense account now, honey. I thought we could all go down to the hotel and have dinner there, and celebrate first with a few cocktails.

LOLA Oh, we can have cocktails, too. Excuse me, just a minute.

(*She hurries to the kitchen and starts looking for the whiskey.* BRUCE *kisses* MARIE)

MARIE (*Whispers*) Now, Bruce, she's been working on this dinner all day. She even cleaned the house for you.

BRUCE (*With a surveying look*) Did she?

MARIE And Doc's joining us. You'll like Doc.

BRUCE Honey, are we going to have to stay here the whole evening?

MARIE We just can't eat and run. We'll get away as soon as we can.

BRUCE I hope so. I got the raise, sweetheart. They're giving me new territory.

(LOLA *is frantic in the kitchen, having found the bottle missing. She hurries back into the living room*)

LOLA You kids are going to have to entertain yourselves awhile 'cause I'm going to be busy in the kitchen. Why don't you turn on the radio, Marie? Get some dance music. I'll shut the door so . . . so I won't disturb you.

(LOLA *does so, then goes to the telephone*)

MARIE Come and see my room, Bruce. I've fixed it up just darling. And I've got your picture in the prettiest frame right on my dresser.

(*They exit and their voices are heard from the bedroom while* LOLA *is phoning*)

LOLA (*At the phone*) This is Mrs. Delaney. Is . . . Doc there? Well, then, is Ed Anderson there? Well, would you give me Ed Anderson's telephone number? You see, he sponsored Doc into the club and helped him . . . you know . . . and . . . and I was a little worried tonight. . . . Oh, thanks. Yes, I've got it. (*She writes down number*) Could you have Ed Anderson call me if he comes in? Thank you.

(*She hangs up. On her face is a dismal expression of fear, anxiety and doubt. She searches flour bin, icebox, closet. Then she goes into the living room, calling to* MARIE *and* BRUCE *as she comes*)

I . . . I guess we'll go ahead without Doc, Marie.

MARIE (*Enters from her room*) What's the matter with Doc, Mrs. Delaney?

LOLA Well . . . he got held up at the office . . . just one of those things, you know. It's too bad. It would have to happen when I needed him most.

MARIE Sure you don't need any help?

LOLA Huh? Oh, no. I'll make out. Everything's ready. I tell you what I'm going to do. Three's a crowd, so I'm going to be the butler and serve the dinner to you two young lovebirds . . . (*The telephone rings*) Pardon me . . . pardon me just a minute. (*She rushes to phone, closing the door behind her*) Hello? Ed? Have you seen Doc? He went out this morning and hasn't come back. We're having company

for dinner and he was supposed to be home early. . . .
That's not all. All this time we've had a quart of whiskey in
the kitchen and Doc's never gone near it. I went to get it
tonight. I was going to serve some cocktails. It was *gone*.
Yes, I saw it there yesterday. No, I don't think so. . . . He
said this morning he had an upset stomach but . . . Oh,
would you? . . . Thank you, Mr. Anderson. Thank you a
million times. And you let me know when you find out anything. Yes, I'll be here . . . yes. (*Hangs up and crosses back
to living room*) Well, I guess we're all ready.

BRUCE   Aren't you going to look at your present?

MARIE   Oh, sure, let's get some scissors.
   (*Their voices continue in bedroom*)

MARIE (*Enters with* BRUCE)   Mrs. Delaney, we think you
should eat with us.

LOLA   Oh, no, honey, I'm not very hungry. Besides, this is
the first time you've been together in months and I think you
should be alone. Marie, why don't you light the candles?
Then we'll have just the right atmosphere.
   (*She goes into kitchen, gets tomato-juice glasses from icebox while* BRUCE *lights the candles*)

BRUCE   Do we have to eat by candlelight? I won't be able
to see.
   (LOLA *returns*)

LOLA   Now, Bruce, you sit here. (*He and* MARIE *sit*) Isn't
that going to be cozy? Dinner for two. Sorry we won't have
time for cocktails. Let's have a little music. (*She turns on
the radio and a Viennese waltz swells up as the curtain falls*)
                                                    CURTAIN

SCENE III

   *Funereal atmosphere. It is about 5:30 the next morn-
ing. The sky is just beginning to get light outside,
while inside the room the shadows still cling heavily to
the corners. The remains of last night's dinner clutter
the table in the living room. The candles have gut-
tered down to stubs amid the dirty dinner plates, and*

the lilacs in the centerpiece have wilted. LOLA *is
sprawled on the davenport, sleeping. Slowly she
awakens and regards the morning light. She gets up
and looks about strangely, beginning to show despair
for the situation she is in. She wears the same spiffy
dress she had on the night before but it is wrinkled
now, and her marcelled coiffure is awry. One silk
stocking has twisted loose and falls around her ankle.
When she is sufficiently awake to realize her situation,
she rushes to the telephone and dials a number.*

LOLA (*At telephone. She sounds frantic*) Mr. Anderson?
Mr. Anderson, this is Mrs. Delaney again. I'm sorry to call
you so early, but I just *had* to. . . . Did you find Doc? . . .
No, he's not home yet. I don't suppose he'll come home till
he's drunk all he can hold and wants to sleep. . . . I don't
know what else to think, Mr. Anderson. I'm scared, Mr.
Anderson. I'm awful scared. Will you come right over? . . .
Thanks, Mr. Anderson.

(*She hangs up and goes to kitchen to make coffee. She
finds some left from the night before, so turns on the fire
to warm it up. She wanders around vaguely, trying to get
her thoughts in order, jumping at every sound. Pours herself a cup of coffee, then takes it to living room, sits and
sips it. Very quietly* DOC *enters through the back way into
the kitchen. He carries a big bottle of whiskey which he
carefully places back in the pantry, not making a sound,
hangs up overcoat, then puts suitcoat on back of chair.
Starts to go upstairs, but* LOLA *speaks*)

Doc? That you, Doc?

(*Then* DOC *quietly walks in from kitchen. He is staggering
drunk, but he is managing for a few minutes to appear as
though he were perfectly sober and nothing had happened.
His steps, however, are not too sure and his eyes are like
blurred ink spots.* LOLA *is too frightened to talk. Her
mouth is gaping and she is breathless with fear*)

DOC Good morning, honey.

LOLA Doc! You all right?

DOC The morning paper here? I wanta see the morning paper.

LOLA Doc, we don't get a morning paper. *You* know that.

DOC Oh, then I suppose I'm drunk or something. That what you're trying to say?

LOLA No, Doc . . .

DOC Then give me the morning paper.

LOLA (*Scampering to get last night's paper from console table*) Sure, Doc. Here it is. Now just sit there and be quiet.

DOC (*Resistance rising*) Why shouldn't I be quiet?

LOLA Nothin', Doc . . .

DOC (*Has trouble unfolding paper. He places it before his face in order not to be seen. But he is too blind even to see*) Nothing, Doc. (*Mockingly*)

LOLA (*Cautiously, after a few minutes' silence*) Doc, are you all right?

DOC Of course, I'm all right. Why shouldn't I be all right?

LOLA Where you been?

DOC What's it your business where I been? I been to London to see the Queen. What do you think of that? (*Apparently she doesn't know what to think of it*) Just let me alone. That's all I ask. I'm all right.

LOLA (*Whimpering*) Doc, what made you do it? You said you'd be home last night . . . 'cause we were having company. Bruce was here and I had a big dinner fixed . . . and you never came. What was the matter, Doc?

DOC (*Mockingly*) We had a big dinner for *Bruce*.

LOLA Doc, it was for you, too.

DOC Well . . . I don't want it.

LOLA Don't get mad, Doc.

DOC (*Threateningly*) Where's Marie?

LOLA I don't know, Doc. She didn't come in last night. She was out with Bruce.

DOC (*Back to audience*) I suppose you tucked them in bed together and peeked through the keyhole and applauded.

LOLA (*Sickened*)   Doc, don't talk that way. Bruce is a nice boy. They're gonna get married.

DOC   He probably *has* to marry her, the poor bastard. Just 'cause she's pretty and he got amorous one day . . . Just like I had to marry *you*.

LOLA   Oh, Doc!

DOC   You and Marie are both a couple of sluts.

LOLA   Doc, please don't talk like that.

DOC   What are you good for? You can't even get up in the morning and cook my breakfast.

LOLA (*Mumbling*)   I will, Doc. I will after this.

DOC   You won't even sweep the floors, till some bozo comes along to make love to Marie, and then you fix things up like Buckingham Palace or a Chinese whorehouse with perfume on the lampbulbs, and flowers, and the gold-trimmed china *my mother* gave us. We're not going to use these any more. My mother didn't buy those dishes for whores to eat off of.
(*He jerks the cloth off the table, sending the dishes rattling to the floor*)

LOLA   Doc! Look what you done.

DOC   Look what I *did*, not *done*. I'm going to get me a drink.
(*Goes to kitchen*)

LOLA (*Follows to platform*)   Oh, no, Doc! You know what it does to you!

DOC   You're damn right I know what it does to me. It makes me willing to come home here and look at you, you two-ton old heifer. (*Takes a long swallow*) There! And pretty soon I'm going to have another, then another.

LOLA (*With dread*)   Oh, Doc! (LOLA *takes phone.* DOC *sees this, rushes for the butcher-knife from kitchen-cabinet drawer. Not finding it, he gets a hatchet from the back porch*) Mr. Anderson? Come quick, Mr. Anderson. He's back. He's *back!* He's got a hatchet!

DOC   God damn you! Get away from that telephone. (*He chases her into living room where she gets the couch between them*) That's right, phone! Tell the world I'm drunk. Tell the

whole damn world. Scream your head off, you fat slut. Holler
till all the neighbors think I'm beatin' hell outuv you. Where's
Bruce now—under Marie's bed? You got all fresh and pretty
for him, didn't you? Combed your hair for once—you even
washed the back of your neck and put on a girdle. You were
willing to harness all that fat into one bundle.

LOLA (*About to faint under the weight of the crushing accusations*) Doc, don't say any more . . . I'd rather you hit
me with an axe, Doc. . . . Honest I would. But I can't stand
to hear you talk like that.

DOC I oughta hack off all that fat, and then wait for Marie
and chop off those pretty ankles she's always dancing around
on . . . then start lookin' for Turk and fix him too.

LOLA Daddy, you're talking crazy!

DOC I'm making sense for the first time in my life. You
didn't know I knew about it, did you? But I saw him coming
outa there, I saw him. You knew about it all the time and
thought you were hidin' something . . .

LOLA Daddy, I didn't know anything about it at all. Honest,
Daddy.

DOC Then *you're* the one that's crazy, if you think I didn't
know. You were running a regular house, weren't you? It's
probably been going on for years, ever since we were married.
   (*He lunges for her. She breaks for kitchen. They struggle
   in front of sink*)

LOLA Doc, it's not so; it's not so. You gotta believe me,
Doc.

DOC You're lyin'. But none a that's gonna happen any more.
I'm gonna fix you now, once and for all. . . .

LOLA Doc . . . don't do that to me. (LOLA, *in a frenzy of
fear, clutches him around the neck holding arm with axe by
his side*) Remember, Doc. It's *me*, Lola! You said I was the
prettiest girl you ever saw. Remember, Doc! It's me! Lola!

DOC (*The memory has overpowered him. He collapses, slowly
mumbling*) Lola . . . my pretty Lola.
   (*He passes out on the floor.* LOLA *stands now, as though*

in a trance. Quietly MRS. COFFMAN *comes creeping in through the back way*)

MRS. COFFMAN (*Calling softly*) Mrs. Delaney! (LOLA *doesn't even hear.* MRS. COFFMAN *comes in*) Mrs. Delaney! Here you are, Lady. I heard screaming and I was frightened for you.

LOLA I . . . I'll be all right . . . some men are comin' pretty soon; everything'll be all right.

MRS. COFFMAN I'll stay until they get here.

LOLA (*Feeling a sudden need*) Would you . . . would you *please,* Mrs. Coffman?
(*Breaks into sobs*)

MRS. COFFMAN Of course, Lady. (*Regarding* DOC) The doctor got "sick" again?

LOLA (*Mumbling*) Some men . . . 'll be here pretty soon . . .

MRS. COFFMAN I'll try to straighten things up before they get here. . . .
(*She rights chair, hangs up telephone and picks up the axe, which she is holding when* ED ANDERSON *and* ELMO HUSTON *enter unannounced. They are experienced AA's. Neatly dressed businessmen approaching middle-age*)

ED Pardon us for walking right in, Mrs. Delaney, but I didn't want to waste a second. (*Kneels by* DOC)

LOLA (*Weakly*) It's all right. . . .
(*Both men observe* DOC *on the floor, and their expressions hold understanding mixed with a feeling of irony. There is even a slight smile of irony on* ED'S *face. They have developed the surgeon's objectivity*)

ED Where is the hatchet? (*To* ELMO *as though appraising* DOC'S *condition*) What do you think, Elmo?

ELMO We can't leave him here if he's gonna play around with hatchets.

ED Give me a hand, Elmo. We'll get him to sit up and then try to talk some sense into him. (*They struggle with the lumpy body,* DOC *grunting his resistance*) Come on, Doc, old

boy. It's Ed and Elmo. We're going to take care of you.
(*They seat him at table*)

DOC (*Through a thick fog*)   Lemme alone.

ED   Wake up. We're taking you away from here.

DOC   Lemme 'lone, God damn it.
    (*Falls forward, head on table*)

ELMO (*To* MRS. COFFMAN)   Is there any coffee?

MRS. COFFMAN   I think so, I'll see.
    (*Goes to stove with cup from drainboard. Lights fire un-
    der coffee and waits for it to get heated*)

ED   He's way beyond coffee.

ELMO   It'll help some. Get something hot into his stomach.

ED   If we could get him to eat. How 'bout some hot food,
Doc?
    (DOC *makes a hideous face*)

ELMO   City Hospital, Ed?

ED   I guess that's what it will have to be.

LOLA   Where you going to take him?
    (ELMO *goes to phone; speaks quietly to City Hospital*)

ED   Don't know. Wanta talk to him first.

MRS. COFFMAN (*Coming in with the coffee*)   Here's the
coffee.

ED (*Taking cup*)   Hold him, Elmo, while I make him swallow this.

ELMO   Come on, Doc, drink your coffee.
    (DOC *only blubbers*)

DOC (*After the coffee is down*)   Uh . . . what . . . what's
goin' on here?

ED   It's me, Doc. Your old friend Ed. I got Elmo with me.

DOC (*Twisting his face painfully*)   Get out, both of you.
Lemme 'lone.

ED (*With certainty*)   We're takin' you with us, Doc.

DOC   Hell you are. I'm all right. I just had a little slip. We all have slips. . . .

ED   Sometimes, Doc, but we gotta get over 'em.

DOC   I'll be O.K. Just gimme a day to sober up. I'll be as good as new.

ED   Remember the last time, Doc? You said you'd be all right in the morning and we found you with a broken collar bone. Come on.

DOC   Boys, I'll be all right. Now lemme alone.

ED   How much has he had, Mrs. Delaney?

LOLA   I don't know. He had a quart when he left here yesterday and he didn't get home till now.

ED   He's probably been through a *couple* of quarts. He's been dry for a long time. It's going to hit him pretty hard. Yah, he'll be a pretty sick man for a few days. (*Louder to* DOC, *as though he were talking to a deaf man*) Wanta go to the City Hospital, Doc?

DOC   (*This has a sobering effect on him. He looks about him furtively for possible escape*)   No . . . no, boys. Don't take me there. That's a torture chamber. No, Ed. You wouldn't do that to me.

ED   They'll sober you up.

DOC   Ed, I been there; I've seen the place. That's where they take the crazy people. You can't do that to me, Ed.

ED   Well, *you're* crazy aren't you? Goin' after your wife with a hatchet.
    (*They lift* DOC *to his feet.* DOC *looks with dismal pleading in his eyes at* LOLA, *who has her face in her hands*)

DOC   (*So plaintive, a sob in his voice*)   Honey! Honey!
    (*LOLA can't look at him. Now* DOC *tries to make a get-away, bolting blindly into the living room before the two men catch him and hold him in front of living-room table*)
Honey, don't let 'em take me there. They'll believe *you*. Tell 'em you won't *let* me take a drink.

LOLA   Isn't there any place else you could take him?

290 William Inge

ED Private sanitariums cost a lotta dough.

LOLA I got forty dollars in the kitchen.

ED That won't be near enough.

DOC I'll be at the meeting tomorrow night sober as you are now.

ED (*To* LOLA) All the king's horses couldn't keep him from takin' another drink now, Mrs. Delaney. He got himself into this; he's gotta sweat it out.

DOC I won't go to the City Hospital. That's where they take the crazy people.
   (*Stumbles into chair*)

ED (*Using all his patience now*) Look, Doc. Elmo and I are your friends. You know that. Now if you don't come along peacefully, we're going to call the cops and you'll have to wear off this jag in the cooler. How'd you like that? (DOC *is as though stunned*) The important thing is for you to get sober.

DOC I don't wanna go.

ED The City Hospital or the City Jail. Take your choice. We're not going to leave you here. Come on, Elmo.
   (*They grab hold of him*)

DOC (*Has collected himself and now given in*) O.K., boys. Gimme another drink and I'll go.

LOLA Oh, no, Doc.

ED Might as well humor him, ma'am. Another drink couldn't make much difference now.
   (MRS. COFFMAN *runs for bottle and glass in pantry and comes right back with them. She hands them to* LOLA)
O.K., Doc, we're goin' to give you a drink. Take a good one; it's gonna be your last for a long, long time to come.
   (ED *takes the bottle, removes the cork and gives* DOC *a glass of whiskey.* DOC *takes his fill, straight, coming up once or twice for air. Then* ED *takes the bottle from him and hands it to* LOLA. *To* LOLA)
They'll keep him three or four days, Mrs. Delaney; then he'll be home again, good as new. (*Modestly*) I . . . I don't

want to pry into personal affairs, ma'am . . . but he'll need you then, pretty bad . . . Come on, Doc. Let's go.

(ED *has a hold of* DOC's *coat sleeve trying to maneuver him. A faraway look is in* DOC's *eyes, a dazed look containing panic and fear. He gets to his feet*)

DOC (*Struggling to sound reasonable*) Just a minute, boys . . .

ED What's the matter?

DOC I . . . I wanta glass of water.

ED You'll get a glass of water later. Come on.

DOC (*Beginning to twist a little in* ED's *grasp*) . . . a glass of water . . . that's all . . .

(*One furious, quick twist of his body and he eludes* ED)

ED Quick, Elmo.

(ELMO *acts fast and they get* DOC *before he gets away. Then* DOC *struggles with all his might, kicking and screaming like a pampered child,* ED *and* ELMO *holding him tightly to usher him out*)

DOC (*As he is led out*) Don't let 'em take me there. Don't take me there. Stop them, somebody. Stop them. That's where they take the crazy people. Oh, God, stop them, somebody. Stop them.

(LOLA *looks on blankly while* ED *and* ELMO *depart with* DOC. *Now there are several moments of deep silence*)

MRS. COFFMAN (*Clears up. Very softly*) Is there anything more I can do for you now, Mrs. Delaney?

LOLA I guess not.

MRS. COFFMAN (*Puts a hand on* LOLA's *shoulder*) Get busy, Lady. Get busy and forget it.

LOLA Yes . . . I'll get busy right away. Thanks, Mrs. Coffman.

MRS. COFFMAN I better go. I've got to make breakfast for the children. If you want me for anything, let me know.

LOLA Yes . . . yes . . . good-bye, Mrs. Coffman.

(MRS. COFFMAN *exits.* LOLA *is too exhausted to move from*

*the big chair. At first she can't even cry; then the tears
come slowly, softly. In a few moments* BRUCE *and* MARIE
enter, bright and merry. LOLA *turns her head slightly to
regard them as creatures from another planet)*

MARIE (*Springing into room.* BRUCE *follows*) Congratulate
me, Mrs. Delaney.

LOLA Huh?

MARIE We're going to be married.

LOLA Married? (*It barely registers*)

MARIE (*Showing ring*) Here it is. My engagement ring.
(MARIE *and* BRUCE *are too engrossed in their own happiness to notice* LOLA'S *stupor*)

LOLA That's lovely . . . lovely.

MARIE We've had the most wonderful time. We danced all
night and then drove out to the lake and saw the sun rise.

LOLA That's nice.

MARIE We've made all our plans. I'm quitting school and
flying back to Cincinnati with Bruce this afternoon. His
mother has invited me to visit them before I go home. Isn't
that wonderful?

LOLA Yes . . . yes, indeed.

MARIE Going to miss me?

LOLA Yes, of course, Marie. We'll miss you very much . . .
uh . . . congratulations.

MARIE Thanks, Mrs. Delaney. (*Goes to bedroom door*)
Come on, Bruce, help me get my stuff. (*To* LOLA) Mrs.
Delaney, would you throw everything into a big box and
send it to me at home? We haven't had breakfast yet. We're
going down to the hotel and celebrate.

BRUCE I'm sorry we're in such a hurry, but we've got a taxi
waiting.
    (*They go into* MARIE'S *room*)

LOLA (*Goes to telephone, dials*) Long-distance? I want to
talk to Green Valley 223. Yes. This is Delmar 1887.
    (*She hangs up.* MARIE *comes from bedroom, followed by*
BRUCE, *who carries suitcase*)

MARIE   Mrs. Delaney, I sure hate to say good-bye to you. You've been so wonderful to me. But Bruce says I can come and visit you once in a while, didn't you, Bruce?

BRUCE   Sure thing.

LOLA   You're going?

MARIE   We're going downtown and have our breakfast, then do a little shopping and catch our plane. And thanks for everything, Mrs. Delaney.

BRUCE   It was very nice of you to have us to dinner.

LOLA   Dinner? Oh, don't mention it.

MARIE   (*To* LOLA)   There isn't much time for good-bye now, but I just want you to know Bruce and I wish you the best of everything. You and Doc both. Tell Doc good-bye for me, will you, and remember I think you're both a coupla peaches.

BRUCE   Hurry, honey.

MARIE   'Bye, Mrs. Delaney! (*She goes out*)

BRUCE   'Bye, Mrs. Delaney. Thanks for being nice to my girl.
    (*They make a hurried exit*)

LOLA   (LOLA *stands a moment in the doorway, automatically waving farewell. Then the telephone rings and she makes a rush to answer it*)   Hello. Hello, Mom. It's Lola, Mom. How are you? Mom, Doc's sick again. Do you think Dad would let me come home for a while? I'm awfully unhappy, Mom. Do you think . . . just till I made up my mind? . . . All right. No, I guess it wouldn't do any good for you to come here . . . I . . . I'll let you know what I decide to do. That's all, Mom. Thanks. Tell Daddy hello.
    (*She hangs up and doesn't move, but sits looking emptily before her*)

                                                        CURTAIN

SCENE IV

It is morning, a week later. The house is neat again. LOLA *is dusting in the living room as* MRS. COFFMAN *enters.*

MRS. COFFMAN   Mrs. Delaney! Good morning, Mrs. Delaney.

LOLA   Come in, Mrs. Coffman.

MRS. COFFMAN   (*Coming in*)   It's a fine day for the games.
I've got a box lunch ready, and I'm taking all the kids to the
Stadium. My boy's got a ticket for you, too. You better get
dressed and come with us.

LOLA   Thanks, Mrs. Coffman, but I've got work to do.

MRS. COFFMAN   But it's a big day. The Spring Relays . . .
All the athletes from the colleges are supposed to be there.

LOLA   Oh, yes. You know that boy, Turk, who used to come
here to see Marie—he's one of the big stars.

MRS. COFFMAN   Is that so? Come on . . . do. We've got a
ticket for you. . . .

LOLA   Oh, no, I have to stay here and clean up the house.
Doc may be coming home today. I talked to him on the
phone. He wasn't sure what time they'd let him out, but I
wanta have the place all nice for him.

MRS. COFFMAN   Well, I'll tell you all about it when I come
home. Everybody and his brother will be there.

LOLA   Have a good time.

MRS. COFFMAN   'Bye, Mrs. Delaney.

LOLA   'Bye.
   (MRS. COFFMAN *leaves, and* LOLA *goes into kitchen. The*
   MAILMAN *comes onto porch and leaves a letter, but* LOLA
   doesn't even know he's there. Then the MILKMAN *knocks*
   on the kitchen door)

LOLA   Come in.

MILKMAN   (*Entering with armful of bottles, etc.*)   I see you
checked the list, lady. You've got a lot of extras.

LOLA   Ya— I think my husband's coming home.

MILKMAN   (*He puts the supplies on table, then pulls out magazine*)   Remember, I told you my picture was going to ap-

pear in *Strength and Health.* (*Showing her magazine*) Well, see that pile of muscles? That's me.

LOLA   My goodness. You got your picture in a magazine.

MILKMAN   Yes, ma'am. See what it says about my chest development? For the greatest self-improvement in a three months' period.

LOLA   Goodness sakes. You'll be famous, won't you?

MILKMAN   If I keep busy on these bar-bells. I'm working now for "muscular separation."

LOLA   That's nice.

MILKMAN   (*Cheerily*) Well, good day, ma'am.

LOLA   You forgot your magazine.

MILKMAN   That's for you.
(*Exits.* LOLA *puts away the supplies in the icebox. Then* DOC *comes in the front door, carrying the little suitcase she previously packed for him. His quiet manner and his serious demeanor are the same as before.* LOLA *is shocked by his sudden appearance*)

LOLA   Docky!
(*Without thinking she assumes an attitude of fear.* DOC *observes this and it obviously pains him*)

DOC   Good morning, honey.
(*Pause*)

LOLA   Are . . . are you all right, Doc?

DOC   Yes, I'm all right. (*An awkward pause. Then* DOC *tries to reassure her*) Honest, I'm all right, honey. Please don't stand there like that . . . like I was gonna . . . gonna . . .

LOLA   (*Tries to relax*)   I'm sorry, Doc.

DOC   How you been?

LOLA   Oh, I been all right, Doc. Fine.

DOC   Any news?

LOLA   I told you about Marie—over the phone.

DOC   Yah.

LOLA   He was a very nice boy, Doc. Very nice.

DOC   That's good. I hope they'll be happy.

LOLA   (*Trying to sound bright*)   She said . . . maybe she'd
come back and visit us some time. That's what she *said*.

DOC   She . . . seemed like such a sweet young girl.

LOLA   Honest, Doc, I didn't know what she and Turk were
up to, all that time. I knew they spooned a lot, and I might
have guessed at other things, but I didn't know.

DOC   I know you didn't, honey.

LOLA   I guess . . . I've always thought that . . . you and I
were the only people . . . in all the world . . . that ever
did anything wrong.

DOC   (*Takes her hand consolingly*)   Now, now. Now, now.
Let's forget it, shall we? (*He looks around the room con-
tentedly*) It's *good* to be home.

LOLA   Is it, Daddy?

DOC   Yah.
   (*Beginning to choke up, just a little*)

LOLA   Did everything go all right . . . I mean . . . did
they treat you well and . . .

DOC   (*Now loses control of his feelings. Tears in his eyes, he
all but lunges at her, gripping her arms, drilling his head into
her bosom*)   Honey, don't ever leave me. *Please* don't ever
leave me. If you do, they'd have to keep me down at that
place all the time. I don't know what I said to you or what I
did, I can't remember hardly anything. But please forgive
me . . . please . . . please . . . And I'll try to make everything up.

LOLA   (*There is surprise on her face and new contentment.
She becomes almost angelic in demeanor. Tenderly she places
a soft hand on his head*)   Daddy! Why, of course I'll never
leave you. (*A smile of satisfaction*) You're all I've got
You're all I ever had. (*Very tenderly he kisses her*)

DOC (*Collecting himself now.* LOLA *sits besides* DOC) I . . . I feel better . . . already.

LOLA (*Almost gay*) So do I. Have you had your breakfast?

DOC No. The food there was terrible. When they told me I could go this morning, I decided to wait and fix myself breakfast here.

LOLA (*Happily*) Come on out in the kitchen and I'll get you a nice, big breakfast. I'll scramble some eggs and . . . You see I've got the place all cleaned up just the way you like it. (DOC *goes to kitchen*) Now you sit down here and I'll get your fruit juice. (*He sits and she gets fruit juice from refrigerator*) I've got bacon this morning, too. My, it's expensive now. And I'll light the oven and make you some toast, and here's some orange marmalade, and . . .

DOC (*With a new feeling of control*) Fruit juice. I'll need lots of fruit juice for a while. The doctor said it would restore the vitamins. You see, that damn whiskey kills all the vitamins in your system, eats up all the sugar in your kidneys. They came around every morning and shot vitamins in my arm. Oh, it didn't hurt. And the doctor told me to drink a quart of fruit juice every day. And you better get some candy bars for me at the grocery this morning. Doctor said to eat lots of candy, try to replace the sugar.

LOLA I'll do that, Doc. Here's another glass of grapefruit juice now. I'll get some candy bars first thing.

DOC The doctor said I should have a hobby. Said I should go out more. That's all that's wrong with me. I thought maybe I'd go hunting once in a while.

LOLA Yes, Doc. And bring home lots of good things to eat.

DOC I'll get a big bird dog, too. Would you like a sad-looking old bird dog around the house?

LOLA Of course, I would. (*All her life and energy have been restored*) You know what, Doc? I had another dream last night.

DOC About Little Sheba?

LOLA Oh, it was about everyone and everything. (*In a rap-
tured tone. She gets bacon from icebox and starts to cook it*)
Marie and I were going to the Olympics back in our old high
school stadium. There were thousands of people there. There
was Turk out in the center of the field throwing the javelin.
Every time he threw it, the crowd would roar . . . and you
know who the man in charge was? It was my father. Isn't
that funny? . . . But Turk kept changing into someone else
all the time. And then my father disqualified him. So he had
to sit on the sidelines . . . and guess who took his place,
Daddy? You! You came trotting out there on the field just
as big as you please . . .

DOC (*Smilingly*) How did I do, Baby?

LOLA Fine. You picked the javelin up real careful, like it
was awful heavy. But you threw it, Daddy, clear, *clear* up
into the sky. And it never came down again. (DOC *looks very
pleased with himself.* LOLA *goes on*) Then it started to rain.
And I couldn't find Little Sheba. I almost went crazy looking
for her and there were so many people, I didn't even know
where to look. And you were waiting to take me home. And
we walked and walked through the slush and mud, and people were hurrying all around us and . . . and . . . (*Leaves
stove and sits. Sentimental tears come to her eyes*) But this
part is sad, Daddy. All of a sudden I saw Little Sheba . . .
she was lying in the middle of the field . . . dead. . . . It
made me cry, Doc. No one paid any attention . . . I cried
and cried. It made me feel so bad, Doc. That sweet little
puppy . . . her curly white fur all smeared with mud, and
no one to stop and take care of her . . .

DOC Why couldn't *you?*

LOLA I wanted to, but you wouldn't let me. You kept saying, "We can't stay here, honey; we gotta go on. We gotta
go on." (*Pause*) Now, isn't that strange?

DOC Dreams are funny.

LOLA I don't think Little Sheba's ever coming back, Doc
I'm not going to call her any more.

DOC Not much point in it, Baby. I guess she's gone for
good.

LOLA   I'll fix your eggs.

(She gets up, embraces DOC, *and goes to stove.* DOC *remains at table sipping his fruit juice. The curtain comes slowly down)*

The
Seven Year
Itch

A Romantic Comedy

by **GEORGE AXELROD**

FOR *Gloria and Peter
and Steven*

THE SEVEN YEAR ITCH

was first presented by Courtney Burr and Elliott Nugent at the Fulton Theatre on the evening of November 20, 1952, with the following cast:

RICHARD SHERMAN	Tom Ewell
RICKY	Johnny Klein
HELEN SHERMAN	Neva Patterson
MISS MORRIS	Marilyn Clark
ELAINE	Joan Donovan
MARIE WHATEVER-HER-NAME-WAS	Irene Moore
THE GIRL	Vanessa Brown
DR. BRUBAKER	Robert Emhardt
TOM MACKENZIE	George Keane
RICHARD'S VOICE	George Ives
THE GIRL'S VOICE	Pat Fowler

Directed by John Gerstad

Set and Lighting by Frederick Fox

Music composed and arranged by Dana Suesse

Production under the supervision of Elliott Nugent

SCENES

Act One

SCENE I About eight o'clock on a summer evening.

SCENE II Immediately following.

Act Two

SCENE I Evening, the following day.

SCENE II Two hours later.

Act Three

The following morning

The action of the play takes place in the apartment of
the Richard Shermans, in the Gramercy Park section of
New York City.
The time is the present.

Act
One

SCENE I

The apartment of the RICHARD SHERMANS, *about half a block from Gramercy Park in New York City.*

We see the foyer, the living room and the back terrace of a four-room apartment—the parlor floor through—in a remodeled private house.

A flight of stairs on the back wall lead to the ceiling where they stop. In one of the earlier phases of remodeling, this apartment and the one above it were a duplex. But now they are rented separately and the ceiling is boarded up.

A door, also on the back wall, leads to the kitchen. French doors, right, open onto the terrace. The terrace, while it increases the rent about thirty dollars a month, is small and rather uninviting. It looks out into the back court and because of the buildings around it you get the feeling of being at the bottom of a well. From the terrace we see some of the skyline of the city and a good deal of the backs of the buildings across the court. On the terrace there is a chaise, a table and a few shrubs.

On the left wall of the living room are high, sliding doors which lead to the bedrooms and bath. There is a fireplace in the living room. The whole apartment has a summer look. The rugs are up and the summer slip covers are on the furniture. The living room contains a piano, bookshelves, a large radio phonograph and a liquor cabinet.

When the curtain rises it is about eight o'clock on an evening in July. It is a hot, airless night. It is not yet completely dark. It grows darker gradually through the scene.

RICHARD SHERMAN, *a young-looking man of thirty-eight, is lying on the chaise on the terrace. He wears a shirt, gabardine pants, loafers and no socks.*

It is hard to know what to say about RICHARD. *He has a crew haircut. He has a good job. He's vice-president in charge of sales at a twenty-five-cent publishing house. He made eighteen thousand dollars last year. He buys his clothes at Brooks.*

At the moment, he has moved a small, portable radio out to the table on the terrace and is listening to the first game of a twi-night double header between Brooklyn and Boston. He is listening to the game and drinking unenthusiastically from a bottle of Seven-Up.

At rise we hear the ball game softly on the radio. We have come in at a rather tense moment. The bases are loaded and Hodges is up. He bunts and is thrown out. RICHARD *is disgusted. He snaps off the radio.*

RICHARD (*Rising*)   Bunt? Two runs behind, the bases loaded and they send Hodges up to bunt!

(*Shaking his head, he goes into the kitchen. He reappears carrying a bottle of raspberry soda. Still appalled*)

Bunt, for God's sake! Well, what are you going to do?

(*He looks around aimlessly for a moment*)

I'm hungry. Well, that's what comes of having dinner at Schrafft's! Schrafft's! I wanted to have dinner in the saloon across the street—but you can't have dinner in a saloon and then not . . . They don't like it. Oh, I suppose I could have ordered a drink and then not drunk it. . . . But I figure it's easier just to eat at Schrafft's.

(*He drops wearily onto the chaise*)

It's hard on a man when the family goes away. It's peaceful, though, with everybody gone. It's sure as hell peaceful.

(*He settles back in the chaise and grins. Music sneaks in very softly, and the light on him dims to a spot*)

Ricky was really upset this morning when they left for the station. It was very flattering. I thought the kid was going to cry. . . .

(*He sits, smiling, remembering the scene. Dream lighting by the front door picks up* HELEN *and* RICKY *leaving*)

RICKY   But what about Daddy? Isn't Daddy coming with us?

HELEN   Daddy'll come up Friday night.

RICKY   But, Mommy, why can't Daddy come up with us now?

HELEN   Poor Daddy has to stay in the hot city and make money. We're going to spend the whole summer at the beach but poor Daddy can only come up week ends.

RICKY   Poor Daddy . . .

HELEN   Daddy is going to work very hard. He's going to eat properly and not smoke like Dr. Murphy told him and he's going to stay on the wagon for a while like Dr. Summers told him, to take care of his nervous indigestion. . . .
   (*In the spot,* RICHARD *drinks from the bottle of raspberry soda. He is somewhat awed by the taste. He looks curiously at the label and then reads it*)

RICHARD   "Contains carbonated water, citric acid, corn syrup, artificial raspberry flavoring, pure vegetable colors and preservative." Since I've been on the wagon, I've had one continuous upset stomach.
   (*He looks sadly at the bottle and drinks some more*)

HELEN   And just to make sure Daddy's all right, Mommy is going to call Daddy at ten o'clock tonight. . . .

RICKY   Poor Daddy . . .
   (*The music fades and so does the dream light by the door.* HELEN *and* RICKY *disappear. The lighting returns to normal*)

RICHARD (*Coming out of his reverie*)   Ten o'clock! I don't even know how I'm going to stay awake till ten o'clock!
   (*He stares moodily off into the growing dusk. Suddenly he notices something in an apartment across the court. He is momentarily fascinated and rises for a better look*)
Hey, lady! I know it's a hot night but . . . You sit out on this terrace, it's like having a television set with about thirty channels all going at once. . . . Don't give me any dirty look, lady. I pay rent for this terrace. If you don't like it, pull your blind down! (*As she apparently does so*) Oh. Well, that's life.

(He yawns. Restlessly, he rises and wanders into the living room. He yawns again and then, suddenly, in mid-yawn, something occurs to him)

Helen has a lot of nerve calling me at ten o'clock. It shows a very definite lack of trust.

What's she think I'm going to do? Start smoking the minute she turns her back? Start drinking? Maybe she thinks I'm going to have girls up here!

You know, that's a hell of a thing!

Seven years, we've been married. And not once have I done anything like that. Not *once!* And don't think I couldn't have, either. Because I could have. But plenty . . .

(Music sneaks in and in dream lighting we see HELEN seated on the couch knitting. She laughs)

Don't laugh. There're plenty of women who think I'm *pretty* attractive, for your information!

HELEN   For instance, who?

RICHARD *(Indignant)*   What do you mean, for instance, who? There've been plenty of them, that's all.

HELEN   Name one.

(There is a considerable pause while he thinks about this)

Go ahead. Just one.

RICHARD   It's hard, I mean just offhand. There're plenty of them, though.

(HELEN laughs. RICHARD is stung)

Well, there's Miss Morris, for instance. She's practically thrown herself at me. You should see the way she gives me the business every time she comes into my office. . . .

(MISS MORRIS, a sexy-looking blonde in a backless summer blouse and a skirt with an exaggerated slit, drifts into the scene carrying a dictation pad and pencil)

She wears those backless things and she's always telling me it's so hot she's not wearing any underwear. . . .

HELEN   It sounds perfectly sordid. Does she sit on your lap when she takes dictation?

RICHARD   Of course not!

(MISS MORRIS sits on his lap)

MISS MORRIS   Good morning, Mr. Sherman.

RICHARD Good morning, Miss Morris.

(MISS MORRIS *runs her fingers through his hair and covers his cheek and neck with little kisses*)

That will be all.

(MISS MORRIS *gets up and drifts away, giving him a private wave and a wink*)

I just happened to bring her up as an example, that's all. Just an example . . .

HELEN I'm quite sure you're a great success with the stenographers in your office.

RICHARD I could be a great success with a couple of your high-class friends if you're going to get snooty about it. Elaine, for instance. You may not know this, but for *two years* that dame has been trying to get me into the sack. . . .

(ELAINE, *a luscious-looking dame in a gold-lamé evening gown, appears on the terrace. She is carrying a glass of champagne*)

The night of your birthday party, she got loaded and went after me right here on the terrace. . . .

(*Dream lighting on* HELEN *dims out*)

ELAINE (*Coming up behind him and draping her arms around his neck*) Do you know something, darling? I look at you and I just melt. You must know that. Men always know . . .

(*Quite casually she tosses her champagne glass off the terrace and grabs him and kisses him violently*)

RICHARD What's the matter? Are you crazy or something?

ELAINE Let's get out of here, darling. Come on. Nobody'll even know we're gone. . . .

RICHARD You don't know what you're saying!

ELAINE Oh, yes, I do! Come on, darling! Let's be a little mad!

(*She drifts away, giving him the eye as she goes*)

RICHARD Now, Elaine may be a little mad, but she's plenty attractive! And *she's* not the only one either! You probably don't even remember that Marie whatever-her-name-was, from the UN who was staying with the Petersons in Westport last summer. . . .

We went swimming together one night. Without any bathing

suits. You didn't know that, did you? It was that Saturday
night the MacKenzies came up and I drove over to the beach
by myself . . .

(MARIE WHATEVER-HER-NAME-WAS *has materialized beside
him. A gorgeous girl in shorts and man's shirt*)

MARIE (*Speaking in rapid but somehow sexy-sounding
French*)   Hello, Dick. You too, without doubt, like to swim
at night. I like it because the wearing of a bathing suit is
unnecessary. . . .
(*She kicks off her shorts and as she talks begins to unbut-
ton her shirt*)

RICHARD   I don't speak very good French, but I knew what
she was talking about.

MARIE   The water at night is magnificent. There is a warm-
ness and a feeling of black velvet. Especially when one is
without bathing costume . . .

RICHARD (*Weakly, unable to take his eyes off the buttons*)
Mais oui. Mais oui.

MARIE   Voilà! Let us go!
(*Her shirt is almost off. The lights dim out just in time*)

RICHARD (*With great self-righteousness*)   We didn't do anything but swim. As a matter of fact, she was plenty disappointed we didn't do anything but swim.
(*The lights have dimmed back to normal*)
So, all I can say is, in the light of the circumstances, I resent
your calling me at ten o'clock to check up on me. If Helen
is going to start worrying about me after seven years, it's
pretty ridiculous, that's all.
(*He rises and begins to pace nervously*)
And she is worried too. Even if she doesn't show it. I don't
know. She probably figures she isn't as young as she used to
be. She's thirty-one years old. One of these days she's going
to wake up and find her looks are gone. Then where will she
be? No wonder she's worried.
Especially since I don't look a bit different than I did when
I was twenty-eight.
It's not my fault I don't. It's just a simple biological fact.
Women age quicker than men. I probably won't look any

different when I'm sixty. I have that kind of a face. Everybody'll think she's my mother.

(*He sighs a mournful sigh and sinks into chair. The downstairs door buzzer rings*)

Now who's that? (*He goes to the foyer and presses the wall
button. Then he opens the front door and peers out calling*)
Hello? Hello? Who is it?

GIRL'S VOICE (*Off stage*)   I'm terribly sorry to bother
you . . .

RICHARD   What?
   (*Then as he sees her, he reacts*)
Oh. Oh. Well, hello . . .

GIRL'S VOICE (*Off stage*)   I feel so silly. I forgot my key. I
locked myself out. So I pressed your bell. I hope you don't
mind.

RICHARD   No. No. I don't mind. No trouble at all.

GIRL'S VOICE (*Off stage*)   I'm awfully sorry.

RICHARD   Don't worry about it. Any time. It's a pleasure.

GIRL'S VOICE (*Off stage*)   Thank you. Well, good-bye . . .

RICHARD   Good-bye . . .
   (*He closes the door. Then, after a moment opens it again
   and peers out, craning his neck to see up the stairs. He
   comes back inside, closes the door. He is shaking his head*)

RICHARD   Where did *that* come from? I didn't know they
made them like that any more. Oh, she must be the one who
sublet the Kaufmans' apartment. I should have asked her in
for a drink. Oh, no, I shouldn't have. Not me, kid.
   (*The telephone rings.* RICHARD *glances at his watch. Then
   hurries to answer it*)
Hello? Oh. Hello, Helen. I wasn't expecting you to call
till ten. Is everything okay? . . . Good. . . . I was just sitting here listening to the ball game. They're two runs behind
and they send Hodges up to bunt. . . . Yeah, I'm sleepy too.
. . . The old place is pretty empty without you. I can't wait
till Friday. Ricky okay? . . . He did? Well, he hasn't done
that for a long time. It was probably just the excitement. . . .

That's nice. No, I don't. . . . Who did you meet at the A&P?

What's Tom MacKenzie doing up there? . . . Look, my advice to you is avoid Tom MacKenzie like the plague. If you keep meeting him at the A&P, switch to Bohack's!

Look, are you sure everything else is all right? Good. . . . Me too. Yeah, I'm pretty tired myself. Good night. . . . Night.

(*He hangs up phone*)

Well, I might as well go to sleep myself. But I'm not sleepy. I suddenly realize I am not even a little bit sleepy. Maybe I could call up Charlie Peterson. No. That's a real bad idea. Under no circumstances should I call up Charlie Peterson. I'll get in bed and read. God knows I've got enough stuff here I'm supposed to read.

(*Picks up brief case and begins to take out manuscripts*) I've got a conference with Dr. Brubaker tomorrow night. It might be amusing if I'd finished his miserable book before I talk to him about it. I don't know why every psychiatrist in America feels he has to write a book. And let's see what else. *The Scarlet Letter.* I read that in school. I don't have to read that again. But I'd better. Dr. Brubaker and *The Scarlet Letter.* It looks like a big night. (*Picks up soda bottle, notices that it is empty*) Well, one more of these for a night cap and we're all set. . . .

(*Sighing heavily, he goes to kitchen for a fresh bottle of soda. He walks back out to the terrace and sits for a moment on the chaise. Automatically, he switches on the radio*)

RADIO VOICE . . . and so as we go into the last half of the eighth inning, Boston is leading, seven to four. In the last of the eighth, for Brooklyn, it'll be Robinson, Hodges and Furillo . . .

(RICHARD *reaches over and snaps off the radio*)

RICHARD   Frankly, I don't give a damn.

(*He rises and walks to the edge of the terrace, looking hopefully toward the apartment across the court*)

(*At that moment there is a violent crash. Apparently from the sky, an enormous iron pot with a plant in it comes plummeting down. It lands with a sickening thud on the chaise where he was sitting a moment before*)

(RICHARD *looks at it in horror-struck silence for a moment or two*)

RICHARD   Look at that damn thing! Right where I was sitting! I could have been killed, for God's sake!

(*Cautiously, with a nervous glance upward, he leans over to examine it*)

Jes-sus!

(*He darts back inside, looks wildly around for a cigarette, finally finds a crumbled pack in the pocket of a raincoat hanging in the hall closet. He starts to light it. Then, stops himself*)

I forgot—I'm not smoking. Oh, the hell with *that!*

(*He lights the cigarette*)

I could have been killed. Just then. Like that. Right now I could be lying out there on the lousy terrace dead. I should stop smoking because twenty years from now it might affect my goddamn lungs!

(*He inhales deeply with great enjoyment*)

Oh, that tastes beautiful. The first one in six weeks.

(*He lets the smoke out slowly*)

All those lovely injurious tars and resins!

(*Suddenly he is dizzy*)

I'm dizzy. . . .

(*He sinks to the piano bench, coughing*)

Another week of not smoking and I'd really've been dead!

(*He picks up the bottle of soda and starts to take a slug of that. He chokes on it*)

The hell with this stuff too!

(*He goes quickly to liquor cabinet and pours an inch or two of whiskey into a glass and belts it down. Then he mixes another one and carries it onto the terrace. He sets the drink on the table and in a very gingerly fashion tries to pick up the pot. It is real heavy*)

My God! This thing weighs a ton! I could have been killed!

(*Suddenly, his anger finds a direction*)

Hey, up there! What's the big idea! You want to kill somebody or something? What do you think you're doing anyway?

GIRL'S VOICE (*From terrace above*)   What's the matter?

RICHARD (*Yelling*)   What's the matter? This goddam cast-iron chamber pot damn near killed me, that's what's the matter. What the hell! . . . Oh. Oh. It's you. Hello.

GIRL'S VOICE   What hap——Oh, golly! The tomato plant fell over!

RICHARD   It sure did.

GIRL'S VOICE   I'm terribly sorry.

RICHARD   That's okay.

GIRL'S VOICE   I seem to be giving you a terrible time tonight. First the door and now this. I don't know what to do. . . .

RICHARD   Don't worry about it. (*He drains drink*) Hey, up there!

GIRL'S VOICE   Yes?

RICHARD   I'll tell you what you can do about it. You can come down and have a drink.

GIRL'S VOICE   But that doesn't seem . . .

RICHARD   Sure it seems . . . Come on now . . . I insist . . .

GIRL'S VOICE   Well, all right . . .

RICHARD   I'll see you in a minute.

GIRL'S VOICE   All right. I'm really terribly sorry. . . .

RICHARD   That's okay. Don't worry about it. As a matter of fact, it's wonderful. See you in a minute . . .

GIRL'S VOICE   All right . . .
    (RICHARD *gallops frantically into the living room. The sound of the telephone brings him up short. He goes quickly to phone and answers it*)

RICHARD   Hi there! Oh. Oh, Helen!
    (*With great, if somewhat forced enthusiasm*)
Well, Helen! This *is* a surprise! And a very pleasant one if I may so! How *are you?*
Sure, sure I'm all right. Why shouldn't I be all right? In what way do I sound funny? I was just out on the terrace listening to the ball game. They're two runs behind and they send Hodges up to bunt. . . . What? Sure . . . Sure I will. Your yellow skirt . . .
    (*As she talks on the other end of the phone he is reaching around straightening up the room*)

Yes, of course I'm listening to you. You want me to send
up your yellow skirt, because you're having Tom MacKenzie
and some people over for cocktails. Good old Tom! How is
he?
No. I haven't been drinking. I just had . . . What? Your
yellow skirt. In the hall closet. On a wire hanger. Sure. By
parcel post. The first thing in the morning. Without fail.
No. I don't feel a bit funny. I was just out on the terrace
listening to the ball game. They're two runs behind and they
send Hodges up . . . Yes . . . well, good night. Good
night. Night.

> (*He hangs up phone. Then, galvanized into action, he
> starts to straighten up the place. In the middle of this he
> realizes he looks a little sloppy himself and he dashes off
> through the bedroom doors. Music swells and the lights
> dim out*)

CURTAIN

SCENE II

> *The music continues through the blackout.*
>
> *After a moment the curtain rises and the lights dim
> back up to normal.*
>
> RICHARD *reappears from the bedroom. He has put
> on the jacket to his pants and is frantically tying his
> tie.*
>
> *He is visibly agitated. He starts to arrange the room
> for his guest. He pauses and turns off a lamp. Catches
> himself and quickly turns it back on again.*

RICHARD   What am I *doing* anyway!
This is absolutely ridiculous. The first night Helen leaves
and I'm bringing dames into the apartment.
Now take it easy. The girl upstairs damn near kills me with
a cast-iron bucket. So I ask her down for a drink. What's
wrong with that?
If Helen was here, she'd do the same thing. It's only polite.
And what the hell is she doing asking Tom MacKenzie over
for cocktails, for God's sake!
Besides, I want to get another look at that girl. She must
be some kind of a model or actress or something.

(He is busily arranging things. Laying out ice and soda. Puffing cushions. Picking up his socks)

There is absolutely nothing wrong with asking a neighbor down for a drink. Nothing.

I just hope *she* doesn't get the wrong idea, that's all. If this dame thinks she's coming down here for some kind of a big time or something—well, she's got a big surprise. One drink and out! That's all! I'm a happily married man, for God's sake!

(He surveys his work)

Maybe we ought to have a little soft music, just for atmosphere.

(He goes to phonograph and starts looking through records)

Let's see. How about the Second Piano Concerto? Maybe Rachmaninoff would be overdoing it a little. This kid is probably more for old show tunes. . . .

(He finds a record: "Just One of Those Things"—it is obviously an old one with a real thirties orchestration. He puts it on and listens to it for a moment or two with great satisfaction)

That's more like it. The old nostalgia. Never misses. . . . *Never misses? What am I trying to do?* I'll call her and tell her not to come. That's all. Why ask for trouble?

(He starts for phone—stops)

I don't even know her phone number. I don't even know her name. What am I doing? And what the hell is she doing? She could have been down here, had her lousy drink, and gone home already!

She's probably getting all fixed up. She'll probably be wearing some kind of a damn evening dress!

Oh, my God! What have I done?

(Very quickly he has another drink)

If anything happens, it happens. That's all. It's up to her. She looked kind of sophisticated. She must know what she's doing.

I'm pretty sophisticated myself. At least I used to be. I've been married so damn long I don't remember.

(Suddenly, he becomes very polished)

Drink?

Thanks.

(*He pours himself a drink*)

Soda?

A dash.

(*He toasts*)

Cheers.

(*He leans nonchalantly against the piano. The "real" lighting begins to dim and music: "Just One of Those Things" fades in. The front door lights up and swings majestically open flooding the room with "dream light." He moves toward the door, almost dancing. In this particular flight of fancy he is very suave, very Noel Coward*)

(*The GIRL is standing in the doorway. She is an extraordinarily beautiful girl in her early twenties. She wears an extravagantly glamorous evening gown. There is a wise, half-mocking, half-enticing smile on her face. She looks like nothing so much as a Tabu perfume ad*)

THE GIRL I came.

RICHARD I'm so glad.

THE GIRL Didn't you know I'd come?

RICHARD Of course. Of course I knew. Won't you come in?

THE GIRL Thank you.

(*She comes in. The door swings closed behind her*)

(RICHARD *turns and we suddenly notice that he is wearing a black patch over one eye*)

RICHARD How lovely you are! Tell me, who are you? What is your name?

THE GIRL Does it matter?

RICHARD No. Of course not. I was a boor to ask.

THE GIRL Why have you invited me here?

RICHARD (*Spoken—like dialogue*) Oh, it was just one of those things. Just one of those foolish things. A trip to the moon—on gossamer wings . . .

THE GIRL How sweet! Oh—a Steinway. Do you play?

RICHARD (*Somewhat wistfully. Thinking, perhaps, of other, happier days*) Just a little now—for myself . . .

THE GIRL   Play something for me. . . .

RICHARD   All right. You'll be sorry you asked. . . .

THE GIRL   I'm sure I'll not . . .

RICHARD (*Sitting at piano*)   You'll see . . .
  (*Very dramatically he prepares to play. His preparations,
  while vastly complicated, do not, however, include raising
  the lid from the keys. Finally he begins to play—or rather
  pantomime playing on the closed lid. We hear, however, the
  opening bars of the C Sharp Minor Prelude played brilliantly*)

RICHARD (*Playing*)   I'm afraid I'm a little rusty.
  (*She is overcome. She sinks to the piano bench beside
  him. He turns to her*)
Tell me, what would you think, if, quite suddenly, I were to
seize you in my arms and cover your neck with kisses?

THE GIRL   I would think: What a mad impetuous fool he is!

RICHARD   And if I merely continued to sit here, mooning at
you, as I have done for the last half hour—what would you
think then?

THE GIRL   I would simply think: What a fool he is!
  (RICHARD *takes her dramatically in his arms. They embrace. He kisses her violently. Music sweeps in and the
  lights black out*)
  (*In the darkness, we hear the sound of the door buzzer. It
  rings twice*)
  (*The lights dim back to normal.* RICHARD *is standing
  where we left him, leaning against the piano, lost in reverie.
  The buzzer rings again and he is jarred back to reality. He
  puts down his drink, and falling all over himself in nervous
  and undignified haste dashes to the door*)

RICHARD   Come in . . . Come in . . .
  (*Revealed in the doorway is* DR. BRUBAKER. *He is a round,
  somewhat messy, imperious man in his middle fifties. He
  carries a large brief case*)

RICHARD (*Completely taken aback*)   Dr. Brubaker!

DR. BRUBAKER   Good evening. I hope I'm not late. Monday
is my day at the clinic plus my regular patients and of course

I'm on The Author Meets the Critic Friday night. I have been preparing my denunciation. I hope I haven't kept you waiting. . . .

RICHARD   Look, Dr. Brubaker. Wasn't our . . . ?

DR. BRUBAKER   Your office sent me the galleys of the last five chapters. I have them here with me. They are a mass of errors. I want to go over the whole thing with you very carefully.

RICHARD   Dr. Brubaker. I'm terribly sorry. Our appointment —I believe it was for tomorrow night. . . .
  (DR. BRUBAKER *has opened his brief case and has begun to spread papers all over the table*)

DR. BRUBAKER   I understand, of course, that your firm wishes to reach as wide an audience as possible. But I must protest —and very strongly—the changing of the title of my book from *Of Man and the Unconscious* to *Of Sex and Violence*. . . .

RICHARD   Dr. Brubaker, I'm terribly sorry. I know how important this is. But I'm afraid our appointment was for tomorrow night.

DR. BRUBAKER   Tomorrow night?

RICHARD   Tuesday night. I understood it was definite for Tuesday night.

DR. BRUBAKER   Good Lord!

RICHARD   And I'm afraid I have someone coming in tonight. Another appointment. With an author. And she'll be here any minute. In fact she's late.

DR. BRUBAKER   Astounding. Really incredible.

RICHARD   It's probably my fault. I probably wasn't clear on the phone.

DR. BRUBAKER   No. No. You were perfectly clear. . . .

RICHARD   I can't understand how it happened.

DR. BRUBAKER   Perfectly simple. Repressed uxoricide.

RICHARD   I beg your pardon?

DR. BRUBAKER   Repressed uxoricide. I came tonight because I want to murder my wife.

RICHARD   I see. . . . Yes . . . Of course . . .

DR. BRUBAKER   A perfectly natural phenomenon. It happens every day.

RICHARD   It does?

DR. BRUBAKER   Certainly. Upon leaving the clinic and being faced with the necessity of returning to my home, I felt a strong unconscious impulse to murder my wife. Naturally, not wanting to do the good woman any bodily harm, my mind conveniently changed our appointment to tonight. What could be more simple?

RICHARD   I see. . . .

DR. BRUBAKER   I am most sorry to have inconvenienced you, sir. . . .

RICHARD   No, no. That's quite all right. . . .

DR. BRUBAKER   And I shall see you here tomorrow evening.

RICHARD   Fine, Doctor. We could just as easily have our conference tonight—except that I do have this other author coming. . . .

DR. BRUBAKER   Of course. I understand perfectly. Oh . . . Have you finished reading the book?

RICHARD   Well, I got as far as Chapter Three. The Meyerholt Case.

DR. BRUBAKER   Meyer*heim*. You read very slowly. Well, sir. Good night.
   (*He turns and starts to go. He is almost to the door when he stops and turns back*)
Sir. I trust you will not be offended if I call to your attention the fact that you are not wearing socks. . . .

RICHARD (*Looking down*)   Good Lord!

DR. BRUBAKER   I was interested in knowing if you were aware of it? And I gather from your expression that you were not. In Chapter Three on Gustav Meyerheim I point out that he invariably removed his socks. Before he struck.

RICHARD Before—he *struck?*

DR. BRUBAKER Yes. Surely you recall Meyerheim. A fascinating character! A rapist! I was certain you would be amused by the coincidence. Until tomorrow then, good evening.

(*The* DOCTOR *bows and exits*)

(RICHARD *looks helplessly down at his sockless ankles, then looks wildly around, finds his socks and struggles into them, muttering angrily as he does so something that sounds vaguely like: "Damn psychiatrists—write books—make a Federal case out of everything. . . . I bet his wife is a nervous wreck—every time he takes off his socks she probably hides in the closet. . . ."*)

(*As he is fighting his way into his loafers the door buzzer sounds*)

RICHARD Coming . . .

(*He dashes to door and opens it.* THE GIRL *is standing in the doorway. Her real-life entrance is very different from the way he imagined it. She is quite lovely but far from the exotic creature he envisioned. She wears a checked shirt and rolled dungarees. She looks at him for a moment and then smiles tentatively*)

THE GIRL Hi.

RICHARD (*He looks at her blankly for an instant*) Hi.

THE GIRL Can I come in?

RICHARD Sure . . . I mean, of course. Please do.

THE GIRL I'm sorry I took so long but I've been watering the garden. I promised the Kaufmans I'd take good care of it, and I'm afraid I kind of neglected it. I didn't even find the hose until tonight.

RICHARD I didn't know the Kaufmans had a garden. . . .

THE GIRL Oh, yes. They do.

RICHARD It must be very nice.

THE GIRL It is. But it's a lot of work. Before I found the hose I'd been using the cocktail shaker—that was the only thing I could find. . . .

RICHARD   The cocktail shaker . . .

THE GIRL   Yes. They have a big glass one. It must hold about a gallon. I'm just sick about the tomato plant. Did it survive, do you think?

RICHARD   I really don't know. We could look at it, I suppose. It's out on the terrace. Right where it landed.

THE GIRL   That's awful. . . . I can't figure out how it happened. . . .
    (RICHARD *leads way to terrace*)

RICHARD   It's right there. I haven't touched it. . . .

THE GIRL   Golly, look at that! I'll pay for it, of course. Do you think you could lift it up . . . ?

RICHARD   Sure.
    (*He lifts the pot off the chaise with a great deal of effort*)
This damn thing weighs a ton. . . . There . . .

THE GIRL   I just thought. If you'd been sitting in that chair . . . When it fell, I mean. It might have, well—practically killed you. . . .

RICHARD   That occurred to me, too.

THE GIRL   I'm really awfully sorry. It's probably criminal negligence or manslaughter or something. You could have sued somebody. Me, probably. Or your family could have. Of course I don't know what they would have collected. If they'd sued me, I mean. But anyway, they'd have had a very good case.

RICHARD   There's no use getting all upset. I wasn't sitting there, thank God, so it's all right. Look, I asked you down for a drink. Would you like one? I mean you really don't look old enough to drink. . . .

THE GIRL   I do, though. I drink like a fish. Do you have Scotch?

RICHARD   Sure. At least I'm pretty sure I do. I've been drinking something for the last half hour. I'm not sure now what it was. I was a little upset. . . .

THE GIRL (*Following him back into the living room*) I don't blame you. You could have been killed, practically. I feel just terrible about it. I mean . . .

RICHARD Let's don't start that again. Let's just have a drink.

THE GIRL All right. I'm glad you're taking it this way. You have every right to be just furious. I know I would be. If somebody practically dropped a tomato plant on my head.

RICHARD Let's see, what I *was* drinking?
 (*Picks up glass and tastes it*)
Bourbon. But we do have Scotch around here somewhere. Yeah—here we are. How do you like it?

THE GIRL Scotch and soda, I guess. That's what you're supposed to say, isn't it? Back home the boys drink Scotch and Pepsi-Cola a lot. Before I knew anything at all, I knew *that* was wrong.

RICHARD That's about as wrong as you can get, yes.

THE GIRL I knew it was. When I was very young I liked it, though. It sort of killed the taste of the Scotch.

RICHARD (*Mixing drink*) I can see how it would tend to do that.

THE GIRL Do you have a cigarette around? I left mine upstairs.

RICHARD Oh, yes. Sure. I'm sorry. Right here.
 (*He takes the crumpled pack from his pocket. There is one left in it*)
It may be a little stale. I haven't been smoking. In fact, before tonight, I hadn't had a cigarette in six weeks.

THE GIRL That's wonderful! I wish I had the will power to stop. I don't, though. I smoke like a chimney. Sometimes three packs a day.

RICHARD My God! That's terrifying.

THE GIRL I know. It doesn't seem to affect me, though. I guess I'm pretty healthy. What made you start aga—— Oh. I'll bet you started smoking after the plant fell down. To steady your nerves.

RICHARD   Well, something like that.

THE GIRL   Now I really *do* feel awful. If I'd just had the sense to move it off the wall. Or call the janitor and have him move it. It's pretty heavy. . . . Oh, I just feel . . .

RICHARD   Please, now, that's enough. Let me get some more cigarettes. I think there's an unopened carton out in the kitchen. Excuse me a minute. . . .
  (*He exits into the kitchen*)
  (*The* GIRL *looks around the apartment then drifts over to the piano. She hits a random note or two.* RICHARD *reappears*)

THE GIRL   Do you play the piano?
  (*For one mad instant,* RICHARD *considers the question. The faraway "Just-a-little-now-for-myself" look comes into his eye. But he quickly suppresses it*)

RICHARD   (*Truthfully*)   I'm afraid not. I'm tone deaf. My wife plays, though. . . .

THE GIRL   Oh, you're married?

RICHARD   Yes. I am.

THE GIRL   I knew it! I could tell. You *look* married.

RICHARD   I do?

THE GIRL   Mmm! It's funny. Back home practically nobody was married. And in New York everybody is. Men, I mean.

RICHARD   That's a remarkable observation.

THE GIRL   It's really true.

RICHARD   I guess so. I never really thought about it.

THE GIRL   (*As he hands her drink*)   Thanks. I think about it quite a lot. This is good. Do you mind if I put my feet up. I'll take my shoes off.

RICHARD   No. Of course not. Go right ahead. Make yourself comfortable.

THE GIRL   Your wife is away for the summer, isn't she?

RICHARD   Yes, as a matter of fact she is. How did you know?

THE GIRL   They all are. It's really amazing.

RICHARD   They *all* are?

THE GIRL   Mmm. Everybody's wife. Back home practically nobody goes away for the summer. Especially anybody's wife.

RICHARD   Have you been away long? In New York, that is?

THE GIRL   Oh, years. Almost a year and a half. It seems like years. I love it. Especially now that I've got my own apartment. When I lived at the club I didn't like it so much. You had to be in by one o'clock. Now I can stay out all night if I want to. I was really glad when they practically asked me to leave.

RICHARD   Why did they practically ask you to leave?

THE GIRL   It was so silly. I used to do modeling when I first came to New York and when this picture of me was published in *US Camera* they got all upset. You should have seen Miss Stephenson's face. She was the house mother.

RICHARD   What was the matter with the picture?

THE GIRL   I was nude.

RICHARD   Oh.

THE GIRL   On the beach with some driftwood. It got honorable mention. It was called "Textures." Because you could see the three different textures. The driftwood, the sand and me. I got twenty-five dollars an hour. And it took hours and hours, you'd be surprised. And the first day the sun wasn't right and I got paid for that too.

RICHARD   That seems only fair.

THE GIRL   Sure. You get paid from the time you're called. No matter how long it takes to make the picture. But I don't do modeling any more. Since I got this steady job . . .

RICHARD   Now you have a steady job?

THE GIRL   I take in washing. . . .

RICHARD   What?

THE GIRL   That's just a joke. I'm on this television program.
The commercial part. First I wash my husband's shirt in
ordinary soap flakes. Then I wash it with Trill. So when
people ask me what I do I always say I take in washing. I'm
on for a minute and forty-five seconds. It's really a very good
part. . . .

RICHARD   Oh, so you're an actress. Is that it?

THE GIRL   Mmm. It's really very interesting. People don't
realize, but every time I wash a shirt on television, I'm appearing before more people than Sarah Bernhardt appeared
before in her whole career. It's something to think about.

RICHARD   It certainly is.

THE GIRL   I wish *I* were old enough to have seen Sarah
Bernhardt. Was she magnificent?
   (RICHARD *is somewhat shaken by this question. For a mo-
   ment he sits there, grinning weakly*)

RICHARD   I really wouldn't know. I'm not quite that old
myself. . . .

THE GIRL   I guess you're really not, are you?

RICHARD   I am thirty-nine. Or I will be the day after tomorrow. At the moment I'm still only thirty-eight.

THE GIRL   The day after tomorrow?

RICHARD   That's right.

THE GIRL   Isn't that amazing? We were born under the same
sign. I was twenty-two yesterday. I didn't do anything about
it, though. I didn't even tell anyone. Oh, I did one thing. I
bought a bottle of champagne. I thought I'd sit there and
drink it all by myself. . . .

RICHARD   That sounds absolutely sad . . .

THE GIRL   Oh, no. It would have been fun. Sitting in my
own apartment drinking champagne. But I couldn't get the
bottle open. You're not supposed to use a corkscrew. You're
supposed to work the cork loose with your thumbs. I just
couldn't seem to do it. I suppose I could have called the
janitor or something. But, somehow, I didn't feel like calling
the janitor to open a bottle of champagne on my birthday.

Look, I got blisters on both thumbs. Well, not really blisters, but I sort of pulled the thumb part away from the nail . . .

RICHARD   It's not really a matter of brute force. It's more of a trick. (*Demonstrating with thumbs*) You kind of get one side and then the other and it finally works loose. . . . You have to have strong thumbs, though. . . .

THE GIRL   I've got a wonderful idea. Let me go up and get it. It's just sitting there in the ice box. We could both drink it. Since we both have birthdays. If you can really get it open . . .

RICHARD   I'm pretty sure I could get it open—but I don't want to drink your . . .

THE GIRL   It would be fun. After I couldn't get it open I sort of lost interest in sitting up there and drinking it alone. Let me go up and get it and we'll have a double birthday party. It's very good champagne. The man said.

RICHARD   I don't really think . . .

THE GIRL   I told him to be sure and give me very good champagne. Because I couldn't tell the difference myself. Wouldn't you like to?

RICHARD   Sure. As a matter of fact, I'd love to. I think we've got some champagne glasses in the kitchen . . .

THE GIRL   Okay. I'll go up and get it. I'll be right back. Should I bring the potato chips too?

RICHARD   Sure. Let's shoot the works!

THE GIRL   That's just the way I felt. I'll be right back.

RICHARD   Okay.

THE GIRL   See you in a minute . . .
 (*She exits, closing the door behind her*)
 (RICHARD *stares after her, somewhat bewildered. He picks up his glass, drains it, shakes his head, picks up her glass and starts toward the kitchen. Suddenly, he stops and turns back, a reflective expression on his face*)

RICHARD   *US Camera* . . .
 (*He puts down the glasses and goes to the bookshelf. He looks for a moment and then finds what he is looking for.*

He takes down a book. It is a very large book, very clearly marked: US Camera. *He begins, in a casual way, to riffle through the pages)*

(*Muttering*) News events . . . Children and Animals . . . The Human Body . . .

(*He turns the pages slowly and then suddenly stops. He stares. He closes the book, puts it back on the shelf, picks up the glasses and goes swiftly into the kitchen. After a moment he comes back again, carrying two champagne glasses. He polishes them, sets them down, starts for the book and stops himself. Instead he pours a little whiskey into one of the champagne glasses, gulps it down, then wipes it out with his handkerchief. Finally he pulls himself together)*

Let's see . . . Birthday party!

(*He starts to fix things up a little bit. Goes to phonograph and looks through records)*

Show tunes . . .

(*He puts on a record: "Falling in Love with Love")*

In seven years I never did anything like this! In another seven years I won't be able to.

(*On this sobering thought, he sits down and stares moodily into space—the music from the record fades softly down)*

HIS VOICE   Hey, Dick. Dickie boy . . .

RICHARD   Yeah, Richard?

HIS VOICE   What do you think you're doing?

RICHARD   I don't know. I don't know what I'm doing.

HIS VOICE   This kid is just a little young, don't you think?

RICHARD   Look, let me alone, will you?

HIS VOICE   Okay. You know what you're doing.

RICHARD   No, I don't. I really don't.

HIS VOICE   Relax. You're not doing anything. Even if you wanted to—you haven't got a chance. . . .

RICHARD   Oh yeah? That's what you think. She seems to like me. She seems kind of fascinated by me.

HIS VOICE She thinks you're that nice Sarah Bernhardt fan who lives downstairs. You're getting older, boy. You got bags under your eyes. You're getting fat.

RICHARD Fat? Where?

HIS VOICE Under your chin there. You're getting a martini pouch. And that crew-cut stuff! You're not kidding anybody. One of these mornings you're going to look in the mirror and that's all, brother. The Portrait of Dorian Gray.
  (RICHARD *examines himself nervously in the mirror. He is only slightly reassured*)

RICHARD Look, pal, I'm going to level with you. This is a real pretty girl—and, as we pointed out, I'm not getting any younger—so . . .

HIS VOICE Okay, pal. You're on your own . . .
  (*He stands there for a moment of nervous indecision. The buzzer sounds. He decides—and with a new briskness in his step heads gaily for the door. He opens the door, admitting the girl. She comes in. She has changed to a sophisticated cocktail dress. She carries champagne and a bag of potato chips*)

THE GIRL Hi. I'm sorry I took so long. I thought I ought to change. I got this dress at Ohrbach's. But I don't think you could tell, could you?

RICHARD You look lovely.
  (*She reacts slightly, sensing a difference in his tone*)

THE GIRL Thank you. Here's the champagne. You can see where I was working on it. . . .

RICHARD Let me take a crack at it. (*He takes bottle and begins to thumb cork*) This is a tough one. . . .

THE GIRL Should I do anything?

RICHARD I don't think so. Just stand well back . . .
  (*He struggles with cork*)

THE GIRL We could call the janitor. He's probably got some kind of an instrument . . .

RICHARD (*Through clenched teeth as he struggles*) No—let's
—keep—the janitor out of this. . . . Damn it . . . This
thing is in here like . . .

THE GIRL I told you. You can just imagine what I went
through. On my birthday and everything.

RICHARD (*He stops to rest*) You know, this is just a lot of
damn chi-chi nonsense. They could put a regular cork in this
stuff and you could just pull it with a corkscrew. . . .
   (*He attacks it again*)
Come on, you stinker!
Hey—I think—watch out—maybe you better get a glass just
in case she . . .
   (*The cork finally pops*)
Catch it! Catch it!
   (*She catches it*)

THE GIRL Got it! Boy, you sure have powerful thumbs. . . .

RICHARD (*He is rather pleased by this*) I used to play a lot
of tennis. . . .

THE GIRL Do you think it's cold enough? I just had it sitting
in the ice box. . . .

RICHARD It's fine. . . . Well, happy birthday.

THE GIRL Happy birthday. (*They touch glasses and drink*)
Is it all right? I mean is that how it's supposed to taste . . . ?

RICHARD That's how.
   (*She takes another tentative taste*)

THE GIRL You know, it's pretty good. I was sort of afraid it
would taste like Seven-Up or something. . . .

RICHARD Hey, I forgot . . .
   (*He leans forward and plants a quick, nervous kiss on her
   forehead*)
Birthday kiss. Happy birthday.

THE GIRL Thank you. Same to you.

RICHARD Maybe we ought to have some music or something.
Since this is a party . . .

THE GIRL That's a good idea. . . .

RICHARD   I've got about a million records here. We can probably find something appropriate. Ready for some more?

THE GIRL   Not quite yet.
  (*He refills his own glass*)

THE GIRL   I've kind of stopped buying records. I mean I
didn't have a machine for so long. Now that I've got one
again—or anyway the Kaufmans have one—I'm all out of
the habit. . . .

RICHARD   Do you like show tunes?

THE GIRL   Sure. Do you have "The King and I"?

RICHARD   I'm afraid I don't. That's a little recent for me. I've
got mostly old Rodgers and Hart and Cole Porter and Gersh-
win. . . . How about this one? From "Knickerbocker Holi-
day."
  (*He is offering a prized possession: The Walter Huston
  recording of "September Song." He puts it on and they
  listen for a moment in silence*)

THE GIRL   Oh, I love that. I didn't even know it was from a
show or anything. I thought it was just a song. . . .

RICHARD   Walter Huston sang it. He had a wooden leg—in
the show. You better have some more champagne. It's really
very good.
  (*He puts a little more in her glass which is still half full.
  He refills his own. She takes off her shoes*)

THE GIRL   This is pretty nice. . . .

RICHARD   Isn't it? It's a lot better than sitting out there listening to the ball game. Two runs behind and they send
Hodges up to bunt!

THE GIRL   Is that bad?

RICHARD   It's awful.

THE GIRL   I didn't know. I was never very good at baseball.
I was going to wash my hair tonight. But after I got through
with the garden I just didn't feel like it.

RICHARD   I was going to bed and read *Of Sex and Violence*
and *The Scarlet Letter*. We're publishing them in the fall and
I'm supposed to read them.

THE GIRL   You're a book publisher?

RICHARD   In a way. I'm the advertising manager for a firm called Pocket Classics. Two bits in any drugstore. I'm supposed to figure out a new title for *The Scarlet Letter*. They want something a little catchier. . . .

THE GIRL   I think I read *The Scarlet Letter* in school. . . . I don't remember much about it. . . .

RICHARD   Neither do I. I sent a memo to Mr. Brady—he's the head of the company—advising him not to change the title. But we had the title tested and eighty per cent of the people didn't know what it meant. So we're changing it . . .
    (*He gets up and fills glass again*)
Do you know what Mr. Brady wanted to call it?
    (*She shakes her head*)
I Was an Adulteress. But he's not going to, thank God. And do you know why? Because we had *it* tested and sixty-three per cent of the people didn't know what *that* meant. I wish you'd drink some more of your champagne. . . .

THE GIRL   No, thanks . . .
    (*She rises and drifts over to the bookcase*)
You've certainly got a lot of books. . . .

RICHARD   There're cases more in the closets. . . .

THE GIRL   (*Suddenly*)   Oh! Look! You've got *US Camera!*

RICHARD   (*A little flustered*)   Do we? I didn't even know it. How about that! *US Camera!*

THE GIRL   (*She takes it down*)   I bet I bought a dozen copies of this. But I don't have a single one left. Boys and people used to keep stealing 'em. . . .

RICHARD   I can't think why. . . .

THE GIRL   Did you ever notice me in it? It's a picture called "Textures."

RICHARD   I'm afraid I didn't. . . .

THE GIRL   I told you about it, don't you remember? See, that's me, right there on the beach. My hair was a little longer then, did you notice?

RICHARD   No, actually—I didn't . . .

THE GIRL   And of course I've taken off some weight. I weighed 124 then. Gene Belding—Gene took the picture—used to call it baby fat.

RICHARD   Baby fat?

THE GIRL   Mmm! I'm much thinner now. . . .
   (*They both study the picture for a moment*)

RICHARD   This was taken at the beach?

THE GIRL   Mmm . . .

RICHARD   *What beach?*

THE GIRL   Right on Fire Island . . . Oh . . . I see what you mean. It was taken very early in the morning. Nobody was even up yet.

RICHARD   Just you and Miss Belding?

THE GIRL   *Mr.* Belding. Gene Belding. With a G . . .

RICHARD   Oh. Well, it certainly is a fine picture.

THE GIRL   I'll autograph it for you if you want. People keep asking me to . . .

RICHARD (*Weakly*)   That would be wonderful. . . . Maybe we'd better have some more champagne. . . .

THE GIRL   Good. You know, this is suddenly beginning to feel like a party. . . .
   (*He refills her glass which is only half-empty and fills his own all the way, emptying the bottle*)
It was awfully sweet of you to ask me down here in the first place. . . .
   (*He drains his glass of champagne—looks at her for a moment*)

RICHARD   Oh, it was just one of those things. Just one of those foolish things. A trip to the moon—on gossamer wings . . . Do you play the piano?

THE GIRL   The piano?

RICHARD   Yeah. Somebody should play the piano. Do you play?

THE GIRL   I really don't. Do you?

RICHARD   Just a little. For myself . . .

THE GIRL   *You* play then . . .

RICHARD   You'll be sorry you asked. . . .
(He sits at piano and after a very impressive moment begins to play "Chopsticks." She listens and is delighted)

THE GIRL   Oh! I was afraid you could *really* play. I can play *that* too!
(She sits on the bench beside him and they play "Chopsticks" as a duet. When they finish)

RICHARD   That was lovely. . . .
(His manner changes)
Tell me, what would you say if, quite suddenly, I were to seize you in my . . . Hey, come here . . .
(He reaches over and takes her in his arms)

THE GIRL   Hey, now wait a minute . . .
(For a moment they bounce precariously around on the piano bench, then RICHARD loses his balance and they both fall off knocking over the bench with a crash and landing in a tangle of arms and legs)

RICHARD   *(Panic-stricken)*   Are you all right? I'm sorry—I don't know what happened—I must be out of my mind. . . .

THE GIRL   I'm fine . . .

RICHARD   I don't know what happened. . . .

THE GIRL   Well, I think I'd better go now. . . .
(Putting on her shoes)

RICHARD   Please don't . . . I'm sorry . . .

THE GIRL   I'd better. Good night . . .

RICHARD   Please . . . I'm so sorry . . .

THE GIRL   That's all right. Good night.
(She goes, closing the door behind her)
(RICHARD looks miserably at the door. Then turns and kicks viciously at the piano bench. He succeeds in injuring his toe. Sadly, still shaking his wounded foot, he limps to the kitchen and reappears a moment later with a bottle of

raspberry soda. He goes to the phonograph and puts on "September Song." He listens to it with morbid fascination. In a melancholy voice he joins Mr. Huston in a line or two about what a long, long while it is from May to December. He shakes his head and crosses sadly to the terrace. He stands there—a mournful figure clutching a bottle of raspberry soda)

(As he stands there, a potted geranium comes crashing down from the terrace above and shatters at his feet)

(He does not even bother to look around. He merely glances over his shoulder and says)

RICHARD *(Quietly)* Oh, now, for God's sake, let's not start that again. . . .

THE GIRL'S VOICE *(From above)* Oh, golly! I was just taking them in so there wouldn't be another accident. I'm really sorry. . . . I mean this is awful. . . . I could have practically killed you again. . . .

RICHARD It doesn't matter. . . .

THE GIRL'S VOICE *(From above)* I'm really sorry. It was an accident. . . . Are you all right . . . ?

RICHARD I'm fine.

THE GIRL'S VOICE *(From above)* Well, good night . . .

RICHARD Good night . . .

THE GIRL'S VOICE *(From above)* Good night. See you tomorrow, maybe. . . .

RICHARD Huh? *(He straightens up)* Yeah! I'll see you tomorrow!

THE GIRL'S VOICE *(From above)* Good night!
(He starts to drink from soda bottle. Stops himself. Puts it down in disgust. Then strides back to living room with renewed vigor. He goes to the liquor cabinet and begins to pour himself another drink. From the phonograph comes the happy chorus of "September Song")
(RICHARD, a peculiar expression on his face, sings cheerfully with the record as)

THE CURTAIN FALLS

Act Two

SCENE I

The same.

It is early evening the following day. RICHARD, *back in full control and very businesslike, is deep in conference with* DR. BRUBAKER.

Both are somewhat tense and it is evident that the conference has been proceeding with difficulty. The DOCTOR *is seated amid a litter of papers and galley sheets.* RICHARD *holds a duplicate set of galleys. As the curtain rises* RICHARD *clears his throat and prepares to renew his attack.*

RICHARD   On page one hundred and ten, Doctor, if we could somehow simplify the whole passage . . .

DR. BRUBAKER   Simplify? In what way simplify?

RICHARD   In the sense of making it—well—simpler. Both Mr. Brady and I have gone over it a number of times, and, to be perfectly frank with you, neither of us has any clear idea of what it's actually about . . .

DR. BRUBAKER   Your Mr. Brady, sir, is, if I may also speak with frankness, a moron.

RICHARD   It is Mr. Brady's business, as an editor, to keep the point of view of the average reader very clearly in mind. If something is beyond Mr. Brady's comprehension, he can only assume that it will also be over the head of our readership.

DR. BRUBAKER   It was, I take it, at Mr. Brady's suggestion that the title of my book was changed from *Of Man and the Unconscious* to, and I shudder to say these words aloud, *Of Sex and Violence.* . . .

RICHARD   That is correct. Mr. Brady felt that the new title would have a broader popular appeal.

DR. BRUBAKER   I regret to inform you, sir, that Mr. Brady is a psychopathic inferior. . . .

RICHARD   Cheer up, Doctor. If you think you've got troubles, Mr. Brady wants to change *The Scarlet Letter* to *I Was an Adulteress*. I know it all seems a little odd to you—but Mr. Brady understands the twenty-five-cent book field. Both Mr. Brady and I *want* to publish worthwhile books. Books like yours. Like *The Scarlet Letter*. But you must remember that you and Nathaniel Hawthorne are competing in every drugstore with the basic writings of Mickey Spillane.

(*As* DR. BRUBAKER *is unacquainted with this author,* RICHARD'S *bon mot gets no reaction*)

DR. BRUBAKER   This is therefore why my book is to be published with a cover depicting Gustav Meyerheim in the very act of attacking one of his victims. . . .

(DR. BRUBAKER *has picked up a large full-color painting of the cover of his book which shows in lurid detail a wild-eyed man with a beard attempting to disrobe an already pretty-well disrobed young lady. It also bears the following line of copy: "Hotter Than the Kinsey Report." Both regard the cover for a moment*)

RICHARD (*With a certain nervous heartiness*)   I must take the responsibility for the cover myself, Doctor. . . .

DR. BRUBAKER   And also for making Meyerheim's victim—all of whom incidentally, were middle-aged women—resemble in a number of basic characteristics, Miss Betty Grable?

RICHARD   I'm afraid so, Doctor. Don't you think there would be something just a little bit distasteful about a book jacket showing a man attempting to attack a middle-aged lady?

DR. BRUBAKER   And it is less distasteful if the lady is young and beautiful?

RICHARD   At least, if a man attacks a young and beautiful girl, it seems more . . . Oh, my God!
  (*He remembers last night and shudders*)

DR. BRUBAKER   I beg you pardon?

RICHARD   Nothing. Doctor, if you don't like the cover, I'll see if I can have it changed. . . .

DR. BRUBAKER   I would be most grateful.

RICHARD   Doctor.

DR. BRUBAKER   Yes?

RICHARD   You say in the book that ninety per cent of the population is in need of some sort of psychiatric help?

DR. BRUBAKER   This is theoretically true. It is not however practical. There is the matter of cost. . . .

RICHARD   With your own patients—are you very expensive?

DR. BRUBAKER   (*His Third Ear has caught the direction this conversation is leading and his defenses go up immediately*) Very.

RICHARD   I'm sure you occasionally make exceptions. . . .

DR. BRUBAKER   Never.

RICHARD   I mean, once in a while a case must come along that really interests you. . . .

DR. BRUBAKER   (*Primly*)   At fifty dollars an hour—all my cases interest me.

RICHARD (*Undaunted*)   I mean if you should run into something really spectacular. Another Gustav Meyerheim, for example . . .

DR. BRUBAKER   If Meyerheim were alive today and desired my help it would cost him fifty dollars an hour, just like anyone else. . . .

RICHARD   Doctor, tell me frankly. Do you think, just for example, that *I* need to be psychoanalyzed?

DR. BRUBAKER   Very possibly. I could recommend several very excellent men who might, perhaps, be a little cheaper.

RICHARD How much cheaper?

DR. BRUBAKER (*Considering*) Ohhhhh . . .

RICHARD I couldn't even afford *that*. . . .

DR. BRUBAKER I thought not. (*He turns back to his papers*) Now to get back to . . .

RICHARD (*Seating himself casually on the couch*) I wondered if possibly you might give me some advice. . . .

DR. BRUBAKER I know. Everyone wonders that.
   (*Still moving casually,* RICHARD *swings his feet onto the couch until he is lying in the classic position*)

RICHARD I'm desperate, Doctor. Last night after you left, I was just sitting there listening to the ball game . . .

DR. BRUBAKER (*Outmaneuvered, but still game*) This fact in itself is not really sufficient cause to undertake analysis . . .

RICHARD No, I don't mean that. I *started out* listening to the ball game and do you know what I ended up doing?

DR. BRUBAKER I have no idea. . . .

RICHARD I ended up attempting to commit what I guess they call criminal assault. . . .

DR. BRUBAKER (*Defeated, he takes a pad and pencil from his pocket*) From the way you phrase it, I assume the attempt was unsuccessful. . . .

RICHARD Thank God! All I did was knock us both off the piano bench. . . .

DR. BRUBAKER (*A flicker of interest—he begins to write*) You attempted to commit criminal assault on a *piano bench*?

RICHARD Yes.

DR. BRUBAKER And on whose person was this obviously maladroit attempt committed?
   (RICHARD *rises and goes to bookshelf. Gets* US Camera *and shows it to* DOCTOR)

RICHARD That's her. Her hair was a little longer then.

DR. BRUBAKER (*After a moment*) Splendid. I congratulate you on your taste. However, you ask for my advice. I give it to you. Do not attempt it again.

(*A brief pause while the* DOCTOR *re-examines the photograph*)

If you *should,* however, give yourself plenty of room to work in. In any case do not attempt it precariously balanced on a piano bench. Such an attempt is doomed from the start. Now, my boy, I must go. I have many things to . . .

RICHARD But look, Doctor—I'm married. I've always been married. Suppose this girl tells people about this. She's likely to mention it to someone. Like my wife.

DR. BRUBAKER This is, of course, not beyond the realm of possibility. In that event I would recommend a course of vigorous denial. It would be simply your word against hers. Very possibly, if you were convincing enough, you could make it stick. And now I must really go. I thank you for your help. It is agreed that I shall make the necessary clarifications in Chapter Eight and you will devote your best efforts to making the cover of my book look less like a French postal card. I shall be in touch with your office the first of next week. . . .

RICHARD If she tells anyone about this—I'll, I'll—kill her! I'll kill her with my bare hands!

DR. BRUBAKER (*Who has started to leave, turns back*) This is also a possible solution. However, I submit that murder is the most difficult of all crimes to commit successfully. Therefore, until you are able to commit a simple criminal assault, I strongly advise that you avoid anything so complex as murder. One must learn to walk before one can run. I thank you again and good night.

(*He exits briskly*)

(RICHARD *stands blankly staring after the good* DOCTOR. *He shakes his head*)

(*Music sneaks in—he turns and there grouped about the couch and coffee table, in "dream lighting" are* HELEN, THE GIRL, MISS MORRIS, ELAINE, MARIE WHATEVER-HER-NAME-WAS *and an unidentified* YOUNG LADY *in brassiere and panties. They all brandish tea cups and in very hen-party fashion are engaged in dishing the dirt about someone. It is, after all, a figment of* RICHARD'S *imagination, so the cups are raised and lowered in unison and the little clucking noises of disapproval are done in chorus*)

THE GIRL (*Very chatty*) Actually, Mrs. Sherman, it was terribly embarrassing. He seemed to go berserk. He'd been sitting playing "Chopsticks" when suddenly he grabbed me and practically tried to tear my clothes off. . . .

ELAINE My dear, the night of your birthday party he made himself perfectly obnoxious right out there on the terrace. I don't like to say this, but he attempted to take advantage of me.

(*All the girls shake their heads and make small clucking noises of shocked disapproval*)

MISS MORRIS It's just terrible, Mrs. Sherman. I'm positively scared to go into his office to take dictation. Why, the way that man looks at me, it makes me feel kinda naked. . . .

(*All drink tea*)

ELAINE I said, Richard darling, at least have the decency not to try something like this practically in front of poor Helen's eyes!

THE GIRL He'd been drinking heavily, of course. . . . He practically guzzled a whole bottle of my champagne. . . .

MARIE (*In French*) Madame! Madame! He was like a human beast! He tore off my belt, he tore off my shirt, he tore off my pants and he chased me into the sea without a bathing costume.

(*All shake heads and "Tsk-tsk." Then the unidentified* YOUNG LADY *in the bra and pants speaks up*)

YOUNG LADY And *me!* I'm not even safe in my own apartment! Every time I start getting ready for bed that man sits out there on the terrace—staring at me! I just hate a Peeping Tom!

HELEN I've always suspected that Richard was not quite sane.

THE GIRL Oh, he's sane, all right. He's just a nasty, evil-minded, middle-aged man. . . .

(RICHARD *can stand it no longer*)

RICHARD   Helen! Listen to me. . . .

> (*The girls raise their tea cups and vanish. Music in and out and lighting back to normal*)

RICHARD (*In a panic, lights a cigarette*)   I've got to do something. That girl's probably told fifty people about this already. If I just sent her some flowers . . . That's no good. . . . I've got to talk to her. Reason with her. Plead with her. Tell her I was drunk, which God knows I was, and beg her not to mention this to anyone or my life could be ruined. . . .

> (*He has found telephone book and is riffling through pages*)

Twelve solid pages of Kaufman . . . Here it is . . . ORegon 3-7221.

> (*He lifts receiver, starts to dial, then stops*)

I can't do it. What can I possibly say to her?

> (*He practices—holding receiver switch down*)

RICHARD (*With great charm*)   My dear Miss—*I don't even know what the hell her name is*—My dear Young Woman—I have simply called to apologize for my absurd behavior last night. It was inexcusable, but I had been drinking. I can barely remember what happened, but I'm under the impression that I made a terrible fool of myself. I beg you to forgive me and put the whole distasteful incident out of your mind.

> (*Stops and puts down phone*)

No good. I can't do it.

And what about Helen? She hasn't called. She's probably heard about it by now. Oh, that's out of the question. How could she possibly have heard anything? But she could have. The word gets around. It's like jungle drums.

If she hasn't heard anything—why hasn't she called?

I could call her. The minute I heard her voice I could tell if she knew anything.

Come on. Call her.

Stop stalling. Pick up the telephone and call her. It's the only way you'll know.

Okay. Okay.

> (*He picks up the phone and dials the Long-Distance Operator*)

Long Distance? I want to call Cohasset. Cohasset, Massachu-

setts 4-2831-J. Yeah . . . My number? ORegon 9-4437.
Thank you.

Okay—fasten your seat belts. . . .

Hello? Hello, Helen? Who? Who is this? Look, I want to talk
to Mrs. Richard Sherman. Is she there? Who is this anyway?
Oh. The baby sitter. Look, this is Mr. Sherman calling from
New York. What do you mean she's out for the evening.
With whom is she out for the evening? Mr. MacKenzie and
some people? *What people?* Well, what *was* the message she
left for me?

Oh. Oh, my God. Her yellow skirt. No, no, I didn't. Something unexpected came up. But tell her I will. The first thing
in the morning. Without fail.

Look, I want to ask you. How did Mrs. Sherman seem? I
mean did she seem upset in any way? Like she'd heard some
bad news or anything like that?

Just about the yellow skirt. Well, good. Tell her I'll send it
up the first thing in the morning. Is Ricky all right? Good.
When Mrs. Sherman comes in, tell her everything is fine
here and I'll talk to her tomorrow. . . . Fine . . . Good-
bye . . . Good-bye.

(He hangs up phone)

Well, thank God!

(He sits down and lights a cigarette)

The only thing I cannot understand is, what the hell is she
doing having dinner with Tom MacKenzie. I wish she
wouldn't hang around with people like that. He gets away
with murder because he's a writer. Well, he's a damn lousy
writer. That last book!

Helen should know better than to go around with people like
that. She isn't even safe.

I know for a positive fact that he's been after her for years.
Tom MacKenzie happens to be a real bum, if you want to
know! And there probably aren't any other people.

She doesn't know what she's getting herself into. She's been
married so long she forgets what it's like.

Helen happens to be a damned attractive woman. A man
like Tom MacKenzie is perfectly capable of making a pass
at her.

(By now he has begun to pace the floor)

And don't think she doesn't know what she's doing. She's

getting older. She's used to me. In many ways I'm probably
very dull. And Tom MacKenzie's a writer. She probably
thinks he's fascinating as hell!

She thought that last book of his was great! All that inwardly-
downwardly-pulsating-and-afterward-her-hair-spilled-across-
the-pillow crap! Strictly for little old ladies at Womrath's.
But Helen is just the kind of middle-aged dame who would
fall for it.

Well, good luck! That's all!

(*Brooding, he sits in easy chair, a grim expression on his
face*)

(*Music sneaks in and the "dream lighting" comes up on
the far side of the stage by the fireplace. We hear the
sound of wind mingled with the music. A door opens and
slams shut and* TOM MACKENZIE *and* HELEN *enter, laughing.*
TOM MACKENZIE *is a handsome, glamorous-type author
with a mustache. He looks quite a lot like his photograph
on the book jackets. He wears a tweed coat with the collar
up and a hunting shirt.* HELEN *wears a sweater and skirt
with a man's raincoat thrown about her shoulders. Both
are very gay*)

HELEN (*As he helps her off with raincoat*)   It's been years
since I took a walk on the beach in the rain. . . .

TOM   I love the rain on the sea. It's so wild and un-
tamed. . . .

HELEN (*Looking around*)   Where are the other people?

TOM   I have a confession to make.

HELEN   Yes?

TOM   There are no other people. Don't be angry.

HELEN (*After a moment*)   I'm not angry.

TOM   I hoped you wouldn't be. Come over here by the fire.

HELEN   I love an open fire.

TOM   I always say, What good is the rain without an open
fire?

RICHARD (*From his chair across the room*)   Oh, brother!

TOM   Let me get you a little whiskey to take out the chill. . . .

HELEN   Thank you . . .
(He pours whiskey from flask. She drinks, then hands the cup to him. He drinks—but first kisses the spot on the cup where her lips have been)

RICHARD *(Muttering scornfully)*   H.B. Warner . . .

TOM   But wait. You're shivering. . . .

HELEN   It's nothing. I'll be warm in a moment. . . .

TOM   No, no . . . You're soaked to the skin. You'll catch your death of cold. . . .

RICHARD   Here it comes. . . .

TOM   Why don't you take off your things and hang them by the fire? I'll get you something dry. . . .

RICHARD *(Appalled)*   He used *that* in his book, for God's sake! As who didn't!

HELEN   All right. Turn your back . . .
(He turns his back and she removes her shoes. She takes off her skirt and hangs it on the fire screen)

TOM   May I turn around now?

HELEN   If you like . . .
(Suddenly, the mood has changed. His voice is now husky with passion)

TOM   Helen, darling!

HELEN   Yes, Tom?

TOM   Did anyone ever tell you that you are a very beautiful woman?

HELEN   No. Not recently anyway . . .

TOM   But surely Richard . . .

HELEN   I'm afraid Richard rather takes me for granted now. . . .

TOM   That blind, utter fool!

HELEN   Oh, darling!

TOM   Darling!
   (*The music swells.* TOM *takes her in his arms*)
   (*Murmuring as he covers her with kisses*)
Inwardly, downwardly, pulsating, striving, now together, ending and unending, now, now, now!
   (*They are in a full mad clinch as the lights black out*)
   (*On his side of the room,* RICHARD *jumps to his feet and angrily pounds the table*)

RICHARD   Okay! If that's the way you want it! Okay!
   (*With great purpose he strides to the telephone. Gets phone book, thumbs through it, finds number and dials. He whistles softly through his teeth. . . . The tune he is whistling might, if he were not tone deaf, almost be "Just One of Those Things." After a moment someone obviously answers the phone*)

RICHARD (*With great charm*)   Hi. Did you know you left your tomato plant down here last night? I could have the janitor bring it back—or—if you want—I was thinking maybe I could . . .
   (*He is talking into the phone with great animation by the time the lights have dimmed and*)

                                       THE CURTAIN IS DOWN

SCENE II

   The same. It is later that evening.
      The apartment is empty. A single light in the foyer.
      After a moment, the sound of a key in the lock and RICHARD *and the* GIRL *enter. He switches on the lights.*

RICHARD   Well, we made it.

THE GIRL   I'm so full of steak I can barely wobble. . . .

RICHARD   Me too.

THE GIRL   I feel wonderful. . . .

RICHARD   Did anyone ever tell you that you have a very, very beautiful digestive tract?

THE GIRL   Yes. But they don't usually say it like that. Mostly they just say: Boy, did you ever stuff yourself!

RICHARD   Would you like a drink or something?

THE GIRL   No, thanks. But you go ahead and have one. Don't mind me . . .

RICHARD   Not me. I'm back on the wagon again. . . .

THE GIRL   This was awfully nice of you. It was enough to have you carry that heavy plant all the way upstairs. You didn't have to ask me out for dinner. I hope you didn't hurt yourself. Or strain something . . .

RICHARD   It wasn't that heavy. I was going to call the janitor to help me, but then I decided not to. . . .

THE GIRL   You're in pretty good shape. . . .

RICHARD   For an old man . . .

THE GIRL   You're not *that* old. You don't look a day over twenty-eight.

RICHARD   I know. . . .

THE GIRL   Anyway it was very nice of you.

RICHARD   I just took a chance and called. I didn't really think you'd be home. You know, I thought you'd be out or something.

THE GIRL   No, I don't go out very much. . . .

RICHARD   That's funny. I should think you'd have a line of suitors halfway round the block. Like Easter show at Radio City . . .

THE GIRL   Last night, I went to the movies by myself. . . .

RICHARD   Last night?

THE GIRL   (*Diplomatically*)   After I left here.

RICHARD   (*Moving the conversation past a trouble spot*)   All by yourself! You must have a boy friend or something. . . .

THE GIRL   I don't go out with most people who ask me. I know it sounds silly but people are always falling desperately

in love with me and everything and it makes things so complicated. I mean, it's just easier to pay the fifty-five cents and
go to the movies by yourself.

RICHARD   It doesn't sound very exciting. . . .

THE GIRL   It is, though. This is the first time I've had my
own apartment and everything.

RICHARD   You went out with me when I asked you. . . .

THE GIRL   Well, that's different. I mean, it's all right going
out with you. After all, you're married.

RICHARD   I see. I *think*.

THE GIRL   No. What I mean is, it's all right to have dinner
with you because you're not likely to fall desperately in love
with me or anything. You're more mature. . . .

RICHARD   I don't feel so—mature. . . .

THE GIRL   Well, you know what I mean.
   (*Pause*)

RICHARD   You're absolutely sure you wouldn't like a drink?

THE GIRL   Absolutely.

RICHARD   I think maybe I'll have one. Just a little one.
   (*He goes to bar and fixes himself a drink*)
Not even a Coke or something?

THE GIRL   Not right now.

RICHARD   Well, happy birthday.
   (*Pause*)

THE GIRL   This certainly is a beautiful apartment.

RICHARD   It's all right. It's a little ridiculous in some ways.
. . . The stairs, for instance . . .

THE GIRL   I think they're beautiful. I like an apartment with
stairs.

RICHARD   But these don't go any place. They just go up to
the ceiling and stop. They give the joint a kind of Jean Paul
Sartre quality.

THE GIRL   I see what you mean. No exit. A stairway to no-where.

RICHARD   I tried to get the landlord to take them out. See, this used to be the bottom half of a duplex. This place and the Kaufmans' were all one apartment. So when he divided them separately he just boarded up the ceiling—or in your case the floor . . .

THE GIRL   Yes, I noticed the place in the floor. I lost an orange stick down the crack. Anyway, I think the apartment's just charming. . . .

RICHARD   Yeah. But we're moving into a larger place in September. . . .

THE GIRL   Oh, that's too bad. But still, people in New York are always moving. You certainly have a lot of books. The last book I read was *The Catcher in the Rye* . . .

RICHARD   The last book I read was *The Scarlet Letter*. Mr. Brady thinks we can sell it. If we make it sound sexy enough.

THE GIRL   Is it sexy? I don't seem to remember.

RICHARD   No. Actually, it's kind of dull. In fact, people are going to want their quarters back. But Mr. Brady feels we can sell it if I can just figure out a way to tell people what The Scarlet Letter is.

THE GIRL   What *is* it?

RICHARD   Well, The Scarlet Letter was a big red "A." For Adultery. Anyone who was convicted of adultery had to wear it.

THE GIRL   How awful!

RICHARD   The cover will be a picture of Hester Prynne with a cigarette hanging out of her mouth. She'll be in a real tight, low-cut dress. Our big problem is—if the dress is cut low enough to sell any copies, there won't be any space on the front for a big red letter . . .

THE GIRL   The publishing business sounds fascinating.

RICHARD   Oh, it is. It is.
  (*Pause*)

THE GIRL   It's getting late. I really ought to go. . . .

RICHARD   You've got plenty of time.

THE GIRL   I guess so. That's the wonderful thing about having my own apartment. I mean at the club you had to be in at one o'clock or they locked the doors.

RICHARD   It sounds barbaric. . . .

THE GIRL   Oh, it practically was. It was really very funny. I mean, all the girls at the club were actresses. So naturally they were always asking each other what they called the big question. . . .

RICHARD   The big question?

THE GIRL   Mmm! They were always asking each other: Would you sleep with a producer to get a part?

RICHARD   That is a big question. . . .

THE GIRL   But it's so silly. If you live at the club anyway. I used to tell them, producers don't even *go* to bed before one o'clock. So the whole thing is academic, if you see what I mean. You'd be surprised how much time they spent discussing it, though.

RICHARD   I can see where they might give the matter some thought.

THE GIRL   Oh, sure. But they never discussed it in a *practical* way. When they asked me, I always used to say: It depends. How big is the part? Is the producer handsome? Things like that . . .

RICHARD   Practical things . . .

THE GIRL   Mmm! I was at the club for eight months and as far as I know no producer ever mentioned the subject to any of the girls.

RICHARD   That must have been very disappointing for them.

THE GIRL   It was.

RICHARD   But what if he was very handsome? And it was a very good part? And you didn't have to be in by one o'clock? What *would* you do?

THE GIRL In that case . . . If I was sure he wouldn't fall desperately in love with me and ask me to marry him and everything.

RICHARD What's so bad about that?

THE GIRL Oh, that would spoil everything. Marrying him, I mean. It would be worse than living at the club. Then I'd have to start getting in at one o'clock again. I mean it's taken me twenty-two years to get my own apartment. It would be pretty silly if the first thing I did was get married and spoil everything. I mean, I want to have a chance to be independent first. For a few years anyway. You can't imagine how exciting it is to live by yourself—after you've had somebody practically running your life for as long as you can remember. . . . You just can't imagine . . .
  (*As* RICHARD *stops listening to the* GIRL *and gradually becomes absorbed in his own thoughts, the lights dim down till there is only a dream spot on* RICHARD)

RICHARD Yes, I can. As a matter of fact we have a great deal in common.

HIS VOICE (*Mockingly—imitating* HELEN'S *tone*) Daddy's going to work very hard. And he's going to stay on the wagon, like Dr. Summers told him. And he's going to eat properly and not smoke, like Dr. Murphy told him. And Mommy is going to call Daddy tonight just to make sure he's all right . . .
Poor Daddy!

RICHARD Poor Daddy!

HIS VOICE The girl is absolutely right. Not want to get married. You—you dope. The minute you were old enough to have any fun—the only thing you could think of to do was to get married.

RICHARD I know. I know. It was a kind of nervousness. But I made the best of it. I've been a pretty good husband. When I think of the chances I've had . . .

HIS VOICE We've been through all this before. . . .

RICHARD I know. I know. I just thought I'd mention it.

HIS VOICE   Has it ever dawned on you that you're kidding yourself?

RICHARD   What do you mean by that?

HIS VOICE   All those dames you could have had if you weren't such a noble husband. The only reason you didn't do anything about 'em is that you didn't want to. . . .

RICHARD   Why didn't I want to?

HIS VOICE   Laziness, pal. Laziness. It was too much trouble. You just didn't want to get involved. Elaine, for instance. It would have taken six months. And all those phone calls and taxis and excuses.

RICHARD   Yeah. (*Pause*) Why does it always have to be so complicated?

HIS VOICE   If you could answer that one, pal-pal, they'd make you President of the United States.
   (RICHARD *sighs and the lights dim back to normal. The* GIRL *is still speaking, unaware of the fact that his mind has been far away*)

THE GIRL   . . . so when you asked me to go out for dinner with you it was all right. You're married and naturally, you don't want to fall desperately in love with anyone any more than I want anyone to fall desperately in love with me. Do you know what I mean?

RICHARD   Sure. It's too much trouble.

THE GIRL   Exactly.

RICHARD   I know just what you mean.

THE GIRL   That's right.

RICHARD   We both happen to be in positions where we can't possibly let ourselves get involved in anything. . . .

THE GIRL   Mmm.

RICHARD   All the damn phone calls and taxis and everything.

THE GIRL   That's right. I mean I certainly wouldn't be sitting alone with some man in his apartment at eleven-thirty at night if he wasn't married.

RICHARD   Certainly not. (*Pause*) When you said about the producer—it would depend on if he were handsome—what did you mean by that? I mean, just out of curiosity . . . what would be your idea of handsome?

THE GIRL   Well, let's see. I really don't know. I suppose he should be tall—and kind of mature-looking . . .

RICHARD   Like me?

THE GIRL   (*Thoughtfully*) Mmmmm . . . (*Pause*) You're not going to start falling desperately in love with me or anything, are you?

RICHARD   No. No. Definitely not. I mean I think you're very pretty and sweet and I certainly enjoyed having dinner with you. But . . .

THE GIRL   That's just the way *I* feel about you. You're very nice-looking and charming and mature. You're someone I can be with and count on him not falling desperately in love with me. . . .

RICHARD   That's right. I'm almost—well—I'm a lot older than you are. And one thing I've learned. Nothing is ever as simple as you think it's going to be. You take the simplest damn thing and, before you know it, it gets all loused up. I don't know how it happens or why it happens but it always happens. . . .

THE GIRL   That's very true. You're absolutely right.
   (*As the* GIRL *stops listening to* RICHARD *and gradually becomes absorbed in her own thoughts the lights dim to a single dream spot on her*)

HER VOICE   Well, what do you think?

THE GIRL   Mmm . . .

HER VOICE   What do you mean—mmm?

THE GIRL   I mean—I don't know . . .

HER VOICE   That's ridiculous. What is there not to know? He certainly is nice—and he's mature without being—you know—decrepit or anything . . .

THE GIRL   He certainly seems well-preserved. . . .

HER VOICE He's sweet and intelligent and married. What more do you want?

THE GIRL I don't know.

HER VOICE You're the one who wants to be the big-deal woman of the world. It's all your idea. It's not as if you were some kind of a virginal creature or something.

THE GIRL Oh—shut up—I mean you make it sound so—so clinical. Besides, you certainly can't count Jerry . . .

HER VOICE What do you mean we can't count Jerry?

THE GIRL Well, I mean it was a big mistake—and it was so —so—and then he got all hysterical and wanted to marry me. . . .

HER VOICE It counts.

THE GIRL I mean you can understand a person wanting to find out something about life and everything before she gets married and all settled down and has to start getting in by one o'clock again. . . . Besides, what makes you think he's interested in me that way? I must seem like some kind of a juvenile delinquent to him. . . .

HER VOICE You're twenty-two years old. And he's interested.

THE GIRL How can you tell?

HER VOICE I can tell. . . .

THE GIRL How?

HER VOICE I can tell. . . . What have you got to lose?

THE GIRL Well, nothing, I guess—if you're really going to make Jerry count.

HER VOICE He counts . . .

THE GIRL Well, then . . .

(The lights come back to normal. RICHARD is still talking, unaware that the GIRL's mind has been far away)

RICHARD . . . what I'm trying to say is, that people who are really mature weigh things more carefully. They impose a discipline on themselves. They understand the cost. . . . I mean, they finally learn that sometimes something that seems

very wonderful and desirable isn't really worth . . . I mean
—all the hysteria it's going to cause . . . (*Pause*) Then, of
course, you can overdo that line of thinking too. I mean a
man—a person—anyone doesn't like to feel he's some kind
of a vegetable or something. You know. What it amounts to
is this: You've got to decide which is the most painful—
doing something and regretting it—or not doing something
and—regretting it. Do you see what I mean?

THE GIRL   I think so. . . .

RICHARD   I didn't mean to start making a speech. Look, are
you sure you don't want a drink?

THE GIRL   No, thanks. Really.
   (*Starts to go*)

RICHARD   Now look, really. It's not late. You don't have to
go yet. . . .

THE GIRL   I really should . . .

RICHARD   Well, whatever you think. Let me take you up to
your door. . . .

THE GIRL   No. That's all right. It's just upstairs. . . .

RICHARD   Well, all right. If you have to go.

THE GIRL   I want to thank you for the dinner. It was
lovely. . . .

RICHARD   It was fun. . . .

THE GIRL   And for carrying that heavy plant all the way
upstairs . . .

RICHARD   It wasn't so heavy. . . .
   (*They have edged almost to the door by now*)

THE GIRL   Well, good night. And thanks—again . . .

RICHARD   Well, good night . . . (*She leans forward and
kisses him lightly on the cheek*) Well, good night . . .
   (*Suddenly they move together in a tight embrace which
   they hold for a moment. She breaks away, then kisses him
   again and in the same motion goes quickly out the door
   closing it behind her*)

(RICHARD *is visibly shaken. He starts after her. Stops himself. Closes the door again. And locks it. He shakes his head and then puts on the chain lock*)

(*Comes inside, starts for the phone, stops again. Tries to pull himself together. Picks up the galley sheets and sits down on the couch and tries to work on them*)

(*As he sits, a square in the ceiling at the top of the stairs lifts out and a moment later the girl appears. She backs down the first few steps, lowering the floor-ceiling back into place. He is oblivious to this. She turns and starts down the stairs. We see that she is carrying a small claw hammer*)

(*Quietly she comes down into the room. She looks at him and smiles. She pauses for a moment*)

THE GIRL (*With a small, ineffectual wave of the hand*) Hi . . .

(RICHARD *almost jumps out of his skin. He sees her. After a moment he sees the hammer and realizes where she has come from. Then, after a long time, he smiles and makes a similar, ineffectual wave of the hand*)

RICHARD Hi . . .

                                                        CURTAIN

Act Three

The same.

It is about eight o'clock the following morning. The blinds on the French doors are drawn, but outside the sun is shining brightly. It is going to be another hot day.

As the curtain rises, RICHARD stands by the French doors. He is in his shirt sleeves. He opens the blinds *and then the doors. He steps out onto the terrace and breathes deeply. He comes back into the living room and notices the girl's shoes. Somewhat tentatively, he picks them up and carries them to the bedroom doors. He stops and listens a moment. He puts the shoes back where he found them and goes to the front door. He listens again, then unlocks the door without unfastening the chain.*

He kneels down and reaching around through the slightly open door fishes in milk and the newspaper. He carries the paper down to the armchair and tries to read. He can't, however.

After a moment he looks up and speaks to himself in a very reassuring voice.

RICHARD   There's not a thing in the world to worry about. Two very attractive, intelligent people happened to meet under circumstances that seemed to be—propitious—and, well, it happened. It was very charming and gay. As a matter of fact it was wonderful. But now it's over.

   (*He rises and starts for the bedroom*)

We'll say good-bye, like two intelligent people. We'll have coffee . . .

   (*He knocks gently on the door. He listens. He knocks again. His calm is rapidly evaporating*)

How can she possibly sleep like that?

What's the matter with her anyway? Maybe she's sick or something. Maybe she's dead.

Maybe the excitement was too much for her and she passed away in her sleep.

Oh, my God! That means the police. And the reporters. "Actress found dead in publisher's apartment"!

   (*He looks desperately around. His eye lights on the staircase*)

No. No. I'll just haul the body upstairs. That's all. Right back upstairs, nail up the floor again and that's all. They'd have no reason to suspect me. I'd wear gloves, of course. They'd never prove a thing.

Now stop it. You're getting hysterical again.

   (*Pause*)

Well, if she isn't dead, why the hell doesn't she just get up
and go home? It's late! It's—late—it's *really* late—it's . . .

   (*He picks up his wrist watch from table*)

. . . *ten after eight?* It seemed later than *that.* . . .

   (*He is somewhat relieved by the time*)

Well. I'll give her another half hour to catch up on her
beauty sleep. Then, I'll very politely wake her. We'll have
coffee like two intelligent people. And then, I'll kiss her
good-bye.

   (*Confidently acting out the scene*)

It's been fun, darling, but now, of course, it's over . . . No
tears—no regrets . . .

   (*He stands waving as if she were walking up the stairs*)

Just good-bye. It's been—swell . . .

   (*He blows a kiss upward, waves and then stands transfixed,
   a foolish expression on his face*)

HIS VOICE   Pal.

RICHARD   Huh?

HIS VOICE   I don't want you to get upset or anything, but it
might not be as easy as all that. You know. Be realistic.

RICHARD   What? What are you talking about?

HIS VOICE   I was just pointing out. Women don't take these
things as lightly as men, you know. There *could* be compli-
cations. For example, suppose she's fallen desperately in love
with you. . . .

RICHARD   She can't do that. It isn't fair. She knows she can't.

HIS VOICE   After all, pal, you had a little something to do
with this yourself. . . .

RICHARD   Don't worry. I can handle it. Just don't worry. I
can be tough if I have to. I can be pretty damn tough. If I
set my mind to it, I can be a terrible heel. . . .

HIS VOICE (*Mocking*) Ha-*ha!*

RICHARD   Shut up . . .

   (*He stands for a moment, setting his mind to being a terrible heel. The lights dim and music sneaks in. "Dream
   lighting" lights up the bedroom doors. They open and the
   girl emerges. She is dressed like an Al Parker illustration*)

for a story called "Glorious Honeymoon" in The Woman's Home Companion. *She is radiant*)

THE GIRL (*Radiantly*) Good morning, my darling . . . Good morning . . . Good morning . . .

RICHARD (*Very tough. He lights a cigarette and stares at her for a moment through ice-blue eyes*) Oh. It's about time you dragged your dead pratt out of the sack. . . .

THE GIRL Oh, darling, darling, darling . . . (*He exhales smoke*) What is it, my darling, you seem troubled . . .

RICHARD Shut up, baby, and listen to me. I got something to tell you.

THE GIRL And I've something to tell you. I've grown older, somehow, overnight. I know now that all our brave talk of independence—our not wanting to get involved—our being —actually—*afraid* of love—it was all childish nonsense. I'm not afraid to say it, darling. I love you. I want you. You belong to me.

RICHARD Look, baby. Let's get one thing straight. I belong to nobody, see. If some dumb little dame wants to throw herself at me—that's her lookout, see. I'm strictly a one-night guy. I've left a string of broken hearts from here to—to Westport, Connecticut, and back. Now, the smartest little move you could make is to pack your stuff and scram. . . .

THE GIRL Go? Not I! Not now! Not ever! Don't you see, my darling, after what we've been to each other . . .

RICHARD I spell trouble, baby, with a capital "T." We're poison to each other—you and me. Don't you see that?

THE GIRL When two people care for each other as we do . . .

RICHARD (*A little "PAL JOEY" creeping in*) What do I care for a dame? Every damn dame is the same. I'm going to own a night club. . . .

THE GIRL That doesn't matter. Nothing matters. This thing is bigger than both of us. We'll *flaunt* our love. Shout it from the highest housetops. We're on a great toboggan. We can't stop it. We can't steer it. It's too late to run, the Beguine has begun . . .

RICHARD (*Weakly*)   Oh, Jesus Christ . . .

THE GIRL (*Coolly taking charge*)   Now then. Do you want to be the one to tell Helen, or shall I?

RICHARD (*With an anguished moan*)   Tell Helen?

THE GIRL   Of course. We must. It's the only way. . . .

RICHARD   No, no, no! You can't do that! You can't!
(*He is now kneeling at her feet, pleading. She puts her arm about his shoulder. From somewhere comes the brave sound of a solo violin which plays behind her next speech*)

THE GIRL   We can and we must. We'll face her together. Hand in hand. Proudly. Our heads held high. Oh, we'll be social outcasts, but we won't care. It'll be you and I together against the world. I'll go and dress now, darling. But I wanted you to know how I felt. I couldn't wait to tell you. Good-bye, for now, my darling. I won't be long . . .
(*As the music swells, she floats off into the bedroom, waving and blowing kisses with both hands. The "dream light" fades out and the lighting returns to normal. RICHARD stands panic-stricken in the middle of the living-room floor. He shakes his head*)

RICHARD   I'm crazy. I'm going crazy. That's all. I've run amok. Helen goes away and I run amok. Raping and looting and . . . (*He notices the cigarette in his hand*) smoking cigarettes . . .
(*He quickly puts out the cigarette*)
What have I done? What did I think I was doing? What did I possibly think I was doing?
Damn it! I begged Helen not to go away for the summer. I begged her!
What am I going to do! That girl in there undoubtedly expects me to get a divorce and marry her.

HIS VOICE   Well, why don't you?

RICHARD   Are you kidding? What about Helen?

HIS VOICE   What about her? Maybe this is all for the best. Maybe this is the best thing that could have happened to you. After all, Helen's not as young as she used to be. In a couple of years you'll look like her son.

RICHARD Now wait a minute. Wait a minute. Helen is still pretty attractive. She happens to be a damn beautiful woman, if you want to know. And we've been through a lot together. The time I was fired from Random House. And when little Ricky was sick—and I caught the damn mumps from him. She's taken a lot of punishment from me, if you want to know. And she's been pretty nice about it . . .

HIS VOICE The point, however, is: Do you love her?

RICHARD Love her? Well, sure. Sure, I love her. Of course I love her. I'm *used to her!*

HIS VOICE Used to her? That doesn't sound very exciting. Of course I imagine when a man enters middle life, he doesn't want someone exciting. He wants someone comfortable. Someone he's *used to* . . .

RICHARD Now, just a second. You've got the wrong idea. Helen's not so—*comfortable*. She's pretty exciting. You should see the way people look at her at parties and on the street and everywhere. . . .

HIS VOICE What people?

RICHARD Men. That's what people. For instance, Tom Mac-Kenzie, if you want to know. When Helen wears that green dress—the backless one with hardly any front—there's nothing comfortable about that at all . . .
  (RICHARD *sinks into chair and leans back*)
She wore it one night last spring when Tom MacKenzie was over—and you just couldn't get him out of here. . . .
  (*Music sneaks in and the lights dim. "Dream lighting" fills the stage*)
It looked like he was going to go home about four different times but he just couldn't tear himself away . . .
  (TOM *and* HELEN *appear.* HELEN *is wearing the green dress. It is everything* RICHARD *has said it is*)

TOM Helen, you look particularly lovely tonight. . . .

HELEN Why, thank you, Tom . . .

TOM You're a lucky boy, Dickie, even if you don't know it.

RICHARD I know all about it and don't call me Dickie. . . .

TOM   Helen—Helen, that name is so like you. "Helen, thy beauty is to me as those Nicaean barks of yore" . . .

HELEN   Gracious . . .

TOM   No, no, I mean it. Stand there a moment. Let me drink you in. Turn around. Slowly, that's it . . . (HELEN *models dress*) You look particularly lovely in a backless gown . . .

RICHARD (*Muttering*)   Backless, frontless, topless, bottomless, I'm on to you, you son of a bitch . . .

TOM (*From across the room*)   What was that, old man?

HELEN (*Quickly*)   Don't pay any attention to Dick. You know what happens to him and martinis. . . .

RICHARD   Two martinis. Two lousy martinis.

HELEN   Dr. Summers has told him time and time again that he should go on the wagon for a while till his stomach gets better. . . .

TOM   That's good advice, Dick. When a man can't handle the stuff he should leave it alone completely. That's what I say. Once a year—just to test my will power—I stop everything.

RICHARD (*He starts to say something, but finally stops himself*)   No comment.

HELEN (*Leaping once again into the breach*)   You really like this dress—do you, Tom?

TOM   I certainly do. It's a Potter original, isn't it?

HELEN   Yes—but that's wonderful! How did you know?

TOM   I'm a bit of an authority on women's clothes. You should really take me with you the next time you go shopping. We could have a bite of lunch first and really make a day of it. . . .
   (*He has finally got to the door*)
Good night, Dick . . .
   (RICHARD *waves unenthusiastically*)
Good night, Helen . . .
   (*He kisses her*)

HELEN   Good night, Tom . . .

TOM   I'll call you one day next week. . . .

HELEN   I'll be looking forward to it. (*She closes the door behind him*) I thought he was never going home . . .

RICHARD   (*In rather feeble imitation of* TOM) "Helen, thy beauty is to me as those Nicaean barks of yore"—is he kidding?

HELEN   You know Tom. He beats his chest and makes noises but it doesn't really mean anything. . . .

RICHARD   I know. His Nicaean bark is worse than his Nicaean bite. . . . (*He is pleasantly surprised by how well this came out*) Hey, that's pretty good. That came out better than I thought it was going to. Nicaean bark—Nicaean bite . . .

HELEN   (*Unfractured*) Actually, in some ways, Tom is very sweet. I mean it's nice to have people notice your clothes. . . .

RICHARD   Notice your clothes! He did a lot more than notice. . . . He practically . . . You know, you really ought to do something about that dress. Just the front part there . . .

HELEN   Do something about it?

RICHARD   I mean sort of . . . (*He gestures ineffectually about raising or tightening or something the front*) I don't know. Maybe we ought to empty the ash trays or something. You should see the way he was looking at you . . .

HELEN   You should have been flattered. Don't you want people to think your wife is attractive?

RICHARD   Sure, but . . . Why don't we clean this place up a little? It looks like a cocktail lounge on West Tenth Street. . . .

(*He picks up an ash tray full of cigarette butts*)
(HELEN *comes over to him*)

HELEN   Darling . . .

RICHARD   We ought to at least empty the ash trays . . .

HELEN   Not now . . .

RICHARD (*Looks at her questioningly*)   Huh?

HELEN   I mean not now . . .
   (*He looks at her for another moment and then very casually tosses away the tray full of butts and takes her in his
   arms*)
   (*The lights black out and the music swells in the darkness*)
   (*When the lights come on again the lighting is back to
   normal and* RICHARD *is leaning back in the chair where we
   left him, a self-satisfied grin on his face*)

HIS VOICE   Then you really do love Helen?

RICHARD   What do you want—an affidavit?

HIS VOICE   Well, good. So that leaves you with only one
problem. I'm warning you, pal, it may not be as easy to get
rid of this girl as you think.

RICHARD   Huh?

HIS VOICE   My dear boy, did you ever hear of a thing called
blackmail?

RICHARD   *Blackmail?*

HIS VOICE   One often hears of unscrupulous young girls who
prey on foolish, wealthy, middle-aged men. . . .

RICHARD   Now, really . . .

HIS VOICE   You got her into bed without any great effort.
Why do you suppose she was so willing?

RICHARD (*Weakly*)   But she said—she told me—she went on
record—she didn't want to get involved . . . (HIS VOICE
laughs coarsely) A minute ago you were saying she was
madly in love with me. . . .

HIS VOICE   *You poor, foolish, wealthy, middle-aged man.*

RICHARD   Wait a minute—in the first place I'm not
wealthy. . . .

HIS VOICE   Blackmail, pal, it happens every day. She'll bleed
you white.

RICHARD   Oh, my God. I'll have to sell the kid's bonds. . . .
Poor Ricky. Poor Helen. There's only one thing to do. Con-

fess everything and throw myself on her mercy. We're both intelligent people. She'll forgive me.

HIS VOICE   I wouldn't be a bit surprised if she shot you dead.

RICHARD   You're out of your mind. Not Helen. If she shot anyone it would much more likely be herself. Oh, my God. She'd probably shoot us both . . . I can't go on torturing myself like this. I'll have to tell her. Oh, she'll be hurt. For a while. But she'll get over it. There's no other way. I've got to tell her and take my chances. . . .
   (*Music and "dream lighting" in*)

RICHARD (*Calling*)   Helen! Helen!

HELEN (*From kitchen*)   Yes, darling . . .

RICHARD   Can you come in here a moment, please? There's something I must tell you.
   (HELEN *enters from the kitchen. This is the domestic, very un-green-dress* HELEN. *She wears an apron and carries a bowl which she stirs with a wooden spoon*)

HELEN (*Sweetly*)   Yes, Dick? I was just making a cherry pie. I know how you hate the pies from Gristede's and I wanted to surprise you. . . .

RICHARD   I don't know how to say this to you. . . .

HELEN   Yes, Dick?

RICHARD   We've been married a long time. . . .

HELEN   Seven years, darling. Seven glorious years. These are sweetheart cherries . . .

RICHARD   And in all that time, I've never looked at another woman. . . .

HELEN   I know that, Dick. And I want to tell you what it's meant to me. You may not know this, darling, but you're terribly attractive to women. . . .

RICHARD   I am?

HELEN   Yes, you funny Richard you—you are. But in all those seven years I've never once worried. Oh, don't I know there are plenty of women who would give their eye teeth to get you. Elaine. Miss Morris. That Marie Whatever-her-

name-was up in Westport. But I trust you, Dick. I always
have. I always will. Do you know something?

RICHARD   What?

HELEN   I . . . Oh, I can't even say it. It's too foolish. . . .

RICHARD   Go ahead. Go ahead, say it. Be foolish.

HELEN   Well—I honestly believe that if you were ever un-
faithful to me—I'd know it. I'd know it instantly.

RICHARD   You would?

HELEN   Oh, yes . . .

RICHARD   How?

HELEN   Wives have ways. Little ways.

RICHARD   And what would you do?

HELEN   Oh, darling, don't be . . .

RICHARD   No. Really. I'm interested. What would you do?

HELEN   Oh, I think I'd probably shoot you dead. Afterwards, of course, I'd shoot myself. Life wouldn't be worth
living after that. . . .

RICHARD   Oh, no!
   (*A pause*)
Helen . . .

HELEN   Yes?

RICHARD   Nothing. Nothing.

HELEN   Yes, there is something. I can tell.

RICHARD   No, now take it easy . . .

HELEN   I can tell. I can suddenly feel it. The vibrations—
something happened while I was away this summer . . .

RICHARD   It was an accident. A crazy accident. There was
this tomato . . . That is—this tomato plant fell down. It
landed right out there on the terrace. But nobody was hurt,
thank God. I didn't want to tell you about it. I was afraid
you'd worry. . . .

HELEN (*Sadly*)   Who was she?

RICHARD   Now, Helen—you're making this up . . .

HELEN (*Turning on him*)   *Who was she!*

RICHARD   Now please, really . . .

HELEN   Then it's true. It is true.

RICHARD   Look, we're both intelligent people. I knew you'd be hurt. But I know that somehow, some day, you'll forgive me. . . . (*He suddenly notices that* HELEN *is holding a revolver in her hand*) Now put that thing down. What are you going to do?

HELEN   You've left me nothing else to do. I'm going to shoot you dead. Then I'm going to kill myself.

RICHARD   But what about—the child?

HELEN   You should have thought of that before. Good-bye, Richard . . .
(*She fires five times*)
(*For a moment,* RICHARD *stands erect, weathering the hail of bullets. . . . Then slowly, tragically, in the best gangster movie tradition—clutching his middle—and making small Bogart-like sounds he sinks to the floor*)

RICHARD (*Gasping—the beads of sweat standing out on his forehead*)   Helen—I'm—going—fast . . . Give me a cigarette. . . .

HELEN (*Always the wife, even in times of crisis*)   A cigarette! You know what Dr. Murphy told you about smoking!

RICHARD   Good-bye . . . Helen . . .
(*She turns and walks sadly to the kitchen. At the door she stops, waves sadly with the wooden spoon, blows one final kiss and as the music swells she exits into kitchen. An instant later we hear the final shot.*
(RICHARD *collapses in a final spasm of agony and the lights black out*)
(*As the lights dim back to reality* RICHARD *is seated where we left him, a horror-struck expression on his face*)

RICHARD   Oh, the hell with *that!* I'll be goddamned if I'll tell her! (*For a moment,* RICHARD *stands shaking his head*) But I've got to . . . I've just got to . . .

(He is heading for the telephone when the sound of the door buzzer stops him)

(He freezes, panic-stricken. Glances quickly at the bedroom. The buzzer sounds again. Then a third time)

(When it is quite clear that whoever it is is not going to go away, RICHARD *presses the buzzer, then opens the door a crack, still leaving the chain fastened)*

RICHARD *(Hoarsely)*   Who is it?

DR. BRUBAKER *(Off stage)*   Once again, sir, I must trouble you . . .

RICHARD   Dr. Brubaker!

DR. BRUBAKER *(Off stage)*   Yes . . .

RICHARD   What is it? What can I do for you?

DR. BRUBAKER *(Through door)*   Last evening, after our conference, I appear to have left your apartment without my brief case.

RICHARD   No, no, Doctor. That's impossible. I'm afraid you're mistaken. I'm quite sure you had it with you. In fact, I remember quite clearly seeing . . .

(He looks wildly around the room and then sees the brief case)

Oh. Oh, there it is. . . . You're right. Isn't that amazing? It's right there. I'm sorry I can't ask you in but the place is kind of a mess and . . .

(He is trying to get the brief case through the door without unfastening the chain. It doesn't fit. He attempts brute force, but it just isn't going to fit. He pounds at it wildly and then finally realizes that he is going to have to open the chain. He does so)

Here you are, Doctor . . . Good-bye . . .

DR. BRUBAKER *(An unstopable force, he moves into the living room)*   I thank you. If you will permit me, I'll just make sure that everything is in order . . .

(Opening the brief case and riffling through the contents)

You can see what a strong unconscious resistance this whole project has stimulated in me. . . . I cannot understand this mass compulsion on the part of the psychiatric profession to write and publish books. . . .

RICHARD Don't worry about it, Doctor. Books by psychiatrists almost always sell well. I'll talk to you again the first of the week. . . .

DR. BRUBAKER Thank you, sir. And once again I must apologize for troubling you. Particularly in the midst of such a delicate situation . . .

RICHARD Yes. Well . . . *What?* What do you mean? What delicate situation?

DR. BRUBAKER I meant only that, as, quite clearly, your second assault on the person of the young lady was more successful than the first, my visit could not have been more inopportune. Good-bye, sir, and good luck!

(DR. BRUBAKER *starts to go.* RICHARD *stops him*)

RICHARD Now wait a minute, Doctor. Now wait a minute. You can't just say something like that and then go . . .

DR. BRUBAKER My boy, I have a full day ahead of me. . . .

RICHARD Look, I can't stand it. You've got to tell me. How did you know—about—what happened?

DR. BRUBAKER In the light of our conversation of last evening, it is quite obvious. I return this morning to find you behind barred doors in an extreme state of sexomasochistic excitement bordering on hysteria. . . .

RICHARD What the hell is sexomasochistic excitement?

DR. BRUBAKER Guilt feelings, sir. Guilt feelings. A state of deep and utter enjoyment induced by reveling in one's guilt feelings. One punishes oneself and one is pardoned of one's crime. And now, my boy, I must really go. Enjoy yourself!

RICHARD Look, this may not seem like very much to you—you spend eight hours a day with rapists and all kinds of—but I've never done anything like this before. . . .

DR. BRUBAKER This is quite obvious.

RICHARD This is the first time. And, by God, it's the last time. . . .

DR. BRUBAKER An excellent decision.

RICHARD I mean, I love my wife!

DR. BRUBAKER   Don't we all? And now, sir . . .

RICHARD   If she ever finds out about this she'll—kill us both.
She'll kill *herself* anyway—and I don't want her to do that.
Maybe it would be better if I didn't tell her. . . .

DR. BRUBAKER   Possibly . . .

RICHARD   But she'd find out some way. I know she would.
What was that you said the other night? There was some
phrase you used. What was it?

DR. BRUBAKER   (*He has wandered over to the bookshelf and
   taken down the copy of* US Camera)
Vigorous denial. This popular theory of the omniscience of
wives is completely untrue. They almost never know. Because they don't want to.

RICHARD   Yeah. Yeah. Vigorous denial. Suppose I denied it.
That's all. She'd have to take my word for it. As a matter of
fact, you know, it's probably a damn good thing this happened. I mean, a couple of days ago—I wasn't even sure if
I did love her. Now I know I do. Helen ought to be damn
glad this happened, if you want to know . . . (*He notices*
DR. BRUBAKER *holding* US Camera) You can take that with
you if you want to . . .

DR. BRUBAKER   No. No, thank you.

RICHARD   You know, suddenly I feel much better. Everything's going to be all right. You're absolutely right, Doctor.
I just won't tell her and everything'll be fine. And if she
should find out, I'll deny it. . . .

DR. BRUBAKER   Vigorously.

RICHARD   Gee, Doctor—I'd like to give you fifty dollars or
something . . .

DR. BRUBAKER   (*Considers this briefly, but rejects it*)   Well
. . . No, no. It will not be necessary . . .
   (*He is casually thumbing through* US Camera *and stops
   at the* GIRL'S *picture*)
However, if the young lady should by any chance suffer any
severe traumatic or emotional disturbances due to your decision to go back to your wife . . . If, in other words, she
appears to be in need of psychiatric aid—I trust you will

mention my name. . . . Thank you once again, sir, and good day . . .

(*He hands* US Camera *back to* RICHARD *and exits.* RICHARD *looks after him thoughtfully for a moment or two. Then, the doors to the bedrooms slide open and* THE GIRL *emerges. She is dressed and is bright and cheerful and very much herself*)

THE GIRL   Hi.

RICHARD   Oh. Hi.

THE GIRL   Golly, I didn't know it was so late. I don't know what happened to me. I've got to be at the studio in half an hour. . . .

RICHARD   The studio . . .

THE GIRL   Sure. The television show. Forty million people are waiting to see me wash my husband's shirt in Trill—that exciting new, no-rinse detergent . . .

RICHARD   Oh.

THE GIRL   Well, I'd better go now. . . .

RICHARD   I was going to make some coffee. . . .

THE GIRL   That's all right. I'll get some on the way.

RICHARD   I don't know how to say this—but you're . . . I mean, I . . .

THE GIRL   I know. Me too . . .

RICHARD   Will I see you—again, I mean?

THE GIRL   I think better not . . .

RICHARD   This whole thing—it's been swell. Only . . .

THE GIRL   Only one thing. We mustn't forget that . . .

RICHARD   What's that?

THE GIRL   This is your birthday.

RICHARD   Gee, that's right. It is.

THE GIRL   Well, I want this to be a happy birthday. . . .

RICHARD   Look. You're not upset about anything, are you?

THE GIRL   No. No, I feel fine. Are you?

RICHARD   Are you sure? I mean, well . . .

THE GIRL   No, really, I feel wonderful. . . . Only . . .
Well, suddenly I feel like maybe it wouldn't be so bad to
have to start getting in at one o'clock again. . . .

RICHARD   Didn't you say—I mean—wouldn't that spoil
everything?

THE GIRL   You don't understand—I mean it would be pretty
nice to have to start getting in at one o'clock again. As soon
as I find someone who's fallen desperately in love with me—
someone who's sweet and intelligent and married—to me
. . . I don't mean you—I mean—you know—someone
who . . .

RICHARD   Someone who never saw Sarah Bernhardt?

THE GIRL   Well, yes . . . Good-bye, and thanks for everything. . . . (*She kisses him lightly on the cheek*) Birthday
kiss. Happy birthday, Richard.

RICHARD   Thank you . . .
      (*She starts up the stairs then turns and stops*)

THE GIRL   Hey—I forgot my hammer.

RICHARD   Yeah—you better take that . . .
      (*Both laugh and are released. She goes up the stairs. The
      trap closes and she is gone*)
      (RICHARD *is a little awed. In a dazed way he wanders over
      to the bar and pours himself a glass of milk. Then, he
      looks at his watch, pulls himself together, picks up* US
      Camera *and heads for bedroom. He puts* US Camera *on
      shelf, starts out. Comes back and drops it behind the row
      of books, hiding it. He starts out again and the door buzzer
      sounds. He goes to the door and opens it.* TOM MACKENZIE
      is standing in the doorway)

TOM   Hi, there . . .

RICHARD   Hello.

TOM   How are you? Hope I didn't wake you . . .

RICHARD   What do you want?

TOM   I'm sorry to bust in on you at this ungodly hour, boy, but I'm here on business. Family business. Got any coffee?

RICHARD   No. What are you doing here? I thought you were up in the country.

TOM   I was. I just drove in this morning. Got an appointment with my agent so Helen asked me to stop by and ask you . . .

RICHARD   Oh! Oh, she did. Well, I'm damn glad she did. I want to talk to you.

TOM   What's the matter with you, boy? You're acting mighty peculiar.

RICHARD   Never mind how *I'm* acting. You think you're pretty fancy with your rain and your damn fireplaces . . .

TOM   What are you talking about? What fireplaces?

RICHARD   You know what fireplaces.

TOM   I don't even have a fireplace.

RICHARD   That's your story.

TOM   I put in radiant heat. It's the latest thing. Cost me three thousand dollars.

RICHARD   Oh, yeah?

TOM   Yeah! They take the coils and they bury them right in the floor. . . . What the hell is all this about fireplaces? Are you drunk or something?

RICHARD   No, I am not drunk! (*From above comes the sound of hammering, a nail being driven into the floor*) She had dinner with you last night, didn't she?

TOM   Sure. Sure. (*More hammering*) What's wrong with that?

RICHARD   And she was wearing that green dress from Clare Potter wasn't she?

TOM   How the hell do I know where she bought that green dress?

RICHARD   Oh, then she *was* wearing it! Worse than I thought!

TOM   You *are* drunk. (*More hammering. This time* TOM *looks up*) What's that?

RICHARD   That's nothing. This used to be a duplex. I just had a glass of milk!

TOM (*Patiently*)   Now see here, old man. Why shouldn't Helen have dinner with me? She's stuck up there in the country while you're down here doing God knows what . . .

RICHARD   What do you mean by that?

TOM   I know what happens with guys like you when their wives are away. Don't forget, I used to be married myself.

RICHARD   I got a good mind to punch you right in the nose.

TOM   Why?

RICHARD   Why—because you're too old—that's why!

TOM   Too old—what are you talking about?

RICHARD   You're getting fat—you look like the portrait of Dorian Gray!

TOM   Drunk. Blind, stinking drunk at nine o'clock in the morning. Where am I getting fat?

RICHARD   Everywhere! You know, there's something really repulsive about old men who run after young wives! Now you get out of here and get back to Helen and tell her I refuse to give her a divorce. . . .

TOM   *A divorce?*

RICHARD   You heard me! You can tell her for me that I'll fight it in every court in the country!

TOM   You're crazy! Helen doesn't want a divorce. . . . (*Yelling, he can no longer control himself*) She wants her yellow skirt!

RICHARD   Her yellow skirt? Oh, my God . . .

TOM (*Bellowing*)   She's having people over for dinner and she needs it!
  (*He exits slamming the door furiously*)

RICHARD   Her yellow skirt . . .
  (*He reaches into hall closet and finds it on the wire hanger.
  Tenderly, he folds it over his arm*)
I'll take her yellow skirt up to her myself. She needs it. She's
having people over for dinner.
People over for dinner? *What* people?
Me! That's what people!
  (*Takes his hat from closet, puts it on his head at a rakish
  angle and with a great flourish exits out the door as*)

                                    THE CURTAIN FALLS

Tea and
Sympathy

by **ROBERT ANDERSON**

THIS IS FOR *Phyllis*

whose spirit is everywhere
in this play and in my life.

AUTHOR'S NOTE

I would like to record here my tremendous debt of gratitude to those persons who helped bring *Tea and Sympathy* so glowingly alive on stage.

It is perhaps not a good selling point for a published volume of a play to say that a playwright writes a play for the theater, for the actors, the director, the designer. But he does. And when he is as brilliantly served by these artists as I have been, he feels a miracle has been brought to pass.

It is not often, I think, that a playwright can say of his produced play, this is the way I wanted it. This is the way I dreamed it would be. I *can* say it. And I can say it because of the devotion to this play of so many creative and wonderful people.

R. A.

was first presented by the Playwrights' Company, in association with Mary K. Frank, at the Ethel Barrymore Theatre, New York City, on September 30, 1953, with the following cast:

(IN ORDER OF APPEARANCE)

LAURA REYNOLDS	Deborah Kerr
LILLY SEARS	Florida Friebus
TOM LEE	John Kerr
DAVID HARRIS	Richard Midgley
RALPH	Alan Sues
AL	Dick York
STEVE	Arthur Steuer
BILL REYNOLDS	Leif Erickson
PHIL	Richard Franchot
HERBERT LEE	John McGovern
PAUL	Yale Wexler

Directed by Elia Kazan

Setting and lighting by Jo Mielziner

Clothes designed by Anna Hill Johnstone

SCENES

Act One

A dormitory in a boys' school in New England.
Late afternoon of a day early in June.

Act Two

SCENE I   Two days later.
SCENE II   Eight-thirty Saturday night.

Act Three

The next afternoon.

Act One

The scene is a small old Colonial house which is now being used as a dormitory in a boys' school in New England.

On the ground floor at stage right we see the house-master's study. To stage left is a hall and stairway which leads up to the boys' rooms. At a half-level on stage left is one of the boys' rooms.

The housemaster's study is a warm and friendly room, rather on the dark side, but when the lamps are lighted, there are cheerful pools of light. There is a fireplace in the back wall, bookcases, and upstage right double doors leading to another part of the house. Since there is no common room for the eight boys in this house, there is considerable leniency in letting the boys use the study whenever the door is left ajar.

The boy's bedroom is small, containing a bed, a chair and a bureau. It was meant to be Spartan, but the present occupant has given it a few touches to make it a little more homelike: an Indian print on the bed, India print curtains for the dormer window. There is a phonograph on the ledge of the window. The door to the room is presumed to lead to the sitting room which the roommates share. There is a door from the sitting room which leads to the stair landing. Thus, to get to the bedroom from the stairs, a person must go through the sitting room.

As the curtain rises, it is late afternoon of a day early in June. No lamps have been lighted yet so the study is in a sort of twilight.

Upstairs in his room, TOM LEE *is sitting on his bed playing the guitar and singing softly and casually, the plaintive song, "The Joys of Love".* . . . TOM *is going on eighteen.*

He is young and a little gangling, but intense. He is wearing faded khaki trousers, a white shirt open at the neck and white tennis sneakers.

Seated in the study listening to the singing are LAURA REYNOLDS *and* LILLY SEARS. LAURA *is a lovely, sensitive woman in her mid to late twenties. Her essence is gentleness. She is compassionate and tender. She is wearing a cashmere sweater and a wool skirt. As she listens to* TOM'S *singing, she is sewing on what is obviously a period costume.*

LILLY *is in her late thirties, and in contrast to the simple effectiveness of* LAURA'S *clothes, she is dressed a little too flashily for her surroundings. . . . It would be in good taste on East 57th Street, but not in a small New England town. . . . A smart suit and hat and a fur piece. As she listens to* TOM *singing, she plays with the martini glass in her hand.*

TOM (*Singing*)   The joys of love
Are but a moment long . . .
The pains of love
Endure forever . . .
    (*When he has finished, he strums on over the same melody very casually, and hums to it intermittently*)

LILLY (*While* TOM *is singing*)   Tom Lee?

LAURA   Yes.

LILLY   Doesn't he have an afternoon class?

LAURA   No. He's the only one in the house that doesn't.

LILLY (*When* TOM *has finished the song*)   Do you know what he's thinking of?

LAURA (*Bites off a thread and looks up*)   What do you mean?

LILLY   What all the boys in this school are thinking about. Not only now in the spring, but all the time . . . Sex!
    (*She wags her head a little wisely, and smiles.*)

LAURA   Lilly, you just like to shock people.

LILLY   Four hundred boys from the ages of thirteen to nineteen. That's the age, Laura. (*Restless, getting up*) Doesn't it give you the willies sometimes, having all these boys around?

LAURA   Of course not. I never think of it that way.

LILLY   Harry tells me they put saltpeter in their food to quiet them down. But the way they look at you, I can't believe it.

LAURA   At me?

LILLY   At any woman worth looking at. When I first came here ten years ago, I didn't think I could stand it. Now I love it. I love watching them look and suffer.

LAURA   Lilly.

LILLY   This is your first spring here, Laura. You wait.

LAURA   They're just boys.

LILLY   The authorities say the ages from thirteen to nineteen . . .

LAURA   Lilly, honestly!

LILLY   You sound as though you were in the grave. How old are you?

LAURA   (*Smiling*)   Over twenty-one.

LILLY   They come here ignorant as all get out about women, and then spend the next four years exchanging misinformation. They're so cute, and so damned intense.
   (*She shudders again*)

LAURA   Most of them seem very casual to me.

LILLY   That's just an air they put on. This is the age Romeo should be played. You'd believe him! So intense! These kids would die for love, or almost anything else. Harry says all their themes end in death.

LAURA   That's boys.

LILLY   Failure; death! Dishonor; death! Lose their girls; death! It's gruesome.

LAURA   But rather touching too, don't you think?

LILLY   You won't tell your husband the way I was talking?

LAURA   Of course not.

LILLY   Though I don't know why I should care. All the boys
talk about me. They have me in and out of bed with every
single master in the school—and some married ones, too.

LAURA (*Kidding her*)   Maybe I'd better listen to them.

LILLY   Oh, never with your husband, of course.

LAURA   Thanks.

LILLY   Even before he met you, Bill never gave me a second
glance. He was all the time organizing teams, planning Mountain Club outings.

LAURA   Bill's good at that sort of thing; he likes it.

LILLY   And you? (LAURA *looks up at* LILLY *and smiles*) Not a
very co-operative witness, are you? I know, mind my own
business. But watch out he doesn't drag his usual quota of boys
to the lodge in Maine this summer.

LAURA   I've got my own plans for him.
   (*She picks up some vacation folders*)

LILLY   Oh really? What?

LAURA   "Come to Canada" . . . I want to get him off on a
trip alone.

LILLY   I don't blame you.

LAURA (*Reflecting*)   Of course I'd really like to go back to
Italy. We had a good time there last summer. It was wonderful
then. You should have seen Bill.

LILLY   Look, honey, you married Bill last year on his sabbatical leave, and abroad to boot. Teachers on sabbatical leave
abroad are like men in uniform during the war. They never
look so good again.

LAURA   Bill looks all right to me.

LILLY   Did Bill ever tell you about the party we gave him
before his sabbatical?

LAURA   Yes. I have a souvenir from it.
   (*She is wearing a rather large Woolworth's diamond ring
   on a gold chain around her neck . . . She now pulls it out
   from her sweater*)

LILLY   I never thought he'd use that Five-and-Dime engagement ring we gave him that night. Even though we gave him an awful ribbing, we all expected him to come back a bachelor.

LAURA   You make it sound as though you kidded him into marrying.

LILLY   Oh, no, honey, it wasn't that.

LAURA (*With meaning*)   No, it wasn't.
   (LAURA *laughs at* LILLY)

LILLY   Well, I've got to go. You know, Bill could have married any number of the right kind of girls around here. But I knew it would take more than the right kind of girl to get Bill to marry. It would take something special. And you're something special.

LAURA   How should I take that?

LILLY   As a compliment. Thanks for the drink. Don't tell Harry I had one when you see him at dinner.

LAURA   We won't be over to the hall. I've laid in a sort of feast for tonight.

LILLY   Celebrating something?

LAURA   No, just an impulse.

LILLY   Well, don't tell Harry anyway.

LAURA   You'd better stop talking the way you've been talking, or I won't have to tell him.

LILLY   Now, look, honey, don't you start going puritan on me. You're the only one in this school I can shoot my mouth off to, so don't change, baby. Don't change.

LAURA   I won't.

LILLY   Some day I'm going to wheedle out of you all the juicy stories you must have from when you were in the theater.

LAURA   Lilly, you would make the most hardened chorus girl blush.

LILLY (*Pleased*)   Really?

LAURA   Really.

LILLY   That's the sweetest thing you've said to me in days. Goodbye.

(*She goes out the door, and a moment later we hear the outside door close*)

LAURA (*Sits for a moment, listening to* TOM'S *rather plaintive whistling. She rises and looks at the Canada vacation literature on the desk, and then, looking at her watch, goes to the door, opens it, and calls up the stairway*)   Tom . . . Oh, Tom.

(*The moment* TOM *hears his name, he jumps from the bed, and goes through the sitting room, and appears on the stairs*)

TOM   Yes?

LAURA (*She is very friendly with him, comradely*)   If it won't spoil your supper, come on down for a cup of tea.

(TOM *goes back into his room and brushes his hair, then he comes on down the stairs, and enters the study. He enters this room as though it were something rare and special. This is where* LAURA *lives*)

(LAURA *has gone out to the other part of the house. Comes to doorway for a moment pouring cream from bottle to pitcher*)

I've just about finished your costume for the play, and we can have a fitting.

TOM   Sure. That'd be great. Do you want the door open or shut?

LAURA (*Goes off again*)   It doesn't make any difference. (TOM *shuts the door. He is deeply in love with this woman, though he knows nothing can come of it. It is a sort of delayed puppy love. It is very touching and very intense. They are easy with each other, casual, though he is always trying in thinly veiled ways to tell her he loves her.* LAURA *enters with tea tray and sees him closing the door. She puts tray on table*)   Perhaps you'd better leave it ajar, so that if some of the other boys get out of class early, they can come in too.

TOM (*Is disappointed*)   Oh, sure.

LAURA (*Goes off for the plate of cookies, but pauses long enough to watch* TOM *open the door the merest crack. She is amused. In a moment, she re-enters with a plate of cookies*)   Help yourself.

TOM   Thanks.
   (*He takes a cookie, and then sits on the floor, near her chair*)

LAURA   Are the boys warm enough in the rooms? They shut down the heat so early this spring, I guess they didn't expect this little chill.

TOM   We're fine. But this is nice.
   (*He indicates low fire in fireplace*)

LAURA   (*Goes back to her sewing*)   I heard you singing.

TOM   I'm sorry if it bothered you.

LAURA   It was very nice.

TOM   If it ever bothers you, just bang on the radiator.

LAURA   What was the name of the song? It's lovely.

TOM   It's an old French song . . . "The Joys of Love" . . .
   (*He speaks the lyric*)
The joys of love
Are but a moment long,
The pain of love
Endures forever.

LAURA   And is that true? (TOM *shrugs his shoulders*) You sang as though you knew all about the pains of love.

TOM   And you don't think I do?

LAURA   Well . . .

TOM   You're right.

LAURA   Only the joys.

TOM   Neither, really.
   (*Teapot whistles off stage*)

LAURA   Then you're a fake. Listening to you, one would think you knew everything there was to know. (*Rises and goes to next room for tea*) Anyway, I don't believe it. A boy like you.

TOM   It's true.

LAURA   (*Off stage*)   Aren't you bringing someone to the dance after the play Saturday?

TOM   Yes.

LAURA   Well, there.

TOM   You.

LAURA   (*Reappears in doorway with teapot*)   Me?

TOM   Yes, you're going to be a hostess, aren't you?

LAURA   Yes, of course, but . . .

TOM   As a member of the committee, I'm taking you. All the committee drew lots . . .

LAURA   And you lost.

TOM   I won.

LAURA   (*A little embarrassed by this*)   Oh. My husband could have taken me.
   (*She sits down again in her chair*)

TOM   He's not going to be in town. Don't you remember, Mountain Climbing Club has its final outing this week-end.

LAURA   Oh, yes, of course. I'd forgotten.

TOM   He's out a lot on that kind of thing, isn't he? (LAURA *ignores his probing*) I hope you're not sorry that I'm to be your escort.

LAURA   Why, I'll be honored.

TOM   I'm supposed to find out tactfully without your knowing it what color dress you'll be wearing.

LAURA   Why?

TOM   The committee will send you a corsage.

LAURA   Oh, how nice. Well, I don't have much to choose from, I guess my yellow.

TOM   The boy who's in charge of getting the flowers thinks a corsage should be something like a funeral decoration. So I'm taking personal charge of getting yours.

LAURA   Thank you.

TOM   You must have gotten lots of flowers when you were acting in the theater.

LAURA   Oh, now and then. Nothing spectacular.

TOM   I can't understand how a person would give up the theater to come and live in a school . . . I'm sorry. I mean, I'm glad you did, but, well . . .

LAURA   If you knew the statistics on unemployed actors, you might understand. Anyway, I was never any great shakes at it.

TOM   I can't believe that.

LAURA   Then take my word for it.

TOM   (*After a moment, looking into the fire, pretending to be casual, but actually touching on his love for* LAURA)   Did you ever do any of Shaw's plays?

LAURA   Yes.

TOM   We got an assignment to read any Shaw play we wanted. I picked *Candida*.

LAURA   Because it was the shortest?

TOM   (*Laughs*)   No . . . because it sounded like the one I'd like the best, one I could understand. Did you ever play Candida?

LAURA   In stock—a very small stock company, way up in Northern Vermont.

TOM   Do you think she did right to send Marchbanks away?

LAURA   Well, Shaw made it seem right. Don't you think?

TOM   (*Really talking about himself*)   That Marchbanks sure sounded off a lot. I could never sound off like that, even if I loved a woman the way he did. She could have made him seem awfully small if she'd wanted to.

LAURA   Well, I guess she wasn't that kind of woman. Now stand up. Let's see if this fits.
     (*She rises with dress in her hands*)

TOM   (*Gets up*)   My Dad's going to hit the roof when he hears I'm playing another girl.

LAURA   I think you're a good sport not to mind. Besides, it's a good part. Lady Teazle in *The School For Scandal*.

TOM (*Puts on top of dress*)   It all started when I did Lady Macbeth last year. You weren't here yet for that. Lucky you.

LAURA   I hear it was very good.

TOM   You should have read a letter I got from my father. They printed a picture of me in the *Alumni Bulletin,* in costume. He was plenty peeved about it.

LAURA   He shouldn't have been.

TOM   He wrote me saying he might be up here today on Alumni Fund business. If he comes over here, and you see him, don't tell him about this.

LAURA   I won't . . . What about your mother? Did she come up for the play?
     (*She helps him button the dress*)

TOM   I don't see my mother. Didn't you know?
     (*He starts to roll up pants legs*)

LAURA   Why no. I didn't.

TOM   She and my father are divorced.

LAURA   I'm sorry.

TOM   You needn't be. They aren't. I was supposed to hold them together. That was how I happened to come into the world. I didn't work. That's a terrible thing, you know, to make a flop of the first job you've got in life.

LAURA   Don't you ever see her?

TOM   Not since I was five. I was with her till five, and then my father took me away. All I remember about my mother is that she was always telling me to go outside and bounce a ball.

LAURA (*Handing him skirt of the dress*)   You must have done something before Lady Macbeth. When did you play that character named Grace?

TOM (*Stiffens*)   I never played anyone called Grace.

LAURA   But I hear the boys sometimes calling you Grace. I thought . . . (*She notices that he's uncomfortable*) I'm sorry. Have I said something terrible?

TOM   No.

LAURA   But I have. I'm sorry.

TOM   It's all right. But it's a long story. Last year over at the movies, they did a revival of Grace Moore in *One Night of Love*. I'd seen the revival before the picture came. And I guess I oversold it, or something. But she was wonderful! . . . Anyway, some of the guys started calling me Grace. It was my own fault, I guess.

LAURA   Nicknames can be terrible. I remember at one time I was called "Beany." I can't remember why, now, but I remember it made me mad. (*She adjusts the dress a little*) Hold still a moment. We'll have to let this out around here. (*She indicates the bosom*) What size do you want to be?

TOM   (*He is embarrassed, but rather nicely, not obviously and farcically. In his embarrassment he looks at* LAURA'S *bosom. then quickly away*)   I don't know. Whatever you think.

LAURA   (*She indicates he is to stand on a small wooden footstool*)   I should think you would have invited some girl up to see you act, and then take her to the dance.

TOM   (*Gets on stool*)   There's nobody I could ask.

LAURA   (*Working on hem of dress*)   What do you mean?

TOM   I don't know any girls, really.

LAURA   Oh, certainly back home . . .

TOM   Last ten years I haven't been home, I mean really home. Summers my father packs me off to camps, and the rest of the time I've been at boarding schools.

LAURA   What about Christmas vacation, and Easter?

TOM   My father gets a raft of tickets to plays and concerts, and sends me and my aunt.

LAURA   I see.

TOM   So I mean it when I say I don't know any girls.

LAURA   Your roommate, Al, knows a lot of girls. Why not ask him to fix you up with a blind date?

TOM   I don't know . . . I can't even dance. I'm telling you this so you won't expect anything of me Saturday night.

LAURA   We'll sit out and talk.

TOM   Okay.

LAURA   Or I could teach you how to dance. It's quite simple.

TOM (*Flustered*)   You?

LAURA   Why not?

TOM   I mean, isn't a person supposed to go to some sort of dancing class or something?
    (*He gets down from footstool*)

LAURA   Not necessarily. Look, I'll show you how simple it is. (*She assumes the dancing position*) Hold your left hand out this way, and put your right hand around my—(*She stops as she sees him looking at her*) Oh, now you're kidding me. A boy your age and you don't know how to dance.

TOM   I'm not kidding you.

LAURA   Well, then, come on. I had to teach my husband. Put your arm around me.
    (*She raises her arms*)

TOM (*Looks at her a moment, afraid to touch this woman he loves. Then to pass it off*)   We better put it off. We'd look kind of silly, both of us in skirts.

LAURA   All right. Take it off, then. No, wait a minute. Just let me stand off and take a look . . . (*She walks around him*) You're going to make a very lovely girl.

TOM   Thank you, ma'am . . .
    (*He kids a curtsy, like a girl, and starts out of his costume. MR. HARRIS, a good-looking young master, comes in the hallway and starts up to Tom's room. On the landing, he knocks on Tom's door*)

LAURA   I wonder who that is?

TOM   All the other fellows have late afternoon classes.

LAURA (*Opens the door wider, and looks up the stairs*)   Yes? Oh, David.

HARRIS (*Turns and looks down the stairs*)   Oh, hello, Laura.

LAURA   I just was wondering who was coming in.
  (TOM *proceeds to get out of the costume*)

HARRIS   I want to see Tom Lee.

LAURA   He's down here. I'm making his costume for the play.

HARRIS   I wonder if I could see him for a moment?

LAURA   Why yes, of course. Tom, Mr. Harris would like to see you. Do you want to use our study, David? I can go into the living room.

HARRIS   No, thanks. I'll wait for him in his room. Will you ask him to come up?
  (*He opens the door and goes in*)

LAURA   (*Is puzzled at his intensity, the urgency in his voice. Comes back in the study*)   Tom, Mr. Harris would like to see you in your room. He's gone along.

TOM   That's funny.

LAURA   Wait a minute . . . take this up with you, try it on in front of your mirror . . . see if you can move in it . . . (*She hands him skirt of costume*) When Mr. Harris is through, bring the costume back.

TOM   (*Anxious over what* HARRIS *wants to see him about*) Yeah, sure. (*He starts out, then stops and picks up a cookie. He looks at her lovingly*) Thanks for tea.

LAURA   You're welcome.
  (TOM *goes to the door as* LAURA *turns to the desk. He stands in the door a moment and looks at her back, then he turns and shuts the door and heads upstairs.* HARRIS *has come into* TOM'S *bedroom, and is standing there nervously clenching and unclenching his hands*)

TOM   (*Off stage, presumably in the study he shares with his roommate*)   Mr. Harris?
  (LAURA *wanders off into the other part of the house after looking for a moment at the Canada vacation material on the desk*)

HARRIS   I'm in here.

TOM (*Comes in a little hesitantly*)   Oh. Hello, sir.
(HARRIS *closes the door to the bedroom.* TOM *regards this action with some nervousness*)

HARRIS   Well?

TOM (*Has dumped some clothes from a chair to his bed. Offers chair to* HARRIS)   Sir?

HARRIS   What did you tell the Dean?

TOM   What do you mean, Mr. Harris?

HARRIS   What did you tell the Dean?

TOM   When? What are you talking about, sir?

HARRIS   Didn't the Dean call you in?

TOM   No. Why should he?

HARRIS   He didn't call you in and ask you about last Saturday afternoon?

TOM   Why should he? I didn't do anything wrong.

HARRIS   About being with me?

TOM   I'm allowed to leave town for the day in the company of a master.

HARRIS   I don't believe you. You must have said something.

TOM   About what?

HARRIS   About you and me going down to the dunes and swimming.

TOM   Why should I tell him about that?

HARRIS (*Threatening*)   Why didn't you keep your mouth shut?

TOM   About what? What, for God's sake?

HARRIS   I never touched you, did I?

TOM   What do you mean, touch me?

HARRIS   Did you say to the Dean I touched you?

TOM (*Turning away from* HARRIS)   I don't know what you're talking about.

HARRIS   Here's what I'm talking about. The Dean's had me on the carpet all afternoon. I probably won't be reappointed next year . . . and all because I took you swimming down off the dunes on Saturday.

TOM   Why should he have you on the carpet for that?

HARRIS   You can't imagine, I suppose.

TOM   What did you do wrong?

HARRIS   Nothing! Nothing, unless you made it seem like something wrong. Did you?

TOM   I told you I didn't see the Dean.

HARRIS   You will. He'll call for you. Bunch of gossiping old busybodies! Well . . . (*He starts for the door, stops, turns around and softens. He comes back to the puzzled* TOM) I'm sorry . . . It probably wasn't your fault. It was my fault. I should have been more . . . discreet . . . Good-bye. Good luck with your music.
   (TOM *hasn't understood. He doesn't know what to say. He makes a helpless gesture with his hands.* HARRIS *goes into the other room on his way out. Three boys, about seventeen, come in from the downstairs hall door and start up the stairs. They're carrying books. All are wearing sports jackets, khaki or flannel trousers, white or saddle rubber-soled shoes*)

AL   I don't believe a word of it.

RALPH (*He is large and a loud-mouthed bully*)   I'm telling you the guys saw them down at the dunes.

AL (*He is* TOM's *roommate, an athlete*)   So what?

RALPH   They were bare-assed.

AL   Shut up, will you? You want Mrs. Reynolds to hear you?

RALPH   Okay. You watch and see. Harris'll get bounced, and I'm gonna lock my room at night as long as Tom is living in this house.

AL   Oh, dry up!

RALPH   Jeeze, you're his roommate and you're not worried.

HARRIS (*Comes out the door and starts down the stairs*)   Hello. (*He goes down stairs and out*)

AL   Sir.

RALPH   Do you believe me now? You aren't safe. Believe me.

STEVE (*He is small,* RALPH's *appreciative audience. He comes in the front door*)   Hey, Al, can I come in watch Mrs. Morrison nurse her kid?

RALPH   You're the loudest-mouthed bastard I ever heard. You want to give it away.

STEVE   It's time. How about it, Al?

AL (*Grudgingly*)   Come on.
(TOM *hears them coming, and moves to bolt his door, but* STEVE *and* RALPH *break in before he gets to the door. He watches them from the doorway.* STEVE *rushes to the bed and throws himself across it, looking out the window next to the bed.* RALPH *settles down next to him*)

AL (*To* TOM *as he comes in*)   Hi. These horny bastards.

STEVE   Al, bring the glasses.
(AL *goes into sitting room*)

RALPH   Some day she's going to wean that little bastard and spoil all our fun.

STEVE   Imagine sitting in a window . . .

TOM (*Has been watching this with growing annoyance*) Will you guys get out of here?

RALPH (*Notices* TOM *for the first time*)   What's the matter with you, Grace?

TOM   This is my damned room.

RALPH   Gracie's getting private all of a sudden.

TOM   I don't want a lot of Peeping Toms lying on my bed watching a . . . a . . .

STEVE   You want it all for yourself, don't you?

RALPH   Or aren't you interested in women?

AL (*Comes back in with field glasses*)   Shut up! (*Looks out window, then realizes* TOM *is watching him. Embarrassed*) These horny bastards.

STEVE (*Looking*)   Geeze!

RALPH (*A bully, riding down on* TOM)   I thought you were going to play ball with us Saturday.

TOM   I didn't feel like it.

RALPH   What *did* you feel like doing, huh?

AL   Will you shut up?

STEVE   Hey, lookit.
  (*Grabs glasses from* AL. AL *leaves room*)

TOM (*Climbing over* STEVE *and* RALPH *and trying to pull the shade*)   I told you to get out. I told you last time . . .

RALPH (*Grabbing hold of* TOM, *and holding him down*)   Be still, boy, or she'll see, and you'll spoil everything.

TOM   Horny bastard. Get out of here.

RALPH   Who are you calling a horny bastard? (*He grabs hold of* TOM *more forcefully, and slaps him a couple of times across the face, not trying to hurt him, but just to humiliate him.* STEVE *gets in a few pokes and in a moment, it's not in fun, but verging on the serious*)   You don't mean that now, boy, do you . . . Do you, Grace? (*He slaps him again*)

AL (*Hearing the scuffle, comes in and hauls* RALPH *and* STEVE *off* TOM)   Come on, come on, break it up. Clear out.
  (*He has them both standing up now,* TOM *still on the bed*)

RALPH   I just don't like that son of a bitch calling me a horny bastard. Maybe if it was Dr. Morrison instead of Mrs. Morrison, he'd be more interested. Hey, wouldn't you, Grace?
  (*He tries to stick his face in front of* TOM, *but* AL *holds him back*)

AL   Come on, lay off the guy, will you? Go on. Get ready for supper.
  (*He herds them out during this. When they have left the room,* TOM *gets up and goes to bureau and gets a handkerchief. He has a bloody nose. He lies down on the bed, his head tilted back to stop the blood*)

AL (*In doorway*)   You all right?

TOM   Yeah.

(RALPH *and* STEVE *go up the stairway singing in raucous voices, "One Night of Love." The downstairs outside door opens, and* BILL REYNOLDS *enters the hall with a student,* PHIL. BILL *is* LAURA'S *husband. He is large and strong with a tendency to be gruff. He's wearing gray flannel trousers, a tweed jacket, a blue button-down shirt. He is around forty*)

BILL   Okay, boy, we'll look forward to—(*He notices* RALPH *still singing. He goes to the bend in the stairs and calls*) Hey, Ralph . . . Ralph!

RALPH   (*Stops singing up out of sight*)   You calling me, Mr. Reynolds, sir?

BILL   Yeah. Keep it down to a shout, will you?

RALPH   Oh, *yes, sir.* Sorry, I didn't know I was disturbing you, Mr. Reynolds.

BILL   (*Comes back and talks with* PHIL *at the bend in the stairway*)   Phil, you come on up to the lodge around . . . Let's see . . . We'll open the lodge around July first, so you plan to come up say, July third, and stay for two weeks. Okay?

PHIL   That'll be swell, sir.

BILL   Frank Hocktor's coming then. You get along with Frank, don't you? He's a regular guy.

PHIL   Oh, sure.

BILL   The float's all gone to pieces. We can make that your project to fix it up. Okay?

PHIL   Thanks a lot, Mr. Reynolds.
(*He goes on up the stairs*)

BILL   See you.
(*He comes in and crosses to phone and starts to call*)

LAURA   (*Off stage*)   Tom?
(BILL *looks around in the direction of the voice, but says nothing*)

LAURA   (*Comes on*)   Oh, Bill. Tom was down trying on his costume. I thought . . . You're early.

BILL   Yes, I want to catch the Dean before he leaves his office. (LAURA *goes up to him to be kissed, but he's too intent on the phone, and she compromises by kissing his cheek*) Hello, this is Mr. Reynolds. Is the Dean still in his office?

LAURA   What's the matter, Bill?

BILL   Nothing very pretty. Oh? How long ago? All right. Thanks. I'll give him a couple of minutes, then I'll call him home. (*Hangs up*) Well, they finally caught up with Harris. (*He goes into the next room to take off his jacket*)

LAURA   What do you mean, "caught up" with him?

BILL   (*Off stage*)   You're going to hear it anyhow . . . so . . . last Saturday they caught him down in the dunes, naked.

LAURA   (*Crosses to close door to hall*)   What's wrong with that?

BILL   (*Enters and crosses to fireplace and starts to go through letters propped there. He has taken off his jacket*)   He wasn't alone.

LAURA   Oh.

BILL   He was lying there naked in the dunes, and one of the students was lying there naked too. Just to talk about it is disgusting.

LAURA   I see.

BILL   I guess you'll admit that's something.

LAURA   I can't see that it's necessarily conclusive.

BILL   With a man like Harris, it's conclusive enough. (*Then casually*)   The student with him was—

LAURA   (*Interrupting*)   I'm not sure I care to know.

BILL   I'm afraid you're going to have to know sooner or later, Laura. It was Tom Lee.
  (TOM *rises from bed, grabs a towel and goes out up the stairs.* LAURA *just looks at* BILL *and frowns*)

BILL   Some of the boys down on the Varsity Club outing came on them . . . or at least saw them . . . And Fin Hadley saw them too, and he apparently used his brains for once and spoke to the Dean.

LAURA   And?

BILL   He's had Harris on the carpet this afternoon, I guess
he'll be fired. I certainly hope so. Maybe Tom too, I don't
know.

LAURA   They put two and two together?

BILL   Yes, Laura.

LAURA   I suppose this is all over school by now.

BILL   I'm afraid so.

LAURA   And most of the boys know.

BILL   Yes.

LAURA   So what's going to happen to Tom?

BILL   (*Takes pipe from mantelpiece and cleans it*)   I know you
won't like this, Laura, but I think he should be kicked out. I
think you've got to let people know the school doesn't stand for
even a hint of this sort of thing. He should be booted.

LAURA   For what?

BILL   Look, a boy's caught coming out of Ellie Martin's rooms
across the river. That's enough evidence. Nobody asks particu-
lars. They don't go to Ellie's rooms to play Canasta. It's the
same here.

LAURA   (*Hardly daring to suggest it*)   But, Bill . . . you
don't think . . . I mean, you don't think Tom is . . . (*She
stops.* BILL *looks at her a moment, his answer is in his silence*)
Oh, Bill!

BILL   And I'm ashamed and sorry as hell for his father. Herb
Lee was always damned good to me . . . came down from
college when I was playing football here . . . helped me get
into college . . . looked after me when I was in college and
he was in law school . . . And I know he put the boy in my
house hoping I could do something with him.
      (*He dials number*)

LAURA   And you feel you've failed.

BILL   Yes. (*He pauses*) With your help, I might say.
      (*Busy signal. He hangs up*)

LAURA   How?

BILL   Because, Laura, the boy would rather sit around here and talk with you and listen to music and strum his guitar.

LAURA   Bill, I'm not to blame for everything. Everything's not my fault.

BILL   (*Disregarding this*)   What a lousy thing for Herb. (*He looks at a small picture of a team on his desk*) That's Herb. He was Graduate Manager of the team when I was a sophomore in college. He was always the manager of the teams, and he really wanted his son to be there in the center of the picture.

LAURA   Why are you calling the Dean?

BILL   I'm going to find out what's being done.

LAURA   I've never seen you like this before.

BILL   This is something that touches me very closely. The name of the school, its reputation, the reputation of all of us here. I went here and my father before me, and one day I hope our children will come here, when we have them. And, of course, one day I hope to be headmaster.

LAURA   Let's assume that you're right about Harris. It's a terrible thing to say on the evidence you've got, but let's assume you're right. Does it necessarily follow that Tom—

BILL   Tom was his friend. Everyone knew that.

LAURA   Harris encouraged him in his music.

BILL   Come on, Laura.

LAURA   What if Tom's roommate, Al, or some other great big athlete had been out with Harris?

BILL   He wouldn't have been.

LAURA   I'm saying what if he had been? Would you have jumped to the same conclusion?

BILL   It would have been different. Tom's always been an off-horse. And now it's quite obvious why. If he's kicked out, maybe it'll bring him to his senses. But he won't change if nothing's done about it. (LAURA *turns away.* BILL *starts to look over his mail again*) Anyway, why are you so concerned over what happens to Tom Lee?

LAURA   I've come to know him. You even imply that I am somewhat responsible for his present reputation.

BILL   All right. I shouldn't have said that. But you watch, now that it's out in the open. Look at the way he walks, the way he sometimes stands.

LAURA   Oh, Bill!

BILL   All right, so a woman doesn't notice these things. But a man knows a queer when he sees one. (*He has opened a letter. Reads*) The bookstore now has the book you wanted . . . *The Rose and The Thorn*. What's that?

LAURA   A book of poems. Do you know, Bill, I'll bet he doesn't even know the meaning of the word . . . queer.

BILL   What do you think he is?

LAURA   I think he's a nice sensitive kid who doesn't know the meaning of the word.

BILL   He's eighteen, or almost. I don't know.

LAURA   How much did you know at eighteen?

BILL   A lot. (*At the desk he now notices the Canada literature*) What are these?

LAURA   What?

BILL   These.

LAURA   Oh, nothing.

BILL   (*He throws them in wastebasket, then notices her look*) Well, they're obviously something.
   (*He takes them out of wastebasket*)

LAURA   (*The joy of it gone for her*)   I was thinking we might take a motor trip up there this summer.

BILL   (*Dialing phone again*)   I wish you'd said something about it earlier. I've already invited some of the scholarship boys up to the lodge. I can't disappoint them.

LAURA   Of course not.

BILL   If you'd said something earlier.

LAURA   It's my fault.

BILL   It's nobody's fault, it's just—Hello, Fitz, Bill Reynolds—
I was wondering if you're going to be in tonight after supper
. . . Oh . . . oh, I see . . . Supper? Well, sure I could talk
about it at supper. . . . Well, no, I think I'd better drop over
alone. . . . All right. I'll see you at the house then . . .
Good-bye.

(LAURA *looks at him, trying to understand him.* BILL *comes
to her to speak softly to her. Seeing him come, she holds out
her arms to be embraced, but he just takes her chin in his
hand*)

BILL   Look, Laura, when I brought you here a year ago, I told
you it was a tough place for a woman with a heart like yours.
I told you you'd run across boys, big and little boys, full of
problems, problems which for the moment seem gigantic and
heartbreaking. And you promised me then you wouldn't get
all taken up with them. Remember?

LAURA   Yes.

BILL   When I was a kid in school here, I had my problems too.
There's a place up by the golf course where I used to go off
alone Sunday afternoons and cry my eyes out. I used to lie
on my bed just the way Tom does, listening to phonograph
records hour after hour. (LAURA, *touched by this, kneels at
his side*) But I got over it, Laura. I learned how to take it.
(LAURA *looks at him. This touches her*) When the headmaster's wife gave you this teapot, she told you what she
tells all the new masters' wives. You have to be an interested
bystander.

LAURA   I know.

BILL   Just as she said, all you're supposed to do is every once
in a while give the boys a little tea and sympathy. Do you remember?

LAURA   Yes, I remember. It's just that . . .

BILL   What?

LAURA   This age—seventeen, eighteen—it's so . . .

BILL   I know.

LAURA   John was this age when I married him.

BILL   Look, Laura . . .

LAURA   I know. You don't like me to talk about John, but . . .

BILL   It's not that. It's . . .

LAURA   He was just this age, eighteen or so, when I married him. We both were. And I know now how this age can suffer. It's a heartbreaking time . . . no longer a boy . . . not yet a man . . . Bill? Bill?

BILL   (*Looks at her awkwardly a moment, then starts to move off*)   I'd better clean up if I'm going to get to the Dean's for supper. You don't mind, do you?

LAURA   (*Very quietly*)   I got things in for dinner here. But they'll keep.

BILL   (*Awkwardly*)   I'm sorry, Laura. But you understand, don't you? About this business? (LAURA *shakes her head, "No."* BILL *stands over her, a little put out that she has not understood his reasoning. He starts to say something several times, then stops. Finally he notices the Five-and-Dime engagement ring around her neck. He touches it*)   You're not going to wear this thing to the dining hall, are you?

LAURA   Why not?

BILL   It was just a gag. It means something to you, but to them . . .

LAURA   (*Bearing in, but gently*)   Does it mean anything to you, Bill?

BILL   Well, it did, but . . .
        (*He stops with a gesture, unwilling to go into it all*)

LAURA   I think you're ashamed of the night you gave it to me. That you ever let me see you needed help. That night in Italy, in some vague way you cried out . . .

BILL   What is the matter with you today? *Me* crying out for help.
        (*He heads for the other room. A knock on study door is heard*)

BILL   It's probably Tom.
        (LAURA *goes to door*)

HERB (*This is* HERBERT LEE, TOM'S *father. He is a middle-sized man, fancying himself a man of the world and an extrovert. He is dressed as a conservative Boston businessman, but with still a touch of the collegiate in his attire—button-down shirt, etc.*) Mrs. Reynolds?

LAURA Yes?

BILL (*Stopped by the voice, turns*) Herb! Come in.

HERB (*Coming in*) Hiya, Bill. How are you, fella?

BILL (*Taking his hand*) I'm fine, Herb.

HERB (*Poking his finger into* BILL'S *chest*) Great to see you. (*Looks around to* LAURA) Oh, uh . . .

BILL I don't think you've met Laura, Herb. This is Laura. Laura, this is Herb Lee, Tom's father.

HERB (*Hearty and friendly, meant to put people at their ease*) Hello, Laura.

LAURA I've heard so much about you.

HERB (*After looking at her for a moment*) I like her, Bill. I like her very much. (LAURA *blushes, and is a little taken aback by this. To* LAURA) What I'd like to know is how did you manage to do it? (*Cuffing* BILL) I'll bet you make her life miserable . . . You look good, Bill.

BILL You don't look so bad yourself.
    (*He takes in a notch in his belt*)

HERB No, *you're* in shape. I never had anything to keep in shape, but you . . . You should have see this boy, Laura.

LAURA I've seen pictures.

HERB Only exercise I get these days is bending the elbow.

LAURA May I get you something? A drink?

HERB No, thanks. I haven't got much time.

BILL You drive out from Boston, Herb?

HERB No, train. You know, Bill, I think that's the same old train you and I used to ride in when we came here.

BILL Probably is.

HERB   If I don't catch the six-fifty-four, I'll have to stay all night, and I'd rather not.

BILL   We'd be glad to put you up.

HERB   No. You're putting me up in a couple of weeks at the reunion. That's imposing enough. (*There is an awkward pause. Both men sit down*) I . . . uh . . . was over at the Dean's this afternoon.

BILL   Oh, he called you?

HERB   Why, no. I was up discussing Alumni Fund matters with him . . . and . . . Do you know about it?

BILL   You mean about Tom?

HERB   Yes.
       (*Looks at* LAURA)

BILL   Laura knows too.
       (*He reaches for her to come to him, and he puts his arm around her waist*)

HERB   Well, after we discussed the Fund, he told me about that. Thought I ought to hear about it from him. Pretty casual about it, I thought.

BILL   Well, that's Fitz.

HERB   What I want to know is, what was a guy like Harris doing at the school?

BILL   I tried to tell them.

HERB   Was there anyone around like that in our day, Bill?

BILL   No. You're right.

HERB   I tried to find the guy. I wanted to punch his face for him. But he's cleared out. Is Tom around?

LAURA   He's in his room.

HERB   How'd he get mixed up with a guy like that?

BILL   I don't know, Herb . . .

HERB   I know. I shouldn't ask you. I know. Of course I don't believe Tom was really involved with this fellow. If I believed

that, I'd . . . well, I don't know what I'd do. You don't
believe it, do you, Bill?

BILL   Why . . .
   (*Looks at* LAURA)

HERB (*Cutting in*)   Of course you don't. But what's the matter? What's happened, Bill? Why isn't my boy a regular fellow?
He's had every chance to be since he was knee-high to a
grasshopper—boys' camps every summer, boarding schools.
What do you think, Laura?

LAURA   I'm afraid I'm not the one to ask, Mr. Lee.
   (*She breaks away from* BILL)

HERB   He's always been with men and boys. Why doesn't
some of it rub off?

LAURA   You see, I feel he's a "regular fellow" . . . whatever
that is.

HERB   You do?

LAURA   If it's sports that matter, he's an excellent tennis
player.

HERB   But Laura, he doesn't even play tennis like a regular
fellow. No hard drives and cannon-ball serves. He's a cut artist.
He can put more damn twists on that ball.

LAURA   He wins. He's the school champion. And isn't he the
champion of your club back home?
   (TOM *comes down the stairs and enters his bedroom with
   the costume skirt and towel*)

HERB   I'm glad you mentioned that . . . because that's just
what I mean. Do you know, Laura, his winning that championship brought me one of my greatest humiliations? I hadn't
been able to watch the match. I was supposed to be in from a
round of golf in time, but we got held up on every hole . . .
And when I got back to the locker room, I heard a couple of
men talking about Tom's match in the next locker section.
And what they said, cut me to the quick, Laura. One of them
said, "It's a damn shame Tom Lee won the match. He's a
good player, all right, but John Batty is such a regular guy."
John Batty was his opponent. Now what pleasure was there
for me in that?

BILL   I know what you mean.

HERB   I *want* to be proud of him. My God, that's why I had him in the first place. That's why I took him from his mother when we split up, but . . . Look, this is a terrible thing to say, but you know the scholarships the University Club sponsors for needy kids . . .

BILL   Sure.

HERB   Well, I contribute pretty heavily to it, and I happened to latch on to one of the kids we help—an orphan. I sort of talk to him like a father, go up to see him at his school once in a while, and that kid listens to me . . . and you know what, he's shaping up better than my own son.
   (*There is an awkward pause. Upstairs* TOM *has put a record on the phonograph. It starts playing now*)

BILL   You saw the Dean, Herb?

HERB   Yes.

BILL   And?

HERB   He told me the circumstances. Told me he was confident that Tom was innocently involved. He actually apologized for the whole thing. He did say that some of the faculty had suggested—though he didn't go along with this—that Tom would be more comfortable if I took him out of school. But I'm not going to. He's had nothing but comfort all his life, and look what's happened. My associates ask me what he wants to be, and I tell them he hasn't made up his mind. Because I'll be damned if I'll tell them he wants to be a singer of folk songs.
   (TOM *lies on the bed listening to the music*)

BILL   So you're going to leave him in?

HERB   Of course. Let him stick it out. It'll be a good lesson.

LAURA   Mightn't it be more than just a lesson, Mr. Lee?

HERB   Oh, he'll take some kidding. He'll have to work extra hard to prove to them he's . . . well, manly. It may be the thing that brings him to his senses.

LAURA   Mr. Lee, Tom's a very sensitive boy. He's a very lonely boy.

HERB   Why should he be lonely? I've always seen to it that he's been with people . . . at camps, at boarding schools.

BILL   He's certainly an off-horse, Herb.

HERB   That's a good way of putting it, Bill. An off-horse. Well, he's going to have to learn to run with the other horses. Well, I'd better be going up.

LAURA   Mr. Lee, this may sound terribly naive of me, and perhaps a trifle indelicate, but I don't believe your son knows what this is all about. Why Mr. Harris was fired, why the boys will kid him.

HERB   You mean . . .
   (*Stops*)

LAURA   I'm only guessing. But I think when it comes to these boys, we often take too much knowledge for granted. And I think it's going to come as a terrible shock when he finds out what they're talking about. Not just a lesson, a shock.

HERB   I don't believe he's as naive as all that. I just don't. Well . . .
   (*He starts for the door*)

BILL   (*Takes* HERB'S *arm and they go into the hall*)   I'm going over to the Dean's for supper, Herb. If you're through with Tom come by here and I'll walk you part way to the station.

HERB   All right. (*Stops on the stairs*) How do you talk to the boys, Bill?

BILL   I don't know. I just talk to them.

HERB   They're not your sons. I only talked with Tom, I mean, really talked with him, once before. It was after a Sunday dinner and I made up my mind it was time we sat in a room together and talked about important things. He got sick to his stomach. That's a terrible effect to have on your boy . . . Well, I'll drop down.
   (*He takes a roll of money from his pocket and looks at it, then starts up the stairs*)

BILL   (*Coming into his study*)   Laura, you shouldn't try to tell him about his own son. After all, if he doesn't know the boy, who does?

LAURA   I'm sorry.

(BILL *exits into the other part of the house, pulling off his tie.* HERB *has gone up the stairs. Knocks on the study door.* LAURA *settles down in her chair and eventually goes on with her sewing*)

AL (*Inside, calls*)   Come in.

(HERB *goes in and shuts the door*)

HERB (*Opens* TOM'S *bedroom door and sticks his head in*) Hello, there.

TOM (*Looks up from the bed, surprised*)   Oh . . . Hi . . .

HERB   I got held up at the Dean's.

TOM   Oh.

(*He has risen, and attempts to kiss his father on the cheek. But his father holds him off with a firm handshake*)

HERB   How's everything? You look bushed.

TOM   I'm okay.

HERB (*Looking at him closely*)   You sure?

TOM   Sure.

HERB (*Looking around room*)   This room looks smaller than I remember. (*He throws on light switch*) I used to have the bed over here. Used to rain in some nights. (*Comes across phonograph*) This the one I gave you for Christmas?

TOM   Yeah. It works fine.

HERB (*Turns phonograph off*)   You're neater than I was. My vest was always behind the radiator, or somewhere. (*Sees part of dress costume*) What's this?

TOM (*Hesitates for a moment. Then*)   A costume Mrs. Reynolds made for me. I'm in the play.

HERB   You didn't write about it.

TOM   I know.

HERB   What are you playing?
(*Looks at dress*)

TOM   You know *The School For Scandal*. I'm playing Lady Teazle.

HERB   Tom, I want to talk to you. Last time we tried to talk, it didn't work out so well.

TOM   What's up?

HERB   Tom, I'd like to be your friend. I guess there's something between fathers and sons that keeps them from being friends, but I'd like to try.

TOM (*Embarrassed*)   Sure, Dad.
   (*He sits on the bed*)

HERB   Now when you came here, I told you to make friends slowly. I told you to make sure they were the right kind of friends. You're known by the company you keep. Remember I said that?

TOM   Yes.

HERB   And I told you if you didn't want to go out for sports like football, hockey . . . that was all right with me. But you'd get in with the right kind of fellow if you managed these teams. They're usually pretty good guys. You remember.

TOM   Yes.

HERB   Didn't you believe me?

TOM   Yes, I believed you.

HERB   Okay, then let's say you believed me, but you decided to go your own way. That's all right too, only you see what it's led to.

TOM   What?

HERB   You made friends with people like this Harris guy who got himself fired.

TOM   Why is he getting fired?

HERB   He's being fired because he was seen in the dunes with you.

TOM   Look, I don't—

HERB   Naked.

TOM   You too?

HERB   So you know what I'm talking about?

TOM   No, I don't.

HERB   You do too know. I heard my sister tell you once. She
warned you about a janitor in the building down the street.

TOM (*Incredulous*)   Mr. Harris . . . ?

HERB   Yes. He's being fired because he's been doing a lot
of suspicious things around apparently, and this finished it. All
right, I'll say it plain, Tom. He's a fairy. A homosexual.

TOM   Who says so?

HERB   Now, Tom—

TOM   And seeing us on the beach . . .

HERB   Yes.

TOM   And what does that make me?

HERB   Listen, I know you're all right.

TOM   Thanks.

HERB   Now wait a minute.

TOM   Look, we were just swimming.

HERB   All right, all right. So perhaps you didn't know.

TOM   What do you mean perhaps?

HERB   It's the school's fault for having a guy like that around.
But it's your fault for being a damned fool in picking your
friends.

TOM   So that's what the guys meant.

HERB   You're going to get a ribbing for a while, but you're
going to be a man about it and you're going to take it and
you're going to come through much more careful how you
make your friends.

TOM   He's kicked out because he was seen with me on the
beach, and I'm telling you that nothing, absolutely nothing
. . . Look, I'm going to the Dean and tell him that Harris did
nothing, that—

HERB (*Stopping him*)   Look, don't be a fool. It's going to be
hard enough for you without sticking your neck out, asking for
it.

TOM But, Dad!

HERB He's not going to be reappointed next year. Nothing you can say is going to change anyone's mind. You got to think about yourself. Now, first of all, get your hair cut. (TOM *looks at father, disgusted*) Look, this isn't easy for me. Stop thinking about yourself, and give me a break. (TOM *looks up at this appeal*) I suppose you think it's going to be fun for *me* to have to live this down back home. It'll get around, and it'll affect me, too. So we've got to see this thing through together. You've got to do your part. Get your hair cut. And then . . . No, the first thing I want you to do is call whoever is putting on this play, and tell them you're not playing this lady whatever her name is.

TOM Why shouldn't I play it? It's the best part in the play, and I was chosen to play it.

HERB I should think you'd have the sense to see why you shouldn't.

TOM Wait a minute. You mean . . . do you mean, you think I'm . . . whatever you call it? Do you, Dad?

HERB I told you "no."

TOM But the fellows are going to think that I'm . . . and Mrs. Reynolds?

HERB Yes. You're going to have to fight their thinking it. Yes.

(TOM *sits on the bed, the full realization of it dawning*)

RALPH (*Sticks his head around the stairs from upstairs, and yells*) Hey, Grace, who's taking you to the dance Saturday night? Hey, Grace!

(*He disappears again up the stairs*)

HERB What's that all about?

TOM I don't know.

(LAURA, *as the noise comes in, rises and goes to the door to stop it, but* AL *comes into the hall and goes upstairs yelling at the boys and* LAURA *goes back to her chair*)

HERB (*Looks at his watch*) Now . . . Do you want me to stay over? If I'm not going to stay over tonight, I've got to catch the six-fifty four.

TOM Stay over?

HERB Yes, I didn't bring a change of clothes along, but if you want me to stay over . . .

TOM Why should you stay over?

HERB (*Stung a little by this*) All right. Now come on down to Bill's room and telephone this drama fellow. So I'll know you're making a start of it. And bring the dress.

TOM I'll do it tomorrow.

HERB I'd feel better if you did it tonight. Come on. I'm walking out with Bill. And incidentally, the Dean said if the ribbing goes beyond bounds . . . you know . . . you're to come to him and he'll take some steps. He's not going to do anything now, because these things take care of themselves. They're better ignored . . .
(*They have both started out of the bedroom, but during the above* HERB *goes back for the dress.* TOM *continues out and stands on the stairs looking at the telephone in the hall*)

HERB (*Comes out of the study. Calls back*) See you Al. Take good care of my boy here. (*Starts down stairs. Stops*) You need any money?

TOM No.

HERB I'm lining you up with a counselor's job at camp this year. If this thing doesn't spoil it. (*Stops*) You sure you've got enough money to come home?

TOM Yes, sure. Look Dad, let me call about the play from here.
(*He takes receiver off hook*)

HERB Why not use Bill's phone? He won't mind. Come on. (TOM *reluctantly puts phone back on hook*) Look, if you've got any problems, talk them over with Bill—Mr. Reynolds. He's an old friend, and I think he'd tell you about what I'd tell you in a spot. (*Goes into master's study*) Is Bill ready?

LAURA He'll be right down. How does the costume work?

TOM I guess it's all right, only . . .

HERB   I'd like Tom to use your phone if he may—to call who-ever's putting on the play. He's giving up the part.

LAURA   Giving up the part?

HERB   Yes. I've . . . I want him to. He's doing it for me.

LAURA   Mr. Lee, it was a great honor for him to be chosen to play the part.

HERB   Bill will understand. Bill! (*He thrusts costume into* LAURA'*s hand and goes off through alcove*) Bill, what's the number of the man putting on the play? Tom wants to call him.
   (LAURA *looks at* TOM *who keeps his eyes from her. She makes a move towards him, but he takes a step away*)

BILL   (*Off stage*)   Fred Mayberry . . . Three-two-six . . . You ready, Herb?

HERB   (*Off stage*)   Yes. You don't mind if Tom uses your phone, do you?

BILL   Of course not.

HERB   (*Comes in*)   When do you go on your mountain-climb-ing week-end, Bill?

BILL   (*Comes in*)   This week-end's the outing.

HERB   Maybe Tom could go with you.

BILL   He's on the dance committee, I think. Of course he's welcome if he wants to. Always has been.

HERB   (*Holding out phone to* TOM)   Tom. (TOM *hesitates to cross to phone. As* LAURA *watches him with concern, he makes a move to escape out the door*) Three-two-six.
   (TOM *slowly and painfully crosses the stage, takes the phone and sits*)

BILL   Will you walk along with us as far as the dining hall, Laura?

LAURA   I don't think I feel like supper, thanks.

BILL   (*Looks from her to* TOM)   What?

HERB   I've got to get along if I want to catch my train.
   (TOM *dials phone*)

BILL   Laura?
   (LAURA *shakes her head, tight-lipped*)

HERB   Well, then, good-bye, Laura . . . I still like you.

LAURA   Still going to the Dean's, Bill?

BILL   Yes. I'll be right back after supper. Sure you don't want to walk along with us to the dining hall?
   (LAURA *shakes her head*)

TOM   Busy.

HERB (*Pats his son's arm*)   Keep trying him. We're in this together. Anything you want? (TOM *shakes his head "No"*) Just remember, anything you want, let me know. (*To* LAURA) See you at reunion time . . . This'll all be blown over by then.
   (*He goes*)

BILL   Laura, I wish you'd . . . Laura!
   (*He is disturbed by her mood. He sees it's hopeless, and goes after* HERB, *leaving door open*)

TOM (*At phone*)   Hello, Mr. Mayberry . . . This is Tom Lee . . . Yes, I know it's time to go to supper, Mr. Mayberry . . . (*Looks around at open door.* LAURA *shuts it*) but I wanted you to know . . . (*This comes hard*) I wanted you to know I'm not going to be able to play in the play . . . No . . . I . . . well, I just can't.
   (*He is about to break. He doesn't trust himself to speak*)

LAURA (*Quickly crosses and takes phone from* TOM)   Give it to me. Hello, Fred . . . Laura. Yes, Tom's father, well, he wants Tom—he thinks Tom is tired, needs to concentrate on his final exams. You had someone covering the part, didn't you? . . . Yes, of course it's a terrible disappointment to Tom. I'll see you tomorrow.
   (*She hangs up.* TOM *is ashamed and humiliated. Here is the woman he loves, hearing all about him . . . perhaps believing the things . . .* LAURA *stands above him for a moment, looking at the back of his head with pity. Then he rises and starts for the door without looking at her.* RALPH *and* STEVE *come stampeding down the stairway*)

RALPH (*As he goes*)   Okay, you can sit next to him if you want. Not me.

STEVE   Well, if you won't . . . why should I?

RALPH   Two bits nobody will.
   (*They slam out the front door.* TOM *has shut the door quickly again when he has heard* RALPH *and* STEVE *start down. Now stands against the door listening*)

AL (*Comes out from his door, pulling on his jacket. Calls*) Tom . . Tom!
   (*Getting no answer, he goes down the stairs and out*)

LAURA   Tom . . .

TOM (*Opens the study door*)   I'll bet my father thinks I'm . . .
   (*Stops*)

LAURA   Now, Tom! I thought I'd call Joan Harrison and ask her to come over for tea tomorrow. I want you to come too. I want you to ask her to go to the dance with you.

TOM (*Turns in anguish and looks at her for several moments. Then*)   You were to go with me.

LAURA   I know, but . . .

TOM   Do you think so too, like the others? Like my father?

LAURA   Tom!

TOM   Is that why you're shoving me off on Joan?

LAURA (*Moving towards him*)   Tom, I asked her over so that we could lick this thing.

TOM (*Turns on her*)   What thing? What thing?
   (*He looks at her a moment, filled with indignation, then he bolts up the stairs. But on the way up,* PHIL *is coming down.* TOM *feels like a trapped rat. He starts to turn down the stairs again, but he doesn't want to face* LAURA, *as he is about to break. He tries to hide his face and cowers along one side going up*)

PHIL   What's the matter with you?
   (TOM *doesn't answer. Goes on up and into the study door.* PHIL *shrugs his shoulders and goes on down the stairs and out.* TOM *comes into his own bedroom and shuts the door and leans against the doorjamb.* LAURA *goes to the partly opened door. Her impulse is to go up to* TOM *to comfort him.*

*but she checks herself, and turns in the doorway and closes
the door, then walks back to her chair and sits down and
reaches out and touches the teapot, as though she were half-
unconsciously rubbing out a spot. She is puzzled and worried. Upstairs we hear the first few sobs from* TOM *as the
lights dim out, and*

THE CURTAIN FALLS

Act Two

SCENE I

The scene is the same.
The time is two days later.
As the curtain rises, AL *is standing at the public telephone fastened to the wall on the first landing. He seems to
be doing more listening than talking.*

AL   Yeah . . . (*He patiently waits through a long tirade*)
Yeah, Dad. I know, Dad . . . No, I haven't done anything
about it, yet . . . Yes, Mr. Hudson says he has a room in his
house for me next year . . . But I haven't done anything
about it here yet . . . Yeah, okay, Dad . . . I know what
you mean . . . (*Gets angry*) I swear to God I don't . . . I
lived with him a year, and I don't . . . All right, okay, Dad
. . . No, don't *you* call. I'll do it. Right now.
   (*He hangs up. He stands and puts his hands in his pocket
   and tries to think this out. It's something he doesn't like*)

RALPH   (*Comes in the house door and starts up the steps*)
Hey, Al?

AL   Yeah?

RALPH   The guys over at the Beta house want to know has it happened yet?

AL   Has what happened?

RALPH   Has Tom made a pass at you yet?

AL (*Reaches out to swat* RALPH)   For crying out loud!

RALPH   Okay, okay! You can borrow my chastity belt if you need it.

AL   That's not funny.

RALPH (*Shifting his meaning to hurt* AL)   No, I know it's not. The guys on the ball team don't think it's funny at all.

AL   What do you mean?

RALPH   The guy they're supposed to elect captain rooming with a queer.

AL (*Looks at him for a moment, then rejects the idea*)   Aw . . . knock it off, huh!

RALPH   So you don't believe me . . . Wait and see. (*Putting on a dirty grin*) Anyway, my mother said I should save myself for the girl I marry. Hell, how would you like to have to tell your wife, "Honey, I've been saving myself for you, except for one night when a guy——" (AL *roughs* RALPH *up with no intention of hurting him*) Okay, okay. So you don't want to be captain of the baseball team. So who the hell cares. I don't, I'm sure.

AL   Look. Why don't you mind your own business?

RALPH   What the hell fun would there be in that?

AL   Ralph, Tom's a nice kid.

RALPH   Yeah. That's why all the guys leave the shower room at the gym when he walks in.

AL   When?

RALPH   Yesterday . . . Today. You didn't hear about it?

AL   No. What are they trying to do?

RALPH   Hell, they don't want some queer looking at them and——

AL   Oh, can it! Go on up and bury your horny nose in your *Art Models* magazine.

RALPH   At least I'm normal. I like to look at pictures of naked girls, not men, the way Tom does.

AL   Jeeze, I'm gonna push your face in in a—

RALPH   Didn't you notice all those strong man poses he's got in his bottom drawer?

AL   Yes, I've noticed them. His old man wants him to be a muscle man, and he wrote away for this course in muscle building and they send those pictures. Any objections?

RALPH   Go on, stick up for him. Stick your neck out. You'll get it chopped off with a baseball bat, you crazy bastard.
     (*Exits upstairs. AL looks at the phone, then up the way RALPH went. He is upset. He throws himself into a few push-ups, using the bannisters. Then still not happy with what he's doing, he walks down the stairs and knocks on the study door*)

LAURA (*Comes from inside the house and opens the door*) Oh, hello, Al.

AL   Is Mr. Reynolds in?

LAURA   Why, no, he isn't. Can I do something?

AL   I guess I better drop down when he's in.

LAURA   All right. I don't really expect him home till after supper tonight.

AL (*Thinks for a moment*) Well . . . well, you might tell him just so's he'll know and can make other plans . . . I won't be rooming in this house next year. This is the last day for changing, and I want him to know that.

LAURA (*Moves into the room to get a cigarette*) I see. Well, I know he'll be sorry to hear that, Al.

AL   I'm going across the street to Harmon House.

LAURA   Both you and Tom going over?

AL   No.

LAURA   Oh.

AL   Just me.

LAURA   I see. Does Tom know this?

AL   No. I haven't told him.

LAURA   You'll have to tell him, won't you, so he'll be able to make other plans.

AL   Yes, I suppose so.

LAURA   Al, won't you sit down for a moment, please? (AL *hesitates, but comes in and sits down. Offers* AL *a cigarette*) Cigarette?

AL (*Reaches for one automatically, then stops*)   No, thanks. I'm in training.
   (*He slips a pack of cigarettes from his shirt pocket to his trousers pocket*)

LAURA   That's right. I'm going to watch you play Saturday afternoon. (AL *smiles at her*) You're not looking forward to telling Tom, are you, Al? (AL *shakes his head, "No"*) I suppose I can guess why you're not rooming with him next year. (AL *shrugs his shoulders*) I wonder if you know how much it has meant for him to room with you this year. It's done a lot for him too. It's given him a confidence to know he was rooming with one of the big men of the school.

AL (*Embarrassed*)   Oh . . .

LAURA   You wouldn't understand what it means to be befriended. You're one of the strong people. I'm surprised, Al.

AL (*Blurting it out*)   My father's called me three times. How he ever found out about Harris and Tom, I don't know. But he did. And some guy called him and asked him, "Isn't that the boy your son is rooming with?" . . . and he wants me to change for next year.

LAURA   What did you tell your father?

AL   I told him Tom wasn't so bad, and . . . I'd better wait and see Mr. Reynolds.

LAURA   Al, you've lived with Tom. You know him better than anyone else knows him. If you do this, it's as good as finishing him so far as this school is concerned, and maybe farther.

AL (*Almost whispering it*)   Well, he *does* act sort of queer, Mrs. Reynolds. He . . .

LAURA   You never said this before. You never paid any attention before. What do you mean, "queer?"

AL   Well, like the fellows say, he sort of walks lightly, if you know what I mean. Sometimes the way he moves . . . the things he talks about . . . long hair music all the time.

LAURA   All right. He wants to be a singer. So he talks about it.

AL   He's never had a girl up for any of the dances.

LAURA   Al, there are good explanations for all these things you're saying. They're silly . . . and prejudiced . . . and arguments all dug up to suit a point of view. They're all after the fact.

AL   I'd better speak to Mr. Reynolds.
     (*He starts for the door*)

LAURA   Al, look at me.
     (*She holds his eyes for a long time, wondering whether to say what she wants to say*)

AL   Yes?

LAURA (*She decides to do it*)   Al, what if I were to start the rumor tomorrow that you were . . . well, queer, as you put it.

AL   No one would believe it.

LAURA   Why not?

AL   Well, because . . .

LAURA   Because you're big and brawny and an athlete. What they call a top guy and a hard hitter?

AL   Well, yes.

LAURA   You've got some things to learn, Al. I've been around a little, and I've met men, just like you—same setup—who weren't men, some of them married and with children.

AL   Mrs. Reynolds, you wouldn't do a thing like that.

LAURA   No, Al, I probably wouldn't. But I could, and I almost
would to show you how easy it is to smear a person, and once
I got them believing it, you'd be surprised how quickly your
. . . manly virtues would be changed into suspicious characteristics.

AL (*Has been standing with his hands on his hips.* LAURA *looks
pointedly at this stance.* AL *thrusts his hands down to his side,
and then behind his back*)   Mrs. Reynolds, I got a chance to
be captain of the baseball team next year.

LAURA   I know. And I have no right to ask you to give up that
chance. But I wish somehow or other you could figure out a
way . . . so it wouldn't hurt Tom.
   (TOM *comes in the hall and goes up the stairs. He's pretty
   broken up, and mad. After a few moments he appears in his
   room, shuts the door, and sits on the bed, trying to figure
   something out*)

AL (*As* TOM *enters house*)   Well . . .

LAURA   That's Tom now. (AL *looks at her, wondering how she
knows*) I know all your footsteps. He's coming in for tea. (AL
starts to move to door) Well, Al? (AL *makes a helpless motion*)
You still want me to tell Mr. Reynolds about your moving next
year?

AL (*After a moment*)   No.

LAURA   Good.

AL   I mean, I'll tell him when I see him.

LAURA   Oh.

AL (*Turns on her*)   What can I do?

LAURA   I don't know.

AL   Excuse me for saying so, but it's easy for you to talk the
way you have. You're not involved. You're just a bystander.
You're not going to be hurt. Nothing's going to happen to
you one way or the other. I'm sorry.

LAURA   That's a fair criticism, Al. I'm sorry I asked you . . .
As you say, I'm not involved.

AL   I'm sorry. I think you're swell, Mrs. Reynolds. You're
the nicest housemaster's wife I've ever ran into . . . I mean
. . . Well, you know what I mean. It's only that . . . (*He is
flustered. He opens the door*) I'm sorry.

LAURA   I'm sorry, too, Al.
     (*She smiles at him.* AL *stands in the doorway for a moment,
     not knowing whether to go out the hall door or go upstairs.
     Finally, he goes upstairs, and into the study door.* LAURA
     stands thinking over what AL *has said, even repeating to her-
     self, "I'm not involved." She then goes into the alcove and
     off*)

AL   (*Outside* TOM'S *bedroom door*)   Tom? (TOM *moves
quietly away from the door*) Tom? (*He opens the door*) Hey.

TOM   I was sleeping.

AL   Standing up, huh? (TOM *turns away*) You want to be
alone?

TOM   No. You want to look. Go ahead.
     (*He indicates the window*)

AL   No, I don't want to look, I . . . (*He looks at* TOM, *not
knowing how to begin . . . He stalls . . . smiling*) Nice
tie you got there.

TOM   (*Starts to undo tie*)   Yeah, it's yours. You want it?

AL   No. Why? I can only wear one tie at a time. (TOM *leaves
it hanging around his neck. After an awkward pause*) I . . .
uh . . .

TOM   I guess I don't need to ask you what's the matter?

AL   It's been rough today, huh?

TOM   Yeah. (*He turns away, very upset. He's been holding it
in . . . but here's his closest friend asking him to open up*)
Jesus Christ! (AL *doesn't know what to say. He goes to* TOM'S
*bureau and picks up his hairbrush, gives his hair a few
brushes*) Anybody talk to you?

AL   Sure. You know they would.

TOM   What do they say?

AL   (*Yanks his tie off*)   Hell, I don't know.

TOM   I went to a meeting of the dance committee. I'm no longer on the dance committee. Said that since I'd backed out of playing the part in the play, I didn't show the proper spirit. That's what they *said* was the reason.

AL (*Loud*)   Why the hell don't you do something about it?

TOM (*Yelling back*)   About what?

AL   About what they're saying.

TOM   What the hell can I do?

AL   Geez, you could . . . (*He suddenly wonders what* TOM *could do*) I don't know.

TOM   I tried to pass it off. Christ, you can't pass it off. You know, when I went into the showers today after my tennis match, everyone who was in there grabbed a towel and . . . and . . . walked out.

AL   They're stupid. Just a bunch of stupid bastards.
     (*He leaves the room*)

TOM (*Following him into sitting room*)   Goddamn it, the awful thing I found myself . . . Jesus I don't know . . . I found myself self-conscious about things I've been doing for years. Dressing, undressing . . . I keep my eyes on the floor . . . (*Re-enters his own room*) Geez, if I even look at a guy that doesn't have any clothes on, I'm afraid someone's gonna say something, or . . . Jesus, I don't know.

AL (*During this,* AL *has come back into the room, unbuttoning his shirt, taking it off, etc. Suddenly he stops*)   What the hell am I doing? I've had a shower today.
     (*He tries to laugh*)

TOM (*Looks at him a moment*)   Undress in your own room, will ya? You don't want them talking about you too, do you?

AL   No I don't.
     (*He has said this very definitely and with meaning*)

TOM (*Looks up at his tone of voice*)   Of course you don't. (*He looks at* AL *a long time. He hardly dares say this*) You . . . uh . . . you moving out?

AL (*Doesn't want to answer*)   Look, Tom, do you mind if I try to help you?

TOM   Hell, no. How?

AL   I know this is gonna burn your tail, and I know it sounds
stupid as hell. But it isn't stupid. It's the way people look at
things. You could do a lot for yourself, just the way you talk
and look.

TOM   You mean get my hair cut?

AL   For one thing.

TOM   Why the hell should a man with a crew cut look more
manly than a guy who—

AL   Look, I don't know the reasons for these things. It's just
the way they are.

TOM (*Looking at himself in bureau mirror*)   I tried a crew
cut a coupla times. I haven't got that kind of hair, or that kind
of head. (*After a moment*) Sorry, I didn't mean to yell at you.
Thanks for trying to help.

AL (*Finds a baseball on the radiator and throws it at* TOM. TOM
smiles, and throws it back)   Look, Tom, the way you
walk . . .

TOM   Oh, Jesus.

AL (*Flaring*)   Look, I'm trying to help you.

TOM   No one gave a goddamn about how I walked till last
Saturday!

AL (*Starts to go*)   Okay, okay. Forget it.
      (*He goes out*)

TOM (*Stands there a few moments, then slams the baseball into
the bed and walks out after* AL *into sitting room*)   Al?

AL (*Off*)   Yeah?

TOM   Tell me about how I walk.

AL (*In the sitting room*)   Go ahead, walk!

TOM (*Walks back into the bedroom.* AL *follows him, wiping
his face on a towel and watching* TOM *walk. After he has
walked a bit*)   Now I'm not going to be able to walk any
more. Everything I been doing all my life makes me look like
a fairy.

AL   Go on.

TOM   All right, now I'm walking. Tell me.

AL   Tom, I don't know. You walk sort of light.

TOM   Light?
  (*He looks at himself take a step*)

AL   Yeah.

TOM   Show me.

AL   No, I can't do it.

TOM   Okay. You walk. Let me watch you. I never noticed how you walked. (AL *stands there for a moment, never having realized before how difficult it could be to walk if you think about it. Finally he walks*) Do it again.

AL   If you go telling any of the guys about this . . .

TOM   Do you think I would? . . . (AL *walks again*) That's a good walk. I'll try to copy it. (*He tries to copy the walk, but never succeeds in taking even a step*) Do you really think that'll make any difference?

AL   I dunno.

TOM   Not now it won't. Thanks anyway.

AL   (*Comes and sits on bed beside* TOM. *Puts his arm around* TOM's *shoulder and thinks this thing out*) Look, Tom . . . You've been in on a lot of bull sessions. You heard the guys talking about stopping over in Boston on the way home . . . getting girls . . . you know.

TOM   Sure. What about it?

AL   You're not going to the dance Saturday night?

TOM   No. Not now.

AL   You know Ellie Martin. The gal who waits on table down at the soda joint?

TOM   Yeah. What about her?

AL   You've heard the guys talking about her.

TOM   Come on, come on.

AL   Why don't you drop in on Ellie Saturday night?

TOM   What do you mean?

AL   Hell, do you want me to draw a picture?

TOM (*With disgust*)   Ellie Martin?

AL   Okay. I know she's a dog, but . . .

TOM   So what good's that going to do? I get caught there, I get thrown out of school.

AL   No one ever gets caught. Sunday morning people'd hear about it . . . not the Dean . . . I mean the fellows. Hell, Ellie tells and tells and tells . . . Boy, you'd be made!

TOM   Are you kidding?

AL   No.

TOM (*With disgust*)   Ellie Martin!

AL (*After a long pause*)   Look, I've said so much already, I might as well be a complete bastard . . . You ever been with a woman?

TOM   What do you think?

AL   I don't think you have.

TOM   So?

AL   You want to know something?

TOM   What?

AL   Neither have I. But if you tell the guys, I'll murder you.

TOM   All those stories you told . . .

AL   Okay, I'll be sorry I told you.

TOM   Then why don't you go see Ellie Martin Saturday night?

AL   Why the hell should I?

TOM   You mean you don't have to prove anything?

AL   Aw, forget it. It's probably a lousy idea anyway.
   (*He starts out*)

TOM   Yeah.

AL (*Stops*) Look, about next—
   (*Stops*)

TOM Next year? Yes?

AL Hap Hudson's asked me to come to his house. He's got
a single there. A lot of the fellows from the team are over
there, and . . . well . . .
   (*He doesn't look at* TOM)

TOM Sure, sure . . . I understand.

AL Sorry I didn't tell you till now, after we'd made our plans.
But I didn't know. I mean, I just found out about the . . . the
opening.

TOM I understand!

AL (*Looks up at last. He hates himself but he's done it, and
it's a load off his chest*) See ya.
   (*He starts to go*)

TOM (*As* AL *gets to door*) Al . . . (AL *stops and looks back.
Taking tie from around his neck*) Here.

AL (*Looks at tie, embarrassed*) I said wear it. Keep it.

TOM It's yours.

AL (*Looks at the tie for a long time, then without taking it,
goes through the door*) See ya.
   (TOM *folds the tie neatly, dazed, then seeing what he's doing,
   he throws it viciously in the direction of the bureau, and
   turns and stares out the window. He puts a record on the
   phonograph*)

BILL (*Comes in to the study from the hall, carrying a pair of
   shoes and a slim book. As he opens his study door, he hears
   the music upstairs. He stands in the door and listens, remembering his miserable boyhood. Then he comes in and closes
   the door*) Laura.
   (*Throws shoes on floor near footstool*)

LAURA (*Off stage, calling*) Bill?

BILL Yes.

LAURA (*Coming in with tea things*) I didn't think you'd be
back before your class. Have some tea.

BILL   I beat young Harvey at handball.

LAURA   Good.

BILL   At last. It took some doing, though. He was after my
scalp because of that D minus I gave him in his last exam.
(*Gives her book*) You wanted this . . . book of poems.

LAURA (*Looks at book. Her eyes shift quickly to the same
book in the chair*)   Why yes. How did you know?

BILL (*Trying to be very offhand about it*)   The notice from
the bookstore.

LAURA   That's very nice of you.
    (*She moves towards him to kiss him, but at this moment,
    in picking some wrapping paper from the armchair, he
    notices the duplicate copy*)

BILL (*A little angry*)   You've already got it.

LAURA   Why, yes . . . I . . . well, I . . . (BILL *picking it
up . . . opens it*) That is, someone gave it to me. (BILL *reads
the inscription*) Tom knew I wanted it, and . . .

BILL (*Looks at her, a terrible look coming into his face. Then
he slowly rips the book in two and hurls it into the fireplace*)
Damn!

LAURA   Bill! (BILL *goes to footstool and sits down and begins
to change his shoes*) Bill, what difference does it make that
he gave me the book? He knew I wanted it too.

BILL   I don't know. It's just that every time I try to do something . . .

LAURA   Bill, how can you say that? It isn't so.

BILL   It is.

LAURA   Bill, this thing of the book is funny.

BILL   I don't think it's very funny.

LAURA (*Going behind him, and kneeling by his side*)   Bill,
I'm very touched that you should have remembered. Thank
you. (*He turns away from her and goes on with his shoes*) Bill,
don't turn away. I want to thank you. (*As she gets no response*

from him, she rises) Is it such a chore to let yourself be thanked? (*She puts her hands on his shoulders, trying to embrace him*) Oh, Bill, we so rarely touch any more. I keep feeling I'm losing contact with you. Don't you feel that?

BILL (*Looking at his watch*)   Laura, I . . .

LAURA (*She backs away from him*)   I know, you've got to go. But it's just that, I don't know, we don't touch any more. It's a silly way of putting it, but you seem to hold yourself aloof from me. A tension seems to grow between us . . . and then when we do . . . touch . . . it's a violent thing . . . almost a compulsive thing. (BILL *is uncomfortable at this accurate description of their relationship. He sits troubled. She puts her arms around his neck and embraces him, bending over him*) You don't feel it? You don't feel yourself holding away from me until it becomes overpowering? There's no growing together any more . . . no quiet times, just holding hands, the feeling of closeness, like it was in Italy. Now it's long separations and then this almost brutal coming together, and . . . Oh, Bill, you do see, you do see. (BILL *suddenly straightens up, toughens, and looks at her.* LAURA *repulsed, slowly draws her arms from around his shoulders*)

BILL   For God's sake, Laura, what are you talking about? (*He rises and goes to his desk*) It can't always be a honeymoon.
    (*Upstairs in his room,* TOM *turns off the phonograph, and leaves the room, going out into the hall and up the stairs*)

LAURA   Do you think that's what I'm talking about?

BILL   I don't know why you choose a time like this to talk about things like . . .

LAURA   . . . I don't know why, either. I just wanted to thank you for the book . . . (*Moves away and looks in book*) What did you write in it?

BILL (*Starts to mark exam papers*)   Nothing. Why? Should I write in it? I just thought you wanted the book.

LAURA   Of course . . . Are you sure you won't have some tea?
    (*She bends over the tea things*)

BILL   Yes.

LAURA (*Straightening up, trying another tack of returning to normality*) Little Joan Harrison is coming over for tea.

BILL No, she isn't. (LAURA *looks inquiringly*) I just saw her father at the gym. I don't think that was a very smart thing for you to do, Laura.

LAURA I thought Tom might take her to the dance Saturday. He's on the committee, and he has no girl to take.

BILL I understand he's no longer on the committee. You're a hostess, aren't you?

LAURA Yes.

BILL I've got the mountain-climbing business this week-end. Weather man predicts rain.

LAURA (*Almost breaks. Hides her face in her hands. Then recovers*) That's too bad. (*After a moment*) Bill?

BILL Yes?

LAURA I think someone should go to the Dean about Tom and the hazing he's getting.

BILL What could the Dean do? Announce from chapel, "You've got to stop riding Tom. You've got to stop calling him Grace?" Is that what you'd like him to do?

LAURA No. I suppose not.

BILL You know we're losing Al next year because of Tom.

LAURA Oh, you've heard?

BILL Yes, Hudson tells me he's moving over to his house. He'll probably be captain of the baseball team. Last time we had a major sport captain was eight years ago.

LAURA Yes, I'm sorry.

BILL However, we'll also be losing Tom.

LAURA Oh?

BILL (*Noticing her increased interest*) Yes. We have no singles in this house, and he'll be rooming alone.

LAURA I'm sorry to hear that.

BILL (*He turns to look at her*)   I knew you would be.

LAURA   Why should my interest in this boy make you angry?

BILL   I'm not angry.

LAURA   You're not only angry. It's almost as though you were, well, jealous.

BILL   Oh, come on now.

LAURA   Well, how else can you explain your . . . your vindictive attitude towards him?

BILL   Why go into it again? Jealous! (*He has his books together now. Goes to the door*) I'll go directly from class to the dining hall. All right?

LAURA   Yes, of course.

BILL   And please, please, Laura . . .
   (*He stops*)

LAURA   I'll try.

BILL   I know you like to be different, just for the sake of being different . . . and I like you for that . . . But this time, lay off. Show your fine free spirit on something else.

LAURA   On something that can't hurt us?

BILL   All right. Sure. I don't mind putting it that way. And Laura?

LAURA   Yes?

BILL   Seeing Tom so much . . . having him down for tea alone all the time . . .

LAURA   Yes?

BILL   I think you should have him down only when you have the other boys . . . for his own good. I mean that. Well, I'll see you in the dining hall. Try to be on time. (*He goes out. LAURA brings her hands to her face, and cries, leaning against the back of the chair. AL has come tumbling out of the door to his room with books in hand, and is coming down the stairs. Going down the hall*) You going to class, Al?

AL   Hello, Mr. Reynolds. Yes I am.

BILL (*As they go*) Let's walk along together. I'm sorry to hear that you're moving across the street next year.

(*And they are gone out the door*)

TOM (*Has come down the stairs, and now stands looking at the hall telephone. He is carrying his coat. After a long moment's deliberation, he puts in a coin and dials*) Hello, I'd like to speak to Ellie Martin, please. (LAURA *has moved to pick up the torn book which her husband has thrown in the fireplace. She is smoothing it out, as she suddenly hears* TOM'S *voice in the hall. She can't help but hear what he is saying. She stands stock still and listens, her alarm and concern showing on her face*) Hello, Ellie? This Tom Lee . . . Tom Lee. I'm down at the soda fountain all the time with my roommate, Al Thompson . . . Yeah, the guys do sometimes call me that . . . Well, I'll tell you what I wanted. I wondered if . . . you see, I'm not going to the dance Saturday night, and I wondered if you're doing anything? Yeah, I guess that is a hell of a way to ask for a date . . . but I just wondered if I could maybe drop by and pick you up after work on Saturday . . . I don't know what's *in* it for you, Ellie . . . but something I guess. I just thought I'd like to see you . . . What time do you get through work? . . . Okay, nine o'clock. (LAURA, *having heard this, goes out through the alcove. About to hang up*) Oh, thanks.

(*He stands for a moment, contemplating what he's done, then he slips on his jacket, and goes to the study door and knocks. After a moment, he opens the door and enters*)

LAURA (*Coming from the other room with a plate of cookies*) Oh, there you are. I've got your favorites today.

TOM   Mrs. Reynolds, do you mind if I don't come to tea this afternoon?

LAURA   Why . . . if you don't want to . . . How are you? (*She really means this question*)

TOM   I'm okay.

LAURA   Good.

TOM   It's just I don't feel like tea.

LAURA   Perhaps, it's just as well . . . Joan can't make it today, either.

TOM   I didn't expect she would. She's nothing special; just a kid.

LAURA   Something about a dentist appointment or something.

TOM   It wouldn't have done any good anyway. I'm not going to the dance.

LAURA   Oh?

TOM   Another member of the committee will stop around for you.

LAURA   What will you be doing?

TOM   I don't know. I can take care of myself.

LAURA   If you're not going, that gives me an easy out. I won't have to go.

TOM   Just because I'm not going?

LAURA   (*In an effort to keep him from going to Ellie*)   Look, Tom . . . now that neither of us is going, why don't you drop down here after supper, Saturday night. We could listen to some records, or play gin, or we can just talk.

TOM   I . . . I don't think you'd better count on me.

LAURA   I'd like to.

TOM   No, really. I don't want to sound rude . . . but I . . . I may have another engagement.

LAURA   Oh?

TOM   I'd like to come. Please understand that. It's what I'd like to do . . . but . . .

LAURA   Well, I'll be here just in case, just in case you decide to come in. (LAURA *extends her hand*) I hope you'll be feeling better.

TOM (*Hesitates, then takes her hand*)   Thanks.

LAURA   Maybe your plans will change.
   (TOM *looks at her, wishing they would; knowing they won't. He runs out and down the hall as the lights fade out on* LAURA *standing at the door*)

                                                    CURTAIN

SCENE II

The time is eight-forty-five on Saturday night.
In the study a low fire is burning. As the curtain rises,
the town clock is striking the three quarter hour. LAURA
is sitting in her chair sipping a cup of coffee. The door
to the study is open slightly. She is waiting for TOM.
She is wearing a lovely but informal dress, and a single
flower. In his room, TOM *listens to the clock strike. He*
has just been shaving. He is putting shaving lotion on
his face. His face is tense and nervous. There is no joy
in the preparations. In a moment, he turns and leaves
the room, taking off his belt as he goes.
After a moment, LILLY *comes to the study door,*
knocks and comes in.

LILLY   Laura?

LAURA   Oh, Lilly.

LILLY (*Standing in the doorway, a raincoat held over her head.*
She is dressed in a low-cut evening gown, which she wears
very well)   You're not dressed yet. Why aren't you dressed
for the dance?

LAURA (*Still in her chair*)   I'm not going. I thought I told you.

LILLY (*Deposits raincoat and goes immediately to look at her-*
self in mirror next to the door)   Oh, for Heaven's sake, why
not? Just because Bill's away with his loathesome little mountain climbers?

LAURA   Well . . .

LILLY   Come along with us. It's raining on and off, so Harry's
going to drive us in the car.

LAURA No, thanks.

LILLY If you come, Harry will dance with you all evening. You won't be lonely, I promise you. (LAURA *shakes her head, "No"*) You're the only one who can dance those funny steps with him.

LAURA It's very sweet of you, but no.

LILLY (*At the mirror*) Do you think this neck is too low?

LAURA I think you look lovely.

LILLY Harry says this neck will drive all the little boys crazy.

LAURA I don't think so.

LILLY Well, that's not very flattering.

LAURA I mean, I think they'll appreciate it, but as for driving them crazy . . .

LILLY After all I want to give them some reward for dancing their duty dances with me.

LAURA I'm sure when they dance with you, it's no duty, Lilly. I've seen you at these dances.

LILLY It's not this . . . (*Indicating her bosom*) it's my line of chatter. I'm oh so interested in what courses they're taking, where they come from and where they learned to dance so divinely.

LAURA (*Laughing*) Lilly, you're lost in a boys' school. You were meant to shine some place much more glamorous.

LILLY I wouldn't trade it for the world. Where else could a girl indulge in three hundred innocent flirtations a year?

LAURA Lilly, I've often wondered what you'd do if one of the three hundred attempted to go, well, a little further than innocent flirtation.

LILLY I'd slap him down . . . the little beast. (*She laughs and admires herself in mirror*) Harry says if I'm not careful I'll get to looking like Ellie Martin. You've seen Ellie.

LAURA I saw her this afternoon for the first time.

LILLY Really? The first time?

LAURA   Yes. I went into the place where she works . . . the soda shop . . .

LILLY   You!

LAURA   Yes . . . uh . . . for a package of cigarettes. (*After a moment she says with some sadness*) She's not even pretty, is she?

LILLY   (*Turns from admiring herself at the tone in* LAURA's *voice*) Well, honey, don't sound so sad. What difference should it make to you if she's pretty or not?

LAURA   I don't know. It just seems so . . . they're so young.

LILLY   If they're stupid enough to go to Ellie Martin, they deserve whatever happens to them. Anyway, Laura, the boys *talk* more about Ellie than anything else. So don't fret about it.

LAURA   (*Arranges chair for* TOM *facing fireplace. Notices* LILLY *primping*) You look lovely, Lilly.

LILLY   Maybe I'd better wear that corsage the dance committee sent, after all . . . right here. (*She indicates low point in dress*) I was going to carry it—or rather Harry was going to help me carry it. You know, it's like one of those things people put on Civil War monuments on Decoration Day.

LAURA   Yes, I've seen them.

LILLY   (*Indicating the flower* LAURA *is wearing*) Now that's tasteful. Where'd you get that?

LAURA   Uh . . . I bought it for myself.

LILLY   Oh, now.

LAURA   It's always been a favorite of mine and I saw it in the florist's window.

LILLY   Well, Harry will be waiting for me to tie his bow tie. (*Starts towards door*) Will you be up when we get back?

LAURA   (*Giving* LILLY *her raincoat*) Probably not.

LILLY   If there's a light on, I'll drop in and tell you how many I had to slap down . . . Night-night.

     (*She leaves.* LAURA *stands at the closed door until she hears*

Tea and Sympathy

439

the outside door close. Then she opens her door a bit. She takes her cup of coffee and stands in front of the fireplace and listens)

TOM (*As* LILLY *goes, he returns to his room, dressed in a blue suit. He stands there deliberating a moment, then reaches under his pillow and brings out a pint bottle of whisky. He takes a short swig. It gags him. He corks it and puts it back under the pillow*)   Christ, I'll never make it.
(*He reaches in his closet and pulls out a raincoat, then turns and snaps out the room light, and goes out. A moment later, he appears on the stairs. He sees* LAURA'S *door partly open, and while he is putting on his raincoat, he walks warily past it*)

LAURA (*When she hears* TOM'S *door close, she stands still and listens more intently. She hears him pass her door and go to the front door. She puts down the cup of coffee, and goes to the study door. She calls*)   Tom? (*After some moments,* TOM *appears in the door, and she opens it wide*)   I've been expecting you.

TOM   I . . . I . . .

LAURA (*Opening the door wide*)   Are you going to the dance, after all?

TOM (*Comes in the door*)   No . . . You can report me if you want. Out after hours. Or . . . (*He looks up at her finally*)   Or you can give me permission. Can I have permission to go out?

LAURA (*Moving into the room, says pleasantly*)   I think I'd better get you some coffee.

TOM (*At her back, truculent*)   You can tell them that, too . . . that I've been drinking. There'll be lots to tell before—(*He stops*)   I didn't drink much. But I didn't eat much either.

LAURA   Let me get you something to eat.

TOM (*As though convincing himself*)   No. I can't stay!

LAURA   All right. But I'm glad you dropped in. I was counting on it.

TOM (*Chip on shoulder*)   I said I might not. When you invited me.

LAURA   I know. (*She looks at him a moment. He is to her a heartbreaking sight . . . all dressed up as though he were going to a prom, but instead he's going to Ellie . . . the innocence and the desperation touch her deeply . . . and this shows in her face as she circles behind him to the door*) It's a nasty night out, isn't it?

TOM   Yes.

LAURA   I'm just glad I'm not going to the dance. (*She shuts the door gently.* TOM, *at the sound of the door, turns and sees what she has done*) It'll be nice just to stay here by the fire.

TOM   I wasn't planning to come in.

LAURA   Then why the flower . . . and the card? "For a pleasant evening?"

TOM   It was for the dance. I forgot to cancel it.

LAURA   I'm glad you didn't.

TOM   Why?
   (*He stops studying the curtains and looks at her*)

LAURA   (*Moving into the room again*)   Well, for one thing I like to get flowers. For another thing . . . (TOM *shakes his head a little to clear it*) Let me make you some coffee.

TOM   No. I'm just about right.

LAURA   Or you can drink this . . . I just had a sip. (*She holds up the cup.* TOM *looks at the proffered coffee*) You can drink from this side.
   (*She indicates the other side of the cup*)

TOM   (*Takes the cup, and looks at the side where her lips have touched and then slowly turns it around to the other and takes a sip*)   And for another thing?

LAURA   What do you mean?

TOM   For one thing you like to get flowers . . .

LAURA   For another it's nice to have flowers on my anniversary.

TOM   Anniversary?

LAURA   Yes.

TOM (*Waving the cup and saucer around*)   And Mr. Reynolds on a mountain top with twenty stalwart youths, soaking wet . . . Didn't he remember?

LAURA (*Rescues the cup and saucer*)   It's not that anniversary. (TOM *looks at her wondering. Seeing that she has interested him, she moves towards him*) Let me take your coat.

TOM (*Definitely*)   I can't—

LAURA   I know. You can't stay. But . . . (*She comes up behind him and puts her hand on his shoulders to take off his coat. He can hardly stand her touch. She gently peels his coat from him and stands back to look at him*) How nice you look!

TOM (*Disarranging his hair or tie*)   Put me in a blue suit and I look like a kid.

LAURA   How did you know I liked this flower?

TOM   You mentioned it.

LAURA   You're very quick to notice these things. So was he.

TOM (*After a moment, his curiosity aroused*)   Who?

LAURA   My first husband. That's the anniversary.

TOM   I didn't know.

LAURA (*Sits in her chair*)   Mr. Reynolds doesn't like me to talk about my first husband. He was, I'd say, about your age. How old are you, Tom?

TOM   Eighteen . . . tomorrow.

LAURA   Tomorrow . . . We must celebrate.

TOM   You'd better not make any plans.

LAURA   He was *just* your age then. (*She looks at him again with slight wonder*) It doesn't seem possible now, looking at you . . .

TOM   Why, do I look like such a child?

LAURA   Why no.

TOM   Men are married at my age.

LAURA   Of course, they are. *He* was. Maybe a few months older. Such a lonely boy, away from home for the first time . . . and . . . and going off to war. (TOM *looks up inquiringly*) Yes, he was killed.

TOM   I'm sorry . . . but I'm glad to hear about him.

LAURA   Glad?

TOM   Yes. I don't know . . . He sounds like someone you *should* have been married to, not . . . (*Stops*) I'm sorry if I . . .
   (*Stops*)

LAURA (*After a moment*)   He was killed being conspicuously brave. He had to be conspicuously brave, you see, because something had happened in training camp . . . I don't know what . . . and he was afraid the others thought him a coward . . . He showed them he wasn't.

TOM   He had that satisfaction.

LAURA   What was it worth if it killed him?

TOM   I don't know. But I can understand.

LAURA   Of course you can. You're very like him.

TOM   Me?

LAURA (*Holding out the coffee cup*)   Before I finish it all? (TOM *comes over and takes a sip from his side of the cup*) He was kind and gentle, and lonely. (TOM *turns away in embarrassment at hearing himself so described*) We knew it wouldn't last . . . We sensed it . . . But he always said, "Why must the test of everything be its durability?"

TOM   I'm sorry he was killed.

LAURA   Yes, so am I. I'm sorry he was killed the way he was killed . . . trying to prove how brave he was. In trying to prove he was a man, he died a boy.

TOM   Still he must have died happy.

LAURA   Because he proved his courage?

TOM   That . . . and because he was married to you. (*Embarrassed, he walks to his coat which she has been holding in her lap*) I've got to go.

LAURA   Tom, please.

TOM   I've got to.

LAURA   It must be a very important engagement.

TOM   It is.

LAURA   If you go now, I'll think I bored you, talking all about myself.

TOM   You haven't.

LAURA   I probably shouldn't have gone on like that. It's just that I felt like it . . . a rainy spring night . . . a fire. I guess I'm in a reminiscent mood. Do you ever get in reminiscing moods on nights like this?

TOM   About what?

LAURA   Oh, come now . . . there must be something pleasant to remember, or someone. (TOM *stands by the door beginning to think back, his raincoat in his hand, but still dragging on the floor*) Isn't there? . . . Of course there is. Who was it, or don't you want to tell?

TOM   (*After a long silence*)   May I have a cigarette?

LAURA   (*Relieved that she has won another moment's delay*) Yes. Of course.
   (*Hands him a box, then lights his cigarette*)

TOM   My seventh-grade teacher.

LAURA   What?

TOM   That's who I remember.

LAURA   Oh.

TOM   Miss Middleton . . .

LAURA   How sweet.

TOM   (*Drops the raincoat again, and moves into the room*) It wasn't sweet. It was terrible.

LAURA   At that time, of course . . . Tell me about her.

TOM   She was just out of college . . . tall, blonde, honey-colored hair . . . and she wore a polo coat, and drove a con-vertible

LAURA   Sounds very fetching.

TOM   Ever since then I've been a sucker for girls in polo coats.

LAURA (*Smiling*)   I have one somewhere.

TOM   Yes, I know.
  (*He looks at her*)

LAURA   What happened?

TOM   What could happen? As usual I made a fool of myself. I guess everyone knew I was in love with her. People I like, I can't help showing it.

LAURA   That's a good trait.

TOM   When she used to go on errands and she needed one of the boys to go along and help carry something, there I was.

LAURA   She liked you too, then.

TOM   This is a stupid thing to talk about.

LAURA   I can see why she liked you.

TOM   I thought she . . . I thought she loved me. I was twelve years old.

LAURA   Maybe she did.

TOM   Anyway, when I was in eighth grade, she got married. And you know what they made me do? They gave a luncheon at school in her honor, and I had to be the toastmaster and wish her happiness and everything . . . I had to write a poem . . . (*He quotes*)
    "Now that you are going to be married,
    And away from us be carried,
    Before you promise to love, honor and obey,
    There are a few things I want to say."
(*He shakes his head as they both laugh*) From there on it turned out to be more of a love poem than anything else.

LAURA (*As she stops laughing*)   Puppy love can be heartbreaking.

TOM (*The smile dying quickly as he looks at her. Then after what seems like forever*)   I'm always falling in love with the wrong people.

LAURA Who isn't?

TOM You too?

LAURA It wouldn't be any fun if we didn't. Of course, nothing ever comes of it, but there are bittersweet memories, and they can be pleasant. (*Kidding him as friend to friend, trying to get him to smile again*) Who else have you been desperately in love with?

TOM (*He doesn't answer. Then he looks at his watch*) It's almost nine . . . I'm late.
   (*Starts to go*)

LAURA (*Rising*) I can't persuade you to stay? (TOM *shakes his head, "No"*) We were getting on so well.

TOM Thanks.

LAURA In another moment I would have told you all the deep, dark secrets of my life.

TOM I'm sorry.
   (*He picks up his coat from the floor*)

LAURA (*Desperately trying to think of something to keep him from going*) Won't you stay even for a dance?

TOM I don't dance.

LAURA I was going to teach you.
   (*She goes over to the phonograph and snaps on the button*)

TOM (*Opens the door*) Some other time . . .

LAURA Please, for me.
   (*She comes back*)

TOM (*After a moment he closes the door*) Tell me something.

LAURA Yes?
   (*The record starts to play, something soft and melodic. It plays through to the end of the act*)

TOM Why are you so nice to me?

LAURA Why . . . I . . .

TOM You're not this way to the rest of the fellows.

LAURA   No, I know I'm not. Do you mind my being nice to you?

TOM   (*Shakes his head, "No"*)   I just wondered why.

LAURA   (*In a perfectly open way*)   I guess, Tom . . . I guess it's because I like you.

TOM   No one else seems to. Why do you?

LAURA   I don't know . . . I . . .

TOM   Is it *because* no one else likes me? Is it just pity?

LAURA   No, Tom, no, of course not . . . It's well . . . it's because you've been very nice to me . . . very considerate. It wasn't easy for me, you know, coming into a school, my first year. You seemed to sense that. I don't know, we just seem to have hit it off.
   (*She smiles at him*)

TOM   Mr. Reynolds knows you like me.

LAURA   I suppose so. I haven't kept it a secret.

TOM   Is that why he hates me so?

LAURA   I don't think he hates you.

TOM   Yes, he hates me. Why lie? I think everyone here hates me but you. But they won't.

LAURA   Of course they won't.

TOM   He hates me because he made a flop with me. I know all about it. My father put me in this house when I first came here, and when he left me he said to your husband, "Make a man out of him." He's failed, and he's mad, and then you came along, and were nice to me . . . out of pity.

LAURA   No, Tom, not pity. I'm too selfish a woman to like you just out of pity.

TOM   (*He has worked himself up into a state of confusion, and anger, and desperation*)   There's so much I . . . there's so much I don't understand.

LAURA   (*Reaches out and touches his arm*)   Tom, don't go out tonight.

TOM   I've got to. That's one thing that's clear. I've got to!

LAURA (*Holds up her arms for dancing*)   Won't you let me teach you how to dance?

TOM (*Suddenly and impulsively he throws his arms around her, and kisses her passionately, awkwardly, and then in embarrassment he buries his head in her shoulder*)   Oh, God . . . God.

LAURA   Tom . . . Tom . . . (TOM *raises his face and looks at her, and would kiss her again*) No, Tom . . . No, I . . . (*At the first "No,"* TOM *breaks from her and runs out the door halfway up the stairs. Calling*) Tom! . . . Tom! (TOM *stops at the sound of her voice and turns around and looks down the stairs.* LAURA *moves to the open door*) Tom, I . . . (*The front door opens and two of the mountain-climbing boys,* PHIL *and* PAUL *come in, with their packs*)

PHIL (*Seeing* TOM *poised on the stairs*)   What the hell are you doing? (TOM *just looks at him*) What's the matter with you?
    (*He goes on and up the stairs*)

TOM   What are you doing back?

PAUL   The whole bunch is back. Who wants to go mountain climbing in the rain?

BILL (*Outside his study door*)   Say, any of you fellows want to go across the street for something to eat when you get changed, go ahead. (PHIL *and* PAUL *go up the stairs past* TOM. BILL *goes into his own room, leaving door open*) Hi. (*He takes off his equipment and puts it on the floor*)

LAURA (*Has been standing motionless where* TOM *has left her*) Hello.

BILL (*Comes to her and kisses her on the cheek*)   One lousy week-end a year we get to go climbing and it rains. (*Throws the rest of his stuff down*) The fellows are damned disappointed.

LAURA (*Hardly paying any attention to him*)   That's too bad.

BILL (*Going up to alcove*)   I think they wanted me to invite them down for a feed. But I didn't want to. I thought we'd be alone. Okay?
    (*He looks across at her*)

LAURA (*She is listening for footsteps outside*)   Sure. (BILL *goes out through alcove.* LAURA *stoops and picks up the rain-*

coat which TOM *has dropped and hides it in the cabinet by the fireplace*)

BILL (*Appears in door momentarily wiping his hands with towel*) Boy it really rained. (*He disappears again.* LAURA *sadly goes to the door and slowly and gently closes it. When she is finished, she leans against the door, listening, hoping against hope that* TOM *will go upstairs. When* TOM *sees the door close, he stands there for a moment, then turns his coat collar up and goes down the hall and out. Off stage as* TOM *starts to go down the hall*) We never made it to the timber-line. The rain started to come down. Another hour or so and we would have got to the hut and spent the night, but the fellows wouldn't hear of it . . . (*The door slams.* LAURA *turns away from the study door in despair. Still off stage*) What was that?

LAURA Nothing . . . Nothing at all.

BILL (*Enters and gets pipe from mantelpiece*) Good to get out, though. Makes you feel alive. Think I'll go out again next Saturday, alone. Won't be bothered by the fellows wanting to turn back.

   (*He has settled down in the chair intended for* TOM. *The school bells start to ring nine.* BILL *reaches out his hand for* LAURA. *Standing by the door, she looks at his outstretched hand, as the lights fade, and*

                                        THE CURTAIN FALLS

Act Three

The time is late the next afternoon.

As the curtain rises, TOM *is in his room. His door is shut and bolted. He is lying on his back on the bed, staring up at the ceiling.*

RALPH (*He is at the phone*) Hello, Mary . . . Ralph . . .
Yeah, I just wanted you to know I'd be a little delayed picking
you up . . . Yeah . . . everyone was taking a shower over
here, and there's only one shower for eight guys . . . No it's
not the same place as last night . . . The tea dance is at the
Inn . . . (*He suddenly looks very uncomfortable*) Look, I'll
tell you when I see you . . . Okay . . . (*Almost whispers it*)
I love you . . . (STEVE, RALPH'S *sidekick, comes running in
from the outside. He's all dressed up and he's got something
to tell*) Yeah, Mary. Well, I can't say it over again . . . Didn't
you hear me the first time? (*Loud so she'll hear it*) Hi, Steve.

STEVE Come on, get off. I got something to tell you.

RALPH Mary—Mary, I'll get there faster if I stop talking now.
Okay? Okay. See you a little after four. (*He hangs up*) What
the hell's the matter with you?

STEVE Have you seen Tom?

RALPH No.

STEVE You know what the hell he did last night?

RALPH What?

STEVE He went and saw Ellie.

RALPH Who are you bulling?

STEVE No, honest. Ellie told Jackson over at the kitchen.
Everybody knows now.

RALPH What did he want to go and do a thing like that for?

STEVE But wait a minute. You haven't heard the half of it.

RALPH Listen, I gotta get dressed.
  (*Starts upstairs*)

STEVE (*On their way up the stairs*) The way Ellie tells it, he
went there, all the hell dressed up like he was going to the
dance, and . . .
  (*They disappear up the stairs.* BILL *after a moment, comes
  in the hall, and goes quickly up the stairs. He goes right
  into* AL *and* TOM'S *main room without knocking. We then
  hear him try the handle of* TOM'S *bedroom door.* TOM *looks
  at the door defiantly and sullenly*)

BILL (*Knocks sharply*) Tom! (*Rattles door some more*) Tom, this is Mr. Reynolds. Let me in.

TOM I don't want to see anyone.

BILL You've got to see me. Come on. Open up! I've got to talk to the Dean at four, and I want to speak to you first.

TOM There's nothing to say.

BILL I can break the door down. Then your father would have to pay for a new door. Do you want that? Are you afraid to see me? (TOM, *after a moment, goes to the door and pulls back the bolt.* BILL *comes in quickly*) Well. (TOM *goes back and sits on the bed. Doesn't look at* BILL) Now I've to have the full story. All the details so that when I see the Dean . . .

TOM You've got the full story. What the hell do you want?

BILL We don't seem to have the full story.

TOM When the school cops brought me in last night they told you I was with Ellie Martin.

BILL That's just it. It seems you weren't *with* her.

TOM (*After a moment*) What do you mean?

BILL You weren't *with* her. You couldn't be *with* her. Do you understand what I mean?

TOM (*Trying to brave it out*) Who says so?

BILL She says so. And she ought to know. (TOM *turns away*) She says that you couldn't . . . and that you jumped up and grabbed a knife in her kitchen and tried to kill yourself . . . and she had to fight with you and that's what attracted the school cops.

TOM What difference does it make?

BILL I just wanted the record to be straight. You'll undoubtedly be expelled, no matter what . . . but I wanted the record straight.

TOM (*Turning on him*) You couldn't have stood it, could you, if I'd proved you wrong?

BILL Where do you get off talking like that to a master?

TOM   You'd made up your mind long ago, and it would have killed you if I'd proved you wrong.

BILL   Talking like that isn't going to help you any.

TOM   Nothing's going to help. I'm gonna be kicked out, and then you're gonna be happy.

BILL   I'm not going to be happy. I'm going to be very sorry . . . sorry for your father.

TOM   All right, now you know. Go on, spread the news. How can you wait?

BILL   I won't tell anyone . . . but the Dean, of course.

TOM   And my father . . .

BILL   Perhaps . . .

TOM (*After a long pause*)   And Mrs. Reynolds.

BILL (*Looks at* TOM)   Yes. I think she ought to know. (*He turns and leaves the room. Goes through the sitting room and up the stairs, calling "Ralph."* TOM *closes the door and locks it, goes and sits down in the chair*)

LAURA (*As* BILL *goes upstairs to* RALPH, *she comes into the master's study. She is wearing a wool suit. She goes to the cupboard and brings out* TOM's *raincoat. She moves with it to the door. There is a knock. She opens the door*)   Oh, hello, Mr. Lee.

HERB (*Coming in, he seems for some reason rather pleased*) Hello, Laura.

LAURA   Bill isn't in just now, though I'm expecting him any moment.

HERB   My train was twenty minutes late. I was afraid I'd missed him. We have an appointment with the Dean in a few minutes . . .

LAURA (*Is coolly polite*)   Oh, I see.

HERB   Have I done something to displease you, Laura? You seem a little . . .

(HERB *shrugs and makes a gesture with his hands meaning cool*)

LAURA   I'm sorry. Forgive me. Won't you sit down?

HERB   I remember that you were displeased at my leaving Tom
in school a week ago. Well, you see I was right in a sense.
Though, perhaps being a lady you wouldn't understand.

LAURA   I'm not sure that I do.

HERB   Well, now, look here. If I had taken Tom out of school
after that scandal with Mr. . . . uh . . . what was his name?

LAURA   Mr. Harris.

HERB   Yes. If I'd taken Tom out then, he would have been
marked for the rest of his life.

LAURA   You know that Tom will be expelled, of course.

HERB   Yes, but the circumstances are so much more normal.

LAURA (*After looking at him a moment*)   I think, Mr. Lee,
I'm not quite sure, but I think, in a sense, you're proud of Tom.

HERB   Well.

LAURA   Probably for the first time you're proud of him because
the school police found him out of bounds with a . . .

HERB   I shouldn't have expected you to understand. Bill will
see what I mean.
    (BILL *starts down the stairs*)

LAURA   Yes. He probably will.
    (BILL *comes in the room*)

HERB   Bill.

BILL   Hello, Herb.
    (HERB *looks from* LAURA *to* BILL. *Notices the coldness
    between them*)

BILL   I was just up seeing Tom.

HERB   Yes. I intend to go up after we've seen the Dean. How
is he?

BILL   All right.

HERB (*Expansive*)   Sitting around telling the boys all about
it.

BILL   No, he's in his room alone. The others are going to the tea dance at the Inn. Laura . . . (*Sees* LAURA *is leaving the room*) Oh, Laura, I wish you'd stay.

(LAURA *takes one step back into the room*)

HERB   I was telling your wife here, trying to make her understand the male point of view on this matter. I mean, how being kicked out for a thing like this, while not exactly desirable, is still not so serious. It's sort of one of the calculated risks of being a man.

(*He smiles at his way of putting it*)

BILL (*Preparing to tell* HERB)   Herb?

HERB   Yes, Bill. I mean, you agree with me on that, don't you?

BILL   Yes, Herb, only the situation is not exactly as it was reported to you over the phone. It's true that Tom went to this girl Ellie's place, and it's true that he went for the usual purpose. However . . . however, it didn't work out that way.

HERB   What do you mean?

BILL   Nothing happened.

HERB   You mean she . . . she wouldn't have him?

BILL   I mean, Tom . . . I don't know . . . he didn't go through with it. He couldn't. (*He looks at* LAURA) It's true. The girl says so. And when it didn't work, he tried to kill himself with a knife in the kitchen, and she struggled with him, and that brought the school cops, and that's that. (LAURA *turns away, shocked and moved.* MR. LEE *sits down in a chair bewildered*) I'm sorry, Herb. Of course the fact that he was with Ellie at her place is enough to get him expelled.

HERB   Does everyone know this?

BILL   Well, Ellie talks. She's got no shame . . . and this is apparently something to talk about.

LAURA (*To* MR. LEE)   Do you still think it will make a good smoking-car story?

BILL   What do you mean?

HERB   Why did he do it? Before, maybe he could talk it down, but to go do a thing like this and leave no doubts.

LAURA   In whose mind?

BILL   Laura, please.

LAURA (*Angry*)   You asked me to stay.

BILL (*Flaring back at her*)   Well, now you've heard. We won't keep you.

LAURA (*Knowing, without asking*)   Why did you want me to hear?

BILL (*Going to her*)   I wanted you to know the facts. That's all. The whole story.
   (LAURA *stands in the alcove*)

HERB   Bill, Bill! Maybe there's some way of getting to this girl so she wouldn't spread the story.

BILL   I'm afraid it's too late for that.

HERB   I don't know. Some things don't make any sense. What am I going to do now?

LAURA (*Re-entering*)   Mr. Lee, please don't go on drawing the wrong conclusions!

HERB   I'm drawing no conclusions. This sort of thing can happen to a normal boy. But it's what the others will think . . . Added to the Harris business. And that's all that's important. What they'll think.

LAURA   Isn't it important what Tom thinks?

BILL   Herb, we'd better be getting on over to the Dean's . . .

HERB (*Indicating upstairs*)   Is he in his room?

BILL   Yes.

HERB   Packing?

BILL   No.

HERB   I told him to come to you to talk things over. Did he?

BILL   No.

HERB   What am I going to say to him now?

BILL   We're expected at four.

HERB   I know. But I've got to go up . . . Maybe I should have left him with his mother. She might have known what to do, what to say . . . (*He starts out*) You want to come along with me?

BILL (*Moving to hall*)   All right.

LAURA (*Serious*)   Bill, I'd like to talk with you.

BILL   I'll be back.
   (*Goes with* HERB *to the landing.* LAURA *exits, taking off her jacket*)

HERB   Maybe I ought to do this alone.

BILL   He's probably locked in his bedroom.
   (HERB *goes up the stairs and inside the study.* BILL *stays in the hall.* TOM, *as he hears his father knocking on the bedroom door, stiffens.* HERB *tries the door handle*)

HERB (*Off, in the study*)   Tom . . . Tom . . . it's Dad. (TOM *gets up, but just stands there*) Tom, are you asleep? (*After a few moments, he reappears on the landing. He is deeply hurt that his son wouldn't speak to him*) I think he's asleep.

BILL (*Making a move to go in and get* TOM)   He can't be . . .

HERB (*Stops*)   Yes, I think he is. He was always a sound sleeper. We used to have to drag him out of bed when he was a kid.

BILL   But he should see you.

HERB   It'll be better later, anyhow.
   (*He starts down the stairs, troubled, puzzled*)

BILL   I'll go right with you, Herb.
   (*They re-enter the study, and* BILL *goes out through the alcove.* HERB *stays in the master's study*)

TOM (*When his father is downstairs, he opens his bedroom door and faintly calls*)   Dad?
   (HERB *looks up, thinking he's heard something but then figures it must have been something else.* RALPH, STEVE *and* PHIL *come crashing down the stairs, dressed for the tea dance, ad libbing comments about the girls at the dance.* TOM

closes his door. When they have gone, he opens it again and calls "Dad" faintly. When there is no response, he closes the door, and goes and lies on the bed)

BILL (*Re-entering*)   Laura, I'm going to the Dean's now with Herb. I'm playing squash with the headmaster at five. So I'll see you at the dining room at six-thirty.

LAURA (*Entering after him*)   I wish you'd come back here after.

BILL   Laura, I can't.

LAURA   Bill, I wish you would.

BILL (*Sees that there is some strange determination in* LAURA'S *face*)   Herb, I'll be with you in a minute. Why don't you walk along?

HERB   All right . . . Good-bye, Laura. See you again.

BILL   You'll see her in a couple of days at the reunion.

HERB   I may not be coming up for it now . . . Maybe I will. I don't know. I'll be walking along. Good-bye, Laura. Tell Tom I tried to see him.
   (*He goes out*)

BILL   Now, Laura, what's the matter? I've got to get to the Dean's room to discuss this matter.

LAURA   Yes, of course. But first I'd like to discuss the boys who made him do this . . . the men and boys who made him do this.

BILL   No one made him do anything.

LAURA   Is there to be no blame, no punishment for the boys and men who taunted him into doing this? What if he had succeeded in killing himself? What then?

BILL   You're being entirely too emotional about this.

LAURA   If he had succeeded in killing himself in Ellie's rooms, wouldn't you have felt some guilt?

BILL   I?

LAURA   Yes, you.

BILL   I wish you'd look at the facts and not be so emotional about this.

LAURA   The facts! What facts! An innocent boy goes swimming with an instructor . . . an instructor whom he likes because this instructor is one of the few who encourage him, who don't ride him . . . And because he's an off-horse, you and the rest of them are only too glad to put two and two together and get a false answer . . . anything which will let you go on and persecute a boy whom you basically don't like. If it had happened with Al or anybody else, you would have done nothing.

BILL   It would have been an entirely different matter. You can't escape from what you are . . . your character. Why do they spend so much time in the law courts on character witnesses? To prove this was the kind of man who could or couldn't commit such and such a crime.

LAURA   I resent this judgment by prejudice. He's not like me, therefore, he is capable of all possible crimes. He's not one of us . . . a member of the tribe!

BILL   Now look, Laura, I know this is a shock to you, because you were fond of this boy. But you did all you could for him, more than anyone would expect. After all, your responsibility doesn't go beyond—

LAURA   I know. Doesn't go beyond giving him tea and sympathy on Sunday afternoons. Well, I want to tell you something. It's going to shock you . . . but I'm going to tell you.

BILL   Laura, it's late.

LAURA   Last night I knew what Tom had in mind to do.

BILL   How did you know?

LAURA   I heard him making the date with Ellie on the phone.

BILL   And you didn't stop him? Then you're the one responsible.

LAURA   Yes, I am responsible, but not as you think. I did try to stop him, but not by locking him in his room, or calling the school police. I tried to stop him by being nice to him, by being affectionate. By showing him that he was liked . . . yes, even

loved. I knew what he was going to do . . . and why he was
going to do it. He had to prove to you bullies that he was a
man, and he was going to prove it with Ellie Martin. Well
. . . last night . . . last night, I wished he had proved it with
me.

BILL   What in Christ's name are you saying?

LAURA   Yes, I shock you. I shock myself. But you are right.
I am responsible here. I know what I should have done. I knew
it then. My heart cried out for this boy in his misery . . . a
misery imposed by my husband. And I wanted to help him
as one human being to another . . . and I failed. At the last
moment, I sent him away . . . sent him to . . .

BILL   You mean you managed to overcome your exaggerated
sense of pity.

LAURA   No, it was not just pity. My heart in its own loneliness
. . . Yes, I've been lonely here, miserably lonely . . . and my
heart in its loneliness cried out for this boy . . . cried out for
the comfort he could give me too.

BILL   You don't know what you're saying.

LAURA   But I was a good woman. Good in what sense of the
word? Good to whom . . . and for whom?

BILL   Laura, we'll discuss this, if we must, later on . . .

LAURA   Bill! There'll be no later on. I'm leaving you.

BILL   Over this thing?

LAURA (*After a moment*)   Yes, this *thing,* and all the other
things in our marriage.

BILL   For God's sake, Laura, what are you talking about?

LAURA   I'm talking about love and honor and manliness, and
tenderness, and persecution. I'm talking about a lot. You
haven't understood any of it.

BILL   Laura, you can't leave over a thing like this. You know
what it means.

LAURA   I wouldn't worry too much about it. When I'm gone,
it will probably be agreed by all that I was an off-horse too, and
didn't really belong to the clan, and it's good riddance.

BILL   And you're doing this . . . all because of this . . . this fairy?

LAURA   (*After a moment*)   This boy, Bill . . . this boy is more of a man than you are.

BILL   Sure. Ask Ellie.

LAURA   Because it was distasteful for him. Because for him there has to be love. He's more of a man than you are.

BILL   Yes, sure.

LAURA   Manliness is not all swagger and swearing and mountain climbing. Manliness is also tenderness, gentleness, consideration. You men think you can decide on who is a man, when only a woman can really know.

BILL   Ellie's a woman. Ask Ellie.

LAURA   I don't need to ask anyone.

BILL   What do you know about a man? Married first to that boy . . . again, a poor pitiable boy . . . You want to mother a boy, not love a man. That's why you never really loved me. Because I was not a boy you could mother.

LAURA   You're quite wrong about my not loving you. I did love you. But not just for your outward show of manliness, but because you needed me . . . For one unguarded moment you let me know you needed me, and I have tried to find that moment again the year we've been married . . . Why did you marry me, Bill? In God's name, why?

BILL   Because I loved you. Why else?

LAURA   You've resented me . . . almost from the day you married me, you've resented me. You never wanted to marry really . . . Did they kid you into it? Does a would-be headmaster have to be married? Or what was it, Bill? You would have been far happier going off on your jaunts with the boys, having them to your rooms for feeds and bull sessions . . .

BILL   That's part of being a master.

LAURA   Other masters and their wives do not take two boys always with them whenever they go away on vacations or weekends.

BILL   They are boys without privileges.

LAURA   And I became a wife without privileges.

BILL   You became a wife . . .
   (*He stops*)

LAURA   Yes?

BILL   You did *not* become a wife.

LAURA   I know. I know I failed you. In some terrible way I've failed you.

BILL   You were more interested in mothering that fairy up there than in being my wife.

LAURA   But you wouldn't let me, Bill. You wouldn't let me.

BILL (*Grabbing her by the shoulders*)   What do you mean I wouldn't let you?

LAURA (*Quietly, almost afraid to say it*)   Did it ever occur to you that you persecute in Tom, that boy up there, you persecute in him the thing you fear in yourself? (BILL *looks at her for a long moment of hatred. She has hit close to the truth he has never let himself be conscious of. There is a moment when he might hurt her, but then he draws away, still staring at her. He backs away, slowly, and then turns to the door*) Bill!

BILL (*Not looking at her*)   I hope you will be gone when I come back from dinner.

LAURA (*Quietly*)   I will be . . . (*Going towards him*) Oh, Bill, I'm sorry. I shouldn't have said that . . . it was cruel. (*She reaches for him as he goes out the door*) This was the weakness you cried out for me to save you from, wasn't it . . . And I have tried. (*He is gone*) I have tried. (*Slowly she turns back into the room and looks at it*) I did try. (*For a few minutes she stands stunned and tired from her outburst. Then she moves slowly to* TOM'S *raincoat, picks it up and turns and goes out of the room and to the stair-landing. She goes to the boy's study door and knocks*) Tom. (*She opens it and goes in out of sight. At* TOM'S *door, she calls again*) Tom. (TOM *turns his head slightly and listens.* LAURA *opens* TOM'S *door and comes in*) Oh, I'm sorry. May I come in? (*She sees she's not going to get an answer from him, so she goes in*) I brought back your raincoat. You left it last night. (*She puts it on chair. She looks at him*) This is a nice room . . . I've never seen it before . . . As a matter of fact I've never been up here in this part of the house. (*Still getting no response, she goes on.* TOM *slowly turns and looks at her back, while she is examining something on the walls. She turns, speaking*) It's very cozy. It's really quite . . . (*She stops when she sees he has turned around looking at her*) Hello.

TOM (*Barely audible*)   Hello.

LAURA   Do you mind my being here?

TOM   You're not supposed to be.

LAURA   I know. But everyone's out, and will be for some time . . . I wanted to return your raincoat.

TOM   Thank you. (*After a pause he sits up on the bed, his back to her*) I didn't think you'd ever want to see me again.

LAURA   Why not?

TOM   After last night. I'm sorry about what happened downstairs.

LAURA (*She looks at him a while, then*)   I'm not.

TOM (*Looks at her. Can't quite make it out*)   You've heard everything, I suppose.

LAURA   Yes.

TOM   Everything?

LAURA   Everything.

TOM   I knew your husband would be anxious to give you the details.

LAURA   He did.
   (*She stands there quietly looking down at the boy*)

TOM   So now you know too.

LAURA   What?

TOM   That everything they said about me is true.

LAURA   Tom!

TOM   Well, it is. isn't it?

LAURA   Tom?

TOM   I'm no man. Ellie knows it. Everybody knows it. It seems everybody knew it, except me. And now I know it.

LAURA   (*Moves towards him*) Tom . . . Tom . . . dear. (TOM *turns away from her*) You don't think that just because . . .

TOM   What else am I to think?

LAURA   (*Very gently*) Tom, that didn't work because you didn't believe in it . . . in such a test.

TOM   (*With the greatest difficulty*)   I touched her, and there was nothing.

LAURA   You aren't in love with Ellie.

TOM   That's not supposed to matter.

LAURA   But it does.

TOM   I wish they'd let me kill myself.

LAURA   Tom, look at me. (TOM *shakes his head*) Tom, last night you kissed me.

TOM   Jesus!

LAURA   Why did you kiss me?

TOM   (*Turns suddenly*) And it made you sick, didn't it? Didn't it?
   (*Turns away from her again*)

LAURA   How can you think such a thing?

TOM   You sent me away . . . you . . . Anyway, when you heard this morning it must have made you sick.

LAURA   (*Sits on edge of bed*)   Tom, I'm going to tell you something. (TOM *won't turn*) Tom? (*He still won't turn*) It was the nicest kiss I've ever had . . . from anybody. (TOM *slowly turns and looks at her*) Tom, I came up to say good-bye. (TOM *shakes his head, looking at her*) I'm going away . . . I'll probably never see you again. I'm leaving Bill. (TOM *knits his brows questioning*) For a lot of reasons . . . one of them, what he's done to you. But before I left, I wanted you to know, for your own comfort, you're more of a man now than he ever was or will be. And one day you'll meet a girl, and it will be right. (TOM *turns away in disbelief*) Tom, believe me.

TOM I wish I could. But a person knows . . . knows inside.
Jesus, do you think after last night I'd ever . . . (*He stops.
After a moment, he smiles at her*) But thanks . . . thanks a
lot. (*He closes his eyes.* LAURA *looks at him a long time. Her
face shows the great compassion and tenderness she feels for
this miserable boy. After some time, she gets up and goes out
the door. A moment later she appears in the hall door. She
pauses for a moment, then reaches out and closes it, and stays
inside.*

TOM, *when he hears the door close, his eyes open. He sees
she has left his bedroom. Then in complete misery, he lies
down on the bed, like a wounded animal, his head at the foot
of the bed.*

LAURA *in a few moments appears in the bedroom doorway.
She stands there, and then comes in, always looking at the
slender figure of the boy on the bed. She closes the bedroom
door.*

TOM *hears the sound and looks around. When he sees she
has come back, he turns around slowly, wonderingly, and lies
on his back, watching her.*

LAURA *seeing a bolt on the door, slides it to. Then she stands
looking at* TOM, *her hand at her neck. With a slight and delicate movement, she unbuttons the top button of her blouse,
and moves towards* TOM. *When she gets alongside the bed, she
reaches out her hand, still keeping one hand at her blouse.* TOM
makes no move. Just watches her.

LAURA *makes a little move with the outstretched hand, asking for his hand.* TOM *slowly moves his hand to hers*)

LAURA (*Stands there holding his hand and smiling gently at
him. Then she sits and looks down at the boy, and after a moment, barely audible*)   And now . . . nothing?
    (TOM'S *other hand comes up and with both his hands he
    brings her hand to his lips*)

LAURA (*Smiles tenderly at this gesture, and after a moment*)
Years from now . . . when you talk about this . . . and
you will . . . be kind.
    (*Gently she brings the boy's hands towards her opened
    blouse, as the lights slowly dim out . . . and . . .*

THE CURTAIN FALLS

THE END

The

Caine Mutiny

Court-Martial

by **HERMAN WOUK**

THIS PLAY IS DEDICATED TO

Charles Laughton

IN ADMIRATION AND GRATITUDE

NOTE

The Caine Mutiny Court-Martial is purely imaginary. No ship named U.S.S. *Caine* ever existed. The records show no instance of a U.S. Navy captain relieved at sea under Articles 184–186. The fictitious figure of the deposed captain was derived from a study of psychoneurotic case histories, and is not a portrait of a real military person or a type; this statement is made because of the existing tendency to seek lampoons of living people in imaginary stories. The author served under two captains of the regular Navy aboard destroyer-minesweepers, both of whom were decorated for valor. One technical note: court-martial regulations have been extensively revised since the Second World War. This trial takes place according to instructions then in force. Certain minor omissions have been made for purposes of brevity; otherwise the play strictly follows procedures stipulated in *Naval Courts and Boards.*

ACKNOWLEDGMENT

The plank owners of the U.S.S. *Caine* include the producer, the director, the stars, and the supporting players of the original production, whose art and constructive wisdom helped so much in refitting the old vessel to navigate in the theatre.

H.W.

THE CAINE MUTINY COURT-MARTIAL

had its first performance in the Granada Theatre, Santa Barbara, California, on October 12, 1953. After a tour across the United States it opened in New York at the Plymouth Theatre on January 20, 1954, with the same cast, as follows:

IN ORDER OF APPEARANCE

LT. STEPHEN MARYK	John Hodiak
LT. BARNEY GREENWALD	Henry Fonda
LT. COM. JOHN CHALLEE	Ainslie Pryor
CAPTAIN BLAKELY	Russell Hicks
LT. COM. PHILIP FRANCIS QUEEG	Lloyd Nolan
LT. THOMAS KEEFER	Robert Gist
SIGNALMAN THIRD CLASS JUNIUS URBAN	Eddie Firestone
LT. (JR. GRADE) WILLIS SEWARD KEITH	Charles Nolte
CAPT. RANDOLPH SOUTHARD	Paul Birch
DR. FORREST LUNDEEN	Stephen Chase
DR. BIRD	Herbert Anderson
STENOGRAPHER	John Huffman
ORDERLY	Greg Roman
MEMBERS OF THE COURT: *	Larry Barton
	Jim Bumgarner
	T. H. Jourdan
	Richard Farmer
	Richard Norris
	Pat Waltz

Produced by Paul Gregory

Directed by Charles Laughton

* Taken from second-night program.

The time of the play is February 1945. The scene is the General Court-Martial Room of the Twelfth Naval District, San Francisco. At the end of Act 2 the scene shifts to a banquet room in the Hotel Fairmont, San Francisco.

from the **NAVY REGULATIONS:**

ARTICLE 184. *Unusual circumstances.* It is conceivable that most unusual and extraordinary circumstances may arise in which the relief from duty of a commanding officer by a subordinate becomes necessary, either by placing him under arrest or on the sick list; but such action shall never be taken without the approval of the Navy Department or other appropriate higher authority, except when reference to such higher authority is undoubtedly impracticable because of the delay involved or for other clearly obvious reason. Such reference must set forth all facts in the case, and the reasons for the recommendation, with particular regard to the degree of urgency involved.

ARTICLE 185. *Conditions to fulfill.* In order that a subordinate officer, acting upon his own initiative, may be vindicated for relieving a commanding officer from duty, the situation must be obvious and clear, and must admit of the single conclusion that the retention of command by such commanding officer will seriously and irretrievably prejudice the public interests. The subordinate officer so acting must be next in lawful succession to command; must be unable to refer the matter to a common superior for one of the reasons set down in Article 184; must be certain that the prejudicial actions of his commanding officer are not caused by secret instructions unknown to the subordinate; must have given the matter such careful consideration, and must have made such exhaustive investigation of all the circumstances, as may be practicable; and finally must be thoroughly convinced that the conclusion to relieve his commanding officer is one which a reasonable, prudent, and experienced officer would regard as a necessary consequence from the facts thus determined to exist.

ARTICLE 186. *Responsibility.* Intelligently fearless initiative is an important trait of military character, and it is not the purpose to discourage its employment in cases of this nature. However, as the action of relieving a superior from command involves most serious possibilities, a decision so to do or so to recommend should be based upon facts established by substantial evidence, and upon the official views of others in a position to form valuable opinions, particularly of a technical character. An officer relieving his commanding officer or recommending such action together with all others who so counsel, must bear the legitimate responsibility for, and must be prepared to justify, such action.

Act
THE PROSECUTION
One

THE SCENE: *The curtain is up when the audience enters the theater. Dimly visible is a gray-draped stage barren except for the chairs, tables, and witness box of a court-martial. The big raised curved judge's bench, Stage Right, is covered with green baize, and behind it on the draperies is a large American flag. Upstage Left is* LIEUTENANT COMMANDER CHALLEE'S *desk. Next to his desk, placed out of the way, is* GREENWALD'S *desk, with two chairs placed on top. Behind, Upstage, is the witness stand: a chair on a raised round platform which rolls on casters. There is a chair for the* ORDERLY, *Stage Center, by the end of the judge's bench, and a chair and small desk for the* STENOGRAPHER, *Downstage Right, below* CAPTAIN BLAKELY'S *place on the bench. The single entrance to the stage is through the curtains, deep Center Stage.*

The start of the play is marked by the dimming of the house lights and the brightening of the stage. THE ORDERLY *and* STENOGRAPHER, *two sailors in dress blues, enter. They pick up* GREENWALD'S *desk and chairs, carry them Downstage Left, and put the chairs in place.* GREENWALD *enters, and as the* ORDERLY *and* STENOGRAPHER *roll the witness stand into place, Center Stage, he puts his brief case down on his desk. Exit the two sailors.* GREENWALD, *a lanky lieutenant in a green flier's uniform with wings and campaign ribbons, strolls to the witness stand. His face is stern and abstracted. He stares at the stand for a few moments, then leans his elbows on the arms of the chair and puts his hand to his face. Enter* MARYK, *a big, powerfully built lieu-tenant in blues, with close-cropped hair. He comes down to the other side of the witness stand and peers at* GREENWALD *for a moment.*

MARYK (*Bursting out*)   What are they doing out there? This is a hell of a long recess. This is the longest recess yet.

GREENWALD   I've seen longer.

MARYK   I thought the trial would be over by now. All they do is swear in somebody, recess, look at a paper, recess, look at another paper, recess, mumble some legal words, recess some more—when does the court-martial start?

GREENWALD   Maryk, take it easy. It's going to be a long trial.

MARYK   But you won't tell me what you're doing, how you're going to conduct my case, what I'm supposed to say—nothing.

GREENWALD   It would only confuse you.

MARYK   I couldn't be more confused than I am.

GREENWALD   Well, you've got something there.

MARYK   I don't like the way you're handling me.

GREENWALD   Good. That makes us even.

MARYK   How's that?

GREENWALD   I don't like handling you.

MARYK   What? Well, then, maybe I'd better—

GREENWALD (*Crossing to desk and taking papers from brief case*)   Maryk, I'd rather be prosecuting you than defending you. I told you that the first time we met. Nevertheless, I'm defending you. If it's humanly possible to win an acquittal in this case I'm going to win you an acquittal. If you want a prediction, I believe I'm going to get you off. But you can't help me. So just leave me be.

MARYK   You're a damn peculiar fish.

GREENWALD   My mother thinks I'm beautiful.

MARYK   That's a hell of a thing to say, you know.

GREENWALD   What?

MARYK   You'd rather be prosecuting me than defending me. How d'you suppose that makes me feel?

GREENWALD (*Looks at him, crosses to him*)   You're nervous.

MARYK   Sure I am.

GREENWALD   I am too, a bit. Sorry.

MARYK   I can ask the court for a different counsel.

GREENWALD   Forget it. I don't take on a case to lose it.

MARYK   You do think I was right to relieve Captain Queeg?

GREENWALD   I can't say that.

MARYK   After everything I told you, you still don't think he was nuts?

GREENWALD   No, I don't.

MARYK   Then I get hung.

GREENWALD   Not necessarily.

MARYK   Maybe I should plead guilty. Eight legal officers advised me to plead guilty. The court would go easy on me—

GREENWALD   I don't care if every legal officer in the Navy says otherwise. I think I can get you off.

MARYK   I'll get all fouled up.

GREENWALD   You'll do nobly. You may come out of this a great naval hero.

MARYK   (*Stares at him*)   Greenwald, is there something eating you?

GREENWALD   I don't know. (*Paces in silence for a moment. Halts*) I'm a damn good lawyer, Maryk, and I'm a pretty poor flyer. Took quite a shellacking at flight school from snotty ensign instructors four or five years younger than me. I didn't like it. Baby-faced kids couldn't do such things to Greenwald the hot-shot lawyer. I used to day-dream about a court-martial coming up on that base. And some poor joe would need defending. And I'd step in, and take over, and twist the Navy's arm, and make it holler Uncle. Now—here's my dream come true. You know something? I don't look forward to twisting the Navy's arm. Not one bit.

MARYK   Scared of the brass, eh?

GREENWALD   Worse.

MARYK   What?

GREENWALD   Respectful.

MARYK   Listen, I put in for transfer to the regulars. I respect the Navy too.

GREENWALD   Maryk, they took us in naked. Just a lot of pink forked animals with belly buttons. And they worked us over, and kicked us around, and put us through a bunch of silly rituals, and stuffed us full of the dullest bloody books in the world, and slapped funny uniforms on us. And there we were all of a sudden with big flaming machines in our hands, sinking U-boats and shooting down Zeroes. A lot of guys take it in stride. Me, it's sort of turned all my old ideas wrong side out. And this is a war that sure needs winning, for my dough.

MARYK   Well, I don't go along with you all the way.

GREENWALD   You don't.

MARYK   There's still a big pile of foolishness connected with the Navy. In fact—I sometimes think the Navy is a master plan designed by geniuses for execution by idiots.

GREENWALD (*Startled*)   You think what?

MARYK (*Self-conscious*)   The Navy is a master plan designed by geniuses for execution by idiots.

GREENWALD   Where'd you hear that?

MARYK (*Injured*)   Couldn't I just have made it up?

GREENWALD   You could just have made up the Gettysburg Address, too. Where'd you hear it?

MARYK (*Grins reluctantly*)   Well, matter of fact, it's one of Tom Keefer's favorite cracks.

GREENWALD (*Nods*)   Ah yes. You echo your novelist friend quite a bit, don't you?

MARYK   Tom's got the keenest mind on the ship. About the keenest I've ever run into.

GREENWALD   He's keen, all right.

MARYK   I'm sure glad Tom is going to testify.

GREENWALD   You are?

MARYK Hell! He knows everything Captain Queeg did. He knows psychiatry. I'm a stoop about those things. I'll foul myself up. Tom Keefer can tell the thing straight.

GREENWALD If I had my way, Lieutenant Thomas Keefer would never appear in this court.

MARYK What?

GREENWALD He's not going to do you any good on the witness stand, Maryk, you mark my word. One man I'd really enjoy prosecuting is Mister Thomas Keefer, the eminent novelist.

MARYK Greenwald, you're not to go pinning anything on Tom Keefer . . . It was my responsibility—

GREENWALD That's right. You did what you did.
   (*Enter the six* COURT MEMBERS, *the* STENOGRAPHER, *and the* ORDERLY, *who take their places*)
Well, here we go . . . It's better you did it out of your own noble judgment than that you took the advice of a sensitive novelist.
   (CHALLEE *enters, and crosses to his desk. Puts his brief case down, looks to the entrance*)

CHALLEE Attention!
   (*All stand to attention as* CAPTAIN BLAKELY *enters and goes to his place in silence. All officers are in dress blues; so are all witnesses in the trial*)

BLAKELY We're spending excessive time in all these recesses.
   (*He rings his desk bell. All sit*)
I appreciate the judge advocate's desire to have the record letter-perfect. But let's get on with the case and hereafter keep technicalities to a minimum.

CHALLEE Aye aye, sir.

BLAKELY (*Holds out paper to* CHALLEE) Court finds the charge and specification in due form and technically correct. Is the accused ready for trial?
   (GREENWALD *motions to* MARYK *to rise.* MARYK *rises*)

MARYK Yes, sir.
   (BLAKELY *nods to* CHALLEE, *who reads from the paper*)

CHALLEE "Charge. Conduct to the prejudice of good order and discipline. Specification. In that Lieutenant Stephen

Maryk, U.S.N.R., on or about 18 December, 1944, aboard the U.S.S. *Caine,* willfully, without proper authority, and without justifiable cause, did relieve from his duty as commanding officer Lieutenant Commander Philip Francis Queeg, U.S.N., the duly assigned commanding officer of said ship, who was then and there in lawful exercise of his command, the United States then being in a state of war." . . . Stephen Maryk, Lieutenant, United States Naval Reserve, you have heard the charge and specification preferred against you; how say you, guilty or not guilty?

MARYK   Not guilty.

GREENWALD (*Rises*)   Accused admits he is Lieutenant Stephen Maryk, U.S.N.R., and that he was the executive officer of the U.S.S. *Caine* on December 18, 1944.

MARYK (*Haltingly*)   The admission is made with my authority.

BLAKELY   Judge advocate, present your case.

CHALLEE (*To* ORDERLY)   Call Lieutenant Commander Queeg. (*Exit* ORDERLY. *He returns in a moment with* QUEEG, *who is tanned, natty, erect, the picture of a correct naval officer. He is a short man in his thirties with scanty hair.* CHALLEE *holds a Bible for him. He places left hand on it and raises right hand*)

BLAKELY (*Stands, raises his right hand*)   You do solemnly swear that the evidence you shall give in this court shall be the truth, the whole truth, and nothing but the truth, so help you God.

QUEEG   I do.

CHALLEE   State your name, rank, and present position.

QUEEG   Philip Francis Queeg, Lieutenant Commander, United States Navy, temporarily assigned to Commandant, Twelfth Naval District, awaiting reassignment by BuPers.

CHALLEE   If you recognize the accused, state as whom.

QUEEG (*Glancing briefly at* MARYK)   Lieutenant Stephen Maryk, U.S.N.R.

The Caine Mutiny Court-Martial

CHALLEE Commander Queeg, on December 18, 1944, were you in command of the U.S.S. *Caine?*

QUEEG I was.

CHALLEE What type of vessel is the *Caine?*

QUEEG Her official designation is high-speed minesweeper. What she is, is a four-piper, one of those flush-deck twelve-hundred-ton destroyers from World War I, fixed up with mine-sweeping gear.

CHALLEE An old ship, then?

QUEEG I guess about the oldest type still doing combatant duty.

CHALLEE What is her primary mission?

QUEEG (*Smiling*) That's a hard one. These old buckets are regarded as pretty expendable. By and large we were doing the usual destroyer duty—anti-submarine screening—also ran the mail, transported marines, carried aviation gas and torpedoes, gave fire support in minor landings, or what have you? Also swept mines now and then.

CHALLEE Commander, on December 18, 1944, were you relieved of command of the *Caine?*

QUEEG (*Slight pause*) Yes.

CHALLEE By whom?

QUEEG By the accused.

CHALLEE Was this a regular relief?

QUEEG It was totally irregular, sir.

CHALLEE How would you describe it?

QUEEG Well, the most charitable description would be that it was an incident, a regrettable incident of temporary and total collapse of military discipline.

CHALLEE Commander, please relate all the facts that bear on this unauthorized relief.

QUEEG Kay, I'll try to do this consecutively, here. The *Caine* sortied from Ulithi Atoll on the sixteenth of December, I

believe, the fifteenth or the sixteenth. We were a screening
vessel with a group of fleet oilers. Our mission was to rendezvous with and refuel Admiral Halsey's fast carrier force in the
Philippine Sea. Kay. Well, we made the rendezvous. And then
this typhoon came along. The fueling was broken off and the
fleet began to maneuver to evade the storm. Now, the storm
was traveling due west—

(*Gestures with hands*)

—so Admiral Halsey set fleet course due south and we
began to make a run for the safe semi-circle.

CHALLEE   What was the date and time of that course change?

QUEEG   That would be early morning of the eighteenth, sir.
Well, as I say, the storm was pretty bad at this point. Visibil-
ity was almost zero. Couldn't see the guide or even the next
ship in the screen, we were just steaming blindly through
rain and spray. And of course with the wind and sea and all,
we had to maneuver pretty smartly with engines and rudder
to hold fleet course and speed. But we were doing fine. My
executive officer, however, pretty early in the game began to
show unusual symptoms of nervousness. And I had to—

CHALLEE   What were these symptoms of nervousness?

QUEEG   Well, for instance, he began talking very early—oh, it
couldn't have been half an hour after the fleet started to run
south—that we should operate independently and come around
north.

CHALLEE   Why did he want to do that?

QUEEG (*With illustrative gestures*)   Well, to give you the picture on that—you see the typhoon was coming at us from the
east. We were on the western edge of it. Now as you know
these blows spin counter-clockwise above the equator. That
means where we were the wind was from due north. Admiral
Halsey, of course, was running south with the wind, to get out
of the storm's path. Now that's in accordance with all existing
storm doctrine from Bowditch on up. But my exec insisted that
the ship was on the verge of foundering, and we'd better come
around and head into the wind—that is, north—if we were to
survive. Of course we weren't in any such bad shape at all.
And that's what I mean by nervousness.

CHALLEE What was your objection to coming north, as the executive officer suggested?

QUEEG Why, everything was wrong with that idea that could be wrong with it, sir. In the first place my orders were to proceed south. My mission was screening. My ship was in no danger and was functioning normally. Why to drop out of station and act independently under those conditions was unthinkable. Coming around to north would have headed the ship directly into the heart of the typhoon. It was not only a senseless suggestion in the circumstances, it was almost suicidal. I might add that I've since checked my decisions of December eighteenth with the finest ship handlers I know up to the rank of rear admiral, and they've unanimously agreed that the only course in that situation was south.

(CHALLEE *glances at* GREENWALD. *He is doodling obliviously.* CHALLEE *hesitates*)

CHALLEE Commander, your last remark was hearsay evidence. That is not acceptable.

QUEEG Oh. I'm sorry, sir. I'm not up on those legal distinctions as much as I should be, I guess.

CHALLEE Perfectly all right.

(CHALLEE *and* BLAKELY *stare at* GREENWALD)

BLAKELY Will defense counsel move to strike out that part of the testimony which was hearsay evidence?

GREENWALD (*Half rises*) All right, sir. I so move.

(*Sits*)

CHALLEE No objection.

(BLAKELY, *with a disgusted look at* GREENWALD, *turns to* STENOGRAPHER)

BLAKELY Strike out the last sentence.

CHALLEE A ship-handling expert will be called, Commander, to testify on that point.

QUEEG I see. I'm very glad to know that, sir. Thank you.

CHALLEE Proceed with your description of the relief.

QUEEG Kay . . . Well, it was just that Maryk kept insisting on coming north, more and more stridently as the weather

deteriorated. Finally I began to be a little concerned about him.
Then suddenly he walked up to me out of a clear sky, and told
me I was on the sick list and he was relieving me. To be honest,
I couldn't believe my ears, and was a little slow in catching on.
It was only when he started shouting orders at the officer of
the deck and countermanding my instructions to the helm that
I began to realize what was going on.

CHALLEE Commander, can you recall anything in your own
bearing or manner that could have provoked your executive
officer's act?

QUEEG Well—truthfully, sir, I cannot. Frankly, I don't think
my bearing or manner had anything to do with it. It was a
pretty scary situation in the wheelhouse. The wind was force
10 to 12, screeching and all that, the waves were mountainous.
The barometer was about as low as it's ever been in the U. S.
Navy history. We took one very bad roll—and I mean a bad
one, and I've done a lot of North Atlantic rolling, too—and I
think Maryk simply went into panic.

CHALLEE Was the *Caine* in grave danger at that moment?

QUEEG I wouldn't say that—no sir. We righted very nicely
from that bad roll. He repeatedly tried to order me off the
bridge, but I stayed right where I was. I gave him orders only
when it seemed necessary for the safety of the ship. In the
situation I thought the chief hazard was any further acts of
frenzy on his part. And to the extent that the *Caine* did come
safely through the storm despite this unprecedented running
amuck of my executive officer, I believe my handling of the
emergency was the correct one.

CHALLEE Did Maryk cite any authority at all when he
relieved you?

QUEEG He mumbled something about Article 184. I didn't
even catch it at the time. Later he said his authority was Articles 184, 185, and 186 of the Naval Regulations.

CHALLEE Are you familiar with those articles?

QUEEG Certainly.

CHALLEE In substance, what do they provide?

QUEEG   Well, as I understand it, they make it possible for an executive officer to take over in an emergency, a highly unusual emergency where the captain is—well, frankly, where the captain's gone absolutely and hopelessly loony.

CHALLEE   Were those articles properly invoked in your situation?

QUEEG (*Smiling wryly*)   Well, I'm sort of an interested party here. But you won't have to take my word for it. I was successfully conning my shop through a typhoon. Fortunately there are a hundred thirty witnesses to that fact, every man who was aboard that ship.

CHALLEE (*Glancing toward* GREENWALD)   There again, sir, you're testifying to the conclusions of others.

QUEEG (*Smiling*)   Sorry. I'm obviously no legal expert. I'll withdraw that last sentence.
   (*With a glance at* BLAKELY)
   BLAKELY *glances annoyed at* GREENWALD, *who seems to be paying no attention, doodling on a scratch pad*)

BLAKELY (*To* STENOGRAPHER)   Strike the last sentence of the answer from the record.

CHALLEE   Have you ever been mentally ill, sir?

QUEEG   No, sir.

CHALLEE   Were you ill in any way when Mister Maryk relieved you?

QUEEG   I was not.

CHALLEE   Did you warn your executive officer of the consequences of his act?

QUEEG   I told him he was performing a mutinous act.

CHALLEE   What was his reply?

QUEEG   That he expected to be court-martialed, but was going to retain command anyway.

CHALLEE   What was the attitude of Lieutenant Junior Grade Keith, the officer of the deck?

QUEEG He was in a state of panic as bad as Maryk's.

CHALLEE What was the attitude of the helmsman?

QUEEG Stilwell was emotionally unbalanced, and for some reason was very devoted to Mister Keith. They both backed up Maryk.

CHALLEE (*Glances at the court*) Is there anything else, Commander Queeg that you care to state in connection with the events of 18 December aboard the *Caine?*

QUEEG Well, I have thought a lot about it all, of course. It's the gravest occurrence in my career, and the only questionable one that I'm aware of. It was an unfortunate freak accident. If the OOD had been anyone but this immature Keith, and the helmsman anyone but Stilwell, I don't think it would have happened. A competent officer of the deck would have repudiated Maryk's orders and a normal sailor at the helm would have disregarded both officers and obeyed me. It was just bad luck that those three men—Maryk, Keith, and Stilwell—were combined against me at a crucial time. Bad luck for me, and I'm afraid worse luck for them.

(MARYK *writes a note to* GREENWALD, *who glances at it negligently, shakes his head, and tears it up*)

BLAKELY The court would like to question the witness. Commander Queeg, you have taken all the prescribed physical and mental examinations incident to entrance to the Academy, graduation, commissioning, promotion, and so forth?

QUEEG Yes, sir, for fourteen years.

BLAKELY Does your medical record contain any history of illness, mental or physical?

QUEEG It does not, sir. My tonsils were removed in the fall of 1938.

BLAKELY Have you ever had an unsatisfactory fitness report, Commander Queeg?

QUEEG Negative, sir. I have one letter of commendation in my jacket.

BLAKELY Now, Commander, can you account for Lieutenant Maryk's opinion that you were mentally ill?

QUEEG (*Smiling*)   Well—that's rather a tough one, sir.

BLAKELY   I appreciate that, but it might be helpful.

QUEEG   Well, sir, I'll have to say that I assumed command of an extremely disorganized and dirty ship. Now that's no reflection on the officer I relieved. The *Caine* had had a year and a half of the most arduous combat duty, and it was understandable. Still, the safety of that ship and its crew demanded its being brought up to snuff. I took many stern measures. Lieutenant Maryk, I may say, from the first, didn't see eye to eye with me at all on this idea of making the *Caine* a taut ship again. Maybe he thought I was crazy to keep trying. I guess that's the picture, sir.

CHALLEE   No more questions.
(*He goes back to his desk.*)
(GREENWALD *rises and approaches* QUEEG)

GREENWALD   Commander Queeg, I should like to ask you whether you have ever heard the expression, "Old Yellowstain."

QUEEG (*Looking genuinely puzzled*)   In what connection?

GREENWALD   In any connection.

QUEEG   Old Yellowstone?

GREENWALD   Old Yellowstain, sir.

QUEEG   I have not.

GREENWALD   You aren't aware, then, that all the officers of the *Caine* habitually referred to you as Old Yellowstain?

CHALLEE (*Jumping to his feet*)   I object to the question! It is impertinent badgering of the witness.

BLAKELY (*Frostily*)   How does defense counsel Greenwald justify this line of questioning?

GREENWALD   If the court please, the nickname, "Old Yellowstain," used by the officers of the *Caine*, will be relevant to the issue of mental competence.

BLAKELY (*Staring very hard at* GREENWALD)   Before ruling, the court wishes to caution defense counsel. This is a most unusual and delicate case. The honor and career of an officer

with an unblemished military record of fourteen years' standing is involved. The defense counsel will have to bear full responsibility for the conduct of his case.
(*Pause*)
Subject to the foregoing comment, the judge advocate's objection is overruled. Court stenographer will repeat the question.

STENOGRAPHER (*Tonelessly*)   "You aren't aware, then, that all the officers of the *Caine* habitually referred to you as Old Yellowstain?"

QUEEG   I am not aware of it.

GREENWALD   No further questions at this time.

BLAKELY   Is that the extent of your cross-examination, Lieutenant Greenwald?

GREENWALD   Commander Queeg will be called as a witness for the defense, sir.

BLAKELY   For the *defense?*

GREENWALD   Yes, sir.
(BLAKELY *stares, shrugs, turns to* CHALLEE, *who shakes his head*)

BLAKELY (*To* QUEEG)   Commander, you'll refrain from conversing with any person whatsoever concerning the details of your testimony today.

QUEEG   Aye aye, sir.

BLAKELY   You're excused, and thank you.

QUEEG   Thank you, Captain.
(QUEEG *goes out.* ORDERLY *stands to attention.* JUDGES *all write notes*)

CHALLEE   Call Lieutenant Thomas Keefer.
(*Exit* ORDERLY. KEEFER *enters, a tall, clever-looking officer, crosses down to* CHALLEE. *Puts hand on Bible*)

BLAKELY   You do solemnly swear that the evidence you shall give in this court shall be the truth, the whole truth, and nothing but the truth. So help you God.

KEEFER   I do so swear.
  (KEEFER *takes witness stand.* ORDERLY *re-enters, sits in his chair Upstage*)

CHALLEE   State your name, rank, and present station.

KEEFER   Thomas Keefer, Lieutenant, U.S.N.R., communication officer of the U.S.S. *Caine.*

CHALLEE   If you recognize the accused, state as whom.

KEEFER   Steve Maryk, Lieutenant Stephen Maryk, executive officer of the *Caine.*

CHALLEE   What is your occupation in civilian life?

KEEFER   I'm a writer.
  (GREENWALD *turns, looks at* KEEFER)

CHALLEE   And has your work been published?

KEEFER   A number of my short stories have been published, yes, sir.
  (*To the court*)
In national magazines.

CHALLEE   Have you done any writing in your spare time while in service?

KEEFER   Yes, I've completed half a war novel.

CHALLEE   What is the title?

KEEFER   *Multitudes, Multitudes.*

BLAKELY   What was that?

KEEFER   *Multitudes, Multitudes,* sir.

BLAKELY   Oh. Thank you. (*Makes a note*)

CHALLEE   And has this novel, *Multitudes, Multitudes,* though incomplete, recently been accepted by a New York publisher?

KEEFER (*A little puzzled*)   Yes.

CHALLEE   I'm asking you these questions to establish your reliability as an observer of personalities.

KEEFER   I understand, sir.

CHALLEE   Now, Lieutenant Keefer, were you serving aboard the *Caine* in your present capacity on December 18, 1944?

KEEFER   Yes, sir.

CHALLEE   Was Captain Queeg relieved of command on that date?

KEEFER   He was, sir.

CHALLEE   By whom?

KEEFER   The accused.

CHALLEE   Describe how you learned that the captain had been relieved.

KEEFER   Well, Mister Maryk passed the word over the loud-speakers for all officers to lay up to the wheelhouse. When we got there he told us that the captain was sick and he had assumed command.

CHALLEE   Did Captain Queeg show any external signs of being sick?
   (KEEFER *shifts in his seat and encounters* MARYK'S *painfully intense glance*)

KEEFER   Well, at the height of a typhoon nobody aboard a four-piper looks very well . . .
   (MARYK *reacts;* GREENWALD *writes a note*)

CHALLEE   Was he raving, or foaming?

KEEFER   No.

CHALLEE   Did he look any worse than, say, Lieutenant Keith?

KEEFER   No, sir.

CHALLEE   Or Maryk?

KEEFER   We were all tired, dripping, and knocked out.
   (MARYK *starts to move,* GREENWALD *passes him the note.* MARYK *turns away from* KEEFER)

CHALLEE   Mister Keefer, did you make any effort to persuade Maryk to restore Queeg to command?

KEEFER   I did not.

CHALLEE   Didn't you feel the seriousness of the situation?

KEEFER   I certainly did, sir.

CHALLEE   Why did you take no remedial action?

KEEFER   I wasn't present when the captain was relieved. Maryk was in full command. The entire ship was obeying his orders. I decided that for the safety of the ship my best course was to obey his orders. That was what I did.

CHALLEE   Mister Keefer, were you aboard the *Caine* throughout the period when Captain Queeg was in command?

KEEFER   Yes.

CHALLEE   Did you ever observe any evidences of insanity in him?
   (KEEFER *hesitates.* GREENWALD *turns in chair, looks at* KEEFER. MARYK *stretches his arms out in tension*)

KEEFER   I don't—I can't answer that question, not being a psychiatrist.
   (GREENWALD *puts his hand on* MARYK'S *arm.* MARYK *pulls away*)

CHALLEE   Well, surely now, Mister Keefer, as a writer you're certainly not wholly ignorant of such matters.

KEEFER   (*Leans back in witness chair*)   Well, I hope not wholly ignorant—no, sir.

CHALLEE   What, for instance, is the Rorschach Test?

KEEFER   I believe that's the inkblot test. The analyst detects psychopathetic tendencies in a person by showing him inkblots and getting the person to say what the shapes resemble.

CHALLEE (*Nods*)   And who is Alfred Adler?

KEEFER   These things are very elementary. Adler split off from Freud. Any college man knows that much, sir.

CHALLEE   A novelist, however, is apt to understand and appreciate these things more than the average man.

KEEFER   Well, our work is the narration of human conduct.
   (GREENWALD *turns, looks at* KEEFER, *then turns away, disgusted*)

CHALLEE   Naturally. Now then, Mister Keefer, with your grasp of such matters—if you saw a man rushing up and down passageways screaming that a tiger was after him when there was no tiger, would you venture to say that that man was temporarily deranged?

KEEFER (*Smiling wryly*) I would, sir.

CHALLEE Did Commander Queeg ever exhibit such behavior?

KEEFER No. Nothing like that.

CHALLEE Did you ever think he might be insane?
    (MARYK *frantically scribbles a note*)

GREENWALD (*rising*) Objection. Witness isn't an expert. Matters of opinion are not admissible evidence.
    (MARYK *pulls at* GREENWALD'S *sleeve, hands him the note.* GREENWALD *sits, reads note, then tears it up*)

CHALLEE (*With a slight smile*) I withdraw the question. Mister Keefer, at any time prior to 18 December were you informed that Maryk suspected Queeg of being mentally ill?

KEEFER Yes, sir.

CHALLEE Describe how you learned this fact.

KEEFER Well—now let me see—two weeks before the typhoon, Maryk showed me a "medical log" he'd kept on Queeg's behavior. He asked me to come with him to the *New Jersey* to report the situation to Admiral Halsey.

CHALLEE Did you consent to go with him?

KEEFER Yes, I did.

CHALLEE Why?

KEEFER He was my superior officer and also my close friend.
    (MARYK *turns away*)

CHALLEE Did you believe that the log justified the relief of Queeg?

KEEFER No—no, when we arrived aboard the *New Jersey*, I told him as forcibly as I could that in my opinion the log would not justify the action.

CHALLEE What was his response?

KEEFER Well, after a lot of arguing, he followed my advice. We returned to the *Caine.*

CHALLEE Were you surprised, two weeks later, when he relieved the captain?

KEEFER I was flabbergasted.

CHALLEE Were you pleased, Mister Keefer?

KEEFER I was badly disturbed. I anticipated that at best he would be involved in grave difficulties. I thought it was a terrible situation.
  (MARYK *turns, rests head on hand*)

CHALLEE No further questions.
  (*Nods at* GREENWALD)

GREENWALD (*Half rises and then sits*) No questions.

BLAKELY Does the defense intend to recall the witness at a later time?

GREENWALD No, sir.

BLAKELY No cross-examination of this highly material witness?

GREENWALD No, sir.

BLAKELY The court will question the witness . . . Mister Keefer, now as to this so-called medical log. The facts it contained, which convinced Lieutenant Maryk that he should report the captain to Admiral Halsey, didn't convince you. Is that right?

KEEFER They did not, sir.

BLAKELY Why not?

KEEFER Sir, it's not something a layman can intelligently discuss.

BLAKELY You've stated you're a close friend of Mister Maryk.

KEEFER Yes, sir.

BLAKELY This court is trying to find out among other things any possible extenuating circumstances for his acts. Did this medical log merely indicate to you that Captain Queeg was a highly normal and competent officer?

KEEFER Sir, speaking from ignorance, it's always seemed to me that mental disability was a relative thing. Captain Queeg was a very strict disciplinarian and extremely meticulous in hunting down the smallest matters. He was not the easiest person in the world to reason with. There were several occasions when I thought he bore down too hard and spent excessive time on small matters. Those were the things that were recorded in the medical log. They were very unpleasant. But to jump from them to a conclusion that the captain was a maniac—no—I was compelled in all honesty to warn Maryk against doing that.

BLAKELY No further questions. You will not discuss your testimony outside this courtroom. Witness excused.

(KEEFER *steps down, turns, and walks out rapidly.* MARYK *looks after him*)

CHALLEE Call Signalman Third Class Urban.

MARYK (*pulls* GREENWALD'S *arm*) Why didn't you cross-examine Tom Keefer? Why did you let him off like that?

GREENWALD It was the only thing to do.

MARYK Why?

GREENWALD It would have made things worse for you. You'll get your chance on the stand.

MARYK I'll never say a word about Tom Keefer. Not me. God damn it, he should have talked himself.

GREENWALD Sure he should. You don't understand, do you?
(*Enter* URBAN, *a little sailor in blues, crosses down to* CHALLEE, *puts hand on Bible*)
Not about Keefer. Not even about yourself.
(BLAKELY *rises, raises right hand*)

BLAKELY You do solemnly swear that the evidence you shall give in this court shall be the truth, the whole truth, and nothing but the truth. So help you God.

URBAN Aye aye, sir.
(URBAN *sits in witness chair.* ORDERLY *re-enters, sits in his chair*)

CHALLEE State your name, rating, and present station.

URBAN Junius Hannaford Urban, Signalman Third Class, U.S.N., of the U.S.S. *Caine*, sir.

CHALLEE   If you recognize the accused, state as whom.

URBAN   Sir?

CHALLEE   Do you recognize the accused?

URBAN   Sir?

CHALLEE   (*Pointing*)   Do you recognize the officer at that table?

URBAN   Which one, sir? There are two.

CHALLEE   Name the one you recognize.

URBAN   That's the exec, sir.

CHALLEE   What's his name?

URBAN   He's Mister Maryk.

CHALLEE   What is he exec of?

URBAN   The ship.

CHALLEE   Name the ship.

URBAN   The *Caine*.

CHALLEE   Thank you.

URBAN   Sorry, sir.

CHALLEE   Urban, on December 18, 1944, were you serving aboard the U.S.S. *Caine* in your present capacity?

URBAN   Is that the day it happened?

CHALLEE   The day what happened?

URBAN   I don't know.

CHALLEE   That was the day of the typhoon.

URBAN   Sure, I was aboard.

CHALLEE   Were you in the pilothouse when Mister Maryk relieved Captain Queeg?

URBAN   Yes, sir.

CHALLEE   Who else was in the wheelhouse at that time?

URBAN   Well, there was the captain and Mister Maryk.

CHALLEE   Yes.

URBAN   And the helmsman.

CHALLEE   His name?

URBAN   Stilwell.

CHALLEE   Who else?

URBAN   The OOD.

CHALLEE   His name.

URBAN   Mister Keith.

CHALLEE   What were you doing in the wheelhouse?

URBAN   I had the watch, sir.

CHALLEE   Urban, describe in your own words how Lieutenant Maryk relieved the captain.

URBAN   He said, "I relieve you, sir."

CHALLEE   What was happening at the time?

URBAN   Well . . . The ship was rolling very bad.

CHALLEE   Urban, describe everything that happened in the ten minutes before Captain Queeg was relieved.

URBAN   Well, like I say, the ship was rolling very bad.
    (*A long silence.* CHALLEE *waits, with his eyes on* URBAN)

CHALLEE   That's all? Did the exec say anything? Did the captain say anything? Did the OOD say anything? Did the ship just roll in silence for ten minutes?

URBAN   Well, sir, it was a typhoon.

BLAKELY   Urban, you're under oath.

URBAN   Well, I think the captain wanted to come north and the exec wanted to come south, or the other way around, or something like that.

CHALLEE   Why did the captain want to come south?

URBAN   I don't know, sir.

CHALLEE   Why did the exec want to come north?

URBAN   Sir, I'm a signalman.

CHALLEE Did the captain act crazy?

URBAN No, sir.

CHALLEE Did the exec seem scared?

URBAN No, sir.

CHALLEE Did the captain?

URBAN No, sir.

CHALLEE Did anyone?

URBAN *I* was goddam scared, sir.
  (*To* BLAKELY, *standing*)
I beg your pardon, sir.
  (*Sits*)

CHALLEE But the captain definitely did not act queer or crazy in any way at any time that morning—correct?

URBAN The captain was the same as always, sir.

CHALLEE (*At the end of his patience*) Crazy, or sane, Urban?

URBAN He was sane, sir, so far as I knew.

BLAKELY Urban, how old are you?

URBAN Twenty, sir.

BLAKELY What schooling have you had?

URBAN One year in high school.

BLAKELY Have you been telling the whole truth here, or haven't you?

URBAN Sir, a signalman isn't supposed to listen to arguments between the captain and the exec.

BLAKELY Did you like the captain?

URBAN (*Miserably*) *Sure* I liked him, sir.

BLAKELY (*To* CHALLEE) Continue your examination.

CHALLEE No further questions.
  (CHALLEE *crosses up to his desk, sits.* GREENWALD *approaches the witness platform, rolling the pencil against his palm*)

GREENWALD   Urban, were you aboard when the *Caine* cut
her own tow cable the time she was towing targets outside
Pearl Harbor?

URBAN   Yes, sir.

GREENWALD   What were you doing at the time that it happened?

URBAN   I was—that is, the captain was eating my—
   (*Catches himself just short of an obscenity, glances in horror at* BLAKELY)
bawling me out—on the bridge, sir.

GREENWALD   What for?

URBAN   My shirttail was out.

GREENWALD   Was the captain very strict on the subject of
shirttails?

URBAN   Sir, he was a nut on—yes, sir. He was very strict on
shirttails, sir.

GREENWALD   (*With an illustrative gesture*)   And while the
captain was discussing your shirttail the ship went right
around in a circle and steamed over its own towline? Is that
the way it hap—
   (CHALLEE *jumps up*)
CHALLEE   Object to this line of questioning. Counsel has
tricked the witness with leading questions into asserting as a
fact that the *Caine* cut a towline, a material point that was
not touched upon in direct examination.

GREENWALD   Please the court, the witness stated he had
never seen the captain do anything crazy. I am attempting to
refute this.

BLAKELY   Defense counsel will have the opportunity to
originate evidence later. Objection sustained. Cross-examination thus far will be stricken from the record.

GREENWALD   Urban, what is a paranoid personality?

URBAN   Huh?

GREENWALD   What is a paranoid personality?

URBAN   Sir?

GREENWALD   Could you recognize a psychotic person?

URBAN   Me?

GREENWALD   No further questions.
   (*Crosses to chair and sits*)

BLAKELY   Urban.
   (URBAN *rises*)
You will not discuss your testimony in this courtroom with anybody, understand?

URBAN   Who, sir? Me, sir? No, sir.

BLAKELY   Excused.

URBAN   Thank you, sir.
   (*Exits*)

CHALLEE   Call Chief Water Tender Budge.
   (*An* ORDERLY *starts out*)

GREENWALD   One moment.
   (ORDERLY *halts*)
If it please the court. I understand that the judge advocate intends to call a dozen members of the crew of the *Caine*.

CHALLEE   That's correct.

GREENWALD   Is the purpose to confirm the testimony of Urban that the captain was never seen to do anything crazy?

CHALLEE   That is the purpose.

GREENWALD   The defense will concede that the testimony of all these witnesses will corroborate Urban's . . . if the judge advocate will concede that these twelve men don't know any more about a paranoid personality than Urban.

CHALLEE (*To* BLAKELY)   I'll gladly accept that concession on those terms, sir.

BLAKELY   Lieutenant Greenwald, you're making a weighty concession.

GREENWALD   By your leave, sir, however, the defense makes that concession.
   (*Sits*)

BLAKELY (*To* STENOGRAPHER) One moment. Don't record that . . . Mister Greenwald.

GREENWALD (*Stands*) Yes, sir?

BLAKELY The court understands that you were appointed as defense counsel by the judge advocate.

GREENWALD Yes, sir.

BLAKELY When were you appointed?

GREENWALD Four days ago, sir.

BLAKELY Do you feel you've had enough time to prepare your case?

GREENWALD Yes, sir.

BLAKELY Did you undertake this assignment willingly?
   (GREENWALD *hesitates*)

CHALLEE (*Rises*) If it please the court. Lieutenant Greenwald accepted the assignment at my earnest request.

BLAKELY I see by your uniform that you're a flying officer.

GREENWALD Yes, sir.

BLAKELY What do you fly?

GREENWALD F6F, sir.

BLAKELY What are you doing on the beach? Were you grounded?

GREENWALD Hospitalized for third degree burns, sir.

BLAKELY (*A little more sympathetically*) I see. How did you get burned?

GREENWALD Crashed a barrier on the U.S.S. *Wasp,* sir.

BLAKELY Did you have a chance to practice much law before the war came along?

GREENWALD (*Hesitantly*) A little, sir.

BLAKELY Court will speak to the accused off the record.
   (GREENWALD *sits, motions to* MARYK *to rise. He does*)

MARYK Yes, sir?

BLAKELY   It seems the court's duty at this point to inquire whether your counsel's conduct of the defense meets with your approval.

(MARYK *hesitates, looking from* GREENWALD *to* BLAKELY. GREENWALD *rises*)

GREENWALD   May it please the court. If the accused answers that question now he must do so on blind faith. I beg the court for an opportunity to speak to my client first.

BLAKELY   We've had too many recesses here.

GREENWALD   Not a recess, sir—a brief delay—two minutes, sir—

BLAKELY   Court will remain in session. We'll have a two-minute pause in the proceedings.

(*Rings the bell*)

GREENWALD   Well, do you want to get rid of me?

MARYK   I don't know.

GREENWALD   Take my word for it. Everything's all right up to now.

MARYK   I think I'm sunk at this point.

GREENWALD   You're not.

MARYK   Fifteen years in the brig—

GREENWALD   You won't go to the brig.

MARYK   Why didn't you cross-examine these twelve guys?

GREENWALD   Two minutes isn't much time to explain elementary trial tactics.

MARYK   Explain one thing and maybe I'll go along with you. Why didn't you cross-examine Tom Keefer?

GREENWALD   Maryk, there isn't time to tell—

MARYK   Tom Keefer knows everything that the captain did. Everything!

GREENWALD   Sure he does.

MARYK   If he wouldn't talk it was up to you to drag it out of him. Wasn't it?

GREENWALD   You don't begin to understand.

MARYK   I don't understand what you're doing, mister, that's
for sure.

GREENWALD   I just happen to want to fight this case.

MARYK   Why? What does it mean to you? You're a total
stranger.

GREENWALD   I want to win it!

MARYK   I want to believe you.

GREENWALD   It's God's truth.

MARYK   You said you'd rather be prosecuting me than defending me. Maybe this is your screwy way of prosecuting me.

GREENWALD   All right.
   (*A hurried glance at the court and at his wrist watch*)
Listen carefully. Implicating Keefer harms you.

MARYK   What?

GREENWALD   Two disgruntled bastards instead of one heroic
exec.
   (MARYK *stares uncomprehending*)
I've got a chance with a lone heroic exec. Making that picture stick is my only chance to win for you. Please try to let
that sink in, Maryk.
   (MARYK *keeps looking at him. Understanding slowly dawns
   on him as* CHALLEE *and* BLAKELY *talk*)

BLAKELY (*Motions to* CHALLEE *to come closer*)   Challee. (*In
a confidential undertone*) What's going on here, Jack? Where'd
you get this bird?

CHALLEE   Sir, Barney Greenwald and I went to Georgetown
Law together. Before the war he was one of the most successful
young lawyers in Washington.

BLAKELY (*Staring at* GREENWALD)   He was? Don't you think
he's putting up a damned queer show?

CHALLEE   Well, yes, sir . . . But he has a reputation for defending the underdog, sir. He used to handle Indian cases back
in Washington—

(GREENWALD *rises, crosses over to* MARYK, *and puts his hand on* MARYK'S *shoulder*)
—where Indians were getting pushed around by the officials —and didn't charge for it.

BLAKELY   Jewish fellow, isn't he?

CHALLEE   Yes, sir. Barney's Jewish.

BLAKELY   Well, maybe he's a hell of a lot smarter than he seems.
(BLAKELY *rings bell.* MARYK *rises.* GREENWALD *crosses back to his chair*)
The court again asks the accused—are you satisfied?

MARYK (*After a long stare at* GREENWALD, *shakily*)   I'm satisfied, sir.

BLAKELY   Court will not reopen this question.

MARYK   I understand, sir. I'm satisfied with Lieutenant Greenwald.

BLAKELY (*Nods to* CHALLEE)   Proceed with your case, Commander Challee.

CHALLEE   Call Lieutenant Keith.
(ORDERLY *goes.* LIEUTENANT (*j.g.*) WILLIS KEITH *enters, a handsome youngster with reddish-blond hair.* CHALLEE *holds Bible for him*)

BLAKELY   You do solemnly swear that the evidence you shall give in this court shall be the truth, the whole truth, and nothing but the truth. So help you God.

KEITH   I do.
(KEITH *takes the stand.* ORDERLY *re-enters, sits*)

CHALLEE   State your name, rank, and present station.

KEITH   Willis Seward Keith, Lieutenant Junior Grade, U.S.N.R., assistant communication officer of the U.S.S. *Caine*.

CHALLEE   If you recognize the accused, state as whom.

KEITH   Steve Maryk, my executive officer on the *Caine*.

CHALLEE   Mister Keith, were you officer of the deck of the *Caine* during the forenoon watch on 18 December, 1944?

KEITH   I was.

CHALLEE   Was the captain relieved of his command during your watch?

KEITH   Yes.

CHALLEE   Do you know why the executive officer relieved the captain?

KEITH   Yes. Captain Queeg had lost control of himself, and the ship was in grave danger of foundering.

CHALLEE   How many years have you served at sea, Lieutenant?

KEITH   One year and three months.

CHALLEE   Do you know how many years Commander Queeg has served at sea?

KEITH   I guess about ten years.

CHALLEE   Which of you is better qualified to judge whether a ship is foundering or not?

KEITH   Myself, sir, if I'm in possession of my faculties and Commander Queeg isn't.

CHALLEE   What makes you think he isn't in possession of his faculties?

KEITH   He wasn't on the morning of December eighteenth.

CHALLEE   Have you studied medicine or psychiatry?

KEITH   No.

CHALLEE   Did the captain foam, or rave, or make insane gestures?

KEITH   No, but what he did do was just as bad.

CHALLEE   Clarify that a bit, if you will.

KEITH   His orders were vague and sluggish and—not appropriate. He insisted on going south, when we had a north wind of ninety miles an hour behind us. With a stern wind that strong the ship couldn't be controlled.

CHALLEE   In your expert opinion as a ship handler, that is.

KEITH   Steve Maryk thought so, and he's an expert ship handler.

CHALLEE   Were you wholeheartedly loyal to your captain or antagonistic to him, prior to 18 December?

KEITH   I was antagonistic to Captain Queeg at certain isolated times.

CHALLEE   At what isolated times were you antagonistic?

KEITH   When Captain Queeg maltreated the men, I opposed him.

CHALLEE   When did the captain ever maltreat the men?

KEITH   Well, for one thing, he systematically persecuted Gunner's Mate Second Class Stilwell.

CHALLEE   In what way?

KEITH   First he restricted him to the ship for six months for reading on watch. He refused to grant him leave in the States when we were back here in December '43. The man was getting anonymous letters about his wife's infidelity. Maryk gave Stilwell a seventy-two-hour emergency leave and he returned a few hours overleave and—

CHALLEE   You say Maryk gave Stilwell a pass. Did Maryk know that the captain had denied leave to Stilwell?

KEITH   Yes, sir.

CHALLEE   Did Maryk check with the captain before issuing this pass?

KEITH   No, sir.

CHALLEE (*Pleased and surprised*)   Are you testifying, Mister Keith, that Maryk deliberately violated his captain's orders?

KEITH (*Rattled*)   Well, I mean it was my fault, actually. I begged him to. I was morale officer, and I thought the man's morale—I mean—

CHALLEE   Mister Keith, we now have your testimony that you and Maryk and Stilwell connived to circumvent an express order of your commanding officer, a whole year before the typhoon of 18 December . . . Now, please tell the court any other instances of maltreatment that occur to you.

KEITH (*Pause*) He cut off the movies for six months just because he wasn't invited to a showing by mistake—he cut off the water at the equator because he said the men were using too much and had to be taught a lesson—and he—

CHALLEE Mister Keith, did the captain ever issue rules or punishments not permitted by regulations?

KEITH He never did anything not allowed by regulations.

CHALLEE You didn't like the captain, did you, Lieutenant?

KEITH I did at first, very much. But I gradually realized that he was a petty tyrant and utterly incompetent.

CHALLEE Did you think he was insane, too?

KEITH Not until the day of the typhoon.

CHALLEE Very well, come to the day of the typhoon. Was your decision to obey Maryk based on your judgment that the captain had gone mad, or was it based on your hatred of Captain Queeg?

KEITH (*Miserably, after a betraying pause and glance at MARYK*) I just don't remember my state of mind that long ago.

CHALLEE (*Contemptuously*) No further questions.
 (*Turns on his heel and sits down*)
 (GREENWALD *rises*)

GREENWALD Mister Keith, you have stated you disliked Captain Queeg.

KEITH I did dislike him.

GREENWALD Did you state under direct examination all your reasons for disliking him?

KEITH Not at all.

GREENWALD State the rest of your reasons now, please.

KEITH Well, for one thing, he extorted a hundred dollars from me—

CHALLEE Objection. The issue in this case is not whether Captain Queeg was a model officer, but whether he was insane on 18 December. Defense counsel hasn't even touched this issue.

GREENWALD   Please the court, this will bear directly on the mental fitness of Captain Queeg to command a naval vessel, and as evidence it is nothing but clarification of Keith's dislike of his commanding officer, a fact established by the judge advocate at great pains in direct examination.

BLAKELY   The objection is overruled.

GREENWALD   Describe this so-called extortion, Mister Keith.

KEITH   Well, this was back last December in San Francisco Bay. The captain had this big crate full of cheap tax-free whiskey from Pearl Harbor that he wanted to sneak into Oakland, avoiding the customs. He appointed me boat officer, and a working party started to load the crate into the gig. It was terrifically heavy. Captain Queeg got excited and screeched a whole bunch of contradictory orders. The sailors got rattled and dropped the crate into the water. It sank like a stone. And I was out a hundred and ten dollars.

GREENWALD   You mean the captain was?

KEITH   No, sir, I was . . . The captain informed me that I was responsible because I was boat officer in charge of the loading. And he asked me to think over what I ought to do about it. Well, I was supposed to go on leave the next day. My girl friend had flown out from New York to be with me. So I went to the captain and I apologized for my stupidity and said I'd like to pay for the lost crate. He took my money gladly. Then he signed my leave papers.

GREENWALD   What further reason did you have for disliking Queeg?

KEITH   (*A pause to gather his nerve*)   My chief reason for disliking Captain Queeg was his cowardice in battle.

GREENWALD   What cowardice?

KEITH   He repeatedly ran from shore batteries—

CHALLEE   (*Infuriated*)   Objection! Counsel is originating evidence beyond the scope of direct examination. He is leading the witness into irresponsible libels of an officer of the Navy!

(BLAKELY *starts looking through Naval Regulations*)

GREENWALD   Please the court, the witness's dislike of Queeg
was not only in the scope of direct examination, it was the key
fact brought out. The witness has confessed ignorance of
psychiatry. Things Queeg did, which caused the witness in
his ignorance to dislike him, may in fact have been the helpless acts of a sick man.

CHALLEE   I respectfully urge my objection, sir!

BLAKELY   One moment
   (JUDGES *write ballots*)
For the benefit of all parties, court will read from the Articles for the Government of the Navy on cowardice.
   (*Reads*)
"The punishment of death, or such other punishment as a
court-martial may adjudge, may be inflicted on any person in
the naval service, who in time of battle, displays cowardice,
negligence, or disaffection, or withdraws from or keeps out of
danger to which he should expose himself . . ."
   (JUDGES *pass ballots to* BLAKELY)
The defense counsel and the witness are warned that they are
on the most dangerous possible ground. In charging an
officer of the United States Navy with an offense punishable
by death, and that the most odious offense in military life,
they take on themselves the heaviest responsibility. The court
now asks defense counsel in view of the foregoing whether
he desires to withdraw his question.

GREENWALD   I do not so desire, sir.

BLAKELY   The court asks the witness to state whether he
desires to withdraw his answers.

KEITH   I do not so desire, sir.

BLAKELY (*With icy gravity*)   Court finds that the question is
within the scope of direct examination, and that the answer
is material. The objection of the judge advocate is overruled.
   (*Tears ballots.*
   (*Nods to* GREENWALD)
Proceed.

GREENWALD   Where and when did Captain Queeg run from
shore batteries?

KEITH   Practically every time we heard gunfire from the beach. I guess the worst time was at Kwajalein. That's where he got the nickname, "Old Yellowstain."

GREENWALD   What did this nickname, "Old Yellowstain," imply?

KEITH   Well, cowardice, of course. It referred to a yellow dye marker he dropped over the side.

GREENWALD   Describe this Yellow Stain incident.

KEITH   Well, I wasn't on the bridge, so I only heard about it afterwards. What happened was that Captain Queeg—

CHALLEE   Objection. Does defense counsel seriously expect to enter these hearsay libels on the record?

GREENWALD   I withdraw the question. Defense will introduce direct evidence on the Yellow Stain incident.

BLAKELY   Strike the question and answer from the record.

GREENWALD   Can you describe incidents of cowardice to which you were an eyewitness?

KEITH   Well, in any combat situation Captain Queeg was always found on the side of the bridge away from the firing. I saw that a dozen times when I was OOD.

GREENWALD   No further questions.
   (*Goes to his seat*)

CHALLEE   Mister Keith, has Commander Queeg been court-martialed by higher authority for any of the alleged acts of cowardice you describe?

KEITH   No.

CHALLEE   Can you cite any official records that will substantiate any of these fantastic and libelous stories you've been telling under the guidance of defense counsel?

KEITH   Official records? No.

CHALLEE   Mister Keith, do you know for a fact that the crate that was lost contained smuggled liquor?

KEITH   It was common knowledge.

CHALLEE Common knowledge. Did you see the liquor in the crate?

KEITH No—

CHALLEE Can you name one person who will testify that they saw liquor in the crate?

KEITH Well, naturally, he was pretty careful about that.

CHALLEE Not one person.

KEITH I just don't know who would have actually seen it.

CHALLEE Mister Keith, you've testified that you hate Captain Queeg. You're reporting as fact every evil rumor about him and you're making wild, irresponsible charges under oath. Isn't that the plain truth about your testimony, Mister Keith?

KEITH I haven't lied once.

CHALLEE Mister Keith, on the morning when the captain was relieved, did you really think he had gone crazy?

KEITH (*Losing assurance*) I said before I can't say for sure what my state of mind was.

CHALLEE No more questions.
  (BLAKELY *looks at* GREENWALD, *who shakes his head*)

BLAKELY (*To* KEITH) You'll not discuss any details of your testimony outside this courtroom, Lieutenant.

KEITH Aye aye, sir.

BLAKELY You're excused.
  (*Exit* KEITH, *with a glance at* MARYK *and a slight despairing shrug*)

CHALLEE Call Captain Southard.
  (*Exit* ORDERLY, *returning with a dapper, lean officer. Close-cropped head, hard-bitten face, three rows of ribbons and stars. Business with Bible*)

BLAKELY You do solemnly swear that the evidence you shall give in this court shall be the truth, the whole truth, and nothing but the truth. So help you God.

SOUTHARD I do.
  (*Takes the witness chair*)

CHALLEE   State your name, rank, and present station.

SOUTHARD   Randolph Patterson Southard, Captain, U. S. Navy, commander, Destroyer Squadron Eight.

CHALLEE   You understand that you've been called as an expert witness on destroyer ship handling?

SOUTHARD   I do.

CHALLEE   State your qualifications.

SOUTHARD   Some twenty years in destroyers. Ten years of commanding all types, from the World War I 4-piper on up to the newest 2200 tonner.

CHALLEE   Now, sir, I'm going to describe a hypothetical ship handling problem for your expert opinion.

SOUTHARD   Very well.

CHALLEE   You're in command of a destroyer in the Philippine Sea. A typhoon blows up without warning, traveling west. You're directly in the path of it. The wind keeps increasing, its direction holding steady from the north. Soon your wind is force 10 to 12, and your seas are mountainous. Under the circumstances, what would you do?

SOUTHARD   I believe I'd execute the classic naval maneuver known as getting the hell out of there.

CHALLEE   *(Smiling)*   How would you go about that, Captain?

SOUTHARD   Well, it's almost rule of thumb. You say the wind's from the north at ninety knots, the center of the typhoon coming at you from the west. Best course is south. You might have to head a couple of points one way or the other, depending on your seas, but there's only one way out of that mess—south.

CHALLEE   But then you have a terribly strong stern wind, don't you?

SOUTHARD   What about it?

CHALLEE   Can a destroyer ride safely downwind in such conditions?

SOUTHARD   She'll ride just as well going downwind as upwind. In fact, with your high freeboard forward, a destroyer tends to back into the wind. Other things being equal, she'll do slightly better going downwind.

CHALLEE   How about turning north in those circumstances and heading into the wind?

SOUTHARD   That would be dubious and dangerous, not to say idiotic.

CHALLEE   Why, Captain?

SOUTHARD   You're heading yourself right back into the path of the typhoon. Unless you're interested in sinking, that's not smart.

CHALLEE   That's all, sir.
  (CHALLEE *crosses to his desk and sits.* GREENWALD *arises*)

GREENWALD   Captain, have you ever conned a ship through the center of a typhoon?

SOUTHARD   Negative. Been on the fringes often but always managed to avoid the center.

GREENWALD   Have you ever commanded a destroyer-mine-sweeper, sir?

SOUTHARD   Negative.

GREENWALD   This case, sir, concerns a destroyer-mine-sweeper at the center of a typhoon—

SOUTHARD   (*Frostily*) I'm aware of that. I've had DMS's under my command in screens, and I've read the book on 'em. They don't differ from destroyers except in details of topside weight characteristics.

GREENWALD   I ask these questions, Captain, because you are the only expert witness on ship handling, and the extent of your expert knowledge should be clear to the court.

SOUTHARD   That's all right. I've handled destroyer types in almost every conceivable situation for ten years. Haven't handled a DMS at the center of a typhoon, no, but I don't know who has besides the skipper of the *Caine*. It's a thousand-to-one shot.

GREENWALD   Will you state without reservation that the rules of destroyer handling would hold for a DMS in the center of a typhoon?

SOUTHARD Well, at the center of a typhoon there are no hard-and-fast rules. That's one situation where it's all up to the commanding officer. Too many strange things happen too fast.

GREENWALD Sir, you remember the hypothetical question of the judge advocate about the typhoon.

SOUTHARD I do.

GREENWALD Now in that situation, I ask you to assume that the winds and seas become worse than any you've ever experienced. Your ship is wallowing broadside. You actually believe your ship is foundering. You're in the last extremity. Would you bring your ship north, into the wind, or continue on south, stern to wind?

SOUTHARD You're getting mighty hypothetical.

GREENWALD Yes, sir. You prefer not to answer that question, Captain?

SOUTHARD I'll answer it. In the last extremity I'd come around to north and head into the wind, if I could. But *only* in the last extremity.

GREENWALD Why, sir?

SOUTHARD Why, because your engines and rudder have the best purchase that way, that's all. It's your last chance to keep control of your ship.

GREENWALD But wouldn't coming north head you back into the path of the storm?

SOUTHARD First things first. If you're on the verge of foundering you're as bad off as you can get. Mind you, you said the last extremity.

GREENWALD Yes, sir, no further questions.
(*Sits*)

CHALLEE (*Rises*) Captain, who in your opinion is the best judge as to whether a ship is in its last extremity?

SOUTHARD There's only one judge. The commanding officer.

CHALLEE Why sir?

SOUTHARD The Navy's made him captain because his knowledge of the sea and of ships is better than anyone else's on the ship. It's very common for some subordinate officers to think the ship is sinking when all they're having is a little weather.

CHALLEE Don't you think, sir, that when his subordinates all agree that the ship is going down the captain ought to listen to them?

SOUTHARD Negative! Panic is a common hazard at sea. The highest function of command is to override it and to listen to nothing but the voice of his own professional judgment.

CHALLEE Thank you, Captain.
  (CHALLEE *sits*)

BLAKELY (*With the smile of an old friend at* SOUTHARD) You will not discuss your testimony outside the courtroom, Captain.

SOUTHARD Understood.

BLAKELY You're excused, and thank you.
  (*Exit* SOUTHARD)

CHALLEE Call Dr. Forrest Lundeen.
  (*Exit* ORDERLY. *Returns with a captain, intelligent plump man in his fifties, rimless glasses. Bible business*)

BLAKELY You do solemnly swear that the evidence you shall give in this court shall be the truth, the whole truth, and nothing but the truth. So help you God.

LUNDEEN I do.
  (*Takes stand*)

CHALLEE State name, rank, and present station.

LUNDEEN Forrest Lundeen, M.D., Captain, U. S. Navy. Head of psychiatry, U. S. Naval Hospital, San Francisco.

CHALLEE Were you the head of the medical board which examined Lieutenant Commander Queeg?

LUNDEEN I was.

CHALLEE How long did your examination last, Doctor?

LUNDEEN We had the commander under constant observation and testing for three weeks.

CHALLEE What was the finding of the board?

LUNDEEN Commander Queeg was discharged with a clean
bill of health.

CHALLEE Doctor, is it possible that two months ago, on
December 18, he was in such a state of psychotic collapse that
relieving him from a naval command would be justified?

LUNDEEN It's utterly impossible.

CHALLEE Is it possible for a sane man to perform offensive,
disagreeble, foolish acts?

LUNDEEN It happens every day. We didn't find that the
commander was a perfect officer.

CHALLEE Yet you still say that to relieve him from naval
command because of mental illness would be unjustified?

LUNDEEN Completely unjustified.

CHALLEE We will place your report in evidence and hear
Dr. Bird. Thank you, Doctor.
    (CHALLEE *glances directly into* GREENWALD'S *eyes, with a
    thin cold grin.* GREENWALD *shuffles toward witness plat-
    form, rubbing his nose with the back of his hand, looking
    down at his feet, and presenting a general picture of
    flustered embarrassment.*)

GREENWALD Dr. Lundeen, my background is legal, not
medical. I hope you'll bear with me if I try to clarify technical
terms.

LUNDEEN Of course, of course.

GREENWALD I'll probably ask some elementary questions.

LUNDEEN (*With an expansive smile*) That's perfectly all
right.

GREENWALD Would you say that Commander Queeg is
absolutely normal?

LUNDEEN Well, normality, you know, is a fiction in psychiatry. No adult is without problems except a happy imbecile.

GREENWALD Describe Commander Queeg's problems.

LUNDEEN Well, you might say the over-all problem is one of inferiority feelings generated by an unfavorable childhood and aggravated by certain adult experiences.

GREENWALD Unfavorable childhood in what way?

LUNDEEN Disturbed background. Divorced parents, financial trouble, schooling problems.

GREENWALD And the aggravating factors in adult life?

LUNDEEN (*Hesitant*) In general, the commander is rather troubled by his short stature, his low standing in his class, and such factors. But the commander is well adjusted to all these things.

GREENWALD Can you describe the nature of the adjustment?

LUNDEEN Yes, I can. His identity as a naval officer is the essential balancing factor. It's the key to his personal security. Therefore he has a fixed anxiety about protecting his standing. That would account for the harshness and ill temper.

GREENWALD Would he be disinclined to admit to mistakes?

LUNDEEN Yes. Of course there's nothing unbalanced in that.

GREENWALD Would he be a perfectionist?

LUNDEEN Such a personality would be.

GREENWALD Suspicious of his subordinates? Inclined to hound them about small details?

LUNDEEN Any mistake of a subordinate is intolerable because it might endanger him.

GREENWALD Yet he will not admit mistakes when he makes them himself.

LUNDEEN You might say he revises reality in his own mind so that he comes out blameless.

GREENWALD Doctor, isn't distorting reality a symptom of mental illness?

LUNDEEN It's a question of degree. None of us wholly faces reality.

GREENWALD   But doesn't the commander distort reality more than, say, you do?

LUNDEEN   That's his weakness. Other people have other weaknesses. It's definitely not disabling.

GREENWALD   If criticized from above, would he be inclined to think he was being unjustly persecuted?

LUNDEEN   It's all one pattern, all stemming from one basic premise, that he must try to be perfect.

GREENWALD   Would he be inclined to stubbornness?

LUNDEEN   Well, you'll have a certain rigidity of personality in such an individual. The inner insecurity checks him from admitting that those who differ with him may be right.

GREENWALD (*Suddenly switching from the fumbling manner to clicking preciseness*)   Doctor, you've testified that the following symptoms exist in the commander's behavior: rigidity of personality, feelings of persecution, unreasonable suspicion, withdrawal from reality, perfectionist anxiety, an unreal basic premise, and an obsessive sense of self-righteousness.

LUNDEEN (*Looking startled, then appreciatively amused*)   All mild, sir, all well compensated.

GREENWALD   Yes, Doctor. Is there an inclusive psychiatric term—one label—for this syndrome?

LUNDEEN   Syndrome? Who said anything about a syndrome? You're misusing a term. There's no syndrome, because there's no disease.

GREENWALD   Thank you for the correction, Doctor. I'll rephrase it. Do the symptoms fall into a single pattern of neurotic disturbance—a common psychiatric class?

LUNDEEN   I know what you're driving at, of course. It's a paranoid personality, but that is not a disabling affliction.

GREENWALD   What kind of personality, Doctor?

LUNDEEN   Paranoid.

GREENWALD   Paranoid, Doctor?

LUNDEEN Yes, paranoid.

(GREENWALD *glances at* CHALLEE, *then looks around slowly one by one at the faces of the* COURT MEMBERS. *He starts back to his desk.* CHALLEE *rises.* GREENWALD *shakes his head at* CHALLEE, *who sits, annoyed. A moment of silence.* GREENWALD *shuffles papers at his desk*)

GREENWALD Doctor, in a paranoid personality like Commander Queeg's—well, let me put this hypothetically. Could a man have a paranoid personality which would not disable him for any subordinate duties, but would disable him for command?

LUNDEEN (*Rather irritated*) It's conceivable.

GREENWALD Is the disabling factor likely to show up in personal interviews?

LUNDEEN With a skilled psychiatrist, yes.

GREENWALD Why is a psychiatrist needed, Doctor? Can't an educated intelligent person, like myself, or the judge advocate, or the court, detect a paranoid?

LUNDEEN (*Sarcastically*) You evidently are not too well acquainted with the pattern. The distinguishing mark of this neurosis is extreme plausibility and a most convincing normal manner on the surface. Particularly in self-justification.

GREENWALD Thank you, Doctor. No more questions.

(*Returns to seat. The other* COURT MEMBERS *look tensely at* BLAKELY)

BLAKELY The court wishes to clear up one point. Doctor, is such a thing possible?

(*Hesitates*)

Well, let me put it this way. Let's say a man with a mild condition is not disabled for all the usual stresses of command. Now let's say the stresses are multiplied manifold by an extreme emergency. Would there be a tendency to make erroneous judgments?

LUNDEEN Well, there might be. Extreme stress does that to almost anybody, sir.

BLAKELY (*Sternly*) It's not supposed to do it to commanding officers.

LUNDEEN No, but practically speaking, sir, they're human, too.

BLAKELY You are not to discuss your testimony outside the courtroom. You're excused.

LUNDEEN Yes, sir.

BLAKELY Thank you, Doctor.
(*Exit* LUNDEEN)

CHALLEE Dr. Bird will be my last witness, sir.
(CHALLEE *nods to* ORDERLY. *Exit* ORDERLY, *returning with a lieutenant, good-looking, young, of an intellectual and ascetic appearance. Bible business.*)

BLAKELY You do solemnly swear that the evidence you shall give in this court shall be the truth, the whole truth, and nothing but the truth. So help you God.

BIRD I do.
(*Takes the stand*)

CHALLEE State your name, rank, and present station

BIRD Allen Winston Bird, M.D., Lieutenant, U.S.N.R. On the psychiatric staff of U. S. Naval Hospital, San Francisco.

CHALLEE Were you a member of the board headed by Dr. Lundeen which recently inquired into the mental health of Lieutenant Commander Queeg?

BIRD Yes. sir.

CHALLEE What was the finding of the board?

BIRD We found that the commander is mentally fit for command now and has never been unfit.

CHALLEE (*After a pause*) Did you find any indication that Commander Queeg had what is known as a paranoid personality?

BIRD Well, I prefer to call it an obsessive personality with paranoid features.

CHALLEE This did not indicate mental unfitness, however?

BIRD Oh, no.

CHALLEE You unanimously agreed, then, Doctor, that Commander Queeg is mentally fit now and must have been mentally fit on 18 December, when he was relieved on the grounds of mental illness?

BIRD That was our unanimous conclusion.

CHALLEE Thank you, Doctor. No further questions.
(GREENWALD *appraises* DR. BIRD *with a cold eye, slowly gets out of his chair, and approaches him*)

GREENWALD Doctor, you have special training in Freudian technique?

BIRD Yes.

GREENWALD In the Freudian analysis is there such a thing as mental illness?

BIRD Well, there are disturbed people and adjusted people.

GREENWALD But *disturbed* and *adjusted* correspond roughly, don't they, to the terms *sick* and *well* as laymen use them?

BIRD Very roughly, yes.

GREENWALD Doctor, would you say Commander Queeg suffers from inferiority feelings?

BIRD Yes, but they are well compensated.

GREENWALD Is there a difference between *compensated* and *adjusted*?

BIRD Most definitely.

GREENWALD Can you explain it?

BIRD (*Smiles and settles back in his chair*) Well—let's say a man has some deep-seated psychological disturbance. He can *compensate* by finding outlets for his peculiar drives. He can never *adjust* without undergoing psychoanalysis.

GREENWALD Has Commander Queeg ever been psychoanalyzed?

BIRD No.

GREENWALD He is, then, a disturbed person.

BIRD   Yes, he is. Not disabled, however, by the disturbance. (*Smiles*)

GREENWALD   How has he compensated?

BIRD   In two ways, mainly. The paranoid pattern, which is useless and not desirable, and his naval career, which is extremely useful and desirable.

GREENWALD   You say his military career is a result of his disturbance?

BIRD   Most military careers are.

GREENWALD   Doctor, did you note any peculiar habit Commander Queeg had? Something he did with his hands?

BIRD   Do you mean rolling the steel balls?

GREENWALD   Yes, describe the habit, please.

BIRD   Well, it's an incessant rolling or rattling of two marbles in his hand—either hand.

GREENWALD   Why does he do it?

BIRD   His hands tremble. He does it to still his hands and conceal the trembling. It makes him feel more comfortable.

GREENWALD   Why do his hands tremble?

BIRD   The inner tension. It's one of the surface symptoms.

GREENWALD   Does this rolling motion have significance in Freudian analysis?

BIRD   It's an obvious sexual symbol, of course. Now, as to the precise meaning, I—

CHALLEE (*Stands*)   How far is this totally irrelevant technical discussion going to be pushed?

BLAKELY (*Scowling*)   Are you objecting to the question?

CHALLEE   I'm requesting the court to set limits to time wasting by the defense.

BLAKELY   Your request is noted.
(*To* GREENWALD)
Proceed with cross-examination.

GREENWALD   Doctor, you have testified that the commander is a disturbed, not an adjusted, person.

BIRD   Yes.

GREENWALD   He is then, in laymen's terms, sick.

BIRD (*Smiles*)   I remember agreeing to the rough resemblance of the terms *disturbed* and *sick*. But by those terms an awful lot of people are sick . . .

GREENWALD   But this trial only has Commander Queeg's sickness at issue. If he's sick, how could your board have given him a clean bill of health?

BIRD   You're playing on words, I'm afraid. We found no disability.

GREENWALD   Doctor, supposing the requirements of command were many times as severe as you believe them to be —wouldn't even this mild sickness disable Queeg?

BIRD   That's absurdly hypothetical, because—

GREENWALD   Is it? Have you ever had sea duty, Doctor?

BIRD   No.

GREENWALD   Have you ever *been* to sea?
   (BIRD *is losing his self-possessed look*)

BIRD   No.

GREENWALD   How long have you been in the Navy?

BIRD   Five months—no, six, I guess, now—

GREENWALD   Have you had any dealings with ships' captains before this case?

BIRD   No.

GREENWALD   On what do you base your estimate of the stresses of command?

BIRD   Well, my general knowledge—

GREENWALD   Do you think command requires a highly gifted, exceptional person?

BIRD   Well, no—

GREENWALD It doesn't?

BIRD Not highly gifted, no. Adequate responses, fairly good intelligence, and sufficient training and experience, but—

GREENWALD Is that enough equipment for, say, a skilled psychiatrist?

BIRD Well, not exactly—

GREENWALD In other words, it takes more ability to be a psychiatrist than the captain of a naval vessel?

BIRD It takes—
  (*Looks toward* BLAKELY)
That is, different abilities are required. You're making the invidious comparison, not I.

GREENWALD Doctor, you've admitted Commander Queeg is sick. The only remaining question is *how* sick. You don't think he's sick enough to be disabled for command. I suggest that since evidently you don't know much about the requirements of command you may be wrong in your conclusion.

BIRD (*Looking like an insulted boy, his voice quivers*) I repudiate your suggestion. You've deliberately substituted the word *sick*, which is a loose, a polarized word, for the correct—

GREENWALD Pardon me, what kind of word?

BIRD Polarized—loaded, invidious . . . I never said sick. My grasp of the requirements of command is adequate or I would have disqualified myself from serving on the board—

GREENWALD Maybe you should have.

CHALLEE (*Rises, shouts*) The witness is being badgered!

GREENWALD I withdraw my last statement. No further questions.
  (GREENWALD *strides to his seat.* CHALLEE *crosses to* BIRD *in witness chair*)

CHALLEE Dr. Bird, defense counsel managed to put words into your mouth that I'm certain you don't mean, and I'd like to—

BIRD   I'm not aware that he succeeded in putting any words
into my mouth.

CHALLEE (*With an exasperated glance at* GREENWALD)   Doctor, he drew the implication from you that Captain Queeg is
sick. Surely you don't—

BIRD   Sir, I'm careful in my use of terminology. I did not
introduce the term *sick*. I don't regard it as a precise term.
Nevertheless, if you're going to use such a loose term, Captain
Queeg, like a vast number of seemingly healthy people, is
sick. However, he is definitely not disabled for command,
which is the only issue here.

CHALLEE   But that sounds like a contradiction, sir, which
surely you don't intend—

BIRD   We live in a sick civilization. The well people are the
exceptions, and Captain Queeg certainly isn't exceptional in
that regard, and furthermore—

CHALLEE (*Hastily, with a worried glance at* BLAKELY)   Thank
you, thank you, Doctor. That certainly clarifies the matter.
No more questions.
    (CHALLEE *goes quickly to his seat*)

BLAKELY   Doctor—
    (*Stares at* BIRD *as though considering questioning him, then
    shrugs*)
Doctor, you will not discuss your testimony outside this courtroom.

BIRD   No, sir.

BLAKELY   Excused.
    (*Exit* BIRD)

CHALLEE   Prosecution rests.
    (BLAKELY *glances at wrist watch, then at* GREENWALD, *who
    comes forward as* CHALLEE *sits*)

BLAKELY   Is defense ready to present its case?

GREENWALD   Yes, sir.

BLAKELY   How many witnesses are you calling?

GREENWALD   Only two, sir. The first is the accused.

BLAKELY Then we can button it all up tomorrow morning.

GREENWALD I believe so, sir.

BLAKELY (*Rings his bell*) Recess until 0900.
  (COURT *rises.* BLAKELY *goes out.* COURT *follows.* ORDERLY *and* STENOGRAPHER *leave.* CHALLEE *gathers his papers.* GREENWALD *sits slumped in his chair, leaning on one hand, doodling*)

CHALLEE (*To* GREENWALD, *when all are gone*) Quite a job you did on Dr. Bird.

GREENWALD (*Looks up; in a weary, flat tone*) Thanks, Jack.

CHALLEE It won't cut any ice.

GREENWALD No?

CHALLEE Captain Blakely's headed up a lot of these courts. He doesn't go for vaudeville.

GREENWALD (*shrugs*) See you tomorrow.

CHALLEE See you tomorrow.
  (*He goes out*)

MARYK Boy, that was marvelous, cutting up that doctor. Wise little bastard.

GREENWALD (*Strolls to witness chair and slumps in it*) Have you ever read it?

MARYK What?

GREENWALD Your friend Tom Keefer's novel.

MARYK Huh?

GREENWALD *Multitudes, Multitudes.* Have you ever read it?

MARYK Tom's novel? No, he's always kept it in a black satchel, locked.

GREENWALD I'd like to read it.

MARYK You would?

GREENWALD I'm sure it exposes this war in all its grim futility, and shows up the regular army and navy officers— just a lot of stupid sadists, bitching up the campaigns, and throwing away the lives of fatalistic, humorous, lovable citizen soldiers. Lots of sexy scenes where the prose becomes rhythmic and beautiful, while the girl gets her pants pulled down.

MARYK   What's eating you?

GREENWALD   I hate this case, do you know? The more so because I want to win it so bad. Because of what I've got to do to win it.

MARYK   I'm beginning to think I've got a chance. You're pretty keen, all right.

GREENWALD (*Gets up and paces*)   Almost as keen as Mr. Keefer?

MARYK (*Abashed*)   You were sure right about him. Why did he do it? He didn't have to implicate himself. He could have said what he really thought of Queeg.

GREENWALD   What, to Blakely? Blakely's sniffing around the edges of Keefer as it is. No sir. Your novelist friend's one course was to clam up. He's smart.

MARYK   You don't like Tom much.

GREENWALD   Well, I look at Keefer and I see my own self of a couple of years ago. Only like in a crazy-house mirror, all distorted and upside down. I'm not amused. Maybe Keefer didn't enjoy sailing under Queeg for half a year. Maybe he'd enjoy it less if the Nazis and the Japs were shaking hands right now at the Mississippi River. I guess what I've found out, Maryk, is that there's a time for everything, including rebellious youth. Possibly you and Mr. Keefer were dead wrong in your timing. In which case the next question is, Who's the real victim in this courtroom? You? Or Captain Queeg?

MARYK   Captain Queeg was nuts!

GREENWALD   You head Dr. Lundeen. It's a question of degree. If you're in a war and your command personnel is stretched thin, maybe you've got to use him because he's got the training. I'll grant you that Captain Queeg was a mean, stupid son of a bitch, but that doesn't mean—

MARYK   Okay!

GREENWALD   Maryk, if that was grounds for deposing your superior officer we wouldn't have an army or a navy. That's a widespread opinion of superior officers.

MARYK   They're not all Queegs.

GREENWALD   Superiors all tend to look like Queeg from underneath. It's an unflattering angle.

MARYK   What do you do when you really get a Queeg?

GREENWALD   You fight the war. Where can we get drunk? I mean drunk.

MARYK   Mister, you've got a day's work to do in court tomorrow.

GREENWALD   I know exactly what I've got to do in court tomorrow. That's why I want to get drunk. Come on, let's go.
     (*They go out. Stage lights fade. House lights come on*)

Act Two   **THE DEFENSE**

SCENE I

THE SCENE: *House lights dim. The lights brighten on an empty stage, the setting unchanged from the end of* ACT I. *Enter* ORDERLY, STENOGRAPHER, GREENWALD, MARYK, CHALLEE, *and the six* COURT MEMBERS. *All take their places, standing.*

CHALLEE   Attention!
     (BLAKELY *enters and goes to his seat*)

BLAKELY (*Rings bell*)   Defense, present your case.
     (*All sit except* GREENWALD)

GREENWALD   I call the accused.
   (MARYK *stands*)

BLAKELY   Does the accused request that he be permitted to testify?

MARYK   I do so request, sir.

BLAKELY   You have the right to do so. You also have the right not to take the stand. If you don't take the stand that fact won't be to your prejudice. If you take the stand you may be subjected to a rigorous cross-examination.

MARYK   I understand that, sir.

BLAKELY   Court stenographer will affirmatively record that the statutory request was made.
   (MARYK *does. Bible business*)
You do solemnly swear that the evidence you shall give in this court shall be the truth, the whole truth, and nothing but the truth. So help you God.

MARYK   I do.
   (MARYK *takes witness stand*)

GREENWALD   State your name, rank, and present station.

MARYK   Stephen Maryk, Lieutenant, U.S.N.R., executive officer of the U.S.S. *Caine*.

GREENWALD   Are you the accused in this court-martial?

MARYK   I am.

GREENWALD   What was your occupation in civilian life?

MARYK   Helping out in my father's fishing business. We own a couple of boats.

GREENWALD   Where?

MARYK   Here in San Francisco.

GREENWALD   Then you were familiar with the problems of ocean-going ship handling before entering the Navy?

MARYK   Well, I've been on the boats since I was fourteen.

GREENWALD   Did you relieve the commanding officer of the *Caine* of his command on December 18, 1944?

MARYK   I did.

GREENWALD   Was the *Caine* in the last extremity when you relieved the captain?

MARYK   It was.

GREENWALD   On what facts do you base that judgment?

MARYK (*Nervous*)   Well, several things, like—well, we were unable to hold course. We broached to three times in an hour.

GREENWALD   Broached to.

MARYK   Yes. Wind and sea took charge and tossed us sideways for ten minutes at a time. We were rolling too steeply for the inclinometer to record. We were shipping solid green water in the wheelhouse. The generators were cutting out. The ship wasn't answering to emergency rudder and engine settings. We were lost and out of control.

GREENWALD   Did you point these things out to the captain?

MARYK   Repeatedly for an hour. I begged him to come north and head into the wind.

GREENWALD   What was his response?

MARYK   Well, mostly a glazed look and no answer or a repetition of his own desires.

GREENWALD   Which were what?

MARYK   I guess to hold fleet course until we went down.

GREENWALD   Mister Maryk, when did you start keeping your medical log on Captain Queeg?

MARYK   Shortly after the Kwajalein invasion.

GREENWALD   Why did you start it?

MARYK   Well, I began to think the captain might be mentally ill.

GREENWALD   Why?

MARYK   That yellow dye marker business.

GREENWALD   Was that the incident in which Captain Queeg acquired the nickname, Old Yellowstain?

MARYK   Yes, it was.

GREENWALD   You witnessed the occurrence yourself?

MARYK   I was navigator. I was right there on the bridge.

GREENWALD   Describe the Yellow Stain incident, please.

MARYK   Well, it was the first morning of the invasion. We were ordered to lead a group of attack boats in to the beach. That is, we had to take them to their line of departure, one thousand yards from the beach. These little boats lay so low in the water they couldn't see to navigate for themselves. They needed a guide to make sure they hit the right island and the right beach. Captain Queeg rang up ten knots and we started to head in toward this island. It had some funny Jap name. Our code name for it was Jacob Island. Well, it was a choppy sea. These assault boats could only make five or six knots. And at that they were shipping solid water, and the marines were getting just about drowned in spray. They began to fall way behind. Naturally they signaled for us to slow down. But the captain just ignored them. We pulled further and further ahead until we could hardly see them. Then, when we were about twenty-five hundred yards from the beach, we heard some gunfire. The captain suddenly yelled, "We're running up on the beach! Reverse course! Make thirty knots!" And while we were turning he threw over one of these yellow dye markers you use to mark water where there's a floating mine or something. So we went barreling out of there. The attack boats were just a lot of specks way off in the distance. All you could see behind us was this big spread of yellow, all over the water.
   (*A long pause*)

GREENWALD   Now, Mister Maryk—
   (BLAKELY *rings his bell*)

BLAKELY   Court wants to question the witness. Lieutenant, how do you know you were twenty-five hundred yards from the beach when you turned?

MARYK   Sir, I was navigating. There wasn't a doubt in the world where we were, by visual plot. And our radar range to the beach was also twenty-five hundred when we turned.

BLAKELY   Did you inform your captain that he was turning fifteen hundred yards short?

MARYK   Sir, I shouted it at him, over and over. He just stood there smiling.

BLAKELY (*Making notes*)   You say these boats signaled to you to slow down.

MARYK   Yes, sir. By semaphore.

BLAKELY   Was the signal reported to your captain?

MARYK   I reported it myself.

BLAKELY   Was he aware of the fact that you were running away from the boats?

MARYK   He was looking right at them, sir. I pointed out that if we got too far ahead, the boats wouldn't know where the line of departure was. That's when he said, "Well, we'll throw over a dye marker, then."

   (BLAKELY *nods to* GREENWALD)

GREENWALD   Mister Maryk, why didn't you go to higher authority at once with your doubts about the captain's mental health?

MARYK   I figured if I only had a record I'd be on stronger ground. So I decided to start the log. I figured if ever I saw that I was all wrong I'd just burn it. I kept it under lock and key.

GREENWALD   What, in your view, made an incident worthy of record in your medical log?

MARYK   Just any act that seemed strange or abnormal. Like the Silex business.

GREENWALD   Describe the Silex business.

MARYK   A mess boy slopped coffee on a Silex and burned it out. None of the mess boys would admit which one did it. So the captain ordered all the officers of the ship to sit as a court of inquiry till we found out who burned out the Silex. I mean in itself it's a silly little thing. But it went on and on for thirty-six hours. All ship's work stopped. There we were, all of us in the wardroom, dying for sleep, needing shaves, and still trying to find out which of those poor colored boys burned out the Silex. By then those kids thought whoever did it was going to get hung. They would have died before telling us. So finally I had to go to the captain and tell him that all the officers admitted they were incompetent investigators and would take cuts in their fitness reports, but they couldn't find out who slopped coffee on the Silex. So, he made a note in his black book and called off the inquiry. Things like that. Or like the water business.

GREENWALD   Describe the water business.

MARYK   It's all in the log. How he cut off the water at the equator for two days for the whole ship. Just because he caught one simple deck hand stealing a drink during water conservation hours. Or plain crazy things, like the strawberry business.

GREENWALD   Describe the strawberry business.

MARYK   Well, there—

CHALLEE   Objection. The so-called medical log was introduced in evidence at the start of these proceedings. All this is just repeating a lot of trivial disloyal gripes.

GREENWALD   If the court concurs, I'll pass over the medical log.

BLAKELY (*With a glance around at the* MEMBERS OF THE COURT, *uneasily*)   Well, let's not take up time here.

GREENWALD   Aye aye, sir.

BLAKELY   Only—there seems to be some confusion about the so-called strawberry business. It started out as a search for a quart of strawberries, didn't it?

MARYK   Yes, sir.

BLAKELY   Then it somehow became a search for a key.

MARYK   That's right.

BLAKELY   How was that?

MARYK   That was on account of the cheese business.

BLAKELY   Cheese business? I don't recall any cheese business.

MARYK That was on the first ship Captain Queeg served on, sir, when he was an ensign. Cheese had been disappearing from ship's stores. He investigated and caught a sailor who had made himself a duplicate key to a padlock on the refrigerator. Well, for catching this cheese thief the captain had gotten a letter of commendation. This was peacetime. Naturally, he was real proud of it. When this strawberry thing came up he insisted it was the same thing, and all we had to do was find out who had made a duplicate key to the wardroom icebox. But of course it was ridiculous. It was the mess boys again. We all knew they'd eaten up this quart of strawberries. It was just the leavings from the wardroom mess, and they were entitled to eat it, that was the custom. But naturally when the captain started to roar around about "those strawberries," why, the boys just froze up and swore they hadn't eaten them. And the captain, he was so steamed up on this key theory, he believed them.

BLAKELY So he ordered the search for the key?

MARYK Yes, sir. We never saw Captain Queeg so happy before or since. He was living the cheese business all over again. He organized the search himself. All ship's work was suspended. We collected every single key on the ship—boxes of keys, barrels of keys, about twenty-eight hundred of them all tagged with the owner's name. Then to make sure we had them all we searched the ship from stem to stern, from the crow's nest to the bilge. We stripped the crew stark-naked, every one of them, and shook out their clothes. We searched their lockers. We crawled into every hole and every space in the ship. We crawled under the boilers and pulled out the lead ballast blocks, two hundred pounds apiece. This went on for three days, and all of it over a key that never existed. Well, when I saw Captain Queeg sitting by the icebox, taking those keys one by one out of the barrels and trying them on the padlock, hours on end, with a gleam in his eye, I gave up. That was when I showed the medical log to Lieutenant Keefer.

BLAKELY Mister Maryk, when Lieutenant Keefer finished reading your medical log, what was his first comment?
    (*All six* COURT MEMBERS *stare intently at* MARYK)

MARYK (*Pause*) Sir, I'm afraid I don't remember.

BLAKELY   Did he encourage you to go to Admiral Halsey?

MARYK   I did that on my own responsibility, sir.

BLAKELY   But he went with you to the *New Jersey?*

MARYK   He did, sir.

BLAKELY   So at first—he didn't discourage you?

MARYK   Well, sir, when we got aboard the *New Jersey* he discouraged me. He said we shouldn't go through with it. And we didn't.

BLAKELY   Would you say his testimony on the subject was substantially correct?

MARYK   Yes, sir. It was all my doing, sir.
    (BLAKELY *nods to* GREENWALD)

GREENWALD   Mister Maryk, when the typhoon was over, did Captain Queeg make any effort to regain command?

MARYK   Yes, on the morning of the nineteenth. The storm had blown out. We'd just sighted the fleet.

GREENWALD   Describe what happened.

MARYK   Well, I was in the charthouse writing up a despatch to report the relief to Admiral Halsey. The captain came in and said, "Do you mind coming to my cabin and having a talk before you send that?" I went below and we talked. It was the same thing at first—about how I'd be court-martialed for mutiny. He said, "You've applied for transfer to the regular navy. You know this means the end of all that, don't you?" Then he went into a long thing about how he loved the Navy and had no other interest in life, and even if he was cleared this would ruin his record. I said I felt sorry for him, and I really did. Finally he came out with his proposal. He said he'd forget the whole thing and never report me. He would resume command, and the whole matter would be forgotten and written off—

GREENWALD   What did you say to the proposal?

MARYK   Well, I was amazed. I said, "Captain, the whole ship knows about it. It's written up in the quartermaster's log and the OOD's log." Well, he hemmed and hawed, and finally said it wouldn't be the first time a penciled rough log had been corrected and fixed up after the fact.

GREENWALD Did you remind him of the rule against erasures?

MARYK Yes, and he kind of laughed and said it was either that or a court-martial for mutiny for me, and a black mark on his record which he didn't deserve. And he didn't see that a few penciled lines were worth all that.

GREENWALD What followed?

MARYK Well he began to plead and beg—he cried at one point—in the end he became terrifically angry, and ordered me out of his cabin. So I sent the despatch.

GREENWALD Then you had the chance, twenty-four hours later, of expunging the whole event from the official record with the captain's knowledge and approval?

MARYK Yes.

GREENWALD Mister Maryk, were you panicky at all during the typhoon?

MARYK I was not.

GREENWALD Now, Lieutenant, you're charged with relieving your captain willfully, without authority, and without justifiable cause. Did you relieve Captain Queeg willfully?

MARYK Yes, I knew what I was doing.

GREENWALD Did you relieve without authority?

MARYK No. My authority was Articles 184, 185, and 186.

GREENWALD Did you relieve without justifiable cause?

MARYK No. My justifiable cause was the captain's mental breakdown at a time when the ship was in danger.

GREENWALD No further questions.
     (*Sits.* CHALLEE *approaches* MARYK)

CHALLEE Mister Maryk, this amazing interview in which the captain offered to falsify official records. Were there any witnesses to it?

MARYK We were alone in the captain's cabin. No.

CHALLEE   This incident at Kwajalein. Did anyone else see this chart which, according to you, indicated your ship turned away from the beach too soon?

MARYK   About an hour after it happened the captain asked to see the chart and took it to his cabin. When I got it back all my bearings and course lines had been erased.

CHALLEE   Then you have no documentary corroboration of this story.

MARYK   No.

CHALLEE   How about the radar men who called off the ranges? Won't they confirm your story?

MARYK   Sir, you can't expect them to remember one single radar range, when they called them by the thousands in every invasion.

CHALLEE   These poor abandoned marines in the assault boats never complained to higher authority of the dastardly conduct of the *Caine?*

MARYK   No.

CHALLEE   Strange.

MARYK   Sir, they landed against machine gun fire. The ones that survived, I don't think they remembered much else besides that landing.

CHALLEE   Mister Maryk, who coined this scurrilous nickname, "Old Yellowstain"?

MARYK   (*A worried glance at* GREENWALD) Well, it just sprang into existence.

CHALLEE   Throughout the ship? Or just among the officers?

MARYK   Among the officers.

CHALLEE   You're sure you didn't coin it yourself?

MARYK   I didn't.

CHALLEE   Mister Maryk, what kind of rating would you give yourself for loyalty to your captain?

MARYK   I think I was a loyal officer.

CHALLEE   Did you issue a seventy-two-hour pass to Stilwell in December '43 against the captain's express instructions?

MARYK   I did.

CHALLEE   Do you call that a loyal act?

MARYK   No.

CHALLEE   You admit to a disloyal act in your first days as executive officer?

MARYK   Yes.

CHALLEE   Mister Maryk—where did you get your schooling?

MARYK   Public schools, San Francisco. And San Francisco University.

CHALLEE   How were your grades in elementary school?

MARYK   Okay.

CHALLEE   Average? Above average? Below average?

MARYK   Average.

CHALLEE   How about your high school grades?

MARYK   Well, I didn't do so good there. Below average.

CHALLEE   What kind of course did you take at college?

MARYK   Business course.

CHALLEE   Any pre-medical courses?

MARYK   No.

CHALLEE   Any psychology or psychiatry courses?

MARYK   No.

CHALLEE   How were your grades at college?

MARYK   I scraped by.

CHALLEE   Below average?

MARYK   Yes.

CHALLEE   Then where did you get all of these highfalutin' ideas about paranoia?

MARYK (*With a worried glance toward* GREENWALD) I—out of books.

CHALLEE What books? Name the titles.

MARYK Medical-type books about mental illness.

CHALLEE Was that your intellectual hobby—reading about psychiatry?

MARYK No.

CHALLEE Then where did you get these books?

MARYK I—borrowed them off ships' doctors here and there.

CHALLEE And with your background, your scholastic record —did you imagine you understood these highly technical scientific works?

MARYK Well, I got something out of them.

CHALLEE What is a conditioned reflex?

MARYK I don't know.

CHALLEE What is schizophrenia?

MARYK I think it's a mental illness.

CHALLEE You think so. What are its symptoms?

MARYK I don't know.

CHALLEE In fact, you don't know what you're talking about when you discuss mental illness, is that right?

MARYK I didn't say I knew much about it.

CHALLEE Have you ever heard the expression, "A little learning is a dangerous thing"?

MARYK Yes.

CHALLEE You got a headful of terms you didn't understand, and on that basis you had the temerity to depose a commanding officer on the grounds of mental illness. Is that correct?

MARYK I didn't relieve him because of what the books said. The ship was in danger—

CHALLEE   Never mind the ship. We're discussing your grasp of psychiatry. Have you heard the diagnosis of the qualified psychiatrists who examined your captain?

MARYK   Yes.

CHALLEE   What was their diagnosis—was he crazy or wasn't he, on 18 December?

MARYK   They say he wasn't.

CHALLEE   But, you, with your whining gripes about straw-berries and Silexes, know better. Mister Maryk, who was the third ranking officer on your ship?

MARYK   Lieutenant Keefer.

CHALLEE   Was he a good officer?

MARYK   Yes.

CHALLEE   Do you consider his mind as good as yours? Or perhaps better?

MARYK   Better.

CHALLEE   You showed this medical log of yours to him.

MARYK   Yes.

CHALLEE   He wasn't convinced by it that the captain was mentally ill.

MARYK   No.

CHALLEE   He talked you out of trying to have the captain relieved.

MARYK   Yes.

CHALLEE   And yet two weeks later—despite the whole weight of naval discipline—despite the arguments of the next officer in rank to you, a superior intellect—despite all this, you went ahead and seized command of your ship?

MARYK   I relieved him because he definitely seemed sick during the typhoon.

CHALLEE   You *still* imagine your diagnosis of Captain Queeg is superior to the doctor's?

MARYK   Only about Queeg on the morning of the typhoon.

CHALLEE   No more questions.

GREENWALD   No re-examination.

BLAKELY   You may step down, Lieutenant.
(MARYK *leaves the stand with a stunned expression and goes to his seat*
(BLAKELY *glances at* GREENWALD)

GREENWALD   Call Lieutenant Commander Queeg.
(*Exit* ORDERLY. *Returns with* QUEEG, *who looks as debonair and assured as on the first day. He hesitates before taking witness chair, expecting to be sworn*)

BLAKELY   Commander, the oath previously taken by you is still binding.

QUEEG   Yes, sir.
(QUEEG *takes witness chair.* GREENWALD *approaches* QUEEG)

GREENWALD   Commander, on the morning of 19 December, did you have an interview in your room with Lieutenant Maryk?

QUEEG   Let's see. That's the day after the typhoon. Yes, I did.

GREENWALD   Was it at your request?

QUEEG   Yes.

GREENWALD   What was the substance of that interview?

QUEEG   Well, as I say, I felt sorry for him. I hated to see him ruining his life with one panicky mistake. Particularly as I knew his ambition was to make the Navy his career. I tried as hard as I could to show him what a mistake he had made. I recommended that he relinquish command to me, and I offered to be as lenient as I could in reporting what had happened.

GREENWALD   You never offered not to report the incident?

QUEEG   How could I? It was already recorded in the logs.

GREENWALD   Were the logs in pencil, or typed, or what?

QUEEG   That would make no difference.

GREENWALD   Were they in pencil, Commander?

QUEEG   Well, let's see. Probably they were—quartermaster log and OOD rough log always are. I doubt the yeoman would have gotten around to typing smooth logs in all the excitement.

GREENWALD   Did you offer to erase the incident from the penciled logs and make no report at all?

QUEEG   I did not. Erasures aren't permitted in penciled logs.

GREENWALD   Lieutenant Maryk has testified under oath, Commander, that you made such an offer. Not only that, but you begged and pleaded and even wept to get him to agree to erase those few pencil lines, in return for which you promised to hush up the incident completely and make no report.

QUEEG (*Calmly and pleasantly*)   That isn't true.

GREENWALD   There isn't any truth in it at all?

QUEEG   Well, it's a distortion of what I told you. My version is the exact truth.

GREENWALD   You deny the proposal to erase the logs and hush up the story?

QUEEG   I deny it completely. That's the part he made up . . . And the weeping and the pleading. That's fantastic.

GREENWALD   You are accusing Mister Maryk of perjury?

QUEEG   I'm not accusing him. He's accused of enough as it stands. You're likely to hear a lot of strange things from Mister Maryk about me, that's all.

GREENWALD   Isn't one of you obviously not telling the truth about that interview?

QUEEG   It appears so.

GREENWALD   Can you prove it isn't you?

QUEEG   Only by citing a clean record of over fourteen years as a naval officer, against the word of a man on trial for a mutinous act.

GREENWALD   Commander, did you ever receive a hundred ten dollars from Lieutenant Junior Grade Keith?

QUEEG   I don't recall offhand that I did.

GREENWALD   He testified that you did.

QUEEG   I did? On what occasion?

GREENWALD   On the occasion of a loss of a crate of yours in San Francisco Bay.

QUEEG   Yes. I remember now. It was over a year ago. December or thereabouts. He was responsible for the loss and insisted on paying, and so he did.

GREENWALD   What was in the crate, Commander, that cost a hundred and ten dollars?

QUEEG   Oh, uniforms, books, navigating instruments—the usual.

GREENWALD   How was Keith responsible for the loss?

QUEEG   Well, he was boat officer and in charge of the loading. He issued foolish and contradictory orders. The men got rattled and the crate fell into the water and sank.

GREENWALD   A wooden crate full of clothes sank?

QUEEG   There were other things in it, I guess. I had some souvenir coral rocks.

GREENWALD   Commander, wasn't the crate entirely full of bottles of intoxicating liquor?

QUEEG (*After a barely perceptible pause*)   Certainly not.

GREENWALD   Keith has testified you charged him for a crate of liquor.

QUEEG   You'll hear plenty of strange distortions about me from Keith and Maryk. They're the two culprits here and they're apt to make all kinds of strange statements.

GREENWALD   Did you make this crate yourself?

QUEEG   No. My carpenter's mate did.

GREENWALD   What was his name?

QUEEG   I don't recall. It'll be on the personnel records. He's been gone from the ship a long time.

GREENWALD Where is this carpenter's mate now, Commander?

QUEEG I don't know. I transferred him to the beach at Funafuti at the request of the commodore for a carpenter. This was back in May.

GREENWALD You don't recall his name?

QUEEG No.

GREENWALD Was it Carpenter's Mate Second Class Otis F. Langhorne?

QUEEG Lang, Langhorne. Sounds right.

GREENWALD Commander, there is a Carpenter's Mate First Class Otis F. Langhorne at present in damage-control school at Treasure Island, right here in the bay. Defense has arranged to subpoena him if necessary.

QUEEG (*Shoots a look at* CHALLEE) You're sure it's the same one?

GREENWALD His service record shows twenty-one months aboard the *Caine*. Your signature is in it. Would it be useful to have him subpoenaed, sir?

CHALLEE Objection to this entire irrelevancy about the crate, and request it be stricken from the record.

GREENWALD The credibility of the witness is being established. I submit to the court that nothing could be more relevant to this trial.

BLAKELY Overruled.
  (*Nods to* STENOGRAPHER)

STENOGRAPHER (*Reads*) "Would it be useful to have him subpoenaed, sir?"

QUEEG Well, it's a question which crate Langhorne nailed up. I had two crates, as I recall now.

GREENWALD Oh?
  (*Pause*)
Well. This is a new angle, not mentioned by Keith. Did Langhorne make both crates, sir?

QUEEG Well, I don't recall whether I had both crates on that occasion or two crates on two different occasions. It's all very trivial and happened a long time ago and I've had a year of combat steaming in between and a typhoon and all this hospital business and I'm not too clear.

GREENWALD Commander, there are many points in this trial which turn on the issue of credibility between yourself and other officers. If you wish I will request a five-minute recess while you clear your mind as well as you can on the matter of these crates.

QUEEG That won't be necessary. Just let me think for a moment, please.

   (*In the silence* BLAKELY'S *pencil makes a thin rattling noise as he rolls it under his palm on the bench.* QUEEG *sits staring from under his eyebrows*)

Kay. I have it straight now. I made a misstatement. I lost a crate in San Diego Harbor back in '38 or '39 I think it was, under similar circumstances. That was the one containing clothes. The crate Keith lost did contain liquor.

GREENWALD Was it entirely full of liquor?

QUEEG I believe it was.

GREENWALD How did you obtain a crate full of whiskey, Commander, in wartime?

QUEEG Bought up the rations of my officers at the wine mess in Pearl Harbor.

GREENWALD You transported this liquor from Pearl to the States in your ship? Do you know the regulations—

QUEEG (*Breaks in*) I'm aware of regulations. The crate was sealed prior to getting under way. I gave it the same locked stowage I gave the medicinal brandy. Liquor was damned scarce and expensive in the States. I'd had three years of steady combat duty. I gave myself this leeway as captain of the *Caine* and it was a common practice and I believe rank has its privileges, as they say. I had no intentions of concealing it from the court and I'm not ashamed of it. I simply mixed up the two crates in my mind.

GREENWALD Keith testified, Commander, that you gave all the orders to the boat crew which caused the loss of the crate.

QUEEG   That's a lie.

GREENWALD   Also that you refused to sign his leave papers until he paid for the loss.

QUEEG   That's another lie.

GREENWALD   It seems to be the issue of credibility again, sir—this time your word against Keith's. Correct?

QUEEG   You'll hear nothing but lies about me from Keith. He has an insane hatred of me.

GREENWALD   Do you know why, sir?

QUEEG   I can't say, unless it's his resentment against fancied injuries to his crony, this sailor Stilwell. Those two were mighty affectionate.

GREENWALD   Affectionate, sir?

QUEEG   Well, it seems to me every time Keith thought I looked cross-eyed at Stilwell there was all kinds of screeching and hollering from Keith as though I were picking on his wife or something. And those two sure ganged up mighty fast to back Maryk when he relieved me.

GREENWALD   Commander, are you suggesting there were abnormal relations between Lieutenant Keith and the sailor Stilwell?

QUEEG   I'm not suggesting a thing. I'm stating plain facts that everybody knew who had eyes to see.

GREENWALD   (*Looking around at* BLAKELY)   Does the court desire to caution the witness about the gravity of the insinuated charge?

QUEEG   (*Nasally*)   I'm not insinuating a thing, sir! I don't know of anything improper between those two men and I deny insinuating anything. All I said was that Keith was always taking Stilwell's part and it's the easiest thing in the world to prove and that's all I said or meant. I resent the twisting of my words.

BLAKELY   Are you going to pursue this—topic?

GREENWALD   No, sir.

BLAKELY   Very well. Go ahead.

GREENWALD   Commander, during the period when the *Caine* was towing targets at Pearl Harbor did you ever steam over your own towline and cut it?

CHALLEE (*Stands*)   Objection! This towline business is the last straw. The tactics of the defense counsel are an outrage on the dignity of these proceedings. He's systematically turning this trial into a court-martial of Commander Queeg.

GREENWALD   Sir, the judge advocate has made it perfectly clear that he thinks he has a prima facie case in the report of the two psychiatrists. But I say it's still up to the court, not to shore-bound doctors, however brilliant, to decide whether the captain of the *Caine* was mentally well enough to retain his self-control and his post during a typhoon.

BLAKELY   The objection is overruled. The witness will answer the question.
   (*Nods to* STENOGRAPHER
   (CHALLEE *appears stunned, sitting down slowly*)

STENOGRAPHER (*Reads*)   "Commander Queeg, during the period when the *Caine* was towing targets at Pearl Harbor did you ever steam over your own towline and cut it?"

QUEEG (*Promptly*)   Kay, now—here's the story on that particular slander. I started to make a turn, when I noticed some anti-aircraft bursts close aboard to starboard. I was gravely concerned that my ship might be within range of somebody's firing. We were in a gunnery area. I was watching the bursts. This same sailor Stilwell, a very dreamy and unreliable man, was at the helm. He failed to warn me that we were coming around the full 360 degrees. I saw what was happening, finally, and instantly reversed course, and I avoided passing over the towline, to my best knowledge. However, the line parted during the turn.

GREENWALD   You say you were distracted by AA bursts. Did anything else distract you?

QUEEG   Not that I recall.

GREENWALD   Were you engaged in reprimanding a signalman named Urban at length for having his shirttail out, while your ship was turning 360 degrees?

QUEEG   Who says that—Keith again?

GREENWALD   Will you answer the question, Commander?

QUEEG   It's a malicious lie, of course.

GREENWALD   Was Urban on the bridge at the time?

QUEEG   Yes.

GREENWALD   Was his shirttail out?

QUEEG   Yes, and I reprimanded him. That took me about two seconds. I'm not in the habit of dwelling on those things. Then there were those AA bursts, and that was what distracted me.

GREENWALD   Did you point out these AA bursts to the officer of the deck or the exec?

QUEEG   I may have. I don't recall. I didn't run weeping to my OOD on every occasion. I may very well have kept my own counsel. And since this shirttail thing has been brought up—I'd like to say that Ensign Keith as morale officer was in charge of enforcing uniform regulations and completely soldiered on the job. When I took over the ship it was like the Chinese Navy. And I bore down on Keith to watch those shirttails and for all I know that's another reason he hated me and circulated all this about my cutting the towline.

GREENWALD   Did you drop a yellow dye marker off Jacob Island on the first morning of the invasion of Kwajalein?

QUEEG   I may have. I don't recall.

GREENWALD   Do you recall what your first mission was during the invasion?

QUEEG   Yes. To lead a group of attack boats to the line of departure for Jacob Island.

GREENWALD   Did you fulfill that mission?

QUEEG   Yes.

GREENWALD   Why did you drop the dye marker?

QUEEG   I don't know for sure that I did drop one. Maybe I dropped one to mark the line of departure plainly.

GREENWALD   How far was the line of departure from the beach?

QUEEG   As I recall, a thousand yards.

GREENWALD Commander, didn't you run a mile ahead of the attack boats, drop your dye marker more than half a mile short, and retire at high speed, leaving the boats to grope their way to the line of departure as best they could?

CHALLEE (*Rises*) The question is abusive and flagrantly leading.

GREENWALD (*Wearily*) I am willing to withdraw the question, in view of the commander's dim memory, and proceed to more recent events.

BLAKELY Court desires to question the witness.
  (GREENWALD *crosses to his desk*)
Commander Queeg, in view of the implications in this line of testimony, I urge you to search your memory for correct answers.

QUEEG I am certainly trying to do that, sir. But these are very small points. I've been through several campaigns since Kwajalein and the typhoon and now all this business—

BLAKELY I appreciate that. It will facilitate justice if you can remember enough to give a few definite answers on points of fact. First of all, were those boats on the line of departure when you turned away from the beach?

QUEEG As near as I could calculate, yes.

BLAKELY In that case, Commander, if they were already on the line, what purpose did the dye marker serve?

QUEEG (*Hesitates*) Well, you might say a safety factor. Just another added mark. Now—maybe I erred in being overcautious and making sure they knew where they were but then again, sir, I've always believed you can't err on the side of safety.

BLAKELY (*Slight acrid impatience*) Did you have the conn?

QUEEG (*Pauses*) As I recall now Lieutenant Maryk had the conn, and I now recall I had to caution him for opening the gap too wide between us and the boats.

BLAKELY How wide?

QUEEG I can't say, but at one point there was definitely too much open water and I called him aside and I admonished him not to run away from the boats.

BLAKELY Didn't you direct him to slow down when you saw the gap widening?

QUEEG Well, but it was all happening very fast and I may have been watching the beach for a few seconds and then I saw we were running away. And so that's why I dropped the marker, to compensate for Maryk's running away from the boats.

BLAKELY (*Pauses, face grave*) These are your factual recollections, Commander?

QUEEG Those are the facts, sir.

BLAKELY (*To* GREENWALD) Resume your examination.

GREENWALD (*Speaks at once*) Commander Queeg, did you make it a practice, during invasions, to station yourself on the side of the bridge that was sheltered from the beach?

QUEEG (*Angrily*) That's an insulting question, and the answer is no, I had to be on all sides of the bridge at once, constantly moving from one side to the other because Maryk was navigator and Keith was my OOD at general quarters and both of them were invariably scurrying to the safe side of the bridge so I was captain and navigator and OOD all rolled in one and that's why I had to move constantly from one side of the bridge to the other. And that's the truth, whatever lies may have been said about me in this court.

(QUEEG *takes two steel balls out of his pocket*)

BLAKELY (*Rings bell*) The court will question the witness.

CHALLEE (*Stands*) Sir, the witness is obviously and understandably agitated by this ordeal, and I request a recess to give him a breathing space—

QUEEG I am not in the least agitated, and I'm glad to answer any and all questions here and in fact I demand a chance to set the record straight on anything derogatory to me in the testimony that's gone before. I did not make a single mistake in fifteen months aboard the *Caine* and I can prove it and my record has been spotless until now and I don't want it smirched by a whole lot of lies and distortions by disloyal officers.

BLAKELY Commander, would you like a recess?

QUEEG   Definitely not, sir. I request there be no recess if it's up to me.

BLAKELY   Very well. I simply want to ask—if the performance of these two officers was so unspeakably bad, why did you tolerate it? Why didn't you beach them? Or at least rotate them to less responsible battle stations?

QUEEG   Well, sir, strange as it may seem, the fact is I'm a very soft-hearted guy. Not many people know that. I never despaired of training those two men up and making naval officers of them. I kept them under my eye just because I wanted to train them up. The last thing I wanted to do was wreck their careers. Not that they had any similar concern for me, either of them.

BLAKELY   Defense counsel . . .

GREENWALD   Commander, on the morning of 18 December, at the moment you were relieved, was the *Caine* in the last extremity?

QUEEG   It certainly was not!

GREENWALD   Was it in grave danger at that moment?

QUEEG   Absolutely not. I had that ship under complete control.
   (*Puts steel balls away*)

GREENWALD   Did you ever indicate to your other officers that it had been your intention to change course and come north at ten o'clock—or fifteen minutes after Maryk did?

QUEEG   (*Pause*)   Yes, I did make that statement, and such had been my intention.

GREENWALD   Why did you intend to abandon fleet course, Commander, if the ship wasn't in danger?

QUEEG   (*After a long silence*)   Well, I don't see any inconsistency there. I've repeatedly stated in my testimony that my rule is safety first. As I say the ship wasn't in danger but a typhoon is still a typhoon and I'd just about decided that we'd do as well coming around to north. I might have executed my intention at ten o'clock and then again I might not have.

GREENWALD   Then Maryk's decision to come north was not a panicky, irrational blunder?

QUEEG   His panicky blunder was relieving me. I kept him from making any disastrous mistakes thereafter. I didn't intend to vindicate myself at the cost of all the lives on the *Caine*.

GREENWALD   Commander Queeg, have you read Lieutenant Maryk's medical log?

QUEEG   Oh, yes, I have read that interesting document, yes, sir, I have. It's the biggest conglomeration of lies and distortions and half-truths I've ever seen and I'm extremely glad you asked me because I want to get my side of it all on the record.

GREENWALD   Please state your version, or any factual comments on the episodes in the log, sir.

QUEEG   Kay. Now, starting right with that strawberry business the real truth is that I was betrayed and thrown and double-crossed by my executive officer and this precious gentleman Mister Keith who between them corrupted my wardroom so that I was one man against a whole ship without any support from my officers . . . Kay. Now, you take that strawberry business—why, if that wasn't a case of outright conspiracy to protect a malefactor from justice—Maryk carefully leaves out the little fact that I had conclusively proved by a process of elimination that someone had a key to the icebox. He says it was the steward's mates who ate the strawberries but if I wanted to take the trouble I could prove to this court geometrically that they couldn't have. It's the water business all over again, like when the crew was taking baths seven times a day and our evaps were definitely on the fritz half the time and I was trying to inculcate the simplest principles of water conservation, but no, Mister Maryk the hero of the crew wanted to go right on mollycoddling them and— Or you take the coffee business . . . No! Well, the strawberry thing first—it all hinged on a thorough search for the key and that was where Mister Maryk as usual with the help of Mister Keith fudged it. Just went through a lot of phony motions that proved nothing and— Like thinking the incessant burning out of Silexes which were government property was a joke, which was the attitude of

everybody from Maryk down, no sense of responsibility
though I emphasized over and over that the war wouldn't last
forever, that all these things would have to be accounted for.
It was a constant battle, always the same thing, Maryk and
Keith undermining my authority, always arguments, though I
personally liked Keith and kept trying to train him up only to
get stabbed in the back when— Kay, I think I've covered the
strawberry business and— Oh, yes, this mess account business.
I had to watch them like a hawk. And believe me I did. They
didn't sneak any fast ones by but it wasn't for not trying. Instead of paying some attention to their accounts and their
inventories which I had to check over and over, always a few
pennies short or a few dollars over—what did it matter to
them, keeping accurate records? Let the captain worry. And
I did, by God. I defy anyone to check over a single wardroom
mess statement or ship's service inventory filed aboard the
U.S.S. *Caine* while I was captain and find a mistake of one
single solitary cent, and I mean I defy a certified public accountant to do it. Kay, what else? There was so much tripe in
that precious log of Mister Maryk's— Oh, yes, the movie
business. Kay. No respect for command was the whole
trouble with that ship, and the movie operator, who had a
disrespectful surly manner anyway, blithely started the movie
without waiting for the arrival of the commanding officer.
And out of that whole ship's crew, officers and men, did one
person call a halt or even notice that the captain wasn't
present? I missed those movies more than they did, but I
banned them and by God I'd do it again. What was I supposed
to do, issue letters of commendation to all of them for this
gratuitous insult to the commanding officer? Not that I took
it personally, it was the principle, the principle of respect for
command. That principle was dead when I came aboard that
ship but I brought it to life and I nagged and I crabbed and
I bitched and I hollered but by God I made it stick while I
was the captain. And as I say—like the Silexes. It wasn't only
the Silexes, it was a matter of respect, when I ask a sailor a
question I want a straight answer and nobody's going to get
away with shifty evasions if I have to hold a court of inquiry
for a week. What do I care for strawberries? It was a question
of principle, pilfering is pilfering, and on my ship—not that
we had so many treats, either. With those slow-motion treas-
urers of ours—not like when I was an ensign, believe me,

they made me jump sure enough—when we did get something pleasant like strawberries once in a blue moon it was an outrage not to have another helping if I felt like it, and I wasn't going to let them get away with that, and I didn't, by God, there was no more of that again on that ship. And so, as I say— Kay, how many of these things have I covered? I can only do this roughly from memory, but you ask me specific questions and I'll tackle them one by one.

(*During this speech* GREENWALD *strolls to his desk and leans against it, listening respectfully. The* COURT MEMBERS *stare at* QUEEG *and at each other and at their wrist watches after a while.* CHALLEE *slouches, biting his nails*)

GREENWALD   It was a very thorough and complete answer, Commander, thank you.

(*Goes to* STENOGRAPHER)

May I have exhibit twelve?

(STENOGRAPHER *hands him a glossy black photostat*)

Commander, I show you an authenticated copy of a fitness report you wrote on Lieutenant Maryk, dated 1 July 1944. Do you recognize it as such?

(QUEEG *takes paper, glances at it*)

QUEEG (*Grumpily*)   Yes.

GREENWALD   By that date, had the following incidents already occurred: the water shortage, the Silex investigation, the suspension of movies—among others?

QUEEG (*Hesitates*)   Well, by then, yes, I think.

GREENWALD   Please read to the court your comment of 1 July on Lieutenant Maryk.

QUEEG (*Stares at the paper. In a choked voice*)   Naturally, not being vindictive, I don't write down every single thing— a fitness report goes into a man's record, and I—I try to go easy, I always have, I always will—

GREENWALD   I appreciate that, sir. Please read your comment.

QUEEG (*Mumbling, hunched over, after a long pause*)   "This officer has if anything improved in his performance of duty since the last fitness report. He is consistently loyal, unflagging, thorough, courageous, and efficient. He is considered at present fully qualified for command of a 1200-ton DMS. His professional zeal and integrity set him apart as an outstanding example for other officers, reserve and regular alike. He cannot be too highly commended. He is recommended for transfer to the regular navy."

GREENWALD   Thank you, Commander. No further questions. (GREENWALD *walks to his desk and sits.* CHALLEE *stands slowly, like an old man with rheumatism. He approaches the witness stand, seems about to speak, then turns to* BLAKELY)

CHALLEE   No cross-examination.

BLAKELY   You are excused, Commander.
(*Exit* QUEEG)

GREENWALD   Defense rests.

BLAKELY   Is the judge advocate ready to present his argument?

CHALLEE   Sir, I believe I'll waive the argument.

BLAKELY   No argument at all?

CHALLEE   If it please the court, I'm at a loss to discuss the case the defense has presented. I have nothing to refute. It's no case at all. It has nothing to do with the charge or the specification. The defense counsel's very first question in this trial was, "Commander, have you ever heard the expression, 'Old Yellowstain'?" That was the key to his entire strategy—which was simply to twist the proceedings around so that the accused would become not Maryk but Commander Queeg. He's dragged out every possible vicious and malicious criticism of the commander from the other witnesses, and forced Queeg to defend himself against them in open court, on the spur of the moment, without advice of counsel, without any of the normal privileges and safeguards of an accused man under naval law.

Can this court possibly endorse the precedent that a captain who doesn't please his underlings can be deposed by them? And that the captain's only recourse afterward is to be placed on the witness stand at a general court-martial to answer every petty gripe and justify all his command decisions to a hostile lawyer taking the part of his insubordinate inferiors? Such a precedent is nothing but a blank check for mutiny. It is the absolute destruction of the chain of command.

However all this doesn't worry me, sir. I'm confident that this court hasn't been impressed by such shyster tactics. I know the court is going to reject this cynical play on its emotions, this insult to its intelligence, and find the specification proven by the facts. I've only this to say, sir. Whatever the verdict on the accused, I formally recommend that defense counsel Greenwald be reprimanded by this court for conduct unbecoming an officer of the Navy—and that this reprimand be made part of his service record.

(CHALLEE *sits*)

BLAKELY   Defense counsel—closing argument?

GREENWALD (*Rises, stands by his desk*)   Please the court, I undertook the defense of the accused very reluctantly, and only at the urging of the judge advocate that no other defense counsel was available. I was reluctant because I knew that the only possible defense was to show in court the mental incompetence of an officer of the Navy. It has been the most unpleasant duty I've ever had to perform. Once having undertaken it, I did what I could to win an acquittal. I thought this was my duty, both as defense counsel appointed by the Navy, and as a member of the bar.

(*Comes forward slowly*)

Let me make one thing clear. It is not, and never has been, the contention of the defense that Commander Queeg is a coward. The entire case of the defense rests on the assumption that no man who rises to command of a United States naval ship can possibly be a coward. And that therefore if he commits questionable acts under fire, the explanation must lie elsewhere. The court saw the bearing of Captain Queeg on the stand. The court can picture what his bearing must have been at the height of a typhoon. On that basis the court will decide the fate of the accused.

(*Sits*)

BLAKELY   Before recessing, the court will rule on the recommendation to reprimand.

(COURT MEMBERS *write their votes and pass papers to him*) Lieutenant Greenwald.

GREENWALD (*rises, comes to Center Stage at attention*)   Yes, sir.

BLAKELY   Lieutenant, this has been a strange and tragic trial. You have conducted your case with striking ingenuity. The judge advocate's remark about "shyster tactics" was an unfortunate personal slur. But your conduct has been puzzling, and it does raise questions. With talent goes responsibility. Has your conduct here been responsible, Lieutenant Greenwald?

(*Glances through votes and tears them up. In a dry cold tone*)

The reprimand, if there's to be one, must come from your own conscience. Counsel's words and acts are privileged within the broad limits of contempt of court. Court finds defense counsel has not been in contempt. Recommendation to reprimand denied.

(*Rings bell*)

Recess.

(*Exit all but* MARYK *and* GREENWALD

(*During next lines* ORDERLY *and* STENOGRAPHER *put back the witness stand and* GREENWALD'S *desk as they were when the play began; then they go out*)

MARYK   What happens now?

GREENWALD   That's the ball game.

MARYK   When do we find out?

GREENWALD   If it's an acquittal, you'll find out in an hour or so. If it isn't they may not publish the findings for weeks.

MARYK   Meantime would I be confined?

GREENWALD   No, hardly.

MARYK   What do you think?

GREENWALD   I'd stick around for an hour or so.

MARYK   You were terrific

GREENWALD   Thanks.

MARYK   You murdered Queeg.

GREENWALD   Yes, I murdered him.

MARYK   I'm grateful to you. Win or lose.

GREENWALD   Okay.

MARYK   What's the matter?

GREENWALD   Not a thing.

MARYK   You bothered by what Challee said? Or Blakely?

GREENWALD   Why should I be? I had a job to do. I did it. That's all.

MARYK   That's the spirit. Look. I want to ask your advice.

GREENWALD   What now?

MARYK   Tom Keefer's throwing a party tonight at the Fairmont Hotel. This morning he got a thousand-buck check— advance on his novel.

GREENWALD   Bully for him. I hope he sells a million copies, and wins the Pulitzer Prize, the Nobel Prize, and the Congressional Medal of Honor, and gets his bust in the Hall of Fame. That'll wrap this thing up in a pink ribbon.

MARYK   We're both invited to the party.

GREENWALD   What!

MARYK   Well, I know what you probably think. But hell, one way or another it's all over. I don't know what I'd have done in Tom's place.

GREENWALD   You'd go to Keefer's party?

MARYK   Tom's always called me a good-natured slob. I'll go if you will. If you think we should.

GREENWALD   (*Staring at him*)   All right. Maybe we'll both go and help Mr. Keefer celebrate.

BLACKOUT.   *Drunken singing of many male voices in the darkness, "I've Got Sixpence."*

SCENE II

THE SCENE: *The scene is the private dining room in
the* FAIRMONT HOTEL. *A long table has been moved on.
It is covered with a green cloth and a garland of
flowers is stretched along the front. A green curtain
masks the center of the courtroom, and the rest is in
darkness. The lights concentrate narrowly on the table.
The table is stacked with bottles of champagne and
glasses, and a huge cake baked in the form of a book.
    Seven officers in blues are grouped around the table,
including* MARYK, KEITH, *and* KEEFER. *They are all
pretty drunk. They are sitting at various angles, waving glasses and bottles, and trying to drown each other
out in the singing of "I've Got Sixpence."* WILLIE
KEITH *is trying desperately to sing, all alone, "Bell
Bottom Trousers."* KEEFER *and* MARYK *tell him he
is singing the wrong song and finally get him to join in
their singing of "Sixpence."* GREENWALD *enters Stage
Left, unnoticed by the group, and stands silently
watching their party.* KEEFER *glances off and sees*
GREENWALD *standing there.*

KEEFER   Quiet!
Quiet! All right, QUIET, you drunken bums of the *Caine!*
Here he is! The guest of honor! Fill your glasses! A toast to
the conquering hero! Greenwald the Magnificent! The man
who won the acquittal!
    (*One of the members of the party walks over to* GREEN-
    WALD *and takes him by the arm and moves* GREENWALD
    closer to the table)

GREENWALD   Party's pretty far along, hey?

KEEFER   A toast I say! to Lieutenant—

KEITH   Make it rhyme, Tom! Like you did at the ship's party!

ALL   Yes, yes. That's right. Rhymes! Rhymes! A toast in
rhyme.

MARYK (*To* GREENWALD) He makes 'em up as he goes along, Barney.

KEITH You've never heard anything like it.

MARYK Come on, Tom.

KEITH Rhymes!

KEEFER Well, I'm a bit drunk to be doing Thomas the Rhymer tonight—
(*Drunken protests from the others*)
But, to honor this great man, I'll try my best. Fill your glasses, I say!

> To Lieutenant Barney Greenwald,
> Who fought with might and main.
> The terror of judge advocates,
> The massive legal brain.

(*They all cheer*)

> Who hit the Navy where it lived
> And made it writhe with pain.
> Who sees through brass and gold stripes
> Like so much cellophane.

(*They all cheer*)

> The man who licked the regulars
> Right on their own terrain,
> Who wrought the great deliverance
> For the galley slaves of the *Caine*.

(*They all cheer*)

> And gave us all the Fifth Freedom—
> Freedom from Old Yellowstain!

(*They all cheer loudly, and burst into "For He's a Jolly Good Fellow." Then, "Speech, Barney, speech," etc.*)

GREENWALD No, no, no. I'm drunker'n any of you. I've been out drinking with the judge advocate—trying to get him to take back some of the dirty names he called me—finally got him to shake hands on the ninth whiskey sour—maybe the tenth—

MARYK   That's good.

GREENWALD   Had to talk loud 'n' fast, Steve—I played
pretty dirty pool, you know, in court—poor Jack Challee.
   (*Peers blearily at cake*)
What's this?

KEEFER   It's a double celebration.

GREENWALD   Cake baked like a book—

KEEFER   A thousand bucks came in the mail today. Advance
on my novel.

GREENWALD   Very nice.
   (*Reads icing*)
Multitudes, Multitudes, by Thomas Keefer—I got something
in the mail, too.

MARYK   What, Barney?

GREENWALD   Medical okay. Orders back to my squadron.
Sailing tomorrow.
   (*They all cheer*)

MARYK   That's great.

GREENWALD   A thousand bucks. Guess I ought to return the
celebrated author's toast, at that—li'l speech—thanks for
that elegant poem, Mr. Keefer. War novel, isn't it?

KEEFER   What else?

GREENWALD   I assume you give the Navy a good pasting?

KEEFER   I don't think Public Relations would clear it, at any
rate.

GREENWALD   Fine. Someone should show up these stodgy,
stupid Prussians. Who's the hero, you?

KEEFER   Well, any resemblance, you know, is purely acci-
dental—
   (*A few laughs*)

GREENWALD   'Course I'm warped, and I'm drunk, but it
suddenly seems to me that if I wrote a war novel I'd try to
make a hero out of Old Yellowstain.
   (*All whoop*)

No, I'm serious, I would. Tell you why. Tell you how I'm warped. I'm a Jew, guess most of you know that. Jack Challee said I used smart Jew-lawyer tactics—'course he took it back, apologized, after I told him a few things about the case he never knew. Well, anyway—the reason I'd make Old Yellowstain a hero is on account of my mother, little gray-headed Jewish lady, fat. Well, sure you guys all have mothers, but they wouldn't be in the same bad shape mine would if we'd of lost this war. See, the Germans aren't kidding about the Jews. They're cooking us down to soap over there. They think we're vermin and should be 'sterminated and our corpses turned into something useful. Granting the premise—being warped, I don't, but granting the premise—soap is as good an idea as any. But I just can't cotton to the idea of my mom melted down to a bar of soap.

(One of the officers, drunker than the rest, mutters thickly something ad lib: "What's all this got to do with Old Yellowstain?" or words to that effect. The others swiftly quiet him. GREENWALD *rides over the interruption)*

Now I'm coming to Old Yellowstain. Coming to him. See, Mr. Keefer, while I was studying law, and you were writing your short stories for national magazines, and little Willie here was on the playing fields of Princeton, why, all that time these birds we call regulars, these stuffy stupid Prussians, they were standing guard on this fat, dumb, and happy country of ours. 'Course they were doing it for dough, same as everybody does what they do. Question is in the last anal—last analysis, what do you do for dough? You and me, for dough, were advancing our free little non-Prussian careers. So, when all hell broke loose and the Germans started running out of soap and figured, well, time to come over and melt down old Mrs. Greenwald, who's gonna stop 'em? Not her boy Barney. Can't stop a Nazi with a lawbook. So, I dropped the lawbooks, and ran to learn how to fly. Stout fellow. Meantime, and it took a year and a half before I was any good, who was keeping Mama out of the soap dish? Tom Keefer? Communication school. Willie Keith? Midshipman school. Old Yellowstain, maybe? Why, yes, even poor sad Queeg. And most of them not sad at all, fellows, a lot of them sharper boys than any of us, don't kid yourself, you can't be good in the Army or Navy unless you're goddamn good. Though maybe not up on Proust, 'n' *Finnegans Wake* 'n' all.

MARYK Barney, forget it, it's all over, let's enjoy the dinner—

GREENWALD Steve, this dinner's a phony. You're guilty. Course you're only half guilty. There's another guy who's stayed very neatly out of the picture. The guy who started the whole idea that Queeg was a dangerous paranoiac—who argued you into it for half a year—who invented the name Old Yellowstain—who kept feeding you those psychiatry books—who pointed out Article 184 and kept hammering it at you—

KEEFER Now wait a minute—

GREENWALD Oh, had to drag it out of Steve, Mister Keefer. Big dumb fisherman, tried to tell me it was all his own idea. Doesn't know the difference between a paranoid and an anthropoid. But you knew. Told him his medical log was a clinical picture of a paranoid. Advised him to go to Halsey. Offered to go with him. Didn't get cold feet till you stood outside Halsey's cabin on the *New Jersey*. Then ducked, and been ducking ever since.

KEEFER (*Angrily*) I don't know where in hell you got all this, but—

GREENWALD Biggest favor you could have done Steve, so far as winning an acquittal went, though I doubt you realized it. But if there's a guilty party at this table, it's you. If you hadn't filled Steve Maryk's thick head full of paranoia and Article 184, why he'd have got Queeg to come north, or he'd have helped the poor bastard pull through to the south, and the *Caine* wouldn't have been yanked out of action in the hottest part of the war. That's your contribution to the good old U.S.A., my friend. Pulling a minesweeper out of the South Pacific when it was most needed. That, and *Multitudes, Multitudes*.

KEEFER Just a minute—you're really drunk—

GREENWALD 'Scuse me, I'm all finished, Mister Keefer. I'm up to the toast. Here's to you. You bowled a perfect score. You went after Queeg and got him. You kept your own skirts all white and starchy. You'll publish your novel proving that the Navy stinks, and you'll make a million dollars and marry Hedy Lamarr. So you won't mind a li'l verbal reprimand from me. What does it mean? I defended Steve because I found out the wrong guy was on trial. Only way I could defend him was to murder Queeg for you. I'm sore that I was pushed into that spot, and ashamed of what I did, and thass why I'm drunk. Queeg deserved better at my hands. I owed him a favor, don't you see? He stopped Herman Goering from washing his fat behind with my mother. So I'm not going to eat your dinner, Mister Keefer, or drink your wine, but simply make my toast and go. Here's to you, Mister *Caine's* favorite author, and here's to your book.

(GREENWALD *throws the wine in* KEEFER'S *face. Shocked murmurs.* KEEFER *crumples*)

You can wipe for the rest of your life, Mister. You'll never wipe off that yellow stain.

MARYK   Barney—

GREENWALD (*A wry smile, a hand brushed on* MARYK'S *head*)
See you in Tokyo, you mutineer.

(GREENWALD *staggers out*)

MODERN LIBRARY GIANTS

A series of sturdily bound and handsomely printed, full-sized library editions of books formerly available only in expensive sets. These volumes contain from 600 to 1,400 pages each.

THE MODERN LIBRARY GIANTS REPRESENT A
SELECTION OF THE WORLD'S GREATEST BOOKS

G55   O'NEILL, EUGENE: *Nine Plays*
G68   PAINE, TOM: *Selected Work*
G86   PASTERNAK, BORIS: *Doctor Zhivago*
G5   PLUTARCH: *Lives* (The Dryden Translation)
G40   POE, EDGAR ALLAN: *Complete Tales and Poems*
G29   PRESCOTT, WILLIAM H.: *The Conquest of Mexico* and *The Conquest of Peru*
G62   PUSHKIN: *Poems, Prose and Plays*
G65   RABELAIS: *Complete Works*
G12   SCOTT, SIR WALTER: *The Most Popular Novels* (Quentin Durward, Ivanhoe & Kenilworth)
G4   SHELLEY & KEATS: *Complete Poems*
G32   SMITH, ADAM: *The Wealth of Nations*
G61   SPAETH, SIGMUND: *A Guide to Great Orchestral Music*
G92   SPENGLER, OSWALD: *The Decline of the West* (one volume)
G91   SPENSER, EDMUND: *Selected Poetry*
G75   STEVENSON, ROBERT LOUIS: *Selected Writings*
G53   SUE, EUGENE: *The Wandering Jew*
G42   TENNYSON: *The Poems and Plays*
G23   TOLSTOY, LEO: *Anna Karenina*—tr. revised
G1   TOLSTOY, LEO: *War and Peace*
G49   TWAIN, MARK: *Tom Sawyer* and *Huckleberry Finn*
G50   WHITMAN, WALT: *Leaves of Grass*
G83   WILSON, EDMUND: *The Shock of Recognition*

MISCELLANEOUS

G77   *An Anthology of Famous American Stories*
G54   *An Anthology of Famous British Stories*
G67   *Anthology of Famous English and American Poetry*
G81   *An Encyclopedia of Modern American Humor*
G47   *The English Philosophers from Bacon to Mill*
G16   *The European Philosophers from Descartes to Nietzsche*
G31   *Famous Science-Fiction Stories*
G85   *Great Ages and Ideas of the Jewish People*
G89   *Great Classical Myths*
G72   *Great Tales of Terror and the Supernatural*
G9   *Great Voices of the Reformation*
G87   *Medieval Epics*
G48   *The Metropolitan Opera Guide*
G46   *A New Anthology of Modern Poetry*
G69   *One Hundred and One Years' Entertainment*
G93   *Parodies: An Anthology from Chaucer to Beerbohm and After*
G90   *Philosophies of Art and Beauty: Readings in Aesthetics from Plato to Heidegger*
G21   *Sixteen Famous American Plays*
G63   *Sixteen Famous British Plays*
G71   *Sixteen Famous European Plays*
G45   *Stoic and Epicurean Philosophers*
G22   *Thirty Famous One-Act Plays*
G66   *Three Famous Murder Novels, Before the Fact,* FRANCIS ILES, *Trent's Last Case,* E. C. BENTLEY, *The House of the Arrow,* A. E. W. MASON
G10   *Twelve Famous Plays of the Restoration and Eighteenth Century* (1660–1820): Dryden, Congreve, Wycherley, Gay, etc.
G56   *The Wisdom of Catholicism*
G59   *The Wisdom of China and India*
G79   *The Wisdom of Israel*